HEY

Watch!

Douglas Hooley

Essential Information Jesus Gave His Followers About His Return

Stay Watchful Bob!

Doug Hooley

A Study of Jesus' Olivet Discourse as Recorded in the Books of Matthew, Mark and Luke

Cover design by Angela Hooley

First Edition

ISBN:-10:1533503125
ISBN-13:978-1533503121

Learn More about Doug Hooley Ministries at doughooley.com

All scripture references utilize the 1611 King James Version of the Bible (public domain). Spelling and grammar are left as per original 1611 version. The Doug Hooley Translation (DHT) of the Olivet Discourse related scriptures is also included.

Because of the ever changing nature of the Internet, web addresses, webpage content, or links contained in *Watch!*, may no longer be valid.

DEDICATION

To my Master: Jesus, who I can't wait to see one day. To my best friend, traveling companion through this world, and love of my life: my wife Angela. And, to my three children: Rachel, Jared, and Megan, who used to sit around the table every month with me putting on stamps and address labels and folding copies of the "Watchful Watchman" newsletter.

Contents

Watch!

ACKNOWLEDGMENTS

I would like to first acknowledge and thank my Lord Jesus who has allowed me to serve Him by writing this book.

Secondly, I would like to recognize my father, Eldon Ray Hooley, who now resides with Jesus. My dad's example taught me how to problem solve and not settle for giving only half my effort.

My great friend and brother in the Lord, Marty Tadlock, has taught me much about God over the years. Marty has always been an encouragement to me to live out my faith. When I have messed that all up, Marty has served as an example of God's grace in action. He has also been kind enough to provide me with editorial suggestions while I was writing this book.

I wish to thank the following beta readers that read *Watch!* prior to its release to the public;

Ron and Ardiss Burch, Rick and Kathy Byers, Dan and Rachel Chase, Debbie Chase, Ed Collins, Loren Corner, Jack Crabtree, Bob Cruzan, Logan Dhonau, Ken Doerksen, David Fenley, Kelly Fenley, Manda Fenley, Tonya Fenley, Dan Frederickson, Cliff Harrold, Ron Heyerly, Martin Heymann, Ryan Hooley, Sally Hooley, John Kennel, Chris and Lindsay Kinman, Cindy Nunez, and John Quigley.

The pre and post reading surveys, comments, suggestions, feedback and encouragement the above group provided was invaluable and helped me to write a better book. May God bless them for their help in this effort.

Finally, my wife Angela has been both a source of encouragement and my sounding board over the years. Together we have literally walked hundreds of miles while talking over what we both have discovered in God's word. I hope there will be some sort of special reward for Angela in eternity for the support she has given me and what she has endured since the day she said, "I do."

Preface

Anyone is welcome to read this book, but I wrote it for those that believe the words contained in the original documents, which make up our Holy Bible to be the inspired words of our Creator. Further, the intended reader of *"Watch!"* knows that a first century carpenter, named Jesus, from Nazareth, a small town next to the Sea of Galilee in Israel, was and is the Messiah, the anointed, and living Son of God. Jesus was executed on a Roman cross for our sins and was resurrected, overcoming Hell and death and making it possible for those who make Him their Lord to live eternally with Him. If we agree on those things, I think you are the perfect intended reader of this book.

I always had an interest in Bible prophecy whenever it was spoken of in my childhood church. I began studying prophecy on my own soon after my wife Angela and I were married in 1982. I made my way through a pretty intensive, but "canned," study on the book of Revelation. I read every Hal Lindsey and Dave Hunt bible prophecy book I could get my hands on. The study of bible prophecy was very exciting to me and I embraced and defended what I had come to believe fervently. However, as I did so, taking the prophecy-related scriptures at face value seemed to raise questions for me that I was never able to really resolve. I simply accepted the theories on how some scriptures should be interpreted "on faith."

In 1993 I was introduced to a word; "hermeneutics." Simply put, hermeneutics have to do with the rules that we follow when we read and attempt to interpret the Bible. At the time, it was my thought that just reading the Bible and trusting the Holy Spirit to guide me, while listening to what good bible teachers had to say, was all that I needed to understand the Bible. I finally came to understand that without applying established rules of interpretation, one could land anywhere one wanted to and support any idea, and life is too short to fool one's self with self-serving doctrines.

In order to set aside my beliefs of personal convenience and comfort (the gospel according to Doug), I was forced to become consistent with how I interpreted what is written in the Bible. The rules I now follow are intended to understand the scriptures not only as the original audience they were written for would have understood them, but also as the Divine Author, God, intended them to be understood in our time.

Unlike the original intended audience, now, 2,000 years after the scriptures were written, we have historical perspective on our side, as well as research aids such as computers, bible software, and Google. The original intended audience, although much more familiar with the language, place it was written, and culture of their day, did not have history on their side. We now have the entire Bible contained in one book. We have lexicons, concordances, dictionaries, word search engines, and the commentaries of countless theologians from the past twenty centuries. These aids allow anyone to accomplish, in some cases minutes, what would have taken a Reformation era theologian, weeks, months, or even years to do.

I have included my own translation of the Olivet Discourse, identified as "DHT," along with the King James Version of the Bible, in the text of this book. I am a student of Koine Greek. I am not even close to being a master of it. The more I study and get to know about the original languages of the Bible, the more I am convinced that no particular modern English translation is "inspired" by God. Although God has preserved accurate records of His Word for us, only the original documents that ultimately led to our modern translations of the Bible were inspired.

Faithful men and women who love God, and have pure motivations, did and do the best they can, taking the words from one language and time, and moving them to another language and time in order to convey the original meaning. But, they are still "only human," and language is a living, evolving commodity. Considering different translations of the Bible and spending time looking at the Bible in the original languages, with the aid of a couple of good lexicons is well worth the serious bible student's time. Please follow along with the scriptures in this book while utilizing your own favorite translation.

Academic treatises on a subject can be dry, difficult to read for many people, and can quickly lead to boredom and frustration. Because of tradition, and the expectations of their peers, even the most well intended academic author sometimes focuses so closely on the "tree" that they miss the fact that the entire forest is now petrified.

Popular books, on the other hand, written for the more casual reader, sometimes seem to assume since a publisher has gone to all the trouble and expense of putting something into print, that the work should be trusted. At risk of alienating both the academic and pop-culture readers with this book, I am striving to land somewhere in the middle.

The dark ages were dark because people completely entrusted the doctrines defining their faith to other people. It is important to listen to wise people that have studied God's Word with pure motivations. However, we should never take other's words as God's Words. My hope is that you will let other people's opinions, and what they teach, inspire you to study the Bible yourself. I am no exception; please check out carefully for yourself what I have written in this book. Make sure in this book, I am keeping scripture in context with surrounding scripture. Every word must fit every verse. Every verse must make sense in every paragraph. Every paragraph must fit the chapter, every chapter the book, and ultimately every book…the Bible.

God will honor your honest search for the truth about what He wants us to know of Him, the world He created, and our future. Fair warning; Truth is often found outside of our "comfort zone." Looking in the Bible to find the truth is the first and most important step, but an ongoing commitment to accurate interpretation of the Bible is equally as important. I trust that readers will hold me accountable through their own personal Bible study. I know ultimately that God Himself will one-day hold me accountable.

1. Introduction

Jesus was very clear in His message: Many Christians living during the period of time just before His return, will be deceived, will be persecuted, and will fall away from the faith. Many who claim to be Christians will one day renounce their faith and betray those they once called brothers and sisters in the Lord. Many will deceive themselves into believing they are servants of Jesus, when in fact it will be Jesus Himself that ends up sentencing them to Hell.

Alarming as this is, the deception Jesus warned about already exists in the Church today. It is the root cause of apathy and acceptance of myths in regards to prophetic scriptures.

What are we, as professed followers of Jesus, to do? Jesus gives us the answer: *Watch!* The words Jesus spoke on the Mount of Olives, and related parallel scriptures, provide enough details to put together a comprehensive picture of "end times" events and the things we *must* do to avoid deception.

Setting the scene for this warning; the Passover in Jerusalem was approaching, Jesus knew His time on earth was growing short. While His death grew nearer, Jesus gave His disciples what *He* considered to be the most crucial information necessary as they would transition from His physical daily presence, to what we all now await…the ultimate day of His return.

Almost 2,000 years later, Jesus' message has become even more urgent. As every day passes and His return grows ever closer, the same information He gave His original disciples is even more crucial for modern day disciples of Christ.

How tragic that one of Satan's greatest victories in our time is that many in the Church avoid studying the very information that Jesus thought was so important for His followers throughout time to know. While many that decide what Christians will hear on Sunday mornings may avoid the topic of "end times prophecy," millions of people, both within the Church and outside of it, are actively searching for answers about the "end of the world." Tragically, in the absence of sound biblical teaching, there are numerous purveyors of misinformation that are providing people with false answers.

Our Internet-rich, 21st century, conspiracy-theory-loving, Western-world culture, has given rise to a number of authors, Christian radio show hosts, and bloggers over the past four decades that have engaged in making bad predictions in regards to the return of Jesus. This has given the study of Bible prophecy a bad reputation. Those who continue to diligently study such things are often dismissed as "end times nuts." To be fair, I have found that some very passionate people, whose principles of biblical interpretation fall outside the envelope of sound hermeneutical practices, are indeed worthy of such a title.

Many well-intentioned people within the Church today can be heard saying things like, "*the Church will be long gone by the time anything bad happens. Most prophecies were written for the benefit of the ones who will be left behind.*" Or, "*Jesus was speaking to the Jews when He said those things on the Mount of Olives, not Christians.*" Or, "*All of those things Jesus was talking about already took place in 70 AD, when the Temple was destroyed. Those prophecies don't concern us.*" There seem to be many reasons some people try to get others to avoid studying and understanding prophetic scriptures.

Today, both intentionally and unintentionally deceptive voices assure followers of Jesus that it is not important to understand what is contained in the Bible regarding the "end of the age." Yet, from Jesus' very own words which make up the Olivet Discourse, He calls out to His Church, with the exact *opposite* message. While many Christians concern themselves primarily with how to get along better in this world here and now, Jesus strongly *commands* His "servants" to live for, and *watch* for, the future day of His return.

Many Christians are confused about what will happen at "the end of the age" and what their role in eternity will be. This confusion comes from lack of knowledge. Lack of knowledge of the truth leaves a vacuum in a person's life. That vacuum leaves them wide open to false teaching. Receiving, accepting and then passing on deceptive teaching, makes one a "well intentioned" teacher of deception. None of this need occur!

According to Jesus on the Mount of Olives, one day many false teachers, false prophets, and people claiming to represent Him will pervade our world and lead people astray. This will happen inside and outside of the Church. A "bad guy," that people have labeled the "Antichrist," will show up on the world scene. This will be really unexpected by many Christians who expected to be "raptured," prior to the Antichrist coming to power. Out of ignorance, some may even support and place themselves in allegiance with this individual. This will be an eternally bad error.

The Antichrist will be a world leader with great military backing and will eventually hunt down and persecute descendants from the tribes of Israel *and* the followers of Jesus. He will fancy himself some sort of "god," and the penalty for not "worshiping" him will be death. Because some Christians ignored the warnings of Jesus, they will have totally missed that this situation will occur. They will not be prepared for this scenario. The results, according to Jesus, are that a large number of people, who said they were Christians, *will* fall away from the faith.

In the midst of wars, out of control inflation, persecution and famine related death, the sun will suddenly go dark, the moon will lose its light, the stars will appear to fall from the sky, and there will be a world-wide earthquake that causes the seas to roar. These things will happen immediately before Jesus shows up in "power and great glory."

Jesus will send out His angels to gather the "elect;" those both dead and alive in Christ, from the "four-corners" of the earth. At that time those who have said, Jesus is their Lord, but are "servants" of Jesus in name only, will deeply regret their life decisions. Their fate will be the same as those who never believed in Jesus at all.

It is only after the Church has been rescued from the planet, that God will begin to pour out His judgment (wrath) on the earth. The elect of God, His Church, were not appointed to suffer this wrath. Things will get really bad for those that are left on the earth, except for a limited number of descendants of the tribes of Israel, who will receive supernatural protection from God.

You may have been taught a much different scenario pertaining to the end of the age, than the one you just read. That is okay. However, there is a great deal riding on your beliefs. If any part of the above scenario is true, it warrants your consideration especially regarding what Jesus had to say on the Mount of Olives.

There is no greater thing for the born-again Disciple of Christ to look forward to than being united with our Messiah, and Savior, Jesus! Yet, in spite of the details given in scripture, most born-again Disciples of Christ are almost completely ignorant of how that entire scene will play out.

Before ascending to Heaven, Jesus established a perpetual Christian educational system when He commanded His disciples, to go and make disciples of others. In creating this system, Jesus expanded the role of His students into that of also being teachers.

Jesus did not give His disciples discretion in the curriculum. He told His disciples to teach "all things" that He had commanded them. "All things" includes what Jesus said to the original disciples on the Mount of Olives regarding His Second Coming.

Followers of Christ have to know the prophetic scripture well enough to know what to watch for, what to be on guard against, how to live "Master-pleasing" lives, and what to teach others. This generation is failing to do so.

Whether you have reached the point that you are teaching others or not, this principle still applies: "once a student of Jesus, always a student of Jesus!" If you have never studied the Olivet Discourse to *a point of understanding* the critical information your Master, Jesus, wanted you to know about His return and the end of the age, this is a perfect time!

The study of what Jesus said about His return and eternity can refocus a believer's entire life and redirect it from focusing on the things of this world, to the things of the everlasting kingdom Jesus will one day bring with Him from Heaven. Setting your mind on things above…is absolutely life changing!

The talk Jesus gave his disciples on the Mount of Olives during His final Passover week on earth has been the source of a great deal of controversy. You may not agree with everything written in this book. However, I am convinced that if you are committed to finding truth, and you carefully and prayerfully consider the points made in the coming chapters, your commitment to being a good, faithful, and "watchful" servant of the Lord Jesus, will grow stronger.

Jesus' words are worthy of not only a quick or even repetitive read through, but of your close study and serious contemplation. I challenge and encourage you to do just that. *Not* with an open mind as to what I have written, but with a mind committed to God's truth.

2. Who, Watch, Where, When and Why?

Jesus was still in the form of a mortal human being, and it was only two days before He would be crucified. It was time for straight and clear answers. It was on the Mount of Olives where the disciples asked Jesus when the fantastic events He had been talking about would take place, and what would be the signs which would signal the "end of the age," and His return to this earth.

Jesus' answers came to be known as, "The Olivet Discourse." "Olivet," because the location the answers were given was on the Mount of "Olives," and "discourse" because what Jesus said, as recorded in the books of Matthew, Mark, and Luke was comprehensive and authoritative.

A Message for Christians and Descendants of Israel

Jesus was speaking to His disciples on the Mount of Olives; They believed in and trusted Jesus to be the authority on the Kingdom of Heaven and how to gain access, through Jesus, to that kingdom. They were what we now call, and the dictionary defines as, "Christians." Jesus was giving this group of Christians, information to pass on to future Christians.

Early in His talk, Jesus confirmed that He was addressing those who follow Him, when He said that His followers now and in the future, will be "hated" for His namesake. This is an important piece to understanding this passage, since many believe the Olivet Discourse was written for the benefit of Jews and *not* the followers of Christ.

At this point in history, and for the past 2,000 years, Jews have not been widely known as followers of Christ. In fact, it was Jewish leaders that were the first to attempt to wipe out the followers of Jesus in the first century. Many Jews still consider Jesus to be one of many false messiahs. Many also consider him to be the most damaging. Judaism rejects any claims that Jesus fulfilled any of the prophecies regarding their messiah. The idea that Jews would accept the teachings of Jesus in the Olivet Discourse or be considered to be His followers in any way is without merit.

It is true that Jesus was born and raised a Jew in every sense. However, it is also true that He has the unique role of being the one and only God; the God of everyone, whether everyone knows it or not. As the Apostle Paul brilliantly revealed, Jesus, who was God in human form, is our High Priest that made salvation possible for the *entire* world, not only Jews, through His sacrifice.

We also know that the original religion of the 12 disciples was Judaism. Although they remained ethnically Jews, the disciples, like the Apostle Paul, parted ways with relying on the Jewish faith for their salvation the day that they decided to follow Jesus and His teaching which says "*no one comes to the father, except through me*" (John 14:6). This indeed made the disciples, "Christians."

Although the disciples may have retained many of their former religious practices, they no longer were counting on the Mosaic Law and animal sacrifices to seek forgiveness for their sins and reconcile themselves to God. That this reconciliation could be obtained through mercy was at the very heart of Jesus' message and was the "good news" delivered to all of humanity. It is the great hope of us all.

The Olivet Discourse was clearly intended to include Christians as the receivers of the message it contains. Having acknowledged that, it is also clear that there is information within the Olivet Discourse that more directly pertains to the descendants of the tribes of Israel which will be alive around the time of Jesus' return. This includes all people, Jew or "Gentile," living in and around the region of "Judea" with Jerusalem at its center.

Although parts of the Olivet Discourse are found in three different Gospels, the Gospel according to Matthew, which contains the most comprehensive account of the discourse, was originally written in the Hebrew language and targeted a Jewish audience. The Book of Matthew appears to have been an attempt to answer the Jews questions about Jesus, who claimed to be their messiah. Yet, to whomever the book was originally addressed matters only as much as does the books of Ephesians or Galatians, originally being letters addressed to the people of Ephesus and Galatia. Both of those letters from the Apostle Paul contain truth that has been relied on and utilized by Christians of all times.

Regardless of whom Jesus was specifically addressing on the Mount of Olives, almost all of the events that Jesus describes during the Olivet Discourse will ultimately affect the entire population of the planet. It is worth paying close attention to what the Son of God said to His Disciples regarding the end of the age. Jerusalem may be the epicenter of end times events, but those events will send enormous shock waves throughout the entire world.

Meant to Be Understood by Anyone

It is often argued that prophecy is too difficult for lay people in the Church to understand. Yet, the four particular disciples Jesus addressed on the Mount of Olives were all fishermen by trade. We know all four could likely read and write, but it was unlikely that they were very well educated. They certainly were not religious authorities, academics, or theologians. Jesus was very perceptive, not a poor communicator, and understood he was speaking to common people.

Although care must be taken to make sure we are appropriately translating what Jesus said across time, space, language, and cultural differences, God's Son intended His words to be everlasting and understood forever. That includes the prophetic scripture contained in the Olivet Discourse.

If you are a follower of Jesus, the Holy Spirit of God resides within you. If you diligently seek the truth of what scripture means, through the Holy Spirit, you will find it. My personal experience is that the Holy Spirit often uses a great deal of study, prayer, meditation, and time to make this happen.

Matthew, Mark, and Luke

As a background, accounts of Jesus' Olivet Discourse are found in all three of the synoptic gospels; Matthew, Mark, and Luke. Although the Apostle John's gospel doesn't include the Olivet Discourse, John was one of the four disciples physically present when it was given. John would later be responsible for authoring the entire Book of Revelation.

Matthew, whose surname was "Levi" (Matt 9:9), was a tax collector and was one of the original twelve disciples of Jesus. He would have been personally present with Jesus the night that the Olivet Discourse was uttered on the Mount of Olives. However, according to the Book of Mark, Matthew is not one of the four specific disciples that went to Jesus "privately" to ask Him the questions that led to the Olivet Discourse.

It is likely that one or more of the four disciples to whom Jesus was directly speaking would have conveyed what they had heard to Matthew and the rest of the disciples. However he heard it,

Matthew wrote by far the most extensive account of what Jesus had to say that night. The date the Book of Matthew was authored is not specifically known. The Ryrie Study Bible puts the authorship date anywhere between 50 and 90 AD. Although disputed, the Gospel of Matthew is thought by some to be the first of the four gospels written.[1]

Mark, also known as "John Mark," was the son of a relatively wealthy woman named Mary, who lived in Jerusalem (Acts 12:12). Mark was the cousin of Barnabas, who was the companion of the Apostle Paul on some of his journeys. Mark was in and out of Paul's life until Paul's death.

Mark was also a companion and friend of the Apostle Peter (1 Peter 5:13). Peter had a front row seat to the Olivet Discourse. Mark's gospel likely contains information that he received from Peter.[2] Undoubtedly Mark would have heard Peter recount numerous times what He had heard from Jesus. Opinions regarding the authorship dates for the Book of Mark range from 61 AD to after 70 AD. [3]

Luke was a physician (Col. 4:14). He was a close friend and companion of the Apostle Paul. As far as we know, Luke would not have been a direct eyewitness to the life of Jesus. He is responsible for writing the Gospel of Luke as well as the Book of Acts. He accomplished documenting the life of Jesus and the beginnings of the Church in the book of Acts through conducting an "investigation" (Luke 1:1-4). He did this as an "orderly attempt" to provide others with confidence in the gospel that they had already received. The Book of Luke was written before the Book of Acts, probably sometime around 60 AD. [4]

There are many, sometimes word for word, similarities between the three gospel accounts of the Olivet Discourse. There is little doubt, since Luke used others as a source for his account that he consulted with at least John Mark. In fact, Luke and Mark were in Rome together between 61 and 63 AD, about the time that the Book of Luke was probably written (Colossians 4:10, 14).[5]

Differences in the text of the three different gospels are explained by different authorship styles and the life experiences and education that the authors brought with them. For example, Dr. Luke is said to have a little bit more of a fascination with medical issues in his gospel than the other authors.

The originally intended audiences for each of the gospels would have also played a part in some of the differences of how each gospel was written. Differences would occur since two authors recorded witness statements rather than what they personally witnessed, and everyone views events through different lenses and from different perspectives. I worked in the law enforcement field for over twenty-five years. I know very well that you can ask five different eyewitnesses to tell you what they saw, and you will get five different stories (perspectives) of the same event, and all of them could be true.

Past, Future, Or Both?

The disciples may have been confused about one of the important recognizable signs Jesus spoke of during the Olivet Discourse. Their possible confusion continues today among many modern day disciples of Christ. From the disciples first century AD perspectives it may have seemed likely that Jesus was speaking of an event that had already taken place in history, yet was again going to take place in the future. It is this prophetic event that is critical to reconciling two very different views on how the Olivet Discourse should be interpreted.

As a backdrop it is important to understand some common current theological positions. "Preterists" are those who believe most of the prophesy given during the Olivet Discourse has already been fulfilled. According to them it was fulfilled around 70 AD when Jerusalem and the Temple fell completely to the Romans under General (and soon to be Emperor) Titus.

The "Futurist" point of view is that most of the prophecies will occur in the future, surrounding the time of the Second Advent (Coming). These two views have caused a great deal of confusion in the Church in how to properly view the Olivet Discourse. In coming chapters, I will offer an explanation on how both views can be considered, for the most part, correct.

Many Warnings

During the Olivet Discourse, Jesus gave clear warnings about false teachers, false messiahs, false signs, persecution, and being deceived. He talked about things that *will not* signal that the world is coming to an end. There are things today, both within the Church, and outside, people look at as apocalyptic signs that the "end" is close at hand. Jesus then went on to instruct His disciples exactly what to watch for, which will indeed signal the end of the age, the rapture of the Church, and His coming.

Jesus also warned of the difficulty of surviving the times at the end of the age. It is clear that His followers will be removed from the earth prior to God's Wrath being poured out on the earth. However, there is no indication that His followers will be saved from difficult times during a period of "tribulation," and persecution at the hands of the Antichrist.

The idea that the Church will go through times of persecution is consistent with what we see in history. Soon after the first time Jesus came, through this present day, a great deal of persecution of the Church has taken place. Many have died horrible deaths for Jesus' namesake. The role of sorrow and suffering in our lives is the topic of another book someday, but much can be said on the subject.

Rapture Only vs. Second Coming

There is no indication to be found in the Olivet Discourse that a "secret" and sudden gathering together of Jesus' followers will occur without any warning. Signs will precede His coming and when He shows up, it will be really loud, out in the open, and for everyone to see. His coming will be accompanied by the rapture of the Church and the beginning of God's wrath being poured out on those that remain behind. The Olivet Discourse and the parallel passages of scripture do not describe two separate Second Comings of Jesus, but one.

Theories, Labels and Definitions

Many systems have been devised as to how to approach bible prophecy regarding the end of the age. "Are you a pretribulation rapturist, a mid-trib, or post triber?" This is the question I most often get when someone learns that I am a student of eschatology; which in layman's terms, means the study of the final events of history. "Are you an Amillennialist or Premillennialist?" is the other question often posed. Most evangelical Christians, since the mid 1800's, when Churches used to teach on this topic, have been taught to be premillennial, pretribulation rapturists, even if they were not aware of these labels.

The following are some greatly simplified definitions that are important to understand:

The "**tribulation period**" is a period of seven years in which the bulk of the prophetic events take place. It is based on scripture from the books of Daniel and Revelation. Things on earth appear to get progressively worse during this period of time. The seven-year period will be discussed in greater detail later in this book.

"Premillennialism" asserts that following the return of Jesus, there will be a literal one thousand-year period of time, the millennium, where Jesus will rule the same earth that we are inhabiting now. It will be a time of peace, long lives, and thriving under King Jesus. It is the "pre"-millennial point of view, because we are now living before (pre) the millennium. This point of view also says that the coming "tribulation period" will take place just before the millennium begins.

"Amillennialism" says that there will be no literal 1000-year period of time that Jesus rules the earth. Typically, Amillennialists say that we have been living in a figurative "millennium" since Jesus came the first time. Based on this theory, Jesus is now ruling over the earth and the Church is "ruling and reigning with Him." Satan is currently "bound up" in Hell and unable to influence the current inhabitants of the earth.

"**Pretribulation rapturists**" believe that prior to any prophetic events taking place, associated with the Second Coming, Jesus will come suddenly, unexpectedly, without warning, and secretly, like a "thief in the night," and take away His true followers in an event known as "the rapture." According to this view, the Church will not suffer under the Antichrist since the Church will not be present on the earth by the time the Antichrist comes to power. This view does not recognize a difference between "trials and tribulation" associated with the end of the age and the "wrath of God." This is the view portrayed in the popular *Left Behind* series by Author, Tim Lahaye.

"**Mid-tribulation rapturists**" believe that the rapture will take place exactly half way through the seven-year tribulation period. The Church will suffer some general troubles, but not all of the prophetic events associated with the end of the age.

"Post-tribulation rapturists" believe that the Church will suffer through all of the events of the tribulation and only then be caught away into the air to meet Jesus, at the end of the seven-year tribulation period, just prior to when the millennial reign of Jesus begins.

I will be discussing some of these points of view in great detail, so it is important to know these terms. However, rather than approaching what is said in the Olivet Discourse from one of these preconceived system approaches, I am going to suggest that we see where the scripture takes us and not worry about labels.

A Composite Picture of the End

The Olivet Discourse does not contain all of the details of the Second Coming or the end of the age, but it contains enough details that when we compare it with other scripture, we can tie certain events together and get a more complete picture. For example, when two different passages are talking about the sun going black, the moon turning red, and the stars falling from the sky, we are probably talking about the same event; especially when it is followed by a great gathering of souls from the earth. When we find these events that tie scripture together, it provides an opportunity to get a more complete picture, since both passages will contain additional details about the same event.

We will attempt to use the Olivet Discourse as a frame work in which to tie other scriptures that appear to be talking about the same events, in order to complete the picture of the end of the age. We will see where that takes us.

Watchfulness

Jesus stated no one would know the exact day or hour of his Second Coming. However, He gave us signs that would occur beforehand and spoke about the importance of being watchful for His return and not being caught off guard.

Although Jesus didn't provide as much detail about what would happen before hand, as our curious minds might have liked, He did give a couple specific and unmistakable signs that would precede His coming. He also stressed the importance of being faithful servants during His absence.

Jesus conveyed short stories or "parables" to the disciples in the Olivet Discourse. In the "*Parable of the Ten Virgins*" Jesus essentially lays out the roles of some major players at the end of the age; Himself, faithful Israel, unfaithful Israel, and the Church. Interpretations of what this parable means have varied greatly. Keys to unlocking this important passage are understanding the characters involved, the cultural wedding practices of Jesus' day, and what other prophetic scripture has to say about the end of the age.

The second parable is known as the "*Parable of the Talents.*" This often-misunderstood parable concerns how Jesus views faithful and unfaithful servants, and what they can expect when He returns. Key to understanding this parable is determining what the "talents" symbolically represent. Here, we will learn that the faithful servants of Jesus will be put in charge of great things and be invited to take part in "the joy of the Lord."

Jesus' last comments concern how He will judge the inhabitants of the Earth that remain at the end of the tribulation period. He uses the imagery of separating out the "Sheep from the Goats." The "sheep," representing those who have done good to the "brothers of Christ," end up inheriting a "kingdom" that has been prepared for them. The "goats," on the other hand, get cast into the "lake of fire."

The short stories Jesus used as examples serve to convey basic principles of the kind of behaviors that Jesus both does and does not value. However, we will see that in context, these stories all pertain to specific groups of people.

Before we begin looking at the Olivet Discourse itself, the next chapter discusses why it is extremely important for every Christian to understand the basics of Jesus' return and the end of the age. Then, since it is so often misused, we will look at how Christians should utilize biblical prophecy.

Notes

3. Why Every Follower of Jesus Needs to Know This Stuff

Unfortunate Instances of Misguided Understanding

On November 18, 1978, 909 people who thought they were living in a time when the end of the world was imminent, followed the direction of their spiritual leader, James Jones, and drank deadly cyanide-laced grape flavored Kool-Aid. Many would have at one time told you they were Christians. It took each of them an average of five terrible minutes to die. Tragically 303 of them were children. They were all completely deceived by their teacher.[6]

On April 19, 1993, following a fifty-one day standoff, seventy-five followers of the Branch Davidian faith, and their leader, David Koresh, perished in a fire. The fire started after the FBI fatally decided to end the standoff by launching a tear gas attack. The Branch Davidian Cult was an offshoot of the Seventh Day Adventist religion. They had all bought into false "end times" teaching. The results of these falsely held beliefs and the horrific consequences speak for themselves.[7]

On March 26, 1997, the bodies of thirty-nine men and women were discovered in Rancho Santa Fe, California, close to San Diego. Each had done the unthinkable and had just ingested cyanide and arsenic, in order to pass from this life, and reach what they believed was an alien space craft following the comet Hale–Bopp, which at the time, was showing its brightest in the night time sky. The thirty-eight "Heaven's Gate" cult members believed the teachings of their leader, Marshall Applewhite. He asserted that the earth was about to be "recycled," and that the only way to survive the process was to leave the planet. These concepts, held deep down at the existential core level of these people, held no truth. "Recycling the earth" and space ships chasing comets, were not part of what Jesus taught is going to happen. [8]

In another example, it is undeniable, that the Abraham, Isaac, and Jacob of the Old Testament did not come to life and return to the earth by the end of the 1920's. Yet, the leader of the Watch Tower organization of that period of time, Judge Joseph Franklin Rutherford, maintained that this would occur. So much so, that the organization purchased a San Diego home for the patriarchs to live in.[9] Today's Jehovah's Witnesses cling to the same principles of prophetic interpretation that deceived the followers of their religion in the 1920's. According to the 2013 Yearbook of Jehovah's Witnesses, there are approximately 7.53 million practicing Jehovah's Witnesses in the world.[10] Their entire religion is based on a version of "end time" teaching that is not what Jesus taught.

Many, who claim to be followers of Jesus, have attempted to name the day and hour of Jesus' return, in direct conflict with what Jesus said. In the eyes of non-believers, this has done great damage to the reputation of Christianity.

William Miller, a Baptist convert and the founder of the Seventh Day Adventist religion, stated that Jesus was going to return between March 21, 1843 and March 21, 1844. [11] He gathered a following of mainstream, church going Baptists, Methodists, and Presbyterians, all adherents to his belief. By 1844, over 100,000 people were counting on Miller's interpretation of prophetic scripture in how they were living their lives; namely, Jesus would return by March 21 1844. When his prediction didn't occur, he modified the date to be October 22. When Jesus again failed to return, many became very disillusioned. All of these people chose to ignore the words of Jesus, who in referencing His own return said, "no one knows the day nor hour."

The late Harold Camping, was an American Christian radio broadcaster, author and evangelist. Mr. Camping gained a great deal of notoriety, and a world-wide following for his multiple famous failed predictions on when Jesus would return to the earth. [12] His latest prediction was that the rapture would take place on May 21, 2011, and that the end of the world would occur five months later on October 21, 2011. Camping said that approximately 200 million inhabitants of the earth would be raptured. It was estimated that his organization, Family Radio, spent about five-million dollars on billboards proclaiming Camping's predictions. Mr. Camping was not independently wealthy. That money was donated by *many* deceived followers, who would call themselves "Christians." Many of them were convinced that the times we live in are what the Bible terms as the "last days."

Bad predictions, misuse of scripture, and deception regarding the Second Advent of Jesus have been going on for thousands of years. Both the chosen and the lost are looking for answers, and where there is lack of accurate information and teaching, they are buying into false teaching.

It is very troubling that those who preach and teach a false picture of the events surrounding the return of Christ, regardless of their good intentions, are contributing to great confusion and the deceiving of Christians. When the events of the tribulation actually unfold one day, those that sit under such false teachers may not recognize what is going on, and become disillusioned.

What a terrible thing it would be for believers to suffer unnecessary persecution because of lack of knowledge. Worse yet, how terrible it would be for them to fall away from the faith because wrong teaching from within the Church has deceived them. Unthinkable? Unfortunately, not; scripture teaches that such deception *will* happen on a large scale.

End Times Popularity

A Google search conducted on January 26, 2014 turned up the results cited below. As you consider the popularity of the subject among the masses, remember the word, "hit" means the number of links to web-pages containing the words typed in to the search engine used, and not the number of people searching out those words.

When I typed in "Apocalyptic books," I got 90,600,000 hits. "Apocalyptic TV shows" resulted in 8,330,000 hits. "Apocalyptic Movies"? 56,300,000 hits, and "End of the world" resulted in 2,110,000,000 hits. Yes, that is over two point one "billion!"

Why are people searching for answers on this important topic on the World Wide Web? Why don't Christians have better knowledge of what Jesus said in regards to His return? It seems like the end of the world as we know it, the judgment of the lost, and the return of the Messiah will be an important enough future event that people would like to know the real story on what is supposed to occur.

Why is this topic so often downplayed and avoided today within the Church? One might think the prophecies were poorly communicated or too difficult for mere humans to understand. Maybe God has lost track of time and people have lost interest in Jesus' return. God is a poor communicator? He can't tell time? Is this blasphemy or is this only paraphrasing common ideas people have in regard to the study of end times events?

God Is Not a Poor Communicator

Our God is not a poor communicator. He created time, space, matter, and all of reality that is including the very language that gave man the ability to understand Him. The Books that make up the Holy Bible were written down by men in the common, everyday language of the time with the expectation that lay people would understand it.

On the Mount of Olives as Jesus was talking about his own return in response to his disciple's questions, He was speaking plainly to them. They were after all, just common people. Just as people communicate with each other every day, Jesus used imagery, common sayings, and metaphors. Most people who lived during His time who had any familiarity with scripture already in existence would have had no problem understanding Him.

Any failure to understand Biblical prophecy is our failure. It is mainly a failure as a result of not applying consistent rules of interpretation that we apply elsewhere when attempting to understand scripture; considering the time period it was written during, the nuances of the original language, context, culture, history, etc. It has been a failure of allowing the scripture to speak for itself. Instead, the well-intended try to make it fit into the "boxes" of tradition, the teachings of particular seminaries, or systems that are the result of someone else's poor methods of understanding scripture, which were built upon another's faulty theories, that they received from yet another, etc.

Why Followers of Jesus Don't Study Bible Prophesy

Too difficult to understand

There are many reasons believers appear to be disinterested or apathetic about the study of the Second Advent. On more than one occasion, a pastor has said to me that "the Book of Revelation is so complicated and difficult to understand that it should only be studied after one has mastered the rest of the Bible." To me this was another way of saying "don't plan on ever studying the book of Revelation." If you were attending this pastor's church, do you think you would feel capable of studying prophetic scriptures on your own?

Too Controversial

Additionally, there are Church leaders who claim, "*matters of prophecy are just too controversial to discuss and can lead to discord among members of the body of Christ.*" "*No one agrees as to how prophecy should be interpreted, therefore we tend to stay away from the subject.*" This is another way of saying that they choose to argue about other things: salvation by faith vs. works, freewill vs. election, submersion vs. sprinkling baptism, grape juice vs. wine at communion, raising hands vs. kneeling during worship, speaking in tongues vs. taking up serpents, tithing, hymns vs. praise choruses, casseroles vs. finger foods at the Sunday potluck, or any number of other highly controversial issues. Anything, instead of making the Second Coming of Christ a part of basic Christian education in their Church.

Not Relevant

Since many main stream Christians in America still believe that Christians will be suddenly raptured without any signs or warning ahead of time, they don't see the point in studying prophetic scriptures that they don't believe pertain to them. They believe those scriptures will be more important to those who have been "left behind."

In his book, *Jesus' Final Warning*, Radio show host and author, Dr. David Jeremiah, recommends that when the believer is confronted by someone who says that they are not interested in prophecy we should read Luke 12:56 to them and show them how Jesus labeled such people "hypocrites." [13] In that scripture Jesus makes a point that some people place more importance on accurately predicting the weather, than they do understanding the predictions found in the bible.

Fear

For some, avoiding prophecy may be a failure of wanting to accept the truth, because sometimes the truth is very hard to hear. The truth may cause fear. I have never seen it, but I have heard that ostriches do the same thing when they get scared: they bury their heads in the sand.

"Apocalyptophobia," is the fear of the end of the world. For the Christian, this is an especially baseless fear. Only this age ends, not the world. Those whom are in Jesus, although they may experience some temporary (albeit severe) hardships and suffering, come out way, way ahead.

Excitement

The truth is just not sensational enough for some. Many fail to understand that the terrible things that fill the headlines every day are simply the result of living in a fallen world. So, rather than being aware of and watchful for the specific signs Jesus actually gave us, many in history, and many today choose to see themselves in a fictional period of time they think to be the "end of the age." After all, "aren't things worse now than ever?" "Aren't we seeing prophecy fulfilled every day?"

In their craving for excitement, they ignore prophetic scripture and instead buy into conspiracy theories that are echoed across talk radio stations and seen on social media. It seems the wilder the better: *"Don't all the shootings in movie theatres and schools, and threats of gun control, tie in with my suspicions that the President is a radicalized Muslim, who is covertly trying to aid ISIS in destroying the West and taking over the world in the name of the Islamic Antichrist?"*

The World is an exciting enough place to live, without involving my imagination to create an apocalyptic facade around me…

Don't want to be labeled an "End Times Nut"

Perhaps so few want to be associated with the study of end times prophecy because there has been so much misunderstanding, improper interpretation, speculation, predictions, and confusion over it.

Personally, I am always hesitant of telling people that I have extensively studied biblical prophecy because of the stigmas and prejudices that go along with the label. Being labeled a "prophecy buff" or "end times nut," is approximately the same in many people's minds as being labeled a "conspiracy theorist." Some, having learned that I am a student of biblical prophecy, have immediately responded with a smile and quoting scripture that "no man knows when Jesus will return," as if the purpose of studying prophecy is to determine the date of Jesus' return. It is not.

Laziness and Wrong or Different Priorities

Given the importance and relevance of the Lord of the universe returning to this planet, most people could stand to at least examine that event in relation to other priorities in life. I am not just talking about recreation and relaxation activities. There are also those who would say, "*I am too busy serving the Lord to understand what the Bible has to say about His Second Coming. It's all about saving souls, teaching others, and feeding people.*" Serving God in such ways is great, but what other critical information about the God that these folks are serving don't they know?

Understanding what Jesus and the prophets had to say about His Coming should be a part of every Christian's basic discipleship education. Passing on *all* that Jesus taught after all, was and is a part of the "Great Commission."

Disobedience and Hypocrisy

Jesus is quite clear when He commands His followers to "watch" for His return. Many Christians are indeed anxious to follow what they believe to be the commands of Jesus. Many people seem to have their favorite commands, which are easy to follow or provide them with gratification.

For the past few years it has been trendy to put a lot of thought in to "What Would Jesus Do" as we attempt to follow Christ, but many Christians would never think to ask "what would Jesus do in regards to studying and understanding prophecy."

Since there is only one Jesus, and He has a unique role, especially in regards to His Second Coming, I tend to think more along the lines of a different saying:

"*What Would Jesus Have Me; A Finite, Sinning, Human, Saved By Grace, With Unique DNA And Life Experiences, Who Cannot Walk On Water Or Ascend Into The Heavenlies On My Own, Do?*"

I know, this phrase, or even the initials, "WWJHMAFSH-SBGWUDNAALEWCWOWOAITHOMOD," just doesn't "sing." Nor would it even fit on a plastic bracelet, and is not as easy to remember as WWJD. However, in the case of the return of Jesus, the answer to this question would be to "watch," just as Jesus commanded.

Unfortunately, all of the above "reasons" for not being well versed at what the Bible has to say about the return of Jesus, stand as evidence of one of Satan's greatest success stories in the last two thousand years of history. What an utter tragedy and failure of the Church.

Representatives of Jesus Should Have Answers About Jesus

Believers and non-believers are both searching for answers and are ready to be taught. Those who claim to be Disciples of Christ should have inside knowledge of what's going on in God's world and should be ready to give an answer to those who ask. They should be familiar with Christ's teaching so they can strike down the lies of the deceiver who seems to be especially active in the area of end times misinformation. Prophetic passages such as the Olivet Discourse provide believers with the answers they need on this important topic.

One would expect that a true child of God would have a great interest in what He has to say regarding Jesus' return to earth. Biblical prophecy may turn out to be of most interest to those followers of Christ who are truly living at the end of this present age. If we are those people, we need to pay extra close attention. If the Messiah does not return in our lifetime, a true disciple of Christ should feel equally as compelled to pass on to the next generation accurate teaching regarding the prophetic scriptures.

Jesus' words to His disciples on the Mount of Olives during the week He would be crucified was out of His own desire to impart essential information that He thought was critical for His followers to know. Representatives of Jesus, should have answers for others based on that information. Jesus said to his followers;

Ye are the light of the world. A city that is set on an hill cannot be hid. Neither do men light a candle, and put it under a bushel, but on a candlestick; and it giveth light unto all that are in the house. Matt 5:14-15 (KJV)

Commanded to Be Watchful

We are encouraged, even commanded in scripture to be "watchful." The Olivet Discourse gives us essential information regarding being watchful. To attempt "watching" without it is like leaving on a trip when you don't know the destination. If you don't know where you are going, how are you going to know what signs to watch for that will inform you of your arrival?

What did Jesus mean when He commanded His disciples to "Watch?" Did He intend for His followers throughout time to hypothesize and speculate in what manner His return would be manifest? Did He mean for them to put together a system that could predict the date of His return? Possibly He meant for us to trust someone else to figure out what it means and maybe read a book from time to time on His Second Coming? Or, perhaps He meant something much different. Perhaps He was only saying to be alert and lead a sober life, ready to meet Him whenever He would happen to "sneak up" on us, possibly catching us "backsliding?"

Although there is other encouragement in the New Testament to be "watchful," by far the most encouragement per square inch comes from Jesus, when He spoke to His disciples on the Mount of Olives.

After His resurrection, as Jesus spoke to His disciples sometime prior to ascending into Heaven, as a part of the "Great Commission," in addition to commanding His disciples to make disciples of others throughout the world, He commanded them to pass on *everything* that He has taught them. "Everything" includes what He taught them on the Mount of Olives the night they asked Him about what will be the sign of His Coming and the end of the age. The information Jesus gave on the Mount of Olives to His disciples regarding the end of the age, is the same information he wants *all* of His disciples throughout time to hear and understand. How many who think they are teaching "all that Jesus commanded" are truly teaching what Jesus said on the Mount of Olives regarding His return?

Watchful Words

There are several different Greek words used in the New Testament for the English word "watch." When Jesus told His disciples to be "watchful" in reference to His Second Coming, the writers of the gospels mainly used two different Greek words to convey the idea of watchfulness. One of those words, "Βλέπω," is transliterated into English as "blepo" (blep'-o). It is a primary verb meaning, "to look at." Blepo is translated in the King James Version of the Bible as the words; "behold, beware, look, perceive, regard, see, sight, take heed." Blepo can mean to be "intent on," or "focused," or "to earnestly contemplate" something.

I believe that when blepo is used in scripture, the reader or hearer should look at what is being referred to with more than their eyes.

The second Greek word Jesus used regularly in speaking of His return is "γρηγορεύω," which is transliterated as "gregoreuo" (gray-gor-yoo'-o) meaning "to keep awake or watch," either literally or figuratively. Gregoreuo is translated in the KJV as the words "be vigilant, wake, (be) watch (-ful)." Its uses in the New Testament have both spiritual and physical applications. This word, more than "blepo," seems to be a more physically proactive form of watchfulness, like being on guard for something, or being on the lookout or staying awake and alert.

According to Luke's gospel there were two additional "watchful" words that were used in order to convey what Jesus said to His disciples during the Olivet Discourse. "Προσέχω," transliterated as "prosecho" (pros-ekh'-o), found in Luke 21:34. Prosecho means "to hold the mind, pay attention to, be cautious about, apply oneself to, adhere to." The other word Luke used for "watch" is "ἀγρυπνέω (Luke 21:36), transliterated as "agrupneo" (ag-roop-neh'-o), meaning to be "sleepless" or "keep awake."

In the Mark 13 account of the Olivet Discourse, the Greek word "blepo" is used six times, in the Luke account, twice, and two times in Matthew 24. "Gregoreuo" is used three times in Mark 13, two times in Matt 24 and is not used in Luke. The specific words used for "watch" vary a little from gospel to gospel because three different writers chose what they thought was the best way to convey the meaning of the words of Jesus. Those words were probably originally spoken by Jesus in the Aramaic language, then translated into the written language of common first century Greek by the different gospel writers (Hebrew in Matthew's case). In all cases, where the words differ, they still mean basically the same thing and are somewhat interchangeable given the repetition of the words and the theme of the passage. They all are communicating, "stay awake, don't miss this, pay attention, focus, and be on the lookout for what I am instructing you about!"

As you can see by the amount of times Jesus uses terms for being alert, awake, aware, on guard, and watchful, within the Olivet

Discourse, the message is clear; Watch! But what does it mean to be watchful?

A simple definition of watchfulness would be *putting wisdom and our knowledge of scripture into action, while we live with expectancy of the return of Christ.*

The spectrum of "watchfulness" within the Church ranges from fanatical sensationalism on one end, seeing "prophecies fulfilled every day," to the other equally off balance approach of taking watchfulness to simply mean that we are merely to live sober Christian lives up until the Lord returns. Whereas the former end of the spectrum contributes to deception and false alarms, the latter promotes an okay lifestyle, but leaves people open to being deceived.

Three Legs of a Watchful Stool

There may be more or fewer "legs" of the metaphorical "watchful stool" I want to build for you here, depending on how you divide up the topic, but three categories (legs) is as basic as I can reduce this important topic.

Leg #1: Knowledge

The first category of being watchful is to *know* what is in the Bible. In regards to the Olivet Discourse, that means to know the signs that will accompany Jesus' coming. As most know very well, the book of Revelation abounds with such signs. The Olivet Discourse is replete with signs as well. We will see that many signs mentioned in both passages are referring to the same sign. This first leg of the "stool" also includes the inverse idea of knowing what to watch for; It may be even more important to know; what are *not* the signs of His coming.

Jesus tells us there are "things" to watch for. After He lists a set of future events, Jesus says of His coming;

So likewise ye, when ye shall see all these things, know that it is near, even at the doors. Matt 24:33 (KJV)

As if Jesus is saying there is no excuse to miss the clarity of what the "things" are, He says;

Behold, I have told you before. Matt 24:25 (KJV)

The number of "things" to know about and watch for are few and easy to learn. They will be difficult to mistake when they occur.

There is little that is more important than knowing what is in God's word. The words contained in the Bible are foundational to how we construct the rest or our lives. To base our lives on anything less than the truth, is a waste of the one life that we were given as a gift from God. Be watchful; guard against deception by knowing God's Word.

Be sober, be vigilant; because your adversary the devil, as a roaring lion, walketh about, seeking whom he may devour: 1 Peter 5:8 (KJV)

<u>Leg #2: Be wise and pay attention: Be on guard for deception and watch for the signs contained in scripture.</u>

Once we know the information contained in the Bible, the practical application of watchfulness is to wisely pay attention to the world around us. We are to constantly be on the lookout for deception. If something or someone in the world is feeding you information that seems to be contrary to what the Bible has taught you, be careful!

In my own life I find that a major application of this type of watchfulness is pointing out sensationalism created by some, apathy about important issues on the part of others, misinterpretation of Biblical prophecy, and hoaxes designed to play on people's fears, ignorance, and emotions.

Playing on people's fears and ignorance sells books and causes them to send in their "seed faith" money. Fear and lack of knowledge causes people to eagerly tune in to the latest Nostradamus special, or, "how the world will end," series.

Jesus starts out his answer to His disciples on the Mount of Olives with the following words;

And Jesus answered and said unto them, take heed that no man deceive you. Matt 24:4 (KJV)

Guarding against deception is not possible without the first leg of the "stool;" knowledge of scripture. In general, the Christian is to guard against all types of false teaching. In the Olivet Discourse, even though it deals specifically with matters of the Second Coming, I believe it includes both encouragement to guard against false teaching having to do with the Second Coming, as well as all other doctrinal matters.

Jesus stresses the importance of watchfulness when He states that the deception will be so intense that even the "elect," the chosen followers of Christ, could be misled.

For there shall arise false Christs, and false prophets, and shall shew great signs and wonders; insomuch that, if it were possible, they shall deceive the very elect. Matt 24:24 (KJV)

The enemy, Satan, has been a deceiver since the Garden of Eden. As far as Satan's interaction with human beings, deception that misleads people into turning away from God's truth is his primary function in the universe. The Bible promises that right up to the end, Satan will be a deceiver. The defense against deception is to know the truth beforehand, then be alert and watchful for things that don't line up with the truth.

Do you know the prophecies well enough to recognize when God has intentionally not provided us with details? Can you tell when humans are filling in the blanks with speculation? I am convinced that this is a great deal of what Jesus is talking about when He refers to "false prophets;" people that attempt to provide detail where God intentionally gives none. This may take the form of Second Coming date setting, or it may take the form of getting specific and attempting to name the Antichrist or be specific about where he comes from, before he is revealed.

Forcing details where there are none can misguide believers as they watch for the return of Jesus. Beyond this, filling in details where there are none in the Bible, or adding human "wisdom" regarding morality and how to live out our lives, may be one of the leading causes of division amongst those Jesus has called to follow Him. Especially when people come to view those non-divinely provided details as important truths. Such practices may be at least partially to blame for 30,000 different Protestant denominations in existence today.

People want to fill in details because we are curious. Curious enough to cause two billion hits on the Internet for a search on the "end of the world." Filling in details where God chose not to give us any is a dangerous business. Besides getting really close to qualifying for being a "false prophecy," those details can end up misleading many people.

Acts of prophecy embellishing aid and abet Satan, the Great Deceiver, by distracting Christians away from watching for what they should be watching for: biblical signs. Instead, those that don't know any better chase after synthesized human theories.

Have you ever read a book or seen a form that had a page that said, "this page intentionally left blank?" I believe sometimes God has intentionally left out details that we would like to have filled in, and so, people tend to fill them in.

The Bible has much to say about how to acquire wisdom. Wisdom can come with age. However, from God's perspective, many old people have died "fools."

An angel once told the Old Testament prophet Daniel that the prophecies He had been given would not be understood until the "time of the end," and that even then, only the wise would understand them. Knowledge of the prophecies is nothing without God given wisdom.

And he said, go thy way, Daniel: for the words are closed up and sealed till the time of the end. Many shall be purified, and made white, and tried; but the wicked shall do wickedly: and none of the wicked shall understand; but the wise shall understand. Dan 12:9-10 (KJV)

Watchful stool leg #3: Abide in Christ

Being watchful is to live with *constant expectancy* that Jesus will return soon. This third essential watchful principal is all about how we approach *abiding in Christ*, or occupying ourselves with His business until we see Him in person, either in our death or at His coming.

Enduring until the end, while we act on behalf of Jesus in His absence, is another strong theme of the Olivet Discourse. Jesus very seldom spoke about prophecies, without somehow relating them to the believer's conduct in the present. He gave us guidelines about how to live right up until the time the prophecies pertaining to the end of the age are fulfilled.

Due to the position of the sun in the solar system and the rotation of the earth, a third of the world stands a good chance of being physically asleep in their beds at the "final trumpet," which will signal Christ's return. But, Jesus is not speaking of physical sleep when he says to "stay awake" and "be alert." He is calling us to be watchful in a way that as His followers would not be ashamed or embarrassed of if He were to walk in the door at any moment. His desire is that He will return and find us being about His business as good and faithful servants.

Prior to retirement, I worked for a medium to large sized County Sheriff's Office for over twenty-five years. I spent fourteen years as a Deputy Sheriff and then started promoting my way up through the ranks, retiring as the Chief Deputy.

I had several different assignments as a Deputy Sheriff. When I was assigned to the Electronic Surveillance Program, the office door I had faced another closed door that lead to the lobby. My desk sat in direct view of that door. At any given moment, if the receptionist pushed the button to unlock the door, anyone could come through without any warning whatsoever. What a gratifying moment it was when someone like my boss's boss came through the door and I was obviously up to my neck in productive pursuits that benefited my employer and demonstrated my enthusiasm for earning the public's trust through fiscal responsibility.

How different it would have been if I would have temporarily forgotten where I was. Then, when the boss walked in the door I had my shoes off, feet on the desk, radio blaring, playing a game on the county computer, while throwing potato chips at my co-worker (*This seldom happened*). My "master" (my boss's boss) would no doubt be very unhappy with what he found when he dropped in.

The Bible is full of descriptions and instructions on exactly what the Master's business is that He wants us to be taking care of in His absence. As He has placed His servants in every walk of life, in every area of the world, in every economic situation, what that business is will look different for everyone.

Attempting to tell followers of Jesus exactly what to do in regards to the Master's business is actually a great strength and focus of many twenty-first century churches. It is also the weakness of some. Whether or not the message of what believers should be doing while the Master is away has been correct, a watchful stool will not easily stand on this one leg alone. We must also be knowledgeable of scripture, and apply that knowledge to the world around us in Godly wisdom.

How Christians View End Times Prophecy Really Matters

There are of course many "end times fanatics" within the Church. Being watchful does not include sitting on your rooftop with your eye to the sky. It does include careful discernment of the times we live in, in light of what the scriptures have to say. It does not include being fanatical about prophecy and consumed by "end times" books, but familiarity with the scriptures regarding the return of Christ is essential in the life of a believer.

There is balance in God's universe. On the other end of the spectrum apart from the fanatics, not much time passes between the times I hear some Christian trying to downplay the importance of future prophetic events. These well intending believers attempt to make a case about how followers of Christ should be focusing our energy on how to get along in this world and best walk with Christ here and now.

I agree that we need to be "present" and deal with what God has placed before us this day. However, one cannot accomplish successfully living here and now as a Christian, if one is living *for* here and now as a Christian. To paraphrase my wife Angela's wise words, *an authentic Christian will live for Christ and not Christianity.*" Have I mentioned how much my wife loves Jesus?

Too many citizens of the Kingdom of God are overly concerned with living as citizens of this present earth, *here and now*, and not more about *there and then.* How to live debt free, how to resolve trouble in relationships, live a "victorious" life, a life free of health problems where putting your faith into action will allow God to shower you with blessings.

There is much to be said for applying scripture to our day to day lives. However, if we believers would place our focus and our hearts more on the world to come that God has in store for us, many of our current day problems would take care of themselves, or at the very least become less important to us.

What if you were going to live forever in a world where you had all the wealth you were ever going to require, and you were never going to get sick? Let us carry this fantasy a little further. What if in that world, you had super powers in addition to living forever and having all the wealth you would ever need? How would this change the way most think about their temporary troubles if their minds truly dwelled on such things? The thing is, the day you were reborn into God's family, that fantasy became a reality that will one day be realized.

One's particular views on matters of eschatology greatly affects what one's doctrinal views are across the board. For example, many Amillennialists (belief that there is not a literal future thousand-year kingdom of Jesus on this earth) believe we are living in an age where Satan is bound up and is not a factor in this present age. This being the case, all the rest of their doctrines are influenced by this belief. Is Satan a spiritual influence in our day or not? How could he be if he is currently bound up in Hell?

Then there is the very popular idea in the Church of a "secret (pre-tribulation) rapture" that *most* evangelical Christians believe in. We see in the Tim Lahaye *Left Behind* series there is a "second chance" doctrine; those who are "left behind" will still have a chance to become saved.

Summary

Ever since Jesus' feet left the Mount of Olives and He ascended into the clouds, people have been looking for answers regarding His Second Coming and the end of the age. Because of lack of knowledge and false teaching, many have been deceived regarding these things. There has been much misunderstanding as to the proper use of biblical prophecy that has led to a great deal of false teaching. Even though it is the Bible itself that warns us of this, it also tells us that this deception will continue into the future, and in fact get worse.

As Servants of Jesus, we are to be "lights" to the world and ready with answers regarding God's plan when people have questions. We are commanded to be watchful pending the return of Jesus; know the signs of His coming, be on guard for deception, and be about His business as any good and faithful servant would be. Finally, how we approach end times prophecies will affect our approach to life as believers in Christ here and now as well as in the future.

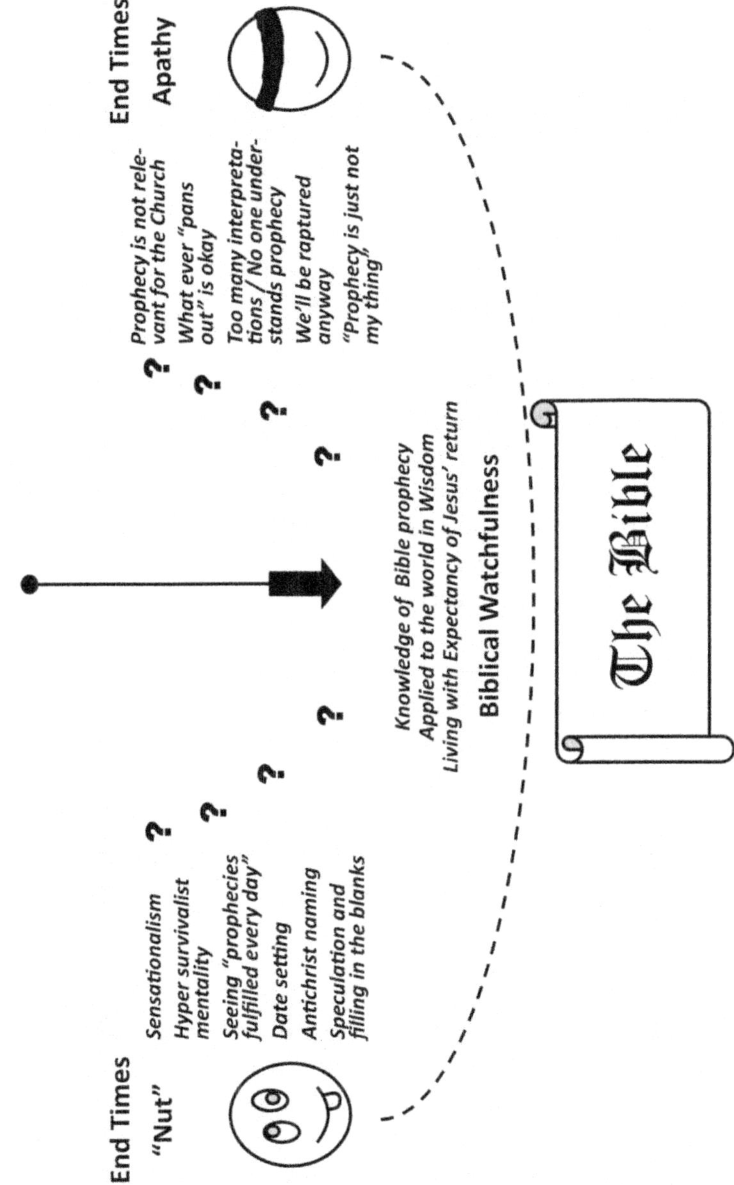
Where Would the Pendulum Find You?
End Times
"Nut"
Sensationalism
Hyper survivalist mentality
Seeing "prophecies fulfilled every day"
Date setting
Antichrist naming
Speculation and filling in the blanks
End Times
Apathy
Prophecy is not relevant for the Church
What ever "pans out" is okay
Too many interpretations / No one understands prophecy
We'll be raptured anyway
"Prophecy is just not my thing"
Knowledge of Bible prophecy
Applied to the world in Wisdom
Living with Expectancy of Jesus' return
Biblical Watchfulness
The Bible

4. The Real Purpose of Prophecy

Before you read on, let's see how well you know your Bible prophecy. Are you prepared to interpret the events that take place around you in light of what the Bible has to say? Try out the following test and see how you do. The answers will follow. Don't cheat! No fair looking up the answers in your Bible or looking ahead in the chapter! Try going by what you already know and have observed in the world around you. No one will ever know but you how you did. Here we go…

Surprise Prophecy Quiz!

Instructions: Nine scenarios follow. Choose one answer based on your knowledge of biblical prophecy.

1. **You have just found out that a third of "mankind" in the continents of Europe and Asia died from pestilence. It completely destroyed their economy. No one was unaffected by this tragedy. What best describes this event?**

a. The fourth seal of Revelation being opened which speaks of plague and death.
b. The third trumpet of Revelation is blown which has to do with something like an asteroid falling on a third of the waters, resulting in poisoning and the subsequent death of "many".
c. The sixth trumpet of Revelation is blown resulting in four "angels" being released that go forward to kill a third of mankind.
d. None of the above.

2. **A government law-enforcement official sits outside of a church during a late evening meeting. With state of the art monitoring equipment, he watches people as they leave the building. His equipment finally registers the presence of the person he has been sent to find. This situation sounds most like:**

a. The persecution of the Church Jesus warned about in Matthew 24.
b. The persecution of the Church that takes place after the mid-point of the tribulation period.
c. The persecution that takes place after the rapture of the church involving those who are "left behind" that come to know the Lord.
d. None of the above.

3. In the midst of constant tragedies and conflict in Israel, a third party steps in to help facilitate peace by co-signing a peace agreement with Israel. This agreement:

a. Is the "covenant" spoken of by the prophet Daniel.
b. Will last for seven years
c. Will last for 1,260 days before it is broken by the Antichrist.
d. All of the above.
e. None of the above

4. Attempting to revive the Roman Empire, a dynamic evil tyrant sets out to destroy every living Jew. This incident:

a. Takes place just after the 3 ½ year mark of the tribulation.
b. Takes place after Satan is cast out of Heaven.
c. Is not mentioned in the bible.
d. Is exactly what Revelation 12:13 speaks of when it talks about the dragon pursuing the woman into the wilderness.
e. None of the above.

5. A well-known world religious leader claims to speak for God Himself and has the full support of the ruling kingdoms, in fact he has twisted his brand of religion to a point where people once again can be put to death for something as simple as possessing a Bible. This situation speaks of:

a. The false prophet.
b. The second beast of Revelation.

c. The first beast of Revelation.
d. The dragon of Revelation.
e. Both a and b.
f. None of the above.

6. In any given four-day period, it is not uncommon to experience 20 earthquakes or more in the area of the Pacific Rim alone. They range from 4.0 magnitude on the Richter scale to 6.0. What the world is experiencing is best described by:

a. Jesus in Matthew 24 when he speaks of earthquakes in "diverse" places.
b. The earthquakes in "various" places spoken of in Mark 13 and Luke 21.
c. The specific set of earthquakes mentioned in the book of Revelation.
d. Both a and c
e. None of the above.

7. On top of all of the other "cash-less" society inventions, there is one that is used to gain entrance to attractions and businesses. Those guarding the gates must first scan the patron's hand for the mark that has been placed there, which is invisible to the naked eye. This situation is probably best described by:

a. The mark of the beast mentioned in Revelation chapter 13.
b. The seal of God spoken of in Revelation chapter 7.
c. The cash-less society that comes about just after the "secret rapture."
d. None of the above.

8. A dynamic evil figure orders his troops to take control of the Temple in Jerusalem. Following this he enters the temple himself and causes pigs to be sacrificed on the altar. He sets up images of false gods in the very Holy of Holies and forces people to worship them. Those who

refuse are threatened with the penalty of death. This clearly:

a. Is the "abomination of desolation" spoken of by Daniel the prophet.
b. Takes place exactly 1,260 days after the Antichrist enters into a covenant with Israel.
c. The action that is a signal for those who are "in Judea" to flee into the hills.
d. The last action that we will be able to see before the severe persecution of the Church takes place.
e. None of the above.

9. People willingly follow the leader of the Western World who actively persecutes Jews and Christians. Christians are being put to death without trials. In spite of his claims that he is some sort of deity, he becomes well known for his sexual immorality. In the middle of executing his political agenda, he subjects a young man to transgender surgery and then marries him. This is:

a. An example of societal decline and people refusing to "love the truth," indicating that we are in the last days.
b. A fulfillment of the prophecy concerning the Antichrist having "no desire for women."
c. Both a & b.
d. None of the above.

The Answers

How do you think you did? Some readers probably couldn't help but notice the similarities of the different scenarios with modern day headlines and events of history. Let's go through the questions.

Question #1, a third of the population dies: What I had in mind was the "Black Death." It was the plague the world experienced from 1348 to about 1351 that wiped out much of the known world's population. It is estimated a third of mankind died during the plague. *Knowing a little history puts things into perspective.* The answer was "None of the above."

Question #2, government monitoring: The government official was me. It was some years back, during my time as a Deputy Sheriff assigned to the "Electronic Surveillance Program." Similar to the program that Martha Stewart was placed on when she got out of prison. I was at work checking on a client who was on "house arrest." She was supposed to be attending an Alcoholics Anonymous meeting in the church. Her ankle bracelet put out a signal that allowed me to confirm she was actually where she was supposed to be without intruding on the meeting. *Sometimes not having all of the information before we draw conclusions is dangerous.* The answer was "None of the above."

Question #3, peace agreement: What I had in mind here was the Oslo Peace Accord agreement of the early 1990s. Israel has entered into many agreements with other countries. Many times they are "confirmed" by other powerful nations such as the US. *It is good to be aware of modern day political developments.* The answer was "None of the above."

Question #4, tyrant attempts to destroy Jews: I was thinking of Hitler when I wrote this question. Although Hitler was obviously not *the* Antichrist that was in power when Christ will return, he *may* have been one of the seven antichrists spoken of by the Apostle John. He certainly had the same characteristics of previous antichrists. *It is important to be familiar with scripture in order to know how everything fits together.* The answer was again "None of the above."

Question #5, religious leader: I had in mind here the Roman Catholic popes of the Middle Ages who caused people to be burned at the stake for possessing a Bible or giving aid to those who translated or printed Bibles, or who did not adhere strictly to the teaching of the Church. The answer is "None of the above."

Question #6, earthquakes: The period of time I looked at for this information was May 4, 2001 to May 7, 2001. I found the information on the United States Geological Services website. You will find roughly the same type of information on any given day, for any given time period. More than anything else I hear people talking about earthquakes in "various places" as proof that we are living in the last days. When you look at the actual data, there has not been any increase in earthquakes since they have been recorded. Only our awareness has increased. *It is important when you hear claims such as this,* *to check them out.* When we make claims, we want them to be credible. The answer again is "None of the above."

Question #7, cash-less society: This technology has existed at Disneyland, among other places, for years. They stamp your hand with ink, which is only visible under a black light. The mark is usually something like Donald Duck. It washes off. We are surrounded by "cash-less" society technology. The only thing is, the Bible never mentions a "cash-less society." *Again, familiarity with scripture is imperative.* "None of the above."

Question #8, dynamic evil figure: In 167 BC, according to historian Josephus, Greek (Seleucid) King Antiochus (IV) Epiphanes desecrated the Temple in Jerusalem before the birth of Christ. Roman General Titus did it again in 70 AD after the resurrection of Christ. Although something like this will one day happen again, I had the historical events in mind. "None of the above."

Question #9, people following an immoral leader: Emperor Nero, circa 66AD, married his slave boy, Sporus, after having him castrated. Nero was a persecutor of Christians perhaps like no other has ever been. As immoral as society had become and bad as things were for Christians and Israel under Emperor Nero, Jesus did not return. In fact, years after Nero's death, under Emperor Constantine, Christianity was legalized and accepted. In that sense, things got better, when it looked like the end. Yet, Rome collapsed. I am not saying that one thing has to do with the other, but in order to address those that say that a nation's acceptance or rejection of "Christianity" is a sign of the impending end of the age, I must point out that it was only after the wide acceptance of Christianity by Rome, that the Roman Empire ultimately collapsed. The answer to question "9" was again, none of the above.

Truthfully, I could have included an answer option on each question that would have said, "not enough information given," and it would have been the correct answer on most questions. The other answer I could have included with some questions is, "the Bible doesn't talk about this or specify that level of detail."

Many Reasons God Gives Us the Inside Scoop

The word "prophecy" can mean a couple different things. It can take the form of any divinely inspired utterance given by a prophet. It doesn't have to be about what is going to happen in the future. The most common way that we define the word is that it concerns the predicting of future events. In the case of bible prophecy, I am writing about the divinely inspired revealing of future events.

It is said that 27% of the Holy Bible is made up of prophecy.[14] There are many reasons why God provided so many prophetic passages to us. I could never say that there is one specific reason for prophecy. However, there are many ways to misuse it as I just illustrated in the above "test." Continuing to look at misuses of prophecy, let's attempt to get at the appropriate use of prophecy through the process of elimination.

Our job as modern day believers, while we await either our death or the return of Jesus, is to be watchful and engaged in doing His business until we see Him. It is not to further prophesy about His return. We are to be *readers* of truth, not *authors*. Trying to predict a specific future, naming names and dates, superimposing nuclear bombs over imagery in Revelation are all examples of misuses of biblical prophecy. Speaking authoritatively about who the Antichrist is or will be, when the Bible only indicates that positive identification is possible after he performs specific acts, is adding to scripture. Those that do so are, or are dangerously close to obtaining the title of a "false prophet." The kind that Jesus warned us about.

Most popular end-times instructional books such as, *The Late Great Planet Earth,* by Hal Lindsey, and *Global Peace,* by the late, Dave Hunt, among others, attempt to fill in information where the Bible does not. Scenarios contained in these books are based on current day (some now historical) trends, technology, and political figures. For example, in his book *Global Peace*, Hunt attempts to make the case that 1980s USSR leader Mikhail Gorbachev is the Antichrist and Pope John Paul II is his false prophet. At least 50% of this prediction died with Pope John Paul II. Mikhail Gorbachev fell from power when the USSR was dissolved in 1991. Although he has since tried to start a new political party in Russia three times since then, it doesn't appear this 84+ year old will be back into the global power arena anytime soon. Predictions like this are very common. The book of Revelation ends with a severe warning to anyone who would add to its contents. Jesus gave us exactly what to watch for, we don't need anyone adding additional details.

It is one thing to attempt to interpret the scripture and discuss possibilities where the scriptures are not clear. It is another to declare a theory to be true, as in God inspired True, with a capital "T," when it is really only a theory. Many unwatchful and unwise Christians have changed their lives based on such things.

Some times when people find out that I study biblical prophecy, they ask, "So who do you think the Antichrist is?" They then seem disappointed somehow or draw the conclusion that I don't know anything about biblical prophecy when I answer "I don't know."

I call this whole issue trying to "pin the tail on the antichrist." Here's how you play: put on a blindfold and wander around a major football stadium full of a hundred million photographs of people and stick a needle in one. Baby pictures and ultrasound images are okay to include since the Antichrist may not even be born yet. Before the Antichrist actually appears someday, you will likely have as much chance sticking the needle in the photograph of the Antichrist as anyone else who is trying to speculate who he may be based on current trends and number crunching.

People Are Looking for A Savior

Why are people attracted to end times books that attempt to fill in the blanks in their minds? In my opinion, one reason is because people are looking for a "savior." In general, people, Christian and non-Christian alike, believe that the events that will take place at the "end of the world" sound like kind of a downer, to say the least. Whether you believe the world will end because of the ozone being depleted, or that the Antichrist will attempt to kill off all the Jews and Christians, for some reason, people pick up on the negativity of how that sounds; THREATENING! People feel as though they will be helpless victims in such a scenario. So, they go looking for a rescuer, or a savior.

Looking for something to save us from the "end of the world" follows the classic model known as the Karpman Drama Triangle. This model was named for the guy who came up with the concept in 1968, Stephen Karpman, M.D. People tend to set up "drama triangles" in their lives when they feel threatened. For example, your boss is mean because he or she won't give you a day off. Your boss is the "persecutor." You look to your co-worker to console you and maybe give you some advice on how to get that day off anyway. He or she is your "rescuer." You of course are the helpless third part of the triangle, the "victim"

In the case of the end of the age, the obvious persecutor is the trials and tribulation associated with that period of time. Those who will be in existence then, potentially us, are the victims. Additional information and details, especially those that may indicate there is a way out of suffering, can be considered the "rescuer." Sometimes this "rescuer" may come in the form of an author of a book, a cult leader, or even the pastor of a church.

Being "rescued," is why many Christians want to hold firmly to the pre-tribulation rapture theory. That belief provides a way out from possible suffering at the hands of the Antichrist. People hold to this theory, most of the time, not because it is supported by a superior scriptural case, but because it promises that they will be rescued.

People go looking for more information to rescue or "save" them from oncoming badness. After all, if there was some hidden information that could save your hide, wouldn't you want to know? I would! The problem is, the Bible provides us with all the information we need regarding the end of the age and the Second Coming of Christ and tells us that the only Savior we can count on is Jesus. No other information will ever possibly serve as our rescuer. Your only hope is to rely on Jesus and be familiar with the information He gave us regarding His return. Come what may, Jesus is our only, one and true rescuer.

People Love Excitement

As pointed out in the last chapter, people fail to study prophecy because the real thing may not be exciting enough for them. This is what drives another misuse of prophecy.

It can be heard on most days as you tune into any number of popular "Christian" television prophecy based shows that the world is ending. It amazes me how many times I have heard the phrase, "we are seeing prophecies being fulfilled every day! How exciting!" How many times can the same prophecy be fulfilled over the last 40 years that has to do with the event of the Lord's return? It is like the Bible saying that people will continue to sin and then every time someone does, it is pointed out as a "fulfilled prophecy."

Such statements seem to be made to sensationalize normal, day to day events as though designed to keep peoples' interest up. This is likely in order to draw support for what some call a "ministry," and others call a "scam."

There actually are prophetic events that will manifest themselves in an ongoing trend. When they occur, it will not be a one-time event. Consider the following:

And then shall many be offended, and shall betray one another, and shall hate one another. And many false prophets shall rise, and shall deceive many. And because iniquity shall abound, the love of many shall wax cold. Matt 24:10-12 (KJV)

This prophecy will come true many times in the last days and will involve many people. The difficulty is figuring out how this prophecy is different than what has occurred in the past and is occurring in our world right now. In order for this to be considered a "hard sign" there would need to be a very dynamic and significant increase in this type of activity.

Whereas one person may write a book, or preach from the pulpit that we are in a time where people are abandoning the truth, turning away from the one true God, and even converting to Islam, I can quickly do the same quality of research on the internet, that brought them to their conclusions and show you how millions are converting to Christianity from Islam. I can show you how Africa will be 50% Christian by the year 2050, and how crime is down in much of the world. I can give you statistics on how life expectancy is longer than ever, and how many, many other things people associate with the end of the world, are not possible to judge from our finite human perspective.

For almost any modern day situation that you may point to as an "end times sign," I can also point to events in history that are more serious or are better examples of what Jesus said that will serve as signs that the end of the age is drawing near. Jesus warns about these types of things in the Olivet Discourse.

It is my opinion that there were very few actual prophecies dealing with the End of the Age that were completely fulfilled in the entire 20th century. Prophecies that I would call "hard signs." I believe there were a couple, and they were very, very significant.

However, we haven't seen countless prophecies "fulfilled," in recent history as the claims of some sensationalists would suggest. Most of what we see is the product of living in a world that is groaning, travailing, and occupied by fallen creatures known as human beings. It is a world where Satan is alive and well, and not yet bound up in Hell. It is a world that has been falling apart since the time of Adam. We must "keep the faith," persevering in watching for the real events revealed by Jesus and the prophets to take place.

Prophecy Function #1: After the Fact Confirmation

I have often compared the Bible in regards to end times events to a template or a stencil that is designed to be held in front of you as the world passes by. Picture holding your Bible out in front of you, opened up wide with the pages facing you. Contained in your wide-open Bible is a series of holes of various shapes and sizes that go completely through the pages and out the other side of the cover. Each of these cutouts represents a scriptural prophetic event. The cutouts are specific in shape and size. Some of the cutouts are very intricate. They would require something very specific to fill them in. Others are very basic and would be more easily filled. However, you would notice that the details of what will fill the cutouts are missing. We have no idea what they will look like. Only the outline of the shapes are present.

Some of the cutouts are stationary and never move on the page. They represent events that God has given enough detail in scripture that we know that they are sequential. Yet there seem to be other events that circle around the open pages, like the hand on a clock because we don't know for sure according to scripture when those events will occur in relation to the others.

As you look through the template, or stencil, you see the world passing by on the other side as we travel through this life one day at a time. Every once in a while you will see something occurring through the template that matches up very well with one of the cut outs. At times you may even see good matches to two or three cutouts all at the same time. They pass by the other side, move into history, and the world does not end.

This biblical template is not meant to be held up at an angle to the side that you are traveling towards, as if you were watching it come down the river. You should not try to look ahead to see what may fill the cutouts. The very angle of trying to look ahead skews the images and puts them out of focus. Trying to use your prophetic template to predict details in the future just will not work. Things will be hidden and out of proportion and you will miss things that are happening right in front of you. You need to keep your template right in front of you and examine the events as they come.

Some attempt to identify ahead of time, based on what they know right now, the events, things, or persons that they believe could possibly be a good match in the future for the cutouts in the prophetic biblical template. They do this not knowing if those events, things, or persons will even be possible or in existence next year. They do this not knowing if a better match will be in existence next year. And, at the risk of sounding very judgmental, they arrogantly do so failing to take into consideration that God's ways are far above our own and His plan is far more detailed and complex, than one that could ever allow us to accurately predict the details of it.

It may be God's will that there will be a world-wide revival. There could be a plague that wipes out a large percentage of the people adhering to any of the world's "fastest growing religions," thereby changing the dynamics of our current situation. The real estate that the United States currently sits on, could go the way of every other kingdom and empire history has ever known and change hands several times. Jesus may not return for decades, centuries, or millennia. Those are details we don't have that the misguided and curious often try to provide.

Filling in detail ahead of time, where none is given distracts believers from their watchful mission. Focusing on unconfirmed theories, even when they are in the realm of the possible and plausible, causes one to narrow one's gaze and leaves him or her susceptible to an attack from behind their self-made blind spot. Where these theories are not accurate, spreading them, supporting them, or teaching about them, as if they are missing details from the Bible, is to spread deception.

Those who are wise will not speculate, for example, about how the late and former Palestinian Authority Chairman Arafat would become the Antichrist because the way he wore his turban resembled a "little horn," which is spoken of in the book of Daniel. Instead, the wise will continue to study the scriptures and evaluate what is taking place in the world in light of those scriptures. They will recognize that the Bible speaks of a few specific events in a specific order, and until those events are manifest they may rule them out as being "end times" events. They are not worth considering any longer.

Earthquakes happen, plagues happen, evil happens. Almost all "watching" comes in the form of ruling out events as being an end time event by utilizing the template method. Any one of the questions in the "test" given at the beginning of this chapter may very well be how an event of the end plays out, but the fact is none of them had anything to do with the Second Coming of Christ. Most of the events mentioned, however, did on some level contribute to people believing that the end was near because of their misconceptions of how bible prophecy is supposed to work. People have been misusing prophecy in this way for nearly two thousand years.

Preterists and Historicists are those that see the events that Jesus spoke of as largely taking place in the past, therefore their interpretations of prophecy break down because they violate the above idea. They pick and choose this event over here to fulfill this prophecy, and that event over there, which happened hundreds of years later, to fulfill something that was supposed to happen earlier. They all ultimately fall short in that the prophetic events were supposed to accompany the Second Coming of Christ. Although there are exceptions, few will argue that they think Jesus has already returned.

One day, *maybe* in our day, those that are watching the world through our "prophetic template," the Holy Bible, *will* find that all of the cutouts are filled with a perfect match. At that time, they can declare, "this is it!" Since the time of Christ there have been many matches to some of the cut outs, but there has never been a perfect match to all of them, and in the correct order. Until that time, we are called to be watchful by continuing to grow in knowledge and understanding of the scriptures, to be aware of what is going on around us in the light of what we learn, and to abide in Christ and do His business until he comes.

It is said that there were over 300 "prophecies" that foretold the first coming of Jesus to this earth a little over 2,000 years ago. However, how many guessed or predicted correctly beforehand the "who, what, where, and when" of the actual circumstances of Jesus' birth? After the fact, after the events have all taken place, all of the prophecies makes sense to anyone who considers them. In this same way, to anyone who is watching, all of the prophecies will make sense once the actual events take place.

Biblical Prophecy Function #2: Our Blessed Hope

Christians would have nothing after this life to look forward to without prophetic scripture. We have been told what is coming and what eternity holds for us. Without this hope, the only thing we would have to look forward to for sure, is possibly waking up tomorrow and doing our best to live our lives in a fallen world. We would have a different kind of "hope" for eternity. One based on our guesses that a good God would surely do something nice for us after we die.

The fact is, that our good God has told us what we can count on if we put our faith and trust in Jesus; eternal life that includes no sickness, pain, or sorrow. We will have the capabilities of our risen Savior, Jesus, who could fly without a plane, walk through walls, walk on water, travel places instantly and either be in the presence of humans in the physical realm, or in Heaven in the spiritual. Although always in a servant role to King Jesus, we will one day rule this earth with Him. Now we know in part, then, we will know everything. All of this is exciting and very cool.

Because of prophecy, even though we know the world is going to get really bad, we know the ultimate "cavalry" rescue scene is going to take place at the end of the story. We know that followers of Jesus will be saved by Him, and that He will justly judge those who have chosen another way. Because of this, we can believe in ultimate justice. We also know that those who are in Christ will not ever suffer the final wrath of God. We know we will one day see our ancestors, family members, and friends who have died, who also placed their hope and trust in Jesus. Because of biblical prophecy, we can know that there is much to look forward to.

Biblical Prophecy Function #3: Instruction

Some biblical prophecy gives instruction on what to do once an event takes place;

When ye therefore shall see the abomination of desolation, spoken of by Daniel the prophet, stand in the holy place, (whoso readeth, let him understand:) Then let them which be in Judaea flee into the mountains: Let him which is on the housetop not come down to take any thing out of his house: Neither let him which is in the field return back to take his clothes. Matt 24:15-18 (KJV)

The reader or hearer of this passage is clearly instructed that when they see the event spoken of here and if they are in the region of Judea that they are to take quick action by fleeing into the mountains. These are very specific and rare prophetic instructions pertaining to the future.

Biblical Prophecy Function #4: Warning

There are perhaps several types of "warnings" given in prophecy, but I consider there to be two main types: conditional, and non-conditional. Conditional being the case of an event taking place based on the actions of those who are receiving the prophecy, and unconditional being the case where an event is going to take place regardless of what anyone does about it. In both cases, the receiver of the prophecy is being warned so that they can be "watchful."

An example of a conditional prophecy follows:

Repent; or else I will come unto thee quickly, and will fight against them with the sword of my mouth. Rev 2:16 (KJV)

Here, Jesus is giving the first century Church in Pergamum an "if-then" like warning. To paraphrase, *"**if** you don't turn around and change your ways, **then** count on some corrective action to be taken."*

Setting aside arguments regarding predestination and God's sovereignty for a moment, salvation itself, on the surface, appears to be based on conditional prophecies: **If** you put your faith in Jesus, **then** you will have eternal life. Of course God knows ahead of time what will occur. It is His story that He has written, He has chosen those who will be "saved," but from our human perspective and understanding, He is giving people a choice with conditional prophecies.

Non-conditional prophecies pertain to such things as the first and Second Coming of Jesus. God has a very specific plan. He graciously lets us know about some of His plans ahead of time, so that we may take appropriate action in response.

With the purposes of prophecy in mind, let us endeavor to not misuse it as we begin to study what Jesus said to His disciples towards the end of a long day, during Passover week, around 2,000 years ago.

5. The Scene

The year was around thirty AD.[15] Jesus and His twelve disciples were about seventy-five miles, a three or four-day journey, away from His hometown of Nazareth. Jesus came here, to Jerusalem, from a place called Ephraim, in the north.

On the "road" the thirteen men went through a sparsely populated valley that was covered in tropical vegetation on both sides. They crossed the Jordan River and passed through the City of Jericho, spending the night there in the house of a tax collector named Zacchaeus (Luke 19:1-7). Jericho, during Jesus' day was a center of Greek paganism. It was a modern city filled with magnificent fountains and gardens.

On the way out of Jericho, a large crowd followed Jesus. As He passed by a couple blind men who were sitting along the road called out to Him to catch his attention. Jesus inquired of them their desire. They respond with a deep desire to see. Jesus touches their eyes and they were both healed (Matthew 20:29). Imagine the first thing you see at that life altering moment is the Savior's face staring back into yours... Later, the last twenty-three miles of the journey from Jericho to Jerusalem would take the group up a dusty winding road that passed by cliffs which towered 4,000 feet high.[16]

The disciples knew this trip they were taking with their Master, Jesus, was different than any trip they had previously undertaken with Him before. Although the twelve didn't understand Jesus at the time, He had told them that as a result of taking this trip to Jerusalem, He would be delivered over to the Gentiles (non-Jews) at which time He would be mocked, spit on, flogged, and then killed. Then He told them that three days after His death, He would rise from the dead (Luke 18:32-33). It is no wonder the disciples didn't understand Jesus; who would take such a trip if they knew those things were going to literally happen. What could Jesus have possibly meant that He would rise three days after being killed?

It is now late Tuesday afternoon and time to start thinking about finding some place to spend the night. Jerusalem is crowded with thousands of pilgrims whom have come here for the annual Passover celebration.

The day started off in Bethany, which lays about one and a half to two miles away at the base of the south-east side of the Mount of Olives (Matthew 21:17). Jesus arrived in Bethany six days prior to the Passover (John 12:1). He most likely spent the last four nights in that location. He may have been staying at Mary, Lazarus, and Martha's house. They were good friends of Jesus. In fact, not very long before, Jesus had raised Lazarus from the dead after he had been in the grave for four days (John 11:1-44). Needless to say, that event caused quite a stir in Bethany and beyond. From that day on, the Jewish religious leaders had determined they needed to kill Jesus (John 11:53). It was right after Jesus raised Lazarus from the dead that he retreated to Ephraim in the north.

Looking for some breakfast on the prior day (Monday morning), Jesus came upon a fig tree that had no figs on it. Figs were not in season, but apparently disappointed, or more likely in order to make a point, Jesus cursed the tree. To the amazement of his disciples, the next morning (Tuesday morning) when they passed by the same tree, they found it withered and dead (Mark 11:12-14 & 20-25). We will see later that this action is important in completely understanding the Olivet Discourse.

This was the third day in a row that Jesus and his disciples had visited the temple in Jerusalem. On Sunday, they came in to a small village named Bethpage, which sat next to Bethany, in the vicinity of the Mount of Olives. Jesus sent two of his disciples to fetch a colt.[17] The colt which the disciples found was that which Jesus rode into Jerusalem. As He did so a large crowd of people laid down palm branches before Him and shouted "Hosanna," a word which originally represented a cry for help to God, but by this time was intended to be a shout of joy and welcome. This word was also associated with deliverance by the Anointed One, the Messiah.[18] A large crowd would have been easier to come by during the Passover week since the population of Jerusalem's metropolitan area would have swollen from its normal approximate 100-200 thousand residents. [19]

After Jesus arrived in Jerusalem on Sunday, He toured the temple. Since it was already late, He went back to Bethany to spend the night (Mark 11:11).

Monday morning, after cursing the fig tree on the walk from Bethany to Jerusalem, Jesus paid a second visit to the Jewish Temple. Arriving there, He flipped over the tables of some dubious vendors, who were charging outrageous fees for exchanging common "dirty" money, for "holy" money. This was money that would have been used for such things as purchasing animals to sacrifice (Matthew 21:10-16). Jesus acted with the authority of a homeowner kicking unwanted people out of His house. It was after all, considered the dwelling place on earth of His Father; the Almighty God.

It was now Tuesday and Jesus had again made the approximate forty-five-minute walk back to Jerusalem from Bethany, walking by the now dead and withered fig tree. As Jesus entered the temple there were probably some nervous moneychangers after the incident the day prior. Jesus spent most of the day teaching in parables, being tested, outwitting the Pharisees, and teaching in the temple. He became very pointed in expressing his disapproval for the Jewish religious leaders, even calling them "blind guides," and "snakes."

How amazed and excited His disciples must have been to witness the events of the last few days. Was this the moment they had anticipated? Massive crowds were following the master shouting blessings. He was validating all His claims by performing miracles right in front of them. People were looking to Jesus as a prophet and quite possibly their Messiah. None of the temple guards attempted to arrest Jesus even though He had caused major disruptions. Jesus was outwitting anyone who dared to question Him. What pride the disciples must have felt in their Master, and likely in themselves, to be associated with Him.

Yet, Jesus knew how the week would progress. He knew by the end of the week, one of His disciples, Judas, would betray Him, and that one of His closest friends, Peter, would deny He even knew Jesus. It was time to speak clearly to his disciples. His time was growing short. By the end of the evening He again revealed to his disciples that he would be crucified in just a couple days (Matthew 26:1-2).

Although they may have gone on to Bethany later that night, for some reason the group decided to spend at least part of this evening on the Mount of Olives rather than immediately going all the way back. The Mount of Olives sits on the opposite side of the Kidron Valley from the temple that they had just exited. Besides garbage dumps and cemeteries, there is a seasonal stream that runs through the valley. The tombs of Jehoshaphat, Absalom, and Zechariah are also there.

A garden called Gethsemane is found at the bottom of the slopes of the Mount of Olives. Jesus would be betrayed and taken captive there in only a couple of days. The Mount of Olives, as you might expect, was covered in olive trees. There would be no shortage of firewood. Hopefully, they would be able to camp in a spot with a good view of the torch lit Temple Mount, across the valley to the west.

Jesus started His public ministry only about three years earlier. Since that time he had likely seldom been apart from His twelve close followers. They had camped together and gathered around campfires many times before. Tonight's topic of conversation would prove to be uniquely interesting.

In less than forty years, General Titus would make the top of the Mount of Olives his base camp for the siege of Jerusalem and the Temple Mount. He would call the Mount, "Lookout Hill." It is from the Mount of Olives that Jesus would ascend into Heaven (Acts 1:12). It is there that Christian tradition says that Jesus will first set His feet back on this earth when He returns. How appropriate that it is there that He would provide His disciples with details about His return!

6. Four Questions for Jesus

"Are you awake?" my wife, Angela, whispered.

"Yep, what time do you think it is?" was my sleepy reply.

"I don't know. The fire is out. It must be close to morning."

This conversation starts off what is a little bit of an embarrassing personal story…

One fall weekend over thirty years ago, before we had children, my wife and I went deer hunting in the Cascade mountains about seventy-five miles away from our home. We spent the chilly night camping by beautiful Timpanogas Lake. We were the only two people in the campground. It was really dark and quiet when both of us found ourselves awake and anticipating getting to the logging unit where we were going to hunt that morning.

The plan was to be there and quietly in place an hour before the sun was set to rise at about 6:45 AM. We would need to be up by about 5:30 in order to make it on time, but there was a problem. This was in the days before cell phones were common, and I had forgotten to bring any sort of time keeping machine like an alarm clock or even my watch. To compound our chrono-challenge, the clock in my 1976 Ford Bronco was broken.

We couldn't risk being late, so Angela and I got up, ate a couple food bars, and drove about fifteen minutes to the logging unit hoping it would contain our four-legged prize. When we got there we waited for the sky to lighten so we could make our way to our stand; there we would wait for a big buck to present itself. Watching the eastern sky, there was no hint of illumination on the horizon.

The radio in the Bronco did work. I attempted to tune in a radio station to try and find out what time it was. The pulsating voices that you hear on distant AM radio stations, as their signal fades in and out, sound the creepiest when you are in the middle of the woods in total darkness. Because radio stations cut their power at a certain hour in the evening, and something to do with the way radio waves travel around at night, I couldn't bring in any of the familiar stations. However, I finally found a station in another state and in a different time zone that didn't completely fade away. We listened and waited for the station to give the time. Just after the news, we heard the announcer say it was 2:30 AM… Mountain Time. That meant it was 1:30 AM, Pacific Time. We were over four hours early!

Feeling really stupid, and tired, we drove back to our camp, and went to sleep, hoping it would be closer to daylight when we woke up the next time. It was. So, how did we do hunting? Did I mention how *beautiful* Timpanogas Lake is? That, and the company of my wife, is what made the whole trip worthwhile…

Of course we laughed about it then, and we still do now, but what happened during that trip is that my young wife and I were woefully unprepared and uninformed. We lacked essential information that left us both stumbling around in the dark and literally *lost in time.* We had no point of reference to the time other than it was dark and later than when we had fallen asleep. In preparing for the trip, I failed to ask some simple questions like, "Did you pack the alarm clock?" or "Have you seen my watch?"

Unlike me, in order to satisfy their curiosity and prepare both themselves and future followers of Jesus, the disciples asked their master some critical questions. Although Jesus provides more information than is asked for, it is these questions that Jesus answers and are the basis of the Olivet Discourse.

The questions the disciples asked seem to be inspired in part by a short conversation which took place just after Jesus and the disciples had left the temple for the day.

A Magnificent Sight

As a reminder, each King James Version of the Olivet Discourse text, will be followed by my own translation, identified as "DHT," (Doug Hooley Translation).

Matthew 24: 1

And Jesus went out, and departed from the temple: and his disciples came to him for to shew him the buildings of the temple. (KJV)

Jesus left the temple and was going away, when His disciples pointed out the buildings of the temple to Him. (DHT)

<u>**Mark 13:1**</u>

And as he went out of the temple, one of his disciples saith unto him, Master, see what manner of stones and what buildings are here! (KJV)

And as He left the temple, one of his disciples said to Him, "Look, Teacher, what remarkable stones and buildings!" (DHT)

<u>**Luke 21:5**</u>

And as some spake of the temple, how it was adorned with goodly stones and gifts, he said, (KJV)

And as some spoke about how the temple was adorned with magnificent stones and offerings, He said, (DHT)

The three gospel accounts above are more than just a record of someone exiting a large, beautiful stone building. It is more than Jesus simply leaving the holy temple in Jerusalem after another day of teaching. Think of this event as the Almighty God, after giving the Jewish leadership one last chance to get it right, departing the temple. God was leaving His "home away from home," once and for all.

The Matthew chapter 24 account of what took place starts with the Greek conjunction "καί," transliterated as "kai." It is the number one used Greek word in the New Testament. Although it can have several meanings, most of the time it simply means "and." In light of the verses at the end of chapter 23, Matthew 24:1 should be taken as a continuation of the story that was being told in chapter 23.

Based on what was said and to whom it was said in chapter 23, I am confident that although short, this was a passionate conversation between Jesus and His disciples. Jesus had just finished His tense discourse on the extremely poor spiritual condition of those in Jewish leadership by saying;

Behold, your house is left unto you desolate. For I say unto you, Ye shall not see me henceforth, till ye shall say, Blessed is he that cometh in the name of the Lord. Matt 23:38-39 (KJV)

It is immediately after Jesus says these things that we see Him leave the temple. In other words, the Messiah was walking out on those whom He had just admonished and leaving them to their now desolate and "godless" temple.

Ezekiel Parallel

The book of Ezekiel (chapters 9-11) tells the story of the Prophet Ezekiel's vision in which he witnesses the Spirit of God moving hesitantly out of the temple, pausing at the threshold, exiting through the east gate and finally hovering over the Mount of Olives to the East. This occurred after God had become disgusted with the actions of His chosen people.

I cannot help but think of Jesus, having become disgusted with the actions of the spiritual leadership of Israel taking the same route as the Spirit of God did in Ezekiel's vision. Like the Spirit of God, Jesus possibly paused at the East gate where His disciples called His attention to the great building. Then again like the Spirit of God, Jesus ascended the slopes of the Mount of Olives, which is the "mountain on the east side of the city."

More Information from Mark and Luke

The books of Luke and Mark add additional details to the scene before Jesus and his disciples left the temple. Jesus decided to have a seat for a moment opposite of the temple treasury. It was there that he noticed the "rich" making their contributions (Mark 12:41). He then called attention to a "poor" widow woman who was putting only a couple coins into the offering. However, this was *all* the money she had. Jesus remarked that this woman had given far more than those who only gave out of their excess. It was only a little while later as Jesus and His disciples left, when taking note of offerings and how the temple was adorned with "goodly stones and offerings," that the disciples called Jesus' attention to the impressive building itself. Just as He was not impressed with those that gave the great riches inside the temple, Jesus did not seem to be impressed with the riches which had been used to pay for the outside of the temple mount structures.

<u>Matthew 24:2</u>

And Jesus said unto them, see ye not all these things? verily I say unto you, there shall not be left here one stone upon another, that shall not be thrown down. (KJV)

And Jesus said to them, "don't you see these things? I'm telling you, not one stone here will be left on another. Every one will be destroyed." (DHT)

<u>Mark 13:2</u>

And Jesus answering said unto him, Seest thou these great buildings? there shall not be left one stone upon another, that shall not be thrown down. (KJV)

And Jesus replied to him, "do you see these great buildings? Not one stone will be left on another that won't be destroyed." (DHT)

<u>Luke 21:6</u>

As for these things which ye behold, the days will come, in the which there shall not be left one stone upon another, that shall not be thrown down. (KJV)

There will come a day when not one of these stones that you are looking at will remain on another. Every one will be destroyed. (DHT)

Maybe the disciples weren't listening to what Jesus was just saying inside the temple a short time earlier as He spoke to the Pharisees. Maybe they didn't get the significance of what was happening, or maybe they were just trying to "cheer up the Master" by distracting Him after just witnessing Him become quite upset with the religious leaders. Whatever the reason, it appears that Jesus' companions were more awe-struck with the physical appearance of the Temple, rather than being concerned about what Jesus had just said. This was the third consecutive day that this group had visited the temple, so they had clearly seen the big buildings and massive stones before.

The Temple *was* amazing. It was considered one of the great structures in the ancient world. It stood in contrast to the typical scene the disciples would have witnessed as fishermen on the shores of the Galilee. This was the third temple built on this site. Some people called it the second, although between Solomon's first temple and King Herod's temple, there was a temple built by Zerubbabel. It was much smaller and lacked the resources and splendor of the first temple. King Solomon built the first. The temple Jesus and the twelve stood in front of that Tuesday was the temple that was rebuilt by King Herod.

First century Historian, Josephus, recorded that in the eighteenth year of his reign, King Herod initiated the reconstruction of the temple, paying for it himself. He laid new a new foundation and constructed the walls out of hard, white stones. He essentially doubled the size of King Solomon's original Temple Mount. One of those foundation stones of the retaining wall, still in place today, weighs over 301 tons! Purple hangings covered the entrances, gold vines with what looked like grape clusters accented the temple. There were large porticoes with 162 Corinthian columns surrounding the temple. The structure the disciples were fixated on was spectacular.

Despite the excitement of the disciples, Jesus seems about as impressed with the temple as He was with the fig tree that He had cursed the day before for bearing no fruit. My guess is that the One who created the universe does not impress easily when it comes to manmade stuff. In response to the disciples, Jesus makes an amazing prophecy about the building made of huge stones; like the unproductive fig tree that was not bearing any fruit, the Temple would be destroyed.

There is no record of Jesus' disciples immediately responding to this prediction. Maybe they were too shocked to make comments right away. Maybe they were afraid that like the fig tree, the destruction was going to take place immediately and they just wanted to get out of the way. Maybe they felt ineffective at their attempts to distract Jesus and seeing how serious He was, they thought it best to be quiet for a while.

This was not the first time Jesus had predicted the destruction of Jerusalem and the temple. Just after He entered the city on a donkey two days earlier, Jesus said:

For the days shall come upon thee, that thine enemies shall cast a trench about thee, and compass thee round, and keep thee in on every side, and shall lay thee even with the ground, and thy children within thee; and they shall not leave in thee one stone upon another; because thou knewest not the time of thy visitation. Luke 19:43-44 (KJV)

Jesus and the twelve took the quarter mile downhill walk eastward from the temple, into the Kidron Valley, and then back up a quarter mile on the other side to possibly the top of the Mount of Olives. If the conversation did continue, it is clear that the disciples still had questions remaining. Later, when they had reached their resting place the disciples must have been talking among themselves. Perhaps that evening they had been looking at the great Temple, softly illuminated by lamp-light across the valley, and were wondering why it was still standing after their Master had cursed it. Whatever led up to the questions, the disciples asked for clarification from Jesus.

Not One Stone Left On Another

Today, there is no Jewish Temple standing on the Temple Mount in Jerusalem. It seems as though Jesus' prophecy was fulfilled in seventy AD when General Titus' troops razed it to the ground. At least that is the claim that the Preterist theory puts forth and some believe…

Still in existence today, and part of the architecture that Jesus and His disciples were talking about, and the disciples were amazed by, is what Josephus specifically referred to as *"the most prodigious work that was ever heard of by man."* [20] The Temple Mount itself, a man made retaining wall structure that still occupies approximately thirty-seven acres. It takes up over five football fields from north to south and six football fields from west to east.

There has been a great deal of repairs made to the retaining wall of the Temple Mount since the first century by the Byzantines, Arabs, Crusaders, and Ottomans. However, there is still a large amount of Herodian masonry intact that would have been present the day that the disciples called Jesus' attention to the structure.

Today, below the "street level" of the Western Wall, known by many as the "Wailing Wall," lay nineteen additional courses of Herodian quarried ashlars. This means that below modern ground level, there are still sixty-eight vertical feet (almost seven stories) of stones, "left upon another," which reach down to the first century street level of Jesus' day.

There are an awful lot of stones "left upon another," to be able to call Jesus' prophecy literally and completely fulfilled. Today, thousands of Jews still worship by the same stones placed by King Herod's masons.

The Book of Revelation indicates that there will one-day be a great earthquake that will level every city in the world, including Jerusalem. In fact, Jerusalem will be split into three parts by this earthquake. The unprecedented quake will be so great as to cause every island and mountain to collapse (Revelation 16:18-20). Unlike General Titus' armies, that future earthquake will likely bring about the complete fulfillment of Jesus' prophecy that "*not one stone will be left on another.*"

Matthew 24:3

And as he sat upon the mount of Olives, the disciples came unto him privately, saying, tell us, when shall these things be? and what shall be the sign of thy coming, and of the end of the world? (KJV)

And, as Jesus sat on the Mount of Olives, the disciples came to him alone and said, "when will these things occur, and what will be the sign of your arrival and presence here, and of the completion of the age?" (DHT)

Mark 13:3-4

And as he sat upon the mount of Olives over against the temple, Peter and James and John and Andrew asked him privately, tell us, when shall these things be? and what shall be the sign when all these things shall be fulfilled? (KJV)

And as He sat on the Mount of Olives, directly opposite the temple, Peter, James, John, and Andrew questioned Him privately, "tell us, when shall these things be, and what shall the sign be when all of these things shall be completed?" (DHT)

<u>Luke 21:7</u>

And they asked him, saying, Master, but when shall these things be? and what sign will there be when these things shall come to pass? (KJV)

And they questioned him, saying, "Master, when shall these things be, and what sign will there be when these things come to pass?" (DHT)

Jerusalem was very crowded every Passover. There were probably many other people camped on the Mount of Olives that night. For all we know Jesus may have been talking to and teaching others besides his closest twelve disciples, but now four of His disciples wanted His "private" attention. They came to Him alone. In the book of Mark, we learn the names of the specific disciples that were interested in having some more answers; Peter, James, John and Andrew.

The documentation varies a little between the three different gospel accounts about the exact questions the disciples asked Jesus. Different commentaries come up with different numbers of questions asked, depending on how the questions are divided up. Some say two questions are asked, some say three. When I combine all three gospels, I come up with the following four questions:

1) When will "these things" happen?
2) What will be the sign that "these things" are about to happen?
3) What will be the sign of your coming and presence back on the earth?
4) What will be the sign of the end of the age?

These "things," (plural) the books of Mark and Luke refer to, imply that it is more than the stones of the temple being knocked over they are inquiring about. In light of Matthew's record of the questions, we can assume that "these things" have to do with the events associated with the Second Coming of Christ ("the sign of your coming and the end of the age").

When will these things happen? It seems clear that the author of Matthew 24 wants us to associate the statement Jesus just made in verse two regarding the destruction of the Temple, with this question. It also seems clear that the disciples for some reason, right or wrong, were linking the Second Coming and the "end of the age" together with the destruction of the temple. Mark specifically uses the word "all" in asking the question regarding the time of fulfillment. Again this is indicating that the events in question are all likely linked together.

Not long before this night, Jesus had informed His disciples that He would one day come with "power and authority." This conversation is recorded in Matthew chapter 16. There, we read that Jesus had just asked His disciples a question regarding who people say that He (Jesus) was. Peter declared Jesus to be the Messiah, the Son of the living God (Matt. 16:16). Jesus then began to tell the disciples what was in store:

From that time forth began Jesus to shew unto his disciples, how that he must go unto Jerusalem, and suffer many things of the elders and chief priests and scribes, and be killed, and be raised again the third day. Matt 16:21 (KJV)

After Peter swears that he will not allow his master to be treated in such a way, Jesus tells the disciples the rest of the story:

For the Son of man shall come in the glory of his Father with his angels; and then he shall reward every man according to his works. Verily I say unto you, there be some standing here, which shall not taste of death, till they see the Son of man coming in his kingdom. Matt 16:27-28 (KJV)

These mind-boggling statements had to have remained on the minds of the disciples. Peter had stated that Jesus is the long awaited Messiah. Jesus confirmed this. Six days after Jesus broke this news to them, Peter, James, and John found themselves standing on a mountain with Jesus where they saw Him undergo an amazing transition in His appearance. At the same time, Moses and Elijah appeared, and a cloud enveloped them. Then came a voice from heaven proclaiming Jesus to be the Son of God (See Matthew 17:2-6). After this overwhelming supernatural experience, Jesus reminded the three disciples again of what will soon happen to Him:

And as they came down from the mountain, Jesus charged them, saying, Tell the vision to no man, until the Son of man be risen again from the dead. Matt 17:9 (KJV)

So, as the disciples sat on the Mount of Olives that Tuesday evening before the Passover, they knew that Jesus was the Messiah, the Son of God, but that he first must die and be raised from the dead before he could return in power and authority. They were naturally very curious about when Jesus would *"come in the glory of His Father with His angels; and would then recompense every man according to his deeds."* The night they sat together on the Mount of Olives, they had to be associating Jesus returning in power and judgment with their Master's prophecy about the destruction of the temple.

Another Important Greek Word: "Parousia"

Sometimes a single word can make a difference when translating scripture. In the New Testament, I counted twelve different Greek words that were translated into the English word "coming." In Matthew 24:3, the disciples asked what the sign of Jesus' "coming" would be. I chose to translate the Greek word Matthew used, "παρουσία," transliterated as "parousia," as "arrival and presence."

Like many foreign language words, parousia does not have a good single word translation into English. Parousia is a noun, not an action word, although it means "to be actively present." The Parousia of Christ represents an "event;" His Second Coming. It does not simply mean "to travel from there to here," like an action word would convey. If the act of the relocation of Jesus is what the writer of Matthew would have wanted to convey, there are several other words that he could have used.

So what difference does the definition of this word make? The difference is that if you use an action word, Jesus could still be on His way. For example, we could say, "Where is Jesus?" the answer could be, "He is *coming*, but not here yet." Using the word parousia means that the event is or will be in play.

The event of His coming (parousia) will take place over an extended period of time. The parousia of Jesus packs a lot of meaning. Much will take place once He has returned. The event of His coming will include many sub-events, such as the signs in the heavens that precede Him, the rapture of the Church, the sealing of His faithful Jewish followers, Armageddon and the defeat of the Antichrist.

After all of the events associated with His return occur, we could still say to Jesus, "your parousia (coming or being here with us) has really been eventful." The disciples, if asking the same question, they did of Jesus on the Mount of Olives in English, may have phrased their question this way: "*What will the sign be of your being present with us again on the earth and all that you will do once you are here?*"

Not The End of the World

In Matthew 24:3, the King James Version of the Bible uses the term, "end of the world," instead of the term "completion of the age," as I translated it. Many other translations use the term, "end of the age." This is another case of many Greek words having more than one meaning, especially when you include the *implied* meanings. The meanings of many Greek words, change according to the words they are grouped with. In this case the word with more than one meaning is, "αἰών," transliterated as "aion."

It is the implied meaning of "aion" that the translators of the King James Version chose when they translated the word as "world." "Aion" means "age," "forever," "perpetuity of time," or "eternity" depending on other words that modify it, and the context in which it is used. As we will see in a later chapter, aion is used in more than one way within the Olivet Discourse.

The word, "world," can imply "Planet Earth." Since we know from other scripture that Planet Earth will still exist after the return of Jesus, the phrase "end of the world," can cause some confusion. It will not be the end of the world. It will be the end, or completion of, this current age we are living in.

There are those who believe that our planet will in fact be destroyed upon the return of Jesus. However, we know for many reasons found in scripture that when Jesus returns, after it is subjected to the events associated with God pouring out His wrath on the inhabitants of the planet, the earth will be renewed and continue to exist for at least another thousand years, before all things "are made new" by Jesus.

It will indeed be a different "age," where the "lion will lay down with the lamb," humans will still be considered "young" at age 100, and "swords will be beaten into plows." The geography of the planet will change based on the judgments God will have carried out, but it will still be planet Earth, and King Jesus will be here in person to rule over it!

Notes

7. Watch!

I attended Buena Vista College (now "University") in Storm Lake, Iowa originally seeking a degree in Music Education. The city of Storm Lake is 2,000 miles away from where I grew up in Oregon. Probably over half of the students drove home each weekend and returned to school on Monday. I would see home once during the school year; on Christmas break.

So, in 1979, before the world of the Internet, texting and Facebook, what did a music student do to kill time on a cold October weekend night in Iowa, when he should have been studying? Naturally, he and three musical friends found some flashlights, a long heavy string, and a couple rolls of aluminum foil and headed for the cornfields to pretend they were a UFO.

The plan was for three of us to appear to be a craft of some sort that had landed in the cornfield. To further give the impression that whatever was in the field was "not from around here," the last guy, let's call him "Bob," was completely covered in aluminum foil, complete with a cone-shaped head. Bob's part was to walk towards the road in zombie-like fashion as soon as the light from an oncoming car started to reflect off his foil suit.

Our deceptive plan worked perfectly. For a while… As the first car approached, I switched on my flashlight and started swinging it in a great circle, taking care not to strike my two friends with it, both of whom were busy on either side of me, blinking their red and green lights on and off. We all felt greatly satisfied when we heard the oncoming car's engine start to slow, as if they were trying to make sense of what they were seeing. Then, how elated we all became when we saw the light reflect off of the "tin man," and the car's engine started racing, as it sped away.

After a couple more successful acts of giving some passing Iowans a story that they could tell their grandchildren, the fourth car that came down the lonely highway kept slowing, when it should have sped back up. Then, it stopped and turned around. I did the logical thing and took off running as fast as I could along with the rest of the flashlight squad. The last thing I remember was looking back and seeing poor "Bob" partially illuminated by the headlights of the stopped car, sprinting across the field towards us as fast as a foil encumbered trumpet player could, aluminum foil flying off all the way.

With all the cell phone calls to 911 this type of thing would generate now, what we four idiots did thirty-seven years ago would be hard to pull off, and I am sure it would be some sort of Homeland Security offense. As fun as it was then, and as fond I am of the memory, now in my mid-'50s, with the life experiences I have had, all I can think about is the liability aspects. What if we would have caused an accident, or someone would have had a heart attack, or what if the corn farmer would have been on his sixth shot of whiskey and blasted the Unidentified Cornfield Object full of twelve gauge shot? It's all fun until someone gets hurt…

Although the deception we attempted to pull off was all in good fun, Jesus warned about an evil deception that will take many forms in order to mislead the elect of God. Deception will be used as a tool of Satan. We bored music education majors put a half an hour of thought into what we were going to do, and spent under five dollars to pull off our low tech attempt at deception. Conversely, Satan has long been making his plans for at least thousands of years and he has all the resources of the worldly system he commands to accomplish them.

Before Jesus answered their questions directly regarding when the temple would fall and when He would return in power, He gave the disciples a warning. He commanded them to be "on guard" for those that would attempt to mislead them and His future followers in years to come. He told them to "watch" for specific events that would be associated with his coming. He also warned them about some events that others would try to associate with His return that will not necessarily indicate that His return was near.

<u>Matthew 24: 4</u>

And Jesus answered and said unto them, take heed that no man deceive you. (KJV)

And Jesus answered them saying, "watch out, that no one deceives you." (DHT)

Mark 13:5

And Jesus answering them began to say, take heed lest any man deceive you: Mark 13:5 (KJV)

And Jesus began to say to them, "watch out, lest you be deceived." (DHT)

Luke 21:8 a

And he said, take heed that ye be not deceived (KJV)

And He said to them, "Watch, that you not be deceived." (DHT)

Jesus starts by commanding his disciples to be watchful. He knew that the circumstances and discussion revolving around His return to earth would be full of deceit. "Watching" in this context implies watching out for deception from others. His beginning admonition is not what to look for as a sign of His coming, but how to guard against deception.

The Greek word in the above verse transliterated as "blepete" (a different form of blepo), which the King James Version of the Bible translated as "take heed," I translated as "watch out," and "watch." It could also be translated as "beware," or "observe and perceive." It implies being aware of what is going on in the world around you, with understanding. Understanding that comes from watching with the worldview that a follower of Jesus is to have. A worldview, which followers of Jesus develop as they study the Word of God, and grow to know Him.

The Greek word for "deception," is "Πλανηθῆτε᾿," transliterated as "planethete." The King James Bible translates this word as "deception" as I did. But the word could also be translated as being led "astray" as in being led astray from the truth. Other ways this word has been translated is to "roam," "wander," or be "seduced." To pull it all together, one could paraphrase Jesus' warning by saying, *"be watchful of the world around you, in light of Jesus' world-view, which is God's truth, so that no one will be able to seduce you into straying from that truth through their deceptions."*

We are lied to and deceived every day. We are bombarded by deception in the media in order to get us to "buy" whatever they are selling. The news is slanted in order to convince us of points of view. Some forms of entertainment, specifically the theatre and cinema, rely on deception. This is not necessarily a bad thing, so long as we understand that we are temporarily and voluntarily suspending reason and reality in favor of being deceived for a couple hours. We watch wide eyed, we tell ourselves it is okay to temporarily believe that cars can be "transformed" into giant robots, or that there may be a zombie apocalypse one day.

People voluntarily and temporarily suspend reason and reality. They allow themselves to be deceived by the media into believing they need many different products that mankind did without for the first several millennia of human history.

It is dangerous when we suspend reason and reality and choose to believe lies because it suits our desires to do so. This can take the form of "burying one's head in the sand." Kids do it when they hide under their covers from the infamous boogieman. Adults do it when they hear a grinding noise come from under the hood of their car and choose to believe that whatever the sound is will just take care of itself.

More on Watchfulness

I discussed being watchful in chapter two. However, the concept of watchfulness cannot be overemphasized since it is a main and reoccurring theme in the Olivet Discourse.

The type of watching the words in the Olivet Discourse imply are absolutely *not* the type that takes place when you are "vegging out" in front of the television. When you passively watch television, your mind wanders from time to time and sometimes you are not even sure what just happened on the show you are watching.

To "watch" as Jesus means it, is to be 5-cups-of-coffee-awake and paying active attention to something that will be the most important event in history. Jesus talks about this type of watchfulness later on in His Olivet Discourse.

For the Son of man is as a man taking a far journey, who left his house, and gave authority to his servants, and to every man his work, and commanded the porter to watch. Watch ye therefore: for ye know not when the master of the house cometh, at even, or at midnight, or at the cockcrowing, or in the morning: Lest coming suddenly he find you sleeping. And what I say unto you I say unto all, Watch. Mark 13:34-37 (KJV)

Who should be watchful? Jesus clears up any confusion here about whom should be watching for his return when he said, "*And what I say to you I say to all: watch.*"

The type and tense of the word "watch" or "stay awake," Jesus uses in this passage (the Greek word transliterated as 'gregoreo') was in the present, active, imperative form. In other words, He was saying, "do it now!" Jesus was *commanding* "all," or everyone to be actively watching for the events that will precede His coming and the end of the age. Commands from Jesus do not get any stronger.

During His Olivet Discourse, Jesus gave us a hint as to one of the reasons why His followers should be watching;

Watch ye therefore, and pray always, that ye may be accounted worthy to escape all these things that shall come to pass, and to stand before the Son of man. Luke 21:36 (KJV)

Paul gives us further encouragement to "watch" and tells us that we don't have to be surprised and caught off guard by Christ's return, in the very classic passage that many misuse to say that Jesus' return will surprise everyone;

But ye, brethren, are not in darkness, that that day should overtake you as a thief. Ye are all the children of light, and the children of the day: we are not of the night, nor of darkness. Therefore, let us not sleep, as do others; but let us watch and be sober. 1 Thess 5:4-6 (KJV)

To be clear, this is the Apostle Paul saying that we who follow the Lord *do not* have to be surprised by Jesus' return sneaking up on us. Those who heed Jesus' warning have the ability to see the signs coming, unlike non-believers, since those who are watchful and "awake," "walk in the light." Remember, you can still stumble even when the lights are on and you are awake if you aren't paying attention to what's going on around you.

For there shall arise false Christs, and false prophets, and shall shew great signs and wonders; insomuch that, if it were possible, they shall deceive the very elect. Matt 24:24 (KJV)

Some may say that it is not possible for the elect (Christians) to be deceived where God is concerned. Yet, Jesus tells us during the Olivet Discourse that this type of deception is possible. The people who say it is not possible may be confusing the issue of "losing their salvation," with the issue of being deceived. Millions of people who call themselves followers of Christ are currently being deceived when they buy into false doctrines. This deception within the Church ranges from non-consequential to extremely serious. This form of deception has been going on since the first advent of Jesus.

For example, the Apostle Paul wrote a letter to the Galatians after they bought into the deception that it was necessary for them to become circumcised in order to be a Christian. This is after they had received specific instruction from Paul in person to the contrary.

All the deceptive doctrines about Jesus that mankind has added to God's truth since the Apostle Paul's day, and what it means to follow Jesus, can and do drive people away from the Church, deafening their ears to the gospel.

If you are truly "saved" or have been "elected" to be ransomed by Jesus from the grips of Satan, you cannot lose that salvation. However, even if you are saved, if you are not "watching," you can still be, and likely will be deceived. There is so much more to being a follower of Christ than "having your salvation in the bag." As Christ-ones living in a world of unbelievers, Jesus said we are to be as "wise as serpents and innocent as doves."

Behold, I send you forth as sheep in the midst of wolves: be ye therefore wise as serpents, and harmless as doves. Matt 10:16 (KJV)

In order to become wise, there is much work to be done. The type of wisdom that Jesus was talking about only comes with knowledge of His word, and understanding of that word. It is so important to know what the truth is. It is only by first knowing the truth that you can positively identify untruth, or deception.

Unless you are familiar with what God has to say about the end of the age, there is a good chance you will be deceived, if you are alive during that time. If you are a leader in your church, family, or other arena and you are deceived, you are a prime candidate for spreading the deception you encounter further. The solution for not being deceived is threefold watchfulness; 1. Gain biblical knowledge about what it is Jesus wants us to know (including the signs of His return) 2. Stay awake and engaged in watching for deception. 3. Faithfully be about Jesus' business until the day you die or He returns.

An Important Note On Being Watchful

It may be true that some are more gifted than others in the interpretation of prophetic scriptures, just like some are gifted in many other areas like music, teaching, preaching, and evangelism. But even if we are not 'gifted' in the area of music, should we still not praise God with all that is within us? Just because we are not all Billy Graham, should we not be able to present the simple gospel and tell others why and what we believe in? Likewise, every Christian should have a basic understanding of the end of the age.

In the military, everyone is expected to be able to recognize the enemy and alert others when they see him approach. Even though everyone in the military has their own specific job to do, they all do their time standing watch. As "soldiers of the cross," we too have our specific jobs to do according to our God given gifts and talents, but we too are *all* called to stand watch and be on guard against deception at all times.

What to Watch for That May Mean It Is Just Another Day

Jesus starts off his teaching on the Mount of Olives not with a list of things that are uniquely associated with His Coming, but with a short message about how some situations and events have always occurred, which people tend to look at as "signs." People interpret these "signs," to mean that something big is about to occur. Jesus is making the point that although many will associate those situations and events with the end of the age, those who are truly "watching" for His return should be careful *not* to make that mistake.

The things Jesus is warning about that do not signal the end of the age have all been occurring regularly since the time that Jesus gave the warning. In fact, all of them have been occurring ever since the beginning of history. Jesus will finish this list by saying, "*See that you are not alarmed, for this must take place,* ***but the end is not yet...***"

How often have you heard modern day prophecy teachers attempting to make a case that the return of Jesus is imminent because of natural phenomenon taking place? Things such as earthquakes "in various places," and other catastrophic, yet natural phenomenon? If you have been around a while, you have read and heard this many times. If you haven't, a quick search on the Internet will verify this is true. According to the number of Google hits I got when I typed in "end times earthquakes," there are literally thousands of examples of people saying that present day earthquakes indicate that we are now in the "last days."

Matthew 24: 5

For many shall come in my name, saying, I am Christ; and shall deceive many. (KJV)

For many will come in my name saying, "I am the Christ," and will deceive many. (DHT)

Mark 13:6

For many shall come in my name, saying, I am Christ; and shall deceive many. (KJV)

For many will come in my name saying that, "I am," and shall deceive many. (DHT)

Luke 21:8b

for many shall come in my name, saying, I am Christ; and the time draweth near: go ye not therefore after them. (KJV)

for many will come in my name, saying, "I am," and the time is close at hand. Do not follow them. (DHT)

False Messiahs

In the three separate gospel accounts above, Jesus is specifically warning about a group of people that will or have come in His name, maybe even declaring that they are the Christ or Messiah. The Gospel of Luke adds a second warning regarding these people who come in the name of Jesus; "*and will say the time is at hand. Do not go after them.*" "The time," which is "at hand," in context is the end of the age. This statement in Luke makes sense in the context of the question that Jesus answers.

I am sure Jesus desires His followers to be on guard for all types of spiritual deception. However, given the context and the extra statement made in the Gospel of Luke, it makes sense that Jesus is specifically telling His followers to watch out for deception about the end of the age and the Second Coming.

In reference to the deceivers who will come, the most conservative approach to this scripture is to say that Jesus is referring only to those false messiahs that say they are Jesus. Paraphrasing Jesus using this interpretation would go like this: "*watch out, for many in the future will say they are actually me, and through deception, with many people, they will get away with it.*"

Surprisingly, Wikipedia lists thirty-two individuals since the 18th century that either themselves or their followers have claimed to be Jesus. They claim to have either been reincarnated as another person who possesses Jesus' spirit, incarnated again as Jesus himself, or that they are Jesus having returned via the Second Coming.[21] Although thirty-two false messiahs (and counting) might qualify for "many" coming in the name of Jesus, it is likely there have been undocumented occurrences over the centuries. This group of fake Jesus' has drawn many followers who were all deceived.

A broader interpretation of this scripture would be those claiming to be the Messiah, but not necessarily Jesus Himself. Wikipedia lists twenty-three false Jewish Messiahs, thirty-four Christian, seven Muslim, and nine "other" messiah claimants spanning the time period from 4 BC to 1994 AD.[22] The list totals seventy-three false messiahs. Some are still living and deceiving today.

A third alternative interpretation would be that Jesus is referring to "many" who would come "in his name." These individuals would claim to have the same authority as Jesus and lead many astray. This, by far, is a much larger group.

The "Vicar of Christ"

I will leave for you to decide for yourself if Jesus' words apply in the following cases or not. As for me, I have determined that I need to be on guard and watchful of anyone who comes speaking with authority "in the name" of Jesus.

Ignatius of Antioch was a Bishop of the Church at Antioch early in the second century AD. He wrote seven letters as he journeyed to Rome to be executed around 110 to 115 AD. [23] It is said the Apostle John taught Ignatius himself. One of his letters contains probably the earliest documentation of the concept of a regular man standing in the place of, and having the authority of God on earth. This position in the Roman Catholic Church, held by the Pope, came to be known as the "Vicar of Christ."

The Epistle of Ignatius to the Magnesians in its sixth chapter says, '*…I exhort you to study to do all things with a divine harmony, while your bishop presides* ***in the place of God***…"[24]

Down through the centuries, the Roman Catholic Pope has claimed to hold the authority of Christ on earth with the power to forgive sins through the sacrament of confession (as any Catholic priest is able). He also claims to have the ability to declare who has made it into heaven, and in days past, declare who should be put to death for heresy.

During the Vatican Council of 1869, the question of the infallibility of the Pope was raised. The bishops ultimately voted whether or not the Pope could speak for God on July 18, 1869. The vote was 533 to 2 that the Pope is indeed "infallible" when he speaks "*ex cathedra.*" According to author Nicolas Cheetam, in his book, *Keepers of the Keys,* speaking "ex cathedra" is defined as when one speaks with "supreme apostolic authority" concerning "faith or morals." [25]

The ruling of the council of 1869 is still adhered to today in the Roman Catholic Church. When the Pope speaks regarding doctrine, he is speaking in the name of, and in the place of, Jesus.

Please understand I am not anti-Catholic. I am convinced that God does not respect man-made, denominational religious boundaries or labels. He looks at every individual's heart and is the one who does the calling and saving. I am only saying that Jesus warned us to watch out for deception from people coming to us in His name and with His authority. Especially when they claim to be "standing in the place of God." "Many" Popes, 266 in fact, have now done so.[26]

The Pope of the Roman Catholic Church is but one example of a formal religious system where a mortal man has been bestowed the authority of God. There have been and continue to be many Protestant and pseudo Christian religions that engage in the same type of practice; giving God-like authority to their leadership, calling them among other things, "prophets" and "apostles."

Islam

It may come as a shock, but Muslims are also waiting for Jesus to return one day. According to Joel Richardson, author of *The Islamic Antichrist* and *Mideast Beast*, adherents to Islam believe that the Christian's Jesus, did not actually die and rise again, but was taken up into Heaven by Allah prior to His death; kind of like what God did with Enoch and Elijah. Muslims also don't believe Jesus to be the Son of God. They believe Him to be a prophet. They think one day Jesus, who they call "Eesa," will miraculously return and tell everyone the truth about what happened 2,000 years ago to compel everyone to follow the Islamic version of the Messiah. The Islamic Messiah is called the "Mahdi."[27]

Given the things that Jesus warned of, this prediction of a person coming in His name is interesting, as are the predictions of the one they call the "Mahdi," However, since what Muslims are waiting for is based on the writings of a false prophet, to give their predictions any credibility whatsoever would be failing to heed the warning of Jesus.

There is no reason to think that Islamic prophecies have any more credibility than the quatrains of Nostradamus or a palm reader in the creepy little shop on the street. In other words, I am not studying Islamic prophecies as if they are an indication of future events, or looking for Islamic prophecies to come true. I do not seek to attempt to fit Islamic prophecies into the prophecies of the Holy Bible. It's unnecessary.

God gave His followers all the information they need within the Holy Bible. If it is in God's plan to include the events spoken of in Islamic prophecy as a part of the deception, then Jesus has already instructed His followers what to do: don't be deceived or seduced, and don't follow after them. As for now, to study false prophecies (contained in the Koran) given by a false prophet (Muhammad), in the name of a false god (Allah), where I give them any credibility, authority, or likelihood of occurring, is to mistakenly "follow after them."

Wars and Rumors of War

Matthew 24:6-7a

And ye shall hear of wars and rumours of wars: see that ye be not troubled: for all these things must come to pass, but the end is not yet. For nation shall rise against nation, and kingdom against kingdom (KJV)

You will hear of wars and rumors of wars. See to it that you are not troubled. For all this must take place, but it is not yet the end. For nation will rise against nation and kingdom against kingdom. (DHT)

Mark 13:7-8a

And when ye shall hear of wars and rumours of wars, be ye not troubled: for such things must needs be; but the end shall not be yet. For nation shall rise against nation, and kingdom against kingdom (KJV)

And when you will hear of wars and rumors of wars, don't be troubled. It must be, but it is not yet the end. For nation shall rise against nation and kingdom against kingdom. (DHT)

Luke 21:9-10

But when ye shall hear of wars and commotions, be not terrified: for these things must first come to pass; but the end is not by and by. Then said he unto them, Nation shall rise against nation, and kingdom against kingdom: (KJV)

But when you will hear of wars and disturbances, don't be terrified, for these things must happen first, but the end is not

soon." Then He said to them, "nation will rise against nation, and kingdom against kingdom. (DHT)

Jesus points out that like deception, "wars, rumors of wars, and disturbances" taking place around you, DOES NOT mean it is the end of the world! "*Don't be troubled. Don't be terrified. These things will happen. The end is not yet. The end is not soon.*"

If you or your loved ones are in the middle of a war, or what seems like a war, there is plenty to be alarmed about in regards to you or your loved one's safety and personal property. There is even much to be troubled about if the war only involved strangers and it was in a far off land. When Jesus says not to be troubled, or alarmed we must again remember the context of the answer He is giving. He is saying, "don't be alarmed, because you think it is the end of the age simply because there is another war breaking out. It is not." War, by itself, does not equal the end of the age.

It is almost incomprehensible how many wars there have been and how many people have died in all of human history. You might want to take a quick look at the casualties of war list found in Wikipedia ("list of all wars by death toll).[28] These (unverified) figures include deaths of civilians from diseases, famine, and atrocities caused by the war as well as deaths of soldiers in battle. On the low end, what is only a partial list of seventy wars that only goes back to 756 AD, comes to over 255 million deaths. The high-end estimate is closer to 400 million deaths associated with war over the last 1,250 years. That is an astonishing average of over 204,000 to 314,000 people dying each year due to war related causes!

Is war a sign of the return of Christ? Archeology and historical documentation agree and confirm the existence of war long before, and ever since the first coming of Christ. Even the Holocaust and Hiroshima did not bring about the return of Jesus. Wars "must take place," and they will definitely play a part in the end of the age, but by themselves they do not indicate that it is the end of the world. Don't look to wars alone as a sign of the end.

Earthquakes Are Normal

<u>Matthew 24:7b-8</u>

and there shall be famines, and pestilences, and earthquakes, in divers places. All these are the beginning of sorrows. (KJV)

And there will be hunger, and pestilence, and earthquakes in places. All of this is the beginning of childbirth-like pain. (DHT)

<u>Mark 13:8b</u>

and there shall be earthquakes in divers places, and there shall be famines and troubles: these are the beginnings of sorrows. (KJV)

and there shall be earthquakes in places, and there shall be hunger and disturbances. These are the beginning of childbirth-like pains. (DHT)

<u>Luke 21:11</u>

And great earthquakes shall be in divers places, and famines, and pestilences; and fearful sights and great signs shall there be from heaven. (KJV)

And there will be mighty earthquakes in places, and hunger, and pestilence and fearful sights and wonders in the sky. They will be exceedingly great. (DHT)

Jesus declares that there will be earthquakes, as well as hunger, and disturbances. These "disturbances," could be likened to civil unrest or uprisings. Sounds like yesterday's news… for the last literal million yesterdays.

Birth Pangs or Childbirth-like pain?

At the end of both the Matthew and Mark passages, a word that translates as "sorrow," or "pain" is used. It has also been translated as "birth pangs." I translate it as "childbirth-like pain." The Greek word is "ὠδίν," transliterated into English as "odin" (o-deen'). It literally means, "the pain of childbirth," as opposed to actual "childbirth" or "birth pangs." [29]

Many interpreters emphasize the "birth pangs" portion of this verse as if to attempt to interpret this as a clue of the timing of Jesus' return. This is to say that once "birth pains" start, they do not stop. They increase in intensity and get closer together up until the child is born. So, those that hold this interpretation conclude that the events Jesus is speaking of; war, earthquakes, famine, etc. will increase in intensity and frequency once they have started, until Jesus returns. They also say once they start, we are in the end times, and they will not end until Jesus returns.

There are at least two things to consider in regards to the "birth pains" interpretation. First, Jesus is saying that the trouble will be painful, at a level that can be likened to "birth pains." Since the Greek word, "odin," refers to a type of pain, and not the event of childbirth, there is really no reason to think the similarities between childbirth and the events Jesus is describing go beyond the pain comparison. From what I understand, childbirth is a top contender for causing the worst pain a human can experience. This comparison makes sense considering the emotional equivalent of a loved one's death from wars, earthquakes, and famines. Those who have lost their loved ones in a tragic way can relate.

The second thing to consider is that even if the "birth pangs" comparison is meant to convey that the events Jesus is referring to will increase in intensity and frequency like child birth. We have no point of reference for when they may have started, or even if they have started. How would we know if they have started? These types of things have always occurred.

One thing childbirth-like pains accomplish is to cause one to pay attention and be watchful of developments. You know the "birth" is going to take place. Will your new baby arrive in an hour, or two days? I believe the point Jesus is trying to make here is that His followers must stay awake and pay attention.

About once or twice a year in regards to earthquakes, the main-stream media picks up on the "we're set to have a big one" theme. They talk about all of the fault lines and the building pressure of the earth's tectonic plates as they interview various geologists and seismologists. Then the modern day dooms-dayers break out their maps showing what the new west coast of the United States is going to look like after "the big one." Montana will have prime coast line property according to these maps. Modern governments appear to love to use this as a reason to justify improving buildings and infrastructure.

In his book, Apocalypse Code, one of the best known Pop-Christian culture, end times authors, Hal Lindsey, implies that we are near the end of the age because of earthquakes when he cites "experts" that say the frequency of earthquakes are increasing. [30]

Are we really seeing a trend today of more earthquakes? I began seriously watching earthquake data almost twenty years ago. During one check of the U.S. Geological website in 1997 I recorded that the Mammoth Lake area in California experienced 944 quakes up to a magnitude of 3.8 in one weekend! In December of 2005 I recorded twenty-one earthquakes ranging from magnitude 2.7 to 6.1 throughout the world in a twenty-four-hour period. When I checked in August 23, 2015, I recorded that there had been twenty-eight earthquakes over a magnitude 2.5 in the preceding twenty-four hours. Three more than in 2005, but less intense. Check out the USGS website if you want to keep an eye on what some call "birth-pangs" yourself. [31]

It seems we are having a lot of earthquakes "these days," but contrary to Mr. Lindsey's claims, at this point, earthquakes have not increased. Only our awareness and the media's sensationalism of earthquakes has increased. Here is the answer to a "frequently asked question" found on the National Geological Survey's website:

> **Question:** *Why are we having so many earthquakes? Has earthquake activity been increasing?*
> **Answer:** *Although it may seem that we are having more earthquakes, earthquakes of magnitude 7.0 or greater have remained fairly constant throughout this century and, according to our records,* ***have actually seemed to decrease in recent years.***

The earthquakes we are experiencing can easily qualify for what Jesus is talking about in Matthew chapter 24; "earthquakes in various places." Because they can be terrifying events, Jesus knew that there would be those people around the world who would say that earthquakes mean that "the end" is near. He was warning us against that deceptive teaching. It turns out Jesus was spot on! End time watchers point to earthquakes all the time as an indicator that the "end is near." Science and historic data tells us that many of the modern day prophecy teachers are giving us alarming and wrong information.

There are several catastrophic earthquakes specifically mentioned in the book of Revelation. In the course of natural events, there may be many more sizable quakes before the quakes mentioned in Revelation take place.

Final word on earthquakes; unless we experience a worldwide earthquake in which "every mountain and island" is "removed from its place," it is just another day in history on planet earth, and not the end (Rev. 6:12-14). However, if we do experience such an earthquake, look up, because Jesus is coming really, really soon afterward!

Famines / Pestilence

Jesus also speaks of "famines" and "pestilence" in the Olivet Discourse. In the Matthew and Mark accounts of the discourse, some translations of the Bible don't include the word which is translated as "pestilence" to the list. This is because some of the ancient documents used in our modern translations of the Bible include the word for "pestilence" (or "disease") and others do not. The word for "disease," or "pestilence" is included in the Luke passage, so it is safe to include it on our list of things that cause the childbirth-like pain of which Jesus spoke. (For a more complete discussion on why I chose to include "disease" in my translation, please see the end notes.)[32]

The Greek word for "famine," can also be translated as "hunger," which is typically a direct result of "famine." Instead of saying "famine and pestilence," one could as easily translate these things as "hunger and disease."

Shortages of food due to the environment, and pestilence or disease are nothing new to the planet:

- In 430 BC an unknown agent killed a quarter of the Athenian troops and a quarter of the population over four years during the Peloponnesian war.

- During the Antonine plague of 165 to 180 AD, an estimated five million people died, with as many as 5,000 people a day dying in Rome.
- That is only half as many as the Plague of Justinian, which started in 541 AD. That plague killed up to 10,000 people per day. In the end, up to a quarter of the human population of the eastern Mediterranean region perished.
- The Black Death plague began in 1348. It killed 20 million Europeans in six years' time. Up to half the population in some areas.
- Cholera has wiped out millions of people over the years across China, India, Russia, Europe and has even reached North America.
- The Spanish Flu killed 25 million people across the world in only six months in 1918 and 1919. Some estimates are twice that high.
- In the 1950's and 60's the Asian and Hong Kong flu epidemics wiped out over 100,000 people. These viruses still circulate today. [33]

Unlike earthquakes, there is some indication in the book of Revelation that very near to the return of Jesus, famine and pestilence will dramatically increase relative to the norm as Jesus breaks "seals" on a "scroll" in Heaven (Revelation 6:7-8). Once the seal related to pestilence is loosed it triggers a quarter of the earth being subjected to severe famine and pestilence.

Discussion of this passage in the book of Revelation is beyond the scope of this book. Even with famine and disease playing a part, be clearly warned that looking at disease and famine as signs of the end of the age, by themselves, is not reliable. The "Black Death" plague, as recorded above wiped out about a third of Europe's population in the mid-fourteenth century, and Jesus did not return.

Signs in the Sky

The Luke account of the Olivet Discourse uniquely states that along with famines, earthquakes, wars and such, will be "fearful signs in the heavens." Later in His Discourse, Jesus will inform the disciples of specific signs in the heavens that will in fact be associated with His return. These same signs are also foretold of in the Old Testament Book of Joel and in the book of Revelation, chapter six. However, here Jesus is still warning about those things that in general have been going on for thousands of years and are not unique to the return of Christ. There are "signs in the heavens" all the time. Solar eclipses, "blood moons," and comets have been frightening the inhabitants of the earth since the beginning of time.

Summary

Earthquakes, wars, civil disturbances, false prophets, famines, pestilence, and astronomical signs have always been around, they are with us now and always will be. These things by virtue of being woven into the fabric of our past and present reality, will also play a part in the coming end of the age. Some of these things will even increase just prior to the return of Jesus. However, since these events all cause calamity and "pain" on relative and subjective scales, we cannot rely on earthquakes, disease, famine, and normal astronomical phenomenon as "hard" signals that the return of Jesus will take place soon. That is the essence of Jesus' warning to His disciples.

With His first warnings out of the way regarding things that will affect all humankind on the earth, Jesus next warns His disciples of something much more personal.

Notes

8. Persecution and Walking Away from The Faith

Though Satan should buffet, though trials should come, let this blest assurance control, That Christ has regarded my helpless estate, and has shed His own blood for my soul…

It Is Well with My Soul
Spafford & Bliss[34]

The next few sentences that Jesus spoke to his disciples on the Mount of Olives as recorded in the books of Matthew, Mark, and Luke speak of a time when Christians will die because of their faith in Jesus. The words that Jesus spoke tell of a test of faith that will clearly separate those who are Christian in name alone, from those who are true disciples of Jesus. These are very hard words for any follower of Jesus to read or hear.

Before we continue, I would like to ask you a question; why does a good and sovereign God allow bad things to happen to good people? I am sure you have at some point thought about, been asked, or heard someone ask this question. I have heard many biblically sound answers to this question. However, I am not going to answer it for you. I would like you to seek the answer and keep it in mind for later in this chapter.

A Troubling Story

I once had a particularly disturbing experience with a friend and coworker about the topic of denying one's faith in the face of severe persecution. I will refer to my friend as "Peter." Somehow, while we were working together the conversation came around to the topic of Christianity. I had seen Peter at a large gathering of Christians before, and I wanted to know about his walk with the Lord. Peter gave me his lifelong summary on his church background. He explained how his current church had been quick to get him involved, even putting him in charge of the fellowship committee.

I said, "So those are all the places you have attended church, and your actions while at Church, but what about your relationship with Jesus? Is Jesus Christ the Lord of your life?"

He said "I would have to say yes, but I often falter." He explained he didn't meet up to his own expectations of what he should be doing as a follower of Christ. "You know," he said, "I am not doing the things that all good Christians do."

After a quick review of the concept of grace with Peter, my curiosity led me to ask some more pointed questions. I asked him what would happen if he were put in the position of either denying Christ or dying. He said he didn't know. Peter said he knew Jesus was real, "and is God, and all that," but he just wasn't sure about his faith in Jesus.

Just a week earlier, someone in the Bible study I was leading at the time, asked the question, "How could a Christian, knowing what the Bible has to say about the mark of the beast, ever take the mark when it meant that you would spend eternity apart from Jesus?" Remembering this question, I applied it to my conversation with Peter.

I asked Peter, "If a representative of the future Antichrist came to your home one day with a firing squad, and presented you with a choice to either die or pledge your allegiance to the Antichrist by taking his mark, thus denying Christ, would you take the mark? Failure to take this mark would result in your immediate death. And remember, the Bible makes it clear that those who will take the mark will be thrown into the lake of fire."

My heart absolutely broke for Peter when he replied, "Yes, I'd take it."

When faced with something tangible right in front of him, that threatens to kill him, Peter stated he would opt for trying to save his life now, when in the end he would lose it for eternity. Years later my prayer continues for "Peter," that he would work out his salvation with "fear and trembling."

It is this exact scenario that I put to Peter, which will most likely be responsible for a great "falling away" of people from the Christian faith during the tribulation period. During the future time of persecution described by Jesus, many who do not possess real faith from God, will turn away from Christianity. Those who read or hear the words of Jesus contained in Matthew 24:9, who are not indwelled by God's Holy Spirit, will choose to interpret these words to mean anything other than what they truly mean.

There will be a future time of great persecution and betrayal directed towards followers of Jesus. Brother will betray brother, and sons will betray their fathers. Because of the level of persecution, those that are not sincere in their beliefs will turn their backs on, or "fall away" from the faith. This persecution will be aggravated by the "Man of sin and lawlessness," AKA; the "Antichrist."

Matthew 24:9

Then shall they deliver you up to be afflicted, and shall kill you: and ye shall be hated of all nations for my name's sake. (KJV)

Then, you will be betrayed and handed over to be persecuted, and you will be killed and hated by all people because of my name. (DHT)

Mark 13:9

But take heed to yourselves: for they shall deliver you up to councils; and in the synagogues ye shall be beaten: and ye shall be brought before rulers and kings for my sake, for a testimony against them. (KJV)

But you watch yourselves: for they will betray and hand you over to councils, and in assemblies you will be beaten, and you will be brought before rulers and kings on my behalf, as a testimony against them. (DHT)

Luke 21:12

But before all these, they shall lay their hands on you, and persecute you, delivering you up to the synagogues, and into prisons, being brought before kings and rulers for my name's sake. (KJV)

Now, before all of these things, they will lay their hands on you and persecute you, betraying and delivering you to the assemblies and prisons, and you will be brought before kings and rulers. (DHT)

Are there more earthquakes now than ever? Has there ever been a time when some war was not taking place in the world? Has there ever been a period in history when disease and famine have not been a factor? Likewise, in the last 2,000 years when have there not been wide spread instances of persecution of both Jews and Christians? In fact, according to Church tradition, almost all of the original disciples of Jesus, with the Apostle John being the possible exception, died a violent, painful, martyr's death, for bearing the name of Jesus as their Lord. Christians, even the most noteworthy, do not live "charmed" lives and are not exempt from harm.

James, the brother of Jesus was thrown off of the Temple in Jerusalem, stoned, and finally clubbed over the head as he was praying for those beating him to death. [35] The Apostle Peter was crucified upside down on a Roman Cross and the Apostle Paul was beheaded for his faith outside of Rome. [36] In 69 AD, Andrew was scourged, and tied to a cross, rather than nailed. It took him two days to die under those circumstances. He preached the gospel to those who passed by as he was dying. [37] Thomas was run through by a spear in India after preaching the gospel there and in Greece. According to Church tradition, Matthew, the author of one of the gospels containing the Olivet Discourse, was stabbed in the back in Ethiopia by a swordsman working for a king whom Matthew criticized for his immoral behavior. John Foxe's Book of Martyrs, first published in 1563, tells the story of thousands of Christians losing their lives because they decided to follow Jesus.

Not Now, But "Then"

These persecution related Olivet Discourse verses might appear to be just another item on Jesus' list of bad stuff which has happened in the past and is going to happen in the future, but it doesn't mean it is the end of the world. That is, if not for one word and a change in tone in the passage. The word is, "then." This simple word is talking about a different period of time in the future from the "now" period of time. To expand on this and paraphrase Jesus said, "*then, during this future period of time you are asking me about, these next things will take place.*" "Then," is meant to denote the future period of time directly pertinent to the question Jesus is answering; "*What will be the sign of your coming and the end of the age?*"

There is a conflict to resolve between the Gospel accounts of this passage. Whereas the Matthew account reads like the persecution in question will take place at a future specific time, in contrast, the Mark passage, simply read by itself could mean the persecution is non-specific, happening before or during a specific time. And, the Luke passage makes it sound like the persecution will take place before all of the events we have already discussed!

The Luke account when read in English can be confusing until it is studied closely. It says, "but, before all this they will lay hands on you…" In our simple understanding, this would mean that "before whatever we were just reading about would occur, this next stuff we are reading about, will take place." That would appear to be in direct contradiction with what I am saying about war, famine, pestilence, and earthquakes having been the norm for the last 2,000 years. Reading Luke in this simple way would mean that persecution must take place before war, famine, pestilence, and earthquakes. How could that be?

The key to understanding the wording found in the Book of Luke, is to understand the uses of the Greek word "δε," transliterated into English as "de." "De," starts off verse 12. It is a conjunction. The Mounce concise Greek English Dictionary has important things to say about this little word. Among other uses, "*it* (δε) *serves also to mark the resumption of an interrupted discourse.*"[38]

In this case, Jesus, has been speaking about something other than the original or main topic, and this word marks a point where they are getting back on track or back to the original subject.

For example, in English Jesus might say, "*now, going back to address "these things" you are asking me about, that will occur in conjunction with My coming.*" This translation makes the most sense in this case. Any other way of reading this sentence in Luke does not reconcile the passage.

In Luke 21:7, the disciples ask when "these things" will occur. Farther down the passage in Luke 21:12, Jesus responds "*now, going back to your original question, before these things you are asking me about will occur, they will lay their hands on you and persecute you…* (my translation),"

It is important to understand the fine parsing out of the Luke passage in order to resolve the conflict with the Matthew and Mark accounts. There is no conflict when the scripture in Luke is translated in this way. We have not changed the meaning of any words as they were written in their original language, only selected a viable alternative which is a normal, natural way to understand the word "de" during the time it was used by Luke in order to convey Jesus' meaning.

We are dealing with one talk alone that Jesus gave, as recorded by three different humans (Matthew, Mark and Luke). When defined by each other and in context, all three gospel accounts can be understood to mean that the persecution spoken of, is a persecution of a future time. Specifically, the time period that occurs just before the end of this age.

We have shifted gears from talking about what Jesus warns His disciples are not signs of the end, to what will be occurring around the time of the end of the age.

"Hard" and "Soft" Signs

Since persecution has always been a part of Jewish and Christian history, can it be looked at as a "sign" that Jesus is about to return? My opinion is yes, and no. In order to explain why I answer this way, I would like to introduce the concept of "hard" signs, and "soft" signs.

What I refer to as a "soft" sign are those things that may be prophetically associated with the end of the age, but are not unique to the end of the age. Soft signs are subjective to mere mortals who are limited in their perspective. We do not have a complete knowledge of what has happened in history, and we certainly do not know what the future holds, outside of what God has told us will occur. Because of this, we do not know if earthquakes, famine, pestilence, disturbances, and persecution are worse now than they have ever been in history. Even if those things are worse now than ever before in history, we do not know if they are going to get better in the future. They may even get worse than they are now before Jesus returns and have nothing to do with the end of the age. God alone has the perspective required. For humans, these "soft" signs, can only be used as secondary evidence to confirm that observable "hard" signs, are the real thing.

"Hard" signs are things that cannot be chalked up to the natural course of events. Hard signs are centered on specific details and generally follow a sequence set out in prophecy. They would defy all odds to occur more than once in the future, so they will not likely do so. Although hard signs are mostly unique events, when related to the future Antichrist, some may have occurred previously in history under a previous antichrist empire. There are relatively very few hard signs. A couple examples would be the Abomination of Desolation (previously occurred under the Greek and Roman empires) and the seven-year covenant that is broken 1,260 days into it (this has never previously occurred). These are very specific signs.

An example of a "soft" sign helping to confirm a "hard" sign would be a great persecution of the Jews and Christians after a future seven-year covenant with Israel is broken by a dynamic, powerful ruler who sets himself up to be worshipped. The soft sign being the persecution, the hard sign, being the covenant related and Antichrist-like activity. So yes, "soft" signs should be watched for, but not relied upon by themselves as being indicative that the return of Jesus is imminent.

We read in the book of Revelation that all of the things Jesus has already mentioned in the Olivet Discourse, which have happened throughout history, will in fact play a part in the last days before the end of the age. However, without the presence of any hard signs, we will only be guessing as to how close we are to Jesus' return.

How Does Persecution Differ from the Other "Soft" Signs?

Jesus is now speaking about "those things" which will take place just prior to His return. One of those things is "persecution." He will soon speak about the Antichrist, the Abomination of Desolation committed by the Antichrist, and his reign of terror. Jesus connects all of those events together. In this way, Jesus is making this future persecution unique to the reign of the Antichrist.

There are specifics given about why this different persecution associated with the end of the age will take place. The Antichrist will expect to be worshipped. He will expect people to take his "mark," in order to be associated with him and be able to buy and sell goods and services. Failure to do so will result in death. Because of this, as people choose temporary survival, a falling away from the faith will occur. Family and friends will betray each other under an extreme Gestapo-like culture, which leads to imprisonment and death penalties. Persecution has always taken place in the past. However, the "soft sign" of persecution, accomplished for the above specific reasons, will be one of the ways that we positively identify the future Antichrist.

Being Hated Because of Jesus

Jesus tells His disciples that because of Him, people (non-followers of Jesus) will "hate" His followers. This situation takes us far beyond the prophetic, end times topic. It happens all the time in our world, as it has all through the last two millennia. Persecution of Christians, followers of Christ, got off to a strong start even before Jesus was crucified. It only got worse from there. The type of persecution Jesus prophesied about, has been fulfilled many times over the last two thousand years, but not ultimately fulfilled, for the last time.

Being hated because of Jesus is not a big selling point in Christian evangelical circles. No one wants to hear about suffering and losing all this world has to offer, on account of belonging to Jesus. What kind of "good news" is that? How can we expect to lead people to Christ with that kind of sales pitch? Of course any Christian who is attempting to "do the Lord's work" and "win souls" for Jesus, is very hesitant about pointing out that to become a follower of Jesus Christ, is to become "hated" by the world.

However, what true believers know far outweighs the extreme challenges of being hated. To be a true believer is to have been given faith by God to believe that His Son is our only hope for salvation. It is for one to know that he or she is reborn as a willing servant of the Lord Jesus Christ, adopted into God's family, and that they then have an eternal, supernatural spirit that is not of this world. It is the Holy Spirit within the re-born followers of Christ, which cannot deny the truth. Come what may. Lose what we may. Be hated by whom we may.

As far as the non-Christian worldview is concerned, it is not "cool" to be a real (not pop-culture) follower of Christ. To follow Christ means that you will not attempt to conform or buy into the self-centered, materialistic, godless, evil society where we live.

Just reading the way that I describe the society we live in should give us a clue why people of the world don't like a true follower of Christ; on the surface, the Christian sounds judgmental. Many Christians *are* unfortunately overtly judgmental. They point fingers and attempt to save the lost, "one sin at a time."

Yet, other Christians may also appear to be overtly judgmental, without ever saying a word or pointing a finger. These Christians rightfully point out, simply through only their life choices, not their words, that the societal system they are surrounded by, the one most people whole-heartedly take part in, is evil. Some Christians appear to stand in judgment of others, only because they choose *not* to participate in the system. They therefore can appear to be "too good" for what is good enough for everyone else.

Christians are called to be "lights unto the world," and true followers of Christ, simply by emulating the one they are following, inherently are a source of "light." That light source can make other people very uncomfortable. Sinners are most comfortable under the cover of darkness and surrounded by like-minded people that will support their sin.

I am not talking about Christians overtly shining the light of truth on people, but passively shining the light, by leading a life pleasing to their Master. I personally don't believe scripture teaches Christians to judge the behaviors of non-Christians. That is the work of God. I am only saying that the ambient "light" that true followers of Christ give off through reflecting Christ's own light, is offensive all by itself to non-believers.

What non-Christians perceive as "judgment" is soon turned back around on the follower of Christ by the non-believer. "Judge not, least you be judged," could not be truer. Because most non-Christians don't understand the concept of grace, and because all humans, including Christians, are weak and self-centered, Christians are called hypocrites as others easily find fault with their lives.

A disciple of Christ will be truly sorry when they have engaged in harmful un-Christ-like activities, while the non-Christian will see no harm, especially because "everyone else is doing it." The non-Christian will see no wrong, because they have not been called by the Holy Spirit to be a people that are "set apart."

Jesus once prayed for His disciples, and all of those who would ever come to know Him. He was quite clear when He prayed in reference to His followers throughout time:

> *I have given them thy word; and the world hath hated them, because they are not of the world, even as I am not of the world.* John 17:14 (*KJV)*

Like Jesus, His followers are no longer of this "world." Those that remain a part of the "world" *will* hate those that are not a part of the world. Those that have been chosen by God, have been purchased out of the world with the very blood of Jesus. Those chosen in this way are called to, and set apart for, a high eternal office of "priesthood." The Apostle Peter wrote:

But ye are a chosen generation, a royal priesthood, an holy nation, a peculiar people; that ye should shew forth the praises of him who hath called you out of darkness into his marvellous light: 1 Pet 2:9 *(KJV)*

Why would a "Royal Priest" engage in activities of the "other master," the world? Why would a "servant" of the Most High, All-seeing, Creator of the Universe, act like they were ignorant of His reality by engaging in activities which are embraced by the world's master, Satan?

There are those that attempt to follow Christ and still engage in following the world's systems. They are "double minded" and therefore "unstable in all their ways" (James 1:8). They are attempting to serve "two masters" and that cannot be done.

Every new believer figuratively has stood at a fork in the road when answering the question of whether or not to follow Jesus' path. As Jesus summons the new believer down the narrow road, they have to make a decision: follow the path of Jesus, or follow the path that leads to destruction. Simply stated, as Jesus put it, if you are not "with Him, you are against Him;"

He that is not with me is against me; and he that gathereth not with me scattereth abroad. Matt 12:30 *(KJV)*

Being hated by the world is very difficult. Especially when the "world" includes your family and coworkers. Maybe even, through life's circumstances, it includes your spouse. Yes, being hated by the world sucks. But, in the end, there is no question it is worth it. The cost-benefit analysis is not even close. It's investing a dollar in this world and receiving a never ending supply of dollars in our account, tax free, that can never be taken away, in the next.

This life is clearly not about the temporary "good times" that the world has to offer. This life is to a high degree about coming to the fork in the road and deciding who you will follow. It is about deciding if you will live by your five senses in this age, or by faith in the eternal age to come.

The person who is not sure that it makes sense to forsake the world and follow Christ down the narrow road, at the cost of being "hated by the world" is truly one that needs to "work out their salvation with fear and trembling" (Philippians 2:12). That is a person who needs to work out if they have received the calling to be set apart (holy) by and for Jesus.

Dying for Jesus in The End

Christian Martyrdom started with the stoning of Stephen mentioned in the book of Acts. It occurred all too often during the reformation, and it continues to this day in such places as Sudan. You now can even watch a video on You Tube of your brothers in Christ being beheaded on a beach by members of the Islamic State in Iraq and Syria (ISIS), if for some reason you would ever choose to do so. People dying for Christ in our time is a tragic reality.

Based on the words of Jesus that follow and several passages in the book of Revelation, there is reason to believe that there will be unprecedented persecution of the followers of Jesus associated with the time just prior to His return. This is not a popular doctrine. Twenty-first century, Western-world Christians do not want to think that it is possible to be put through a time of suffering. They would prefer that God would miraculously keep them from such a painful inconvenience those before them have suffered.

Jesus Wouldn't Allow That, Would He?

Visiting a church one Sunday several years ago, my wife Angela and I noticed that one of the Sunday school classes that followed the service was going to be about the Second Coming of Christ. We thought it would be interesting to hear what they had to say.

It was soon made clear that the knowledge of the husband and wife teaching the class was gained through their reading a couple popular end times books. I recognized the teaching. They quoted Hal Lindsey and the late Dave Hunt. I asked them to tell me why they believed in the theory which says that Jesus will "secretly catch away" His Church prior to any persecution, trials, or tribulations taking place. They told me it was true because the Church is the "Bride of Christ," and that, "Jesus is a gentleman," who would "never allow anything bad to happen to His Bride."

This same reason was given as substantiation of the pretribulation rapture theory by Dr. David Jeremiah in his book *Jesus' Final Warning*. This reasoning is a real tough sell for me, given what scriptures and 2,000 years of Christian martyrdom have to say. I firmly believe, as Dr. Jeremiah does, that the elect followers of Christ are not appointed to suffer the wrath of God or His judgment. Where we part ways is that I separate out the events of the future tribulation period. First, there are those things that will take place as a consequence of living in a fallen world especially under the future Antichrist. Then, there will be those events that are actually the results of God pouring out His wrath on the world during the great and terrible "Day of the Lord." The Church will clearly not be present for the latter.

How is it that anyone thinks they can explain away what Jesus had to say about the persecution of His followers? It is easy if you are willing to believe in a myth that has been handed down by those in authority in the Church. The myth says that the Church will be caught away from the earth prior to any trials, tribulation, or persecution associated with the end of the age.

Such is the case with the classic "pretribulation" rapture theory, which a large percentage of evangelical Christians believe to be true without even really knowing why. Since that theory came into popularity in the mid 1800's, it has been handed down from generation to generation and included in popular reference Bibles. Naturally, if it is in print in the Bible, it must be right, isn't it?

If Jesus is not addressing His Church in the Matthew 24:9, Mark 13:9, and Luke 21:12 passages regarding persecution "because of His namesake," who then is He addressing according to the pretribulation rapture theory? Pretribulation rapture theory advocate, and longtime preacher, author, and radio-evangelist, Dr. J Vernon McGee states the following, "*Obviously, He* (Jesus) *is not addressing the church but the nation Israel. The affliction He is talking about is anti-Semitism on a worldwide scale.*[39]

Jews have certainly been persecuted since the time of Christ. Millions have died for their faith. They are still God's chosen people and have an extremely important part to play in the future. According to the Book of Revelation, this will include enduring great persecution in the end. Yet, this question must be answered: since when are Jews hated because they are associated with the name of Jesus? Jesus, is the Messiah they rejected.

First century Jews were some of the leading persecutors of the followers of Jesus. This included the Apostle Paul, before his miraculous conversion to Christianity. The words Jesus is speaking here are words of warning to His followers: Christians. This would include the group of believers that some call "Messianic Jews:" those ethnic Jews that come to accept Jesus as their Lord and Messiah. Earlier in the day, when Jesus found himself giving this talk on the Mount of Olives, He had left the Temple after being rejected by the Jewish leaders. People of the Jewish faith are clearly not people who would be persecuted for "Jesus' namesake."

The "good news" of all this is that the persecution of followers of Christ, past, present and future, is a very temporary affliction that cannot do harm to that part of a Christian that will live forever.

Mark 13:11

But when they shall lead you, and deliver you up, take no thought beforehand what ye shall speak, neither do ye premeditate: but whatsoever shall be given you in that hour, that speak ye: for it is not ye that speak, but the Holy Ghost. (KJV)

But when they take you, and deliver you over to the custody of others, don't take any thought beforehand about what to say, but speak whatever you are given at that time, because it is not you that speaks, but the Holy Spirit. (DHT)

Luke 21:13-15

And it shall turn to you for a testimony. Settle it therefore in your hearts, not to meditate before what ye shall answer: For I will give you a mouth and wisdom, which all your adversaries shall not be able to gainsay nor resist. (KJV)

And it will come down to your testimony on my behalf. Therefor purpose beforehand not to premeditate what defense

to make. For I will give you a mouth and wisdom that all of your adversaries won't be able to reply to or oppose. (DHT)

You may have noticed that we skipped Mark 13:10. We will discuss that verse in the next chapter.

Both Mark and Luke record instructions from Jesus regarding what to do in case you are taken into captivity for *His* sake. Although Matthew chapter 24 does not contain a parallel passage, the Book of Matthew is not silent on these instructions. This passage is almost identical to the passage found in Matthew 10:16-22, where Jesus was preparing to send out His 12 disciples on a mission;

Behold, I send you forth as sheep in the midst of wolves: be ye therefore wise as serpents, and harmless as doves. But beware of men: for they will deliver you up to the councils, and they will scourge you in their synagogues; And ye shall be brought before governors and kings for my sake, for a testimony against them and the Gentiles. But when they deliver you up, take no thought how or what ye shall speak: for it shall be given you in that same hour what ye shall speak. For it is not ye that speak, but the Spirit of your Father which speaketh in you. And the brother shall deliver up the brother to death, and the father the child: and the children shall rise up against their parents, and cause them to be put to death. And ye shall be hated of all men for my name's sake: but he that endureth to the end shall be saved. Matt 10:16-22 (KJV)

These instructions were given to Jesus' disciples as they were sent out during Jesus' day. The similar instructions in the Olivet Discourse differ in that they were intended for not only the disciple's time but also for the end of time when Jesus would not be physically present on the earth. We know this because the context of Jesus' statements in the Olivet Discourse relate to His coming, and the end of the age. However, the Matthew 10 passage again illustrates that persecution, because of the name of Jesus, has been around as long as He has. The same instructions are recorded yet another time in Luke 12:11-12.

Only a couple of days after He delivered His message on the Mount of Olives, Jesus put His own instructions into action as He stood before the Chief Priest after He had been taken captive. This captivity of course, ended in His death on the cross.

I have been taught over the years, via various Christian sources, that it is God's wish that we are comfortable and healthy and that we are to rely on the Holy Spirit in times such as the above scripture mentions in order to allow the Holy Spirit to *rescue us*. God may certainly choose to rescue a follower of Jesus for His Holy purpose. However, to those that believe that the instructions of Jesus are a technique designed to "get you off the hook," by way of the Holy Spirit giving you words of wisdom to utter, please remember how this technique worked out for the Messiah Himself. Jesus was beaten and put to death on a Roman cross. You can read about His court testimony in Matthew 26:59-68.

It is clear that the purpose of the Holy Spirit giving utterances to us is not necessarily intended to save ourselves. Rather the intervention of the Holy Spirit will provide followers of Christ who are being persecuted the wisdom and words to enable them to give their testimony on behalf of Jesus, to those who are doing the persecuting.

Betrayal

Mark 13:12-13a

Now the brother shall betray the brother to death, and the father the son; and children shall rise up against their parents, and shall cause them to be put to death. And ye shall be hated of all men for my name's sake (KJV)

Now brother will betray brother to death and the father his son. And children will rise up against their parents and shall cause them to be put to death. And you will be detested by everyone on account of my name. (DHT)

Luke 21:16-17

And ye shall be betrayed both by parents, and brethren, and kinsfolks, and friends; and some of you shall they cause to be put to death. And ye shall be hated of all men for my name's sake. (KJV)

And you will be betrayed both by parents, brothers, relatives and friends. And they will cause some of you to be put to death. And you will be detested by everyone on account of my name. (DHT)

In the Matthew ten passage cited above, Jesus sends out His disciples to do His work and warns them that they will be betrayed. We find this theme again repeated in Luke chapter twelve when Jesus points out that His first coming, 2,000 years ago, would not result in unity between all, but rather division:

Suppose ye that I am come to give peace on earth? I tell you, Nay; but rather division: For from henceforth there shall be five in one house divided, three against two, and two against three. The father shall be divided against the son, and the son against the father; the mother against the daughter, and the daughter against the mother; the mother in law against her daughter in law, and the daughter in law against her mother in law. Luke 12:51-53 (KJV)

Persecution of His followers, division because of Jesus, and adversity was foretold by Jesus and is as old as Christianity itself. It is not unique to what will occur during the end of the age. Yet, it is important to realize that it will take place right up until the end of the age.

Look at the following passage from the book of Revelation. It records a scene the Apostle John witnessed unfolding in Heaven. God the Father is seated on a throne. Before the throne, there is an altar. As the Apostle John recalls his vision, Jesus has been found to be the only one qualified to take a scroll from the hand of God, and loose its seven seals. The scroll, once completely unsealed will reveal the Will of God in the form of "the Day of the Lord" judgments to be poured out on the earth. As Jesus breaks each seal, things happen.

And when he (Jesus) *had opened the fifth seal, I saw under the altar the souls of them that were slain for the word of God, and for the testimony which they held: And they cried with a loud voice, saying, how long, O Lord, holy and true, dost thou not judge and avenge our blood on them that dwell on the earth? And white robes were given unto every one of them; and it was said unto them, that they should rest yet for a little season, until their fellow servants also and their brethren, that should be killed as they were, should be fulfilled.* Rev 6:9-11 (KJV)

The fifth seal of this heavenly scroll is broken and what, or who, do we see? Martyred "servants," before the throne of God in Heaven. They had been killed because of the testimony they maintained regarding their Master, Jesus. They are told that they need to be patient until a number more of "their brethren" would also be killed in the same manner prior to God avenging their blood. These disembodied souls were in the very presence of God making their requests known. The answer they were given is that God would not take action based on their request. It was instead the Will of God that more of their "fellow servants," be slain because of their testimony.

Why are "brothers betraying brothers," even when it means their own family members will be put to death? In the coming verses of the Olivet Discourse, Jesus will introduce the character of the Antichrist. By comparing scripture with scripture, we start to put together a picture in which we see the Antichrist being the driving force behind such persecution and betrayal. He provides very strong external motivation for betraying followers of Christ. They do so in order to save their own lives and perhaps the lives of their loved ones. Both Mark and Luke record that this hatred driven persecution is directed specifically at those who keep God's commandments; Jews, and those that bear the name of Jesus: Christians.

A Great Falling Away

The future persecution of the Church will be vast. It will be extremely difficult to be a Christian. We've talked about the persecution of Christians but here we are talking about a specific time when there will be a great "falling away" from the faith.

Many have fallen away from the faith in the past as a result of persecution. Many have fallen away because the seeds of salvation that were planted with them never took root. However, this future occurrence of leaving the Christian faith will apparently occur on a scale large enough to be recognizable. So much so both Jesus and Paul use it as a sign of the approaching end of the age.

Matthew 24:10

And then shall many be offended, and shall betray one another, and shall hate one another. (KJV)

And at that time many will fall away, and shall betray one another, and hate one another. (DHT)

Persecution is nothing new to the Church, and like earthquakes, wars, and disease, persecution of the Church alone should not be taken as a sign of the end of the age. However, it is at this point in the Olivet Discourse that it appears that Jesus is changing His focus on things that *will be* unique to the period of His Second Coming. In the ultimate fulfillment of what Jesus is talking about, the "falling away" from the faith appears to be a noteworthy occurrence associated with persecution and the end of the age.

The Greek word that Matthew used to record what Jesus said (probably originally spoken in the Aramaic language) is "σκανδαλίζω." It is transliterated into the English language as "skandalizō." We get our word, "scandal" from it. In the original language, one of the ways the word was used is "to offend, shock, excite a feeling of repugnance." It also can mean to be "enticed to sin," or to "falter or fall away." It can mean causing a person to distrust someone or something that they should trust. This interpretation is the way the word was used in Jesus' parable of the seeds and the sower in Matthew chapter 13.

In Matthew chapter 13, Jesus tells a story about a person who scattered some seed, and what happened to the seeds.

And he spake many things unto them in parables, saying, Behold, a sower went forth to sow; And when he sowed, some seeds fell by the way side, and the fowls came and devoured them up: Some fell upon stony places, where they had not much earth: and forthwith they sprung up, because they had no deepness of earth: And when the sun was up, they were scorched; and because they had no root, they withered away. Matt 13:3-6 (KJV)

A little later, Jesus defined what the story of the seeds and the sower meant. In regards to the seeds that fell on rocky soil, he said the following:

But he that received the seed into stony places, the same is he that heareth the word, and anon (immediately) *with joy receiveth it; Yet hath he not root in himself, but dureth for a while: for when tribulation or persecution ariseth because of the word, by and by he is **offended*** (skandalizō). *Matt 13:20-21 (KJV)* (Definition, emphasis and transliteration added)

Interpreting the Greek word transliterated as "skandalizō," to mean, "fall away," in light of the context of persecution found in the Olivet Discourse immediately surrounding this word, and the use of the word in the *Parable of the Sower*, makes perfect sense. Some people will fall away from the faith after suffering tribulation and persecution, just as Jesus said in Matthew chapter 13 and Matthew 24.

Falling Away Event Also Written About by The Apostle Paul

Although Matthew is the only author that documented this particular statement regarding "falling away," in the Olivet Discourse, it is not the only place we read about a "falling away" from the faith in regards to the Second Coming of Jesus. The Apostle Paul's correspondence to the believers in Thessalonica about the Second Coming of Jesus actually utilizes the future falling away from the faith as a sign.

*Now we beseech you, brethren, by the coming of our Lord Jesus Christ, and by our gathering together unto him, that ye be not soon shaken in mind, or be troubled, neither by spirit, nor by word, nor by letter as from us, as that the day of Christ is at hand. Let no man deceive you by any means: for that day shall not come, except there come a **falling away** first, and that man of sin be revealed, the son of perdition; Who opposeth and exalteth himself above all that is called God, or that is worshipped; so that he as God sitteth in the temple of God, shewing himself that he is God. Remember ye not, that, when I was yet with you, I told you these things? 2 Thess 2:1-5 (KJV)* (Emphasis Added).

The English Standard Version of the Bible, and several other versions translate the Greek word, "αποστασία," transliterated into English as "apostasia," (ap-os-tas-ee'-ah) as the English word, "rebellion." Other translations, such as the American Standard Version and King James Version, translate it as "falling away." Yet others, such as the New American Standard Version, translate the word as "apostasy." The word means to "defect from the truth, to fall away, or forsake." [40]

The only other time "apostasia" is used in the Bible is in Acts 21:21 where it is translated as "forsake." It is used there referencing the "forsaking of beliefs." Remember the meaning of the Greek word transliterated as "skandalizo," includes distrusting that which should be trusted, or to forsake or fall away from something.

A wrong interpretation of this or any other word brings to mind wrong images. The word "rebellion" for example, in our time may either bring to mind anything from some sort of paramilitary uprising, to teenagers experiencing another round of hormone driven differences of opinions with their parents. The word "rebellion" is only accurate in that it is a rebellion of individuals, once Christian in name, coming against the Christian faith.

The reason I take up so much space to carefully define this word, is that there are those that say that this "falling away," that Paul wrote of, is actually the "rapture" of the church. They incorrectly believe the Apostle Paul is talking about the "departure" of the church from the *earth* instead of the departure of many in the church from the faith and *truth*. This however, is a misuse of the word and would be a unique use of the word in the Bible.

Being secretly "taken away" by a third party, is a long way from an individual falling away, or departing from the truth, or rebelling. This interpretation is particularly absurd when you consider that Paul is saying in this same passage that the rapture, or as he put it, "our gathering together unto him," will not occur until "there comes a falling away first." Secondly, the falling away is tied to the revealing of the Antichrist. In other words, according to Paul, a "falling away" (from the faith) and the revealing of the Antichrist must first take place before followers of Christ will be gathered to Jesus.

Paul uses strong language as if to say, "*make no mistake, like I told you before, you won't miss the Second Coming because there are two obvious things that will happen before it; the falling away, and the revealing of the Antichrist.*"

To further make the case that this particular "falling away" is a specific event in the future and not just an ongoing trend through history, the word "apostasy" as used in II Thessalonians 2, has the definite article (like "the" as opposed to "a" when referring to a thing). It is not just *any* falling away throughout history, it is *the* falling away. It is a specific, definitive, event. It is no coincidence that it is mentioned in conjunction with another specific identifiable event; the revealing of the Antichrist:

… and the man of sin is revealed, the son of perdition, who opposes and exalts himself above all that is called God….

We will soon see this "son of perdition" referred to by Jesus in the next couple of verses of Matthew 24.

The time of the apostasy will be the time for many, who have been Christian's in name only, to decide what side of the fence they are on. According to the book of Revelation, the Antichrist will cause all people to take his "mark" in order to buy, sell, or trade (Rev. 13:16-17). People will also have the option of either worshipping the Antichrist or dying (Rev. 13:15). Of course worshiping the Antichrist is not an acceptable option for the true follower of Jesus.

Historical Life or Death Decisions

This won't be the first time this sort of definitive, forced decision making process regarding one's faith at the hand of a powerful world leader will have taken place. In 168 BC the Greek Seleucid leader, Antiochus Epiphanes IV, who is thought by many to be a foreshadow of the future Antichrist, caused the Jews to choose his ways or die. To choose his ways meant denying God and defiling themselves, by among many other things, making sacrifices to false gods. Many Jews were agreeable to doing so in order to save their lives.

Likewise, in the Roman Empire, in the first two centuries after Christ ascended into Heaven, when certain Caesars were in power, faith-based tests of allegiance were administered. When it was discovered that someone might be a Christian, he or she was questioned about their faith after they were advised that there was a death penalty for being a Christian. If she or he denied their faith, as proof, they were asked to make a sacrifice to a false god. Again many chose to save their lives by making the sacrifice. [41]

What does the Bible say about denying your faith?

Whosoever therefore shall confess me before men, him will I confess also before my Father which is in heaven. But whosoever shall deny me before men, him will I also deny before my Father which is in heaven. Matt 10:32-33 (KJV)

If we suffer, we shall also reign with him: if we deny him, he also will deny us: 2 Tim 2:12 (KJV)

Then said Jesus unto his disciples, if any man will come after me, let him deny himself, and take up his cross, and follow me. For whosoever will save his life shall lose it: and whosoever will lose his life for my sake shall find it. For what is a man profited, if he shall gain the whole world, and lose his own soul? or what shall a man give in exchange for his soul? Matt 16:24-26 (KJV)

Falling Away vs. Losing One's Salvation

As we have seen, there will be those who "fall away" from the faith. How do we reconcile this with the doctrine of "once saved always saved?" There will be those who say they are Christians beforehand that will take the infamous "mark of the beast," spoken of in the Book of Revelation, in order to save either their lives or the lives of their children. They will have believed or at least said that they believed that Jesus was real, and that He rose from the dead. They will have even prayed the sinner's prayer. But, in the end, they will deny Christ by taking the Antichrist's mark instead of trusting God's word and patiently enduring until the end, even if it would have meant dying.

Is "falling away" from the faith, the same as one losing their salvation? By taking the mark of the beast, even though someone prayed the "sinner's prayer," and in light of God's grace, are they destined for the lake of fire? Is this saying that you can lose your salvation? Absolutely not! It is not a question of whether or not someone can *lose* his or her eternal life. The very words "eternal life" mean just that! How do you end an eternal life? How can *eternal,* be conditional? If it is conditional, and you can lose it, it never really was eternal. Thank God that we are saved by his grace, because of what Jesus did for us once and for all. When he saves us, it's a done deal… eternally!

No, it's not a question of whether one can lose one's salvation. It's a question of whether or not one was "saved" in the first place. God is the only judge of this. He is the one who searches hearts and minds (Rev 2:23).

For by grace are ye saved through faith; and that not of yourselves: it is the gift of God: Not of works, lest any man should boast. Eph 2:8-9 (KJV)

It is through this faith that we obtain God's gift of salvation by His grace, and by God given faith alone. There is nothing you or I can physically do to obtain this grace, or to pay God back for it.

Remember the *Parable of the Sower*, discussed above? The seeds that fell on the rocky soil were likened to a person who "hears the word, and immediately and joyfully joy accepts it." However, because that person has no solid foundation or "root" within himself concerning the faith, he or she endures for a while, professing to be a Christian, but when trouble and persecution come, they fall away from the faith, even though they seem to know it is the truth.

Being "Saved": Understanding what it means to confess "Jesus as Lord."

When discussing this issue with other believers I have asked them "What is the simplest instructions we have in the Bible on how to become saved?" The number one answer is found in the book of Romans, where it says:

> *That if thou shalt confess with thy mouth the Lord Jesus, and shalt believe in thine heart that God hath raised him from the dead, thou shalt be saved.* Rom 10:9 (KJV)

This verse that is contained in the Apostle Paul's first century letter to the Church in Rome, contains a two-part procedure that leads to eternal life; #1 Confess with your mouth. #2 Believe in your heart. Many people have confessed with their mouths that "Jesus is Lord," for anyone present to hear, but believing in your heart is impossible for other people to judge.

Even having both confessed, and believed, it will still come down to an understanding of what it actually means to confess "Jesus as Lord." It goes way beyond merely putting the syllables together, expelling some air and uttering the words as though it is a magical spell or formula that forces God Almighty's hand to "save" anyone who utters them.

How many 21st century earth dwellers really understand the historical meaning of the word "lord?" Have they really pondered the meaning of the commitment they are making when they utter the words? Have those who are "making disciples" appropriately educated their potential proselytes about the commitment behind the words they are saying?

The Greek word used for "Lord" in Romans 10:9 is transliterated as "kurios" (koo'-ree-os). It means "supreme in authority," or "controller." This particular word is translated in the King James Version of the New Testament as God, Lord, Master, and Sir. When we confess Jesus as Lord, we are asking Him to be and agreeing that He will forevermore will be, the "supreme authority and controller" in our lives as our God and Master. We are saying, "not my will, Lord, but your will be done in my life."

God knows when we understand the complete meaning and ramifications behind the words we say when we name Jesus as our "Lord." It is at that point when Jesus uses the blood that He has already shed to purchase us out of slavery to sin and this world and makes us His servant. That is the moment of eternal salvation when the "seed that was planted" takes root and will not be blown away or uprooted.

Many people believe that Jesus really walked the face of the earth 2,000 years ago and did rise from the dead. They believe the facts as stated in the Bible. But then Satan believes the facts doesn't he? (See James 2:19). Why then aren't Satan or his minions "saved" if that is all it takes? The problem is, even though Satan knows these things about Jesus to be true, he has made himself his own lord.

Lucifer being the lord of his own life, shares the same fundamental problem with all of those who have never made Jesus the true Lord of their life. They believe the biblical facts with their minds, and have spoken the words, but still remain the "lord" of their own lives.

People may even "believe in their hearts" that Jesus is "Lord" in the larger sense that they acknowledge His authority over everything. They will confess this in every way, except for how they actually intend to lead their own life. This group of people may stand out as appearing to be very hypocritical.

Some in this group will attempt to hide what they are doing, others will at least be honest and say, "I know I'm going to Hell." They may be one of those who believe they are beyond God's reach because of what they have done, or they may just be knowingly and intentionally taking their own Hell-bound path to spite God. Whatever the reason, *understanding* and *acknowledging* that Jesus is Lord and believing He was raised from the dead, does not seem to get at the full meaning of Roman's 10:9.

You can't serve two masters, whether it is "God and money," or God and yourself. If you have chosen to follow Him, Jesus demands to be your Lord. Scripture does not say, "If you confess with your mouth that Jesus was real," but rather that Jesus is the "absolute authority and controller" in your life, through being your "Lord."

None of this is to say that the true follower of Jesus, the one who has made Jesus his or her Lord, will have a life that looks perfect. Jesus does not purchase His followers out of slavery to the world and sin based on their qualifications. He purchases them regardless of sin and character flaws. He purchases the low and high functioning, the young and the old, the physically grossly deformed and the beautiful, the very weak and the very strong, the capable and the incapable, the bald and hairy, the sick and healthy, and the intelligent and the illiterate. He also purchases the weak and strong willed.

He takes those He purchases, those bond servants who have truly made the decision to follow Him, and turns them into the new person that He wants them to be over time. They bring with them all the flaws and sin they had before. They may keep their flaws until they lay dying, but as they lay dying they are still resolved to follow their Master, Jesus, who has long forgiven and forgotten their sins.

It is those Christians in name only, who have not made Jesus their Lord and Master, which will fall away from the faith during the tribulation and persecution of the end. They may have even attended church for 40 years and served on every committee known, but they won't have the God given faith and strength needed to overcome.

Work Out Your Salvation?

It is with the above things in mind that I believe we need to "work out our salvation with fear and trembling."

Wherefore, my beloved, as ye have always obeyed, not as in my presence only, but now much more in my absence, work out your own salvation with fear and trembling. Phil 2:12 (KJV)

Philippians 2:12 does not mean that you are to work out your own path to salvation. There is only one way; through Jesus. This verse does not say "*Work for* your salvation with fear and trembling." Salvation is a gift from God. You can't earn it, and will never deserve it. Likewise, the verse does not say "*Work off* your salvation with fear and trembling." To try to pay God back for what His Son did would just be a terrible insult to Him. We could never pay Him back. What the Word is instructing us to do is to examine ourselves.

In your mind, when you are completely honest with yourself, do you clearly have it resolved that you want His will to be done in your life over your own? When you walk into the throne room of your own being, who do you see sitting there? Is it Jesus, or you?

You do not have anything to prove to any other human being in regards to these questions or this issue. It is God only that can judge you. No human knows the struggle of another human in this regard. What we do know, is if you are someone who has been called by the Holy Spirit, and you truly do make Jesus your Lord, that the Holy Spirit will literally take up residence inside you and make these questions much easier to answer.

Life after the Cross

What about Peter? The Apostle Peter denied that he knew Jesus three times, and on him, Christ "built His Church." True story. I am not suggesting that there should be no room for human failure and therefore the grace and forgiveness of God. After all, "The spirit may be willing, but the flesh is weak" (Matthew 26:41).

If you were to ask Peter the same questions about Christ after the resurrection of Jesus, and the indwelling of the Holy Spirit, you would have most likely received a much different answer from him than when he originally denied Jesus. Now, having both the entire written Word of God, the indwelling of the Holy Spirit, and Satan being defeated by the Risen Savior, life on earth after the cross, is very different.

It is those people who have heard the Word, received it, but not made Jesus their Lord who Jesus is talking about in His *Parable of the Sower* in Matthew 13:20-21. It is those same people who have not made Jesus the final absolute authority in their lives that will cry out to Him in the end, in the following manner. Jesus said:

Not every one that saith unto me, Lord, Lord, shall enter into the kingdom of heaven; but he that doeth the will of my Father which is in heaven. Many will say to me in that day, Lord, Lord, have we not prophesied in thy name? and in thy name have cast out devils? and in thy name done many wonderful works? And then will I profess unto them, I never knew you: depart from me, ye that work iniquity. Matt 7:21-23 (KJV)

Where Is the Hope? Jesus Will Overcome for His Followers

Persecution, the Antichrist, suffering, and betrayal; where is the hope in all of this? If you have been elected by God and have been given faith by him, there is no way you will fail the test. In that hour of testing, it is His very own Holy Spirit that will take the test for you.

The overcoming of any test or trial of the end of the age is completely reliant on Jesus, who has already overcome. It is a God given gift of faith. If we are not in Him, if He is not truly our Lord, then we are on our own, and will fail. Remember II Timothy 2:12 mentioned above? To refresh your memory:

If we suffer, we shall also reign with him: if we deny him, he also will deny us: 2 Tim 2:12 (KJV)

What is amazing and gives us hope is what follows in the next verse:

If we believe not, yet he abideth faithful: he cannot deny himself. II Tim 2:13 (KJV)

Once we are saved by God's great free gift, we are indwelled by His Holy Spirit, who cannot deny Himself. By God's own power, He will overcome for us. When we would be found faithless on our own and not have the will to stand firm for Christ, He will remain faithful and not allow us to deny Him. Jesus said:

To him that overcometh will I grant to sit with me in my throne, even as I also overcame, and am set down with my Father in his throne. Rev 3:21 (KJV)

Sitting next to Jesus on His throne? Talk about hope? I would be thrilled with groveling on the floor outside the door of the throne room. Jesus is the over-comer. Those who make Him their Lord and are His possessions will overcome because He already overcame for us.

False Prophets

Matthew 24:11

And many false prophets shall rise, and shall deceive many. (KJV)

And many false prophets shall rise up and shall deceive many. (DHT)

If one were to just quickly read through this passage, one may think that Jesus is simply emphasizing what He had just said a few sentences earlier in verse five when He said:

For many shall come in my name, saying, I am Christ; and shall deceive many. Matt 24:5 (KJV)

One may also think that this statement seems a little random in the middle of a passage that is talking about persecution and falling away from the faith. However, Jesus is actually giving us some insight as to why the persecution, betrayal, and falling away, is taking place and why we will see an increase in wickedness and "love growing cold"; "false prophets" will have something to do with it.

The Greek word for "false prophet" is "ψευδοπροφῆται," transliterated as "pseudoprofetai." This is a word made up of three root words; "pseudo," meaning "false" or "untrue," "pro," meaning "before," or "fore," and "phemi," meaning "to say" or "speak one's mind." Literally, all together it means "a foreteller of untruths."

A false prophet can come in many forms, a false Messiah being only one of them. They can come in the form of a teacher of untruths from both within and outside of the Church. They can be overt, like Muhammad, and covert, like someone who attempts to introduce false teaching into the Church. Institutions of learning and the media are full of false teaching. Just a little while later in the

Olivet Discourse, Jesus will tell us that these false prophets will be so effective, that they may even be able to "fool the elect."

Force and deception will be used to convince people that the smart thing to do is to pledge their allegiance to the Antichrist and become a part of his ungodly system. People will be so convinced of this that they will be willing to betray their family in order to be a part of the Antichrist's system.

There will be far more than one false prophet that will "deceive many" people. However, we are told in the book of Revelation that the Antichrist will have help in convincing the people that they should follow him. His help will come from a single person referred elsewhere in scripture as "the false prophet" (Revelation 16:13, 19:20, 20:10). This chief among false prophets will be able to perform what appear to be miraculous signs. Referring to this false prophet, the Apostle John, author of the Book of Revelation, wrote:

And he (the False Prophet) *doeth great wonders, so that he* (the False Prophet) *maketh fire come down from heaven on the earth in the sight of men, and deceiveth them that dwell on the earth by the means of those miracles which he* (the False Prophet) *had power to do in the sight of the beast* (the Antichrist)*; saying to them that dwell on the earth, that they should make an image to the beast,* (the Antichrist) *which had the wound by a sword, and did live. Rev 13:13-14 (KJV)* (My words added in parentheses).

Love Will Grow Cold

The falling away from the faith, and betraying those who remain in the faith go hand in hand. It becomes easier to "betray" when you have no love for someone. Jesus indicates that because of the increase of wickedness, that the love of "many," not just a few, will "grow cold." Because of what the rest of the passage says, this may be referring to love for God, or to the love for those we call family and friends.

Matthew 24:12

And because iniquity shall abound, the love of many shall wax cold. (KJV)

And because lawlessness will abound, the love of many will be made cold. (DHT)

The correlation between the increase of lawlessness and "love growing cold" is interesting. The sequence seems to be that tribulation, persecution and deception, leads to a great falling away of the faith. A departure from the Christian faith leads to wickedness or lawlessness, and this lawlessness leads to love growing cold. Love growing cold, leads to the betrayal of others. The betrayal of others leads to their persecution, which contributes to this end of the age cycle.

The King James Version of the Bible uses the antiquated term "wax," saying that the "love of many will wax cold." The original meaning of the Greek word used means to cool something down by blowing on it or having air move over a surface to cause cooling by means of evaporation. This definition brings to mind something other than just passive cooling down, like when you take a teakettle off a burner. It denotes more action, like when you dump a cold bucket of water on something.

Here is the good news; For those that do not fall away from the faith, there is a promise…

Matthew 24:13

But he that shall endure unto the end, the same shall be saved. (KJV)

But the one who patiently suffers to the end, that same person will be saved. (DHT)

Mark 13:13b

but he that shall endure unto the end, the same shall be saved. (KJV)

but the one that patiently suffers to the end, that same person will be saved. (DHT)

Luke 21:18-19

But there shall not an hair of your head perish. In your patience possess ye your souls. (KJV)

But not a hair on your head will be lost. Through your patient endurance, you will gain your soul. (DHT)

In the midst of betrayal and persecution, there is a promise from Jesus that if you endure, you will "gain life." Surely Jesus is not talking about saving one's physical life. 2,000 years of people dying for their faith in Jesus and numerous scriptures on this topic indicate that this is not the case. This scripture is clearly referring to eternal life. If you know Jesus as your Lord and Savior, you have already gained eternal life. Although your physical body likely will die one day, the reborn spirit inside you right now, will never see death.

In Jesus' letter to the seven churches as recorded in the book of Revelation by the Apostle John, there are several promises made in regards to eternal life as a result of being faithful. For example:

Fear none of those things which thou shalt suffer: behold, the devil shall cast some of you into prison, that ye may be tried; and ye shall have tribulation ten days: be thou faithful unto death, and I will give thee a crown of life. He that hath an ear, let him hear what the Spirit saith unto the churches; He that overcometh shall not be hurt of the second death. Rev 2:10-11 (KJV)

He that overcometh, the same shall be clothed in white raiment; and I will not blot out his name out of the book of life, but I will confess his name before my Father, and before his angels. Rev 3:5 (KJV)

Luke's documentation of the Olivet Discourse includes the statement *that "not one hair on your head will be harmed."* Yet, it may very well be that one may have their physical hair on their head harmed as a result of persecution. Suffering physical harm is a temporary problem. To think that this verse could possibly mean that one who is faithful will not suffer physical harm would be taking this verse out of context and missing the point about eternal life and salvation that Jesus is making. The rest of the surrounding scriptures are talking about physically suffering and even dying for the cause of Christ.

Does this mean this verse represents one of those "un-resolvable conflicts" within scripture? No.

I don't have as much hair on my head as I used to. I don't look to this promise to restore my physical hair or hold on to what remains. This sounds silly, but if we take some scripture literally, rather than how we would take someone communicating with us in a normal, natural, customary sense, taking use of hyperbole into consideration, it is where we end up; with a full head of hair, if we are faithful. To be really literal, it means that you may die from the persecution, but the hair on your head will be thick and full!

What Jesus is really talking about is not fearing or succumbing to those that can do harm to your physical body, but rather fearing God, who controls your eternal status.

And fear not them which kill the body, but are not able to kill the soul: but rather fear him which is able to destroy both soul and body in hell. Matt 10:28 (KJV)

A Big Objection

The main objection typically raised by those who believe in a pretribulation rapture is that God would not allow His Beloved Church to suffer trials and tribulations like the intense persecution described under the rule of the Antichrist. Pretribulationists argue that since God would not allow such terrible persecution of His Church, the rapture must take place prior. Below are three counter arguments for you to consider.

It is time for you to answer the question I put forward at the beginning of this chapter; Why would a good and sovereign God allow bad things to happen to good people? The answer to that question, whatever it is, is my first argument against those that say God would not allow His Church to suffer persecution associated with the end of the age. So you tell me, why will God allow the end of the age Church go through severe persecution? Does God love the people who will make up the last days Church more than He does the mother that today is dying of cancer, or the child who drowns in the lake? Why doesn't He rescue them, and the children around the world that are dying of malnutrition?

Secondly, I have another question for you to answer; Is God going to love and care more for His future Church than He has loved and cared for His past or present Church? Will He think more of their physical wellbeing than Jesus' disciples who all, save possibly one, died painful deaths for his name's sake? Were all of those persecuted under the Roman Empire who were being torn to shreds in the Coliseum less deserving of God's rescue from persecution? How about the thousands that have suffered and died for Christ since then?

Finally, I will point out that it is not up to mortal human beings to decide ultimate good. It is God's plan, not man's. It is not mankind's place to say what seems logical, humane, or just and then determine scriptural doctrines based on our finite point of view. No matter how compassionate and logical we believe that point of view to be it is still God's decision. Our place is to accept what the Bible tells us about God's plan and then to trust Him, even if it looks like there is pain in store.

Aren't we talking about a God, that in His wisdom and perfect will cursed mankind to death because Adam disobeyed God? Isn't it also the same Almighty God, who sent His Only Son to painfully die on a Roman cross to atone for our sins? Were there not six million of God's "chosen people" that perished in World War Two and the hands of an Antichrist-like maniac?

Are we not talking about the God who is calling out a "Holy Nation" of people from among the world who live by faith and willingly follow His Son, no matter what the consequences? Didn't God tell us in His Word that He would conform those people into the image of His Son? As many Christians around the world today will attest, while suffering and watching their brothers and sisters die for the name of Jesus at the hands of evil persecutors, sometimes God's plan includes extreme pain and even the death of the ones He loves dearly.

To continue to believe that God would not allow those He loves dearly to suffer according to His purposes is to engage in cognitive dissonance. Especially when confronted by scripture that clearly says the Church will suffer severe persecution during the end of the age and by historical accounts of cruel persecution of Christians throughout the past twenty centuries. The facts do not line up with the fantasy. My prayer is that those who hold to this baseless theory will give up the doctrine of comfort and convenience in favor of the truth and be given faith to trust the Almighty God, whatever may come.

SUMMARY

The end of the age will bring with it the persecution of those that follow Jesus. Followers of Jesus will be "hated." This persecution will lead to a great falling away from the faith, separating out those who never really knew Jesus as their Lord. Those who are closest to Christians, their own family in some cases, will betray them. The love of many will grow cold during this period of time. Some followers of Jesus will go to prison or be put to death for their faith.

Those who remain faithful to Jesus until the end, even if it means they will lose their physical life, will gain eternal life. Jesus cannot deny Himself, and through the Holy Spirit of God, those that belong to Jesus will overcome.

9. Good News for Everyone!

The Lord is not slack concerning his promise, as some men count slackness; but is longsuffering to us-ward, not willing that any should perish, but that all should come to repentance. 2 Peter 3:9 (KJV)

"How are we doing in China?" The Almighty asked.

One of the twenty-four elders surrounding the throne of God replied. "Well, my Lord, with it now being okay for families there to have two children rather than one, we are a little worried about people contributing enough money to be able to publish enough Bibles in the Chinese language in order to keep up with the birth rate."

"Sure. Well, what about the satellite program to send the gospel into Uzbekistan?"

A second elder around the throne cleared his throat and responded, "Yes, Lord, there may be a little delay on that project. Uh, the, uh, rocket carrying the satellite exploded in the sky after takeoff, causing a bit of a setback."

"Hmmm," The Lord turned His head and set his gaze to the far end of where the elders were seated. "How about heart stirrings? Where are we at with people feeling the call to be missionaries?"

"Uh, heart stirrings are down 17% Lord," the elder answered. "It appears we are having a hard time competing with Instagram and other social media."

"Right, right." The Almighty said quietly, and then paused contemplatively. Suddenly, the heavens shook and thunder and lightning burst forth from the throne as the Creator of the Universe boomed, "We are never going to get my Son back to that planet at this rate!"

How absolutely absurd to think that such a conversation could ever occur in the throne room of the Almighty Lord of the Universe. Equally absurd is to think that in order to accomplish His purposes, God could ever be dependent upon the intellect, resources, or actions of the human beings that He created from the dust.

When God tells us in His word that something is going to happen unconditionally, it is going to happen, and it will happen precisely at the appointed time. The next thing Jesus says in the

Olivet Discourse, is one of those things that will happen with, or without us.

<u>**Matthew 24:14**</u>

And this gospel of the kingdom shall be preached in all the world for a witness unto all nations; and then shall the end come. (KJV)

And this gospel of the kingdom shall be proclaimed throughout all of the world, as a testimony to all peoples, and then the end will come. (DHT)

<u>**Mark 13:10**</u>

And the gospel must first be published among all nations. Mark 13:10 (KJV)

And the gospel must first be publicly proclaimed to all peoples. (DHT)

This statement regarding preaching the gospel to "all the world," almost seems a little out of place in the context of what we have read so far. On the surface, it makes what sounds like a conditional statement; "*Jesus isn't coming back until you get out there and spread the gospel!*" However, this statement was made here because it directly relates to what Jesus was just saying about His return and His follower's persecution. Here is Mark's version of the statement again along with the verses preceding and following it.

But take heed to yourselves: for they shall deliver you up to councils; and in the synagogues ye shall be beaten: and ye shall be brought before rulers and kings for my sake, for a testimony against them. ***And the gospel must first be published among all nations.*** *But when they shall lead you, and deliver you up, take no thought beforehand what ye shall speak, neither do ye premeditate: but whatsoever shall be given you in that hour, that speak ye: for it is not ye that speak, but the Holy Ghost. Mark 13:9-11 KJV* (Emphasis added)

The statement about proclaiming the gospel to all nations appears to be a part of the larger statement regarding bearing witness during persecution. With that in mind, in context, it looks like at least one way the gospel will be spread, before "the end" comes, is through the testimony of those followers of Jesus that are brought to trial and stand before government officials. At the time in which that occurs, Jesus said the Holy Spirit will speak through His followers. The main message the Holy Spirit will proclaim, considering the surrounding scripture, is that of the "gospel of the kingdom."

Mark's account of this statement in the Olivet Discourse, leaves out the part about the gospel being spread to the "whole world," as well as the part about the "end" occurring after it is accomplished.

If the Matthew version of scripture is to be taken close to literally, the "whole world" hearing the gospel indicates that there will be other avenues for the gospel to be spread. There will be more ways of spreading the gospel than court of law or testimony before "governors and kings."

The original Greek word used to express "the whole world," originally only meant the Greek or Hellenized world, or later, the world under Roman authority. The idea is that what is involved is the "known" or "inhabited" world. By inference it means the entire inhabited world.

The statement recorded in Matthew, "and then the end shall come," clearly ties the Olivet Discourse to the end of the age. Not, as Preterists would have us believe, only the destruction of the Temple in Jerusalem in 70 AD.

As pointed out earlier, this is not the first place where we find documentation of Jesus speaking of the spreading the gospel of the kingdom. Matthew chapter 10 contains an account of Jesus sending his disciples out to spread the gospel in Israel. However, in contrast, Jesus is now telling the same disciples that the gospel will be spread not only to Israel and Jews, but beyond, to the entire world and all peoples.

The "Mystery"

There are two important differences between Jesus' statement on the Mount of Olives about the spreading of the gospel, compared to what happened in Matthew chapter 10. First, when Jesus speaks of the gospel being spread in the Olivet Discourse, it is not a command to the disciples to do anything. Jesus is telling His disciples that *it will be* spread. The statement is silent in this passage as to how spreading the gospel to the entire world will occur. Mark only hints that the spreading of the gospel will come about as a result of persecution.

The second and perhaps most important difference is that in Matthew chapter 10, Jesus specifically instructed the disciples to go only to the "house of Israel" and not to the nations of the Gentiles ("the whole world" and "all people").

These twelve Jesus sent forth, and commanded them, saying, go not into the way of the Gentiles, and into any city of the Samaritans enter ye not: But go rather to the lost sheep of the house of Israel. And as ye go, preach, saying, the kingdom of heaven is at hand. Matt 10:5-7(KJV)

During the Olivet Discourse, Jesus tells the Disciples that His gospel, the gospel of the Kingdom that He has been teaching about for the last few years, must now be spread to the *entire world,* and not just the Nation of Israel. Earlier in the same day that Jesus delivered this message, He hinted to the religious leaders of Israel about this change.

O Jerusalem, Jerusalem, thou that killest the prophets, and stonest them which are sent unto thee, how often would I have gathered thy children together, even as a hen gathereth her chickens under her wings, and ye would not! ***Behold, your house is left unto you desolate.*** *For I say unto you, Ye shall not see me henceforth, till ye shall say, Blessed is he that cometh in the name of the Lord. Matt 23:37-39 (KJV)* (Emphasis added)

The startling announcement made here by Jesus is that God would now be looking outside of the house of Israel for "chosen people." This is the same thing that the Apostle Paul was speaking of in the following passage when Paul refers to the "Mystery," which was made known to him and was delivered through him. Paul wrote of the "mystery" to the Church in Ephesus, and the Church in Colossae.

Paul to the Ephesians

If ye have heard of the dispensation of the grace of God which is given me to you ward: How that by revelation he made known unto me **the mystery***; (as I wrote afore in few words, Whereby, when ye read, ye may understand my knowledge in* **the mystery** *of Christ) Which in other ages was not made known unto the sons of men, as it is now revealed unto his holy apostles and prophets by the Spirit;* ***That the Gentiles should be fellow heirs, and of the same body, and partakers of his promise in Christ by the gospel:*** *Whereof I was made a minister, according to the gift of the grace of God given unto me by the effectual working of his power. Unto me, who am less than the least of all saints, is this grace given, that I should preach among the Gentiles the unsearchable riches of Christ; And to make all men see what is the fellowship of* **the mystery***, which from the beginning of the world hath been hid in God, who created all things by Jesus Christ: Eph 3:2-9 (KJV)* (Emphasis added)

Paul to the Colossians

Who now rejoice in my sufferings for you, and fill up that which is behind of the afflictions of Christ in my flesh for his body's sake, which is the church: Whereof I am made a minister, according to the dispensation of God which is given to me for you, to fulfil the word of God; Even **the mystery** *which hath been hid from ages and from generations, but now is made manifest to his saints:* ***To whom God would make known what is the riches of the glory of this mystery among the Gentiles; which is Christ in you, the hope of glory:*** *Whom we preach, warning every man, and teaching every man in all wisdom; that we may present every man perfect in Christ Jesus: Col 1:24-28 (KJV)* (Emphasis added)

Simply put, the "mystery" is that Gentiles (non-Jews) would have the ability to become a chosen and special people who can spend eternity with Jesus in His Kingdom. The "gospel" or "good news" that would be spread to all nations is that the blood that Jesus would spill (From Paul's perspective, *did* spill), was an atonement for the sins of all mankind, if they will accept it.

The "mystery" does not replace Jews with Gentiles. Nor does it take away from the special relationship Jews have with God, the role they played in God's plan, or will play in the future. That relationship will always be unique and very special.

The End of the Mystery / The Beginning of Jesus' Kingdom on Earth

Scripture indicates that the "mystery" is limited in time and will one day come to an end. It began at the cross of Jesus, and will conclude at some time in the future when Jesus returns to establish His Kingdom on this earth. God has predestined that an exact number of "Gentiles" will be called to Himself. That is what is meant in the following passage, when the Apostle Paul writes of the "fullness of the Gentiles."

Paul to the Romans

For I would not, brethren, that ye should be ignorant of this ***mystery****, lest ye should be wise in your own conceits; that blindness in part is happened to Israel,* ***until the fullness of the Gentiles be come in.*** *Rom 11:25 (KJV)* (Emphasis added)

Paul wrote a great deal about the "mystery" in Romans chapter 11. There, he used similar language regarding the "times of the Gentiles," as Jesus did:

And they shall fall by the edge of the sword, and shall be led away captive into all nations: and Jerusalem shall be trodden down of the Gentiles, ***until the times of the Gentiles be fulfilled.*** *Luke 21:24 (KJV)* (Emphasis added)

These passages speak about a future time, when Israel will turn back to God and recognize that Jesus was and is their Messiah. This will occur after all of the Gentile people of the world who were predestined to be called by God from among all of the nations, have been set apart for Himself. Setting aside any debate of freewill vs. predestination, only God knows who all of those people are. The last Gentile to be called is only known to God. Once that number has been realized, the "fullness of the Gentiles" will have "come in." That will only take place, as Jesus has said, after "this gospel" has been "preached to all nations." It is then that the "end shall come."

This end of "the mystery" and the end of the age is clearly spoken of in the book of Revelation:

And the angel which I saw stand upon the sea and upon the earth lifted up his hand to heaven, and sware by him that liveth for ever and ever, who created heaven, and the things that therein are, and the earth, and the things that therein are, and the sea, and the things which are therein, that there should be time no longer: But in the days of the voice of the seventh angel, when he shall begin to sound, ***the mystery of God should be finished, as he hath declared to his servants the prophets.*** *Rev 10:5-7 (KJV)* (Emphasis added)

The "mystery is fulfilled" or finished, when the "fullness of the Gentiles has come in." The "seventh angel," seen in the above scripture, sounds his trumpet and the fulfillment of this "mystery of God" is announced. The next thing that happens in sequence in the Book of Revelation is the establishment of the Kingdom of Jesus on this earth.

And the seventh angel sounded; and there were great voices in heaven, saying, the kingdoms of this world are become the kingdoms of our Lord, and of his Christ; and he shall reign for ever and ever. Rev 11:15 (KJV)

What is "This Gospel of the "Kingdom?"

If someone were to ask you to explain the "gospel" to him or her, what would you say? "Gospel" literally means "good news." Having even the simplest understanding of the gospel has to play a part in anyone coming to salvation. What is your understanding of it? Knowing the gospel is also critical to a Christian's ability to "spread the gospel," as we, His modern disciples, have been instructed by Jesus to do.

The Apostle Paul summed up the basic components of what the gospel is, as most understand it today, from our perspective in time, in his first letter to the Church in the ancient city of Corinth:

Paul to the Corinthians

Moreover, brethren, I declare unto you ***the gospel which I preached unto you****, which also ye have received, and wherein ye stand; By which also ye are saved, if ye keep in memory what I preached unto you, unless ye have believed in vain. For I delivered unto you first of all that which I also received,* ***how that Christ died for our sins*** *according to the scriptures;*

And that he was buried, ***and that he rose again the third day according to the scriptures:*** *1 Cor 15:1-4 (KJV) (My emphasis added)*

If I had to put what I understand as the gospel into one sentence, it would be based on the above scripture. Jesus, (God in human form) through His sacrificial actions, provided anyone who will make Jesus his or her Lord, a way to be eternally in right standing with God. This is truly "good news," to say the least. Yet, none of what Paul was talking about in his letter to the Church in Corinth had occurred at the time Jesus was speaking to His disciples on the Mount of Olives about the "gospel of the kingdom."

What would the disciples, who sat with Jesus on the Mount of Olives, had understood Jesus to mean when He referred to "this gospel of the kingdom" being preached? Likewise, what was the gospel they were teaching to the Nation of Israel after Jesus instructed them to do so in Matthew chapter 10?

Certainly the disciples might have thought about the gospel a little differently since they were listening to someone who had not yet died on a Roman cross, nor had risen in a glorified body, or conquered Hell and Death. They did not have the advantage of the historical documentation as we do in the form of the Bible as our guide. These disciples had not yet received the indwelling of the Holy Spirit, nor the many faith building experiences they would have in the coming years.

The Apostle John had not yet written 1 John 1:9.

If we confess our sins, he is faithful and just to forgive us our sins, and to cleanse us from all unrighteousness. 1 John 1:9 (KJV)

The Apostle Paul had not yet written Romans 10:9.

That if thou shalt confess with thy mouth the Lord Jesus, and shalt believe in thine heart that God hath raised him from the dead, thou shalt be saved. Romans 10:9 (KJV)

Gospel of the Kingdom

The Book of Matthew records that Jesus himself spread the "gospel of the kingdom."

And Jesus went about all Galilee, teaching in their synagogues, and preaching the gospel of the kingdom, and healing all manner of sickness and all manner of disease among the people. Matt 4:23 (KJV)

And Jesus went about all the cities and villages, teaching in their synagogues, and preaching the gospel of the kingdom, and healing every sickness and every disease among the people. Matt 9:35 (KJV)

Important Components of the Gospel of the Kingdom

What Jesus was talking about as He spread the "gospel of the kingdom" is a fascinating study, far outside of the scope of this book. However, since Jesus refers to the "gospel of the kingdom" in the Olivet Discourse, we need to have a basic understanding of it.

The scripture passage that contains perhaps the most concise information on the topic is found in the Gospel of John, chapter three. There Jesus explains to a man named Nicodemus, one must be "born again" to access the Kingdom of God (John 3:3). Jesus relays that He Himself is the Son of God (John 3:16), and that belief and trust in Him is key to salvation (John 3:15).

Jesus cryptically hints that He will be crucified when He says that the "Son of Man," (Jesus) must be "lifted up," meaning, on a cross (John 3:14). Some also believe that being "lifted up," may be referring to the resurrection. He also points out that those who do not believe in Him are condemned (John 3:18). Certainly these are all of the important components of the gospel before and after the cross.

The Jews of Jesus' day were expecting a messiah to come and establish a kingdom on this earth. Under the rule of the messiah they had in mind, the Jews expected a golden era, spoken of by the Old Testament prophets. However, Jesus came and spoke of a spiritual kingdom: The Kingdom of Heaven, or referred to elsewhere as the Kingdom of God (John 3:4-8). The good news was and is that one can enter the Kingdom of Heaven, at any time, without the overthrow of any government, by being born again (John 3:3). Not a physical rebirth, but a spiritual one. This spiritual rebirth, comes about through belief in who Jesus is, and in what He says.

This understanding of the Gospel of the Kingdom takes nothing away from the importance of the death and resurrection of Jesus. It is only because of His death and resurrection, that salvation was made possible.

The Book of Mark, starts off with the words, "*the beginning of the gospel of Jesus Christ, the Son of God.*" Mark 1:1 (ESV). Whereas some have attempted to parse out differences between the gospel of Jesus Christ from the gospel of the "Kingdom of God" or "Kingdom of Heaven," I think that the two are utterly dependent on each other and inseparable. You can't have one without the other.

As "First Citizen" of the Kingdom of Heaven, Jesus is our example of what all citizens of that kingdom should strive to be like. As the one who spoke authoritatively on the Kingdom of Heaven, having been the only one who descended from there (John 3:13), He is *the* Prophet of the Kingdom of Heaven, testifying as to what He personally knows of that Kingdom. As the one who ultimately atoned for our sins making it possible for mere humans to become spiritually reborn and enter the Kingdom of Heaven, He is *the* High Priest of the Kingdom of Heaven (Hebrews 5:1-10). Because all authority in both Heaven and Earth has been given to Jesus, He is *the* King of the Kingdom of Heaven (Matthew 28:18 & Ephesians 1:22).

Finally, "this gospel of the Kingdom," includes the good news of His bringing the Kingdom of Heaven to this earth. That is the essence of what the Olivet Discourse is about; *the good news of the Kingdom of Heaven coming to earth.* The Old Testament prophecies are rich with descriptions of the future golden era when Jesus establishes His Millennial Kingdom on this earth. That is what made the "news" so "good" to first century Jews.

Most first century Jews knew about the Old Testament prophecies, which talked about the future Messianic Kingdom. Then, there He was; Jesus, the Messiah in person to tell them how simple it was for them to have a part of that Kingdom. Likewise, His gospel still proclaims that simple message to us today.

A Prophecy Abused

Well intended people have misused the prophecy Jesus gave on the Mount of Olives, pertaining to the gospel being spread to all nations, in an attempt to support many different gospel-spreading ministries. Some claim that Jesus "can't return" until we "get out there and do our job" of spreading the gospel to all the nations. This has taken many forms. I have personally witnessed this on a number of occasions. For example:

- *"We need to give money so we can install satellite dishes in China so we can preach the gospel there. It is only when the gospel has reached all the world that it will be possible for Jesus to return."*
- *"We need to give money to a prison ministry so the people in jail can hear the gospel. It is only after every inmate has had the opportunity to hear the gospel that Jesus may return."*
- *"We need to give money to print bibles in every known language. Once we have done so, then Jesus may return."*
- *"Have you considered the mission field? You know the gospel must be preached in every corner of the earth before Jesus can return."*

A Humanly Impossible Task

There are many problems with the logic of those that say Jesus "can't" return until the gospel has been preached to the entire world. Is Jesus stating every geographical inch of the world must have first had a missionary trod upon it prior to his return, or do we only need to merely set foot in every "nation?" Do we go by the geo-political maps of the first century, or the twenty first century? Once this has occurred, if it hasn't already, do we need to start over preaching the gospel, since although the places are the same, the inhabitants of the earth are constantly changing?

Is Jesus saying that every human being in the world must have been presented with the gospel prior to His return? Out of fairness, do babies need to grow up to an age where they can understand the gospel when they hear it? What do we do in a world where there is a new person born every eight seconds? Are we going to need to come up with a system where we have a missionary present for the birth of every child, making it possible for Jesus to return? What about countries that have had the gospel preached, but long ago forgot that it ever occurred? Does that count?

We are called to spread the gospel, but believing that God is depending on mankind to come up with a system to get out His good news before He can return is as absurd as the made up story I started this chapter with.

The fullness of the gentiles will occur and the mystery will be complete at a precise predetermined time by God. God uses humans as tools to bring about His will and has used many faithful missionaries over the centuries to spread His gospel. However, the fullness of the Gentiles and the completion of the "mystery" will not depend on the efforts of mankind. Regardless of this, Christians are still commanded to do their part in spreading the Gospel.

Already Accomplished According to Paul

According to the Apostle Paul, the gospel has already been spread to "every creature," on the earth:

For the hope which is laid up for you in heaven, whereof ye heard before in the word of the truth of ***the gospel;*** *Which is come unto you,* ***as it is in all the world;*** *and bringeth forth fruit, as it doth also in you, since the day ye heard of it, and knew the grace of God in truth Col 1:5-6 (KJV)* (My emphasis added)

If ye continue in the faith grounded and settled, and be not moved away from the hope of ***the gospel,*** *which ye have heard, and* ***which was preached to every creature which is under heaven;*** *whereof I Paul am made a minister; Col 1:23 (KJV)* (Emphasis added)

No one knows for sure how many people lived on the planet in the first century AD, or how the population was dispersed. Estimates by the fourth century AD in the Roman Empire alone runs between 50 and 60 million people. It is likely that in the above passages of Paul's letter to the Colossians, that he was *not* writing about personal missionary contact being made with every person on the planet. Far more likely, was that he was writing about something supernatural. The following passage from the Book of Romans, again written by Paul, may give us a clue.

So, as much as in me is, I am ready to preach the gospel to you that are at Rome also. For I am not ashamed of the gospel of Christ: for it is the power of God unto salvation to every one that believeth; to the Jew first, and also to the Greek. For therein is the righteousness of God revealed from faith to faith: as it is written, the just shall live by faith. For the wrath of God is ***revealed from heaven*** *against all ungodliness and unrighteousness of men, who hold the truth in unrighteousness;* ***Because that which may be known of God is manifest in them; for God hath shewed it unto them. For the invisible things of him from the creation of the world are clearly seen, being understood by the things that are made, even his eternal power and Godhead; so that they are without excuse:***

Because that, when they knew God, they glorified him not as God, neither were thankful; but became vain in their imaginations, and their foolish heart was darkened. Rom 1:15-21 (KJV) (Emphasis added)

Whether people acknowledge it or not, all have had the reality of God revealed to them. This being the case, they will either accept it, and seek Him, or reject it and harden their hearts against Him. Rejecting God, they become "vain in their imaginations." If you "seek" the real God, scripture tells us that "you will find" Him.

The Final Spreading of the "Eternal Gospel" to the Whole World

Whether what Paul wrote qualifies for satisfying what Jesus spoke about on the Mount of Olives or not, in the book of Revelation we see the "eternal gospel" being miraculously preached throughout the entire world prior to "the end coming." Here is what the apostle John witnessed in his vision as recorded in the book of Revelation:

And I saw another angel fly in the midst of heaven, ***having the everlasting gospel*** *to preach unto them that dwell on the earth, and to every nation, and kindred, and tongue, and people, saying with a loud voice, Fear God, and give glory to him; for the hour of his judgment is come: and worship him that made heaven, and earth, and the sea, and the fountains of waters. Rev 14:6-7 (KJV)* (Emphasis added)

This event will be the ultimate and final fulfillment of what Jesus is referring to on the Mount of Olives when He says, *"And this gospel of the kingdom shall be preached in the whole world for a witness to all the nations, and then the end shall come."* God will miraculously assure that the entire world has heard the "eternal" gospel prior to the end of the age and His judgment being poured out on the earth. Everyone, in spite of their lack of knowledge of theology will be presented with the essentials in what is known as the "eternal gospel."

The gospel has been defined in different ways throughout history. "Dispensationalists," say that God has changed His plan several times over the years as to how man can be reconciled to Him. They say that God had one plan for salvation for Adam (don't eat from the forbidden tree), another for the generations that followed him (just do the right thing), another for the Jews who followed after Moses (follow the law), etc. However, throughout all times, all of these "dispensations" or chapters in time, fall under one plan; God's one and only plan, that He has always had, which has been boiled down greatly and is referred to in the Book of Revelation as the "eternal gospel."

The gospel, which has always been, regardless of how theologians have diced it up; "*fear God and give Him Glory…and worship him who made heaven and earth…*"

Jesus, is the first name of the only true God that exists in the universe. Jesus, who was there at creation, the King of the Kingdom of Heaven, is the God that is to be given "glory," to be "worshiped," and to be "feared." It is only through the sacrifice that God the Son made on the cross that reconciliation with the God of the eternal gospel was made possible.

The word "eternal" as used in Revelation 14:6, means "perpetual" and ongoing. It means it always has been, and always will be.[42] The "eternal gospel" written of in the Book of Revelation is not a special gospel that will only apply to those in the future, rather it is a gospel that was in existence before, during, and after the first advent of the Messiah. It is a gospel that is not in conflict with anything that Moses, the prophets, Jesus, or the Apostles said.

The eternal gospel per Revelation 14:7 is to fear, or have reverence for, the Creator of the Universe and to worship Him. Literally, this form of worship can be compared to when a faithful dog is licking the hand of its master.[43] It means to have humble and complete adoration and submission for the Creator. This is part of the simple gospel that was taught by Jesus, Moses, and Paul. Jesus summed up the essence of all of the Old Testament "law" for us when He answered one of His disciples' questions:

> *Master, which is the great commandment in the law? Jesus said unto him, thou shalt love the Lord thy God with all thy heart, and with all thy soul, and with all thy mind. This is the first and great commandment. And the second is like unto it, thou shalt love thy neighbour as thyself. On these two commandments hang all the law and the prophets.* Matt 22:36-40 (KJV)

The "mystery" or "Paul's gospel," did nothing more than to say that this gospel was meant for all of the nations, and not only the

Jews. That was the same announcement Jesus made when He said that the gospel of the kingdom, which was once to be taken only to the Jews, will now be taken to the entire world.

For there is no difference between the Jew and the Greek: for the same Lord over all is rich unto all that call upon him. Romans 10:12 (KJV)

Scripture is clear that it is only through Jesus that humans can be reconciled to God. It is His blood sacrifice that made reconciliation with God and eternal life with Him possible.

Where is Jesus in the "Eternal Gospel?"

Based on the sequence of events found in scripture, I believe that the "eternal gospel" of Revelation is proclaimed in conjunction with the return of Jesus. There will be phenomenal, catastrophic, supernatural, worldwide, and unmistakable events that take place with the "sign of the Son of Man" occurring in the heavens.

Jesus shows up, and the eternal gospel will be proclaimed. *Jesus is the eternal gospel.* The eternal gospel will be proclaimed by the angel, like a caption on television, on behalf of the one who just showed up to the planet! Any details that the Apostle John may have omitted from the eternal gospel that he witnessed in his vision will be filled in by the presence of the one who the gospel is about, Jesus. It will be clear; the one who shows up with power and authority in the sky, Jesus, is the God who is to be "feared" and "worshiped."

Behold, he cometh with clouds; and every eye shall see him, and they also which pierced him: and all kindreds of the earth shall wail because of him. Even so, Amen. I am Alpha and Omega, the beginning and the ending, saith the Lord, which is, and which was, and which is to come, the Almighty. Rev 1:7-8 (KJV)

The Great Commission

During the Olivet Discourse, Jesus *is not* commanding His disciples to spread the gospel. He is telling them that *it will be* spread. However, as pointed out above, just because God miraculously fulfills the prophecy of the gospel being spread to the entire world through the Eternal Gospel Angel, and just because Paul says it has already been accomplished, it does not let the followers of Jesus out of their responsibility to spread the gospel.

After His resurrection and prior to ascending to heaven, Jesus told His disciples to participate in this mission; to go to all nations and spread the gospel. Now, after His death, burial, and resurrection, the entire gospel His followers are to spread certainly does include the historical components of Jesus' sacrifice and what it means.

And he said unto them, go ye into all the world, and preach the gospel to every creature. Mark 16:15 (KJV)

Summary

Although the gospel was taken to Israel first, Jesus made the announcement that the "gospel of the Kingdom," will be preached to all nations, not just Israel. He said that this would occur prior to the "end" of the age. The gospel of the Kingdom of Heaven being taken to "all the world," as opposed to only the nation of Israel, is what Paul refers to as the "mystery." When the last appointed Gentile (non-Jew) has "came in" the mystery will be complete and the end of this age will occur.

The "gospel of the Kingdom" is the gospel that Jesus taught about during His time on earth. Although the Gospel of the Kingdom would have been thought of differently by His disciples, whom were hearing this prophecy before Jesus died on the cross, it contained all of the same essential components. Ultimately it is what Jesus did by dying on the cross; making atonement for our sins, overcoming death and hell, and rising to eternal life in a glorified body that makes it possible for anyone to enter into the Kingdom of Heaven.

In spite of the "Great Commission" for the followers of Jesus to spread the gospel to the whole world, the Olivet Discourse's mention of the "gospel being preached to all the nations," was not a command. According to God's will as recorded in the scriptures, the Gospel *will be* proclaimed throughout the entire world. The scripture does not say how that will be accomplished, but only that it will happen.

God Himself will assure that the "eternal gospel" is miraculously preached to the entire world prior to the end of the age. We see this idea supported by the Apostle Paul's statements to the

Church in Colossae and Rome. We also see it occurring in the book of Revelation, when an angel flies through the heavens proclaiming the eternal gospel to all creation just prior to Jesus establishing the Kingdom of Heaven on this earth.

The "eternal gospel" spoken of in Revelation is the Gospel of "fearing" God the Creator and worshipping Him. It is a gospel that has existed since the time of Adam and will exist throughout eternity. In this case, this proclamation of the gospel accompanies the return of Jesus, *who is the eternal gospel.* Like a text that accompanies a picture in the dictionary, the final proclamation of the gospel will stand like a caption under the scene of the Second Coming of Jesus.

Notes

10. Recycling and Prophecy
(The way the world works)

I once attended a risk-management-training program, for Criminal Justice professionals. The popular speaker's main theme was "*if something is predictable, it is preventable.*" I get what he was talking about and mostly agree with him, but predicting that the sun will rise tomorrow and that Jesus will return someday, blows some rather large holes in his thesis. Both things are not preventable.

This seminar instructor gets paid very well to travel around the United States and inform his trainees they can use what they have learned from the past to prevent things from happening in the future. To support his claims, the speaker kept coming back to what I believe *is* a rock solid principle. He phrased it a number of ways, but essentially, it is that *"history repeats itself."* Another way of putting it is that there is nothing that will occur in the future, that has not in some way already occurred in the past. I recognized his words.

It turns out that even his training curriculum is just history repeating itself. For millennia philosophers and those who study history have stated, "*history repeats itself*." Even the guy, who thought he was the first to say, "history repeats itself," was probably repeating someone else.

Emperor and stoic philosopher, Marcus Aurelius, observed that there is "nothing new under the Sun." In his writings, Marcus Aurelius said;

Consider the past; the great shifts in political supremacy. You may foresee also the things, which will be. For they will certainly keep the same form; they cannot possibly deviate from the order in which they take place now. Accordingly, to have contemplated human life for forty years is the same as to have contemplated it for ten thousand years. For what more will you see?[44]

The wise King Solomon, who preceded Roman Emperor Marcus Aurelius by over a millennium, was already pointing out that because we live in a world of cycles, there is" nothing *new under the sun.*"

The thing that hath been, it is that which shall be; and that which is done is that which shall be done: and there is no new thing under the sun. Is there anything whereof it may be said, See, this is new? it hath been already of old time, which was before us. There is no remembrance of former things; neither shall there be any remembrance of things that are to come with those that shall come after. Eccl 1:9-11 (KJV)

With the general warnings regarding the end of the age now behind us in the Olivet Discourse, Jesus is going to move on to a subject that may have initially confused His Disciples. The same subject still causes confusion and division today. Because of this, I want to first discuss the concept that "history repeats itself."

The Way Things Work

Observing and quantifying the way things work in God's Universe is what we sometimes call "science." Science and faith are often at odds. As the co-authors of the Bible documented, God sometimes chose to work outside of what is scientifically provable in the natural world. This is the case whenever He accomplished deeds that only one who exists outside of the bounds of nature could accomplish. However, God "supernaturally" created the universe in such a way that He could also accomplish His will through "natural" means. One thing God created into His universe is what we know as a "cycle."

One of the foundational building blocks of the interpretive approach I utilize in this discussion, is based on an observation of one of the scientifically provable principles found in God's Universe; "history repeats itself." The very definition of "science" is built on this principle. Cycles are a part of what can be thought of as a component of God's "operating system." Gravity, the temperature at which water freezes and the laws of thermodynamics are also included in this operating system.

When we understand that God created a universe that works in cycles, we can resolve some of the points of contention between various camps of end times theorists. History repeating itself explains how Preterists, those who believe that most prophetic scriptures have been fulfilled in the past, can be correct at the same time that Futurists; those who believe that most prophetic scriptures will be fulfilled in the future.

The issues that lead to contention between Preterists and Futurists are the same issues that contribute to why many tend to "spiritualize" prophecy. Those who say that prophetic scripture may not be taken literally or interpreted as other scripture. They believe that because a literal fulfillment seems so unlikely, prophecy must be taken metaphorically in order to understand it properly.

Cycles in Science, Philosophy, & History

Creation itself shouts out to us that God's world works in cycles; seasons, the geologic, hydrologic, astronomic, and atmospheric cycles of nature are everywhere to be seen.

Within the human body there are many cycles; circulatory, menstrual, respiratory, sleep, etc. Animals hibernate according to a cycle.

The "science" of Cultural Anthropology points to a cycle of the rise and fall of civilizations: Simplicity> Rise in complexity> Decrease in Marginal Returns (non-sustainability)> Collapse> Simplicity> repeat...[45]

Most of history repeating itself goes unnoticed by people. Because our lives are relatively short, we view our time on earth as unique. We think we are the first generation to have difficulty with raising our children, we think crime is worse now than ever, we think society is more immoral than ever, we think government is more corrupt than ever, we think people have abandoned the truth for the first time, etc.

Cycles in Other Religions

Emperor Aurelius was not the only one outside of the Judeo-Christian world to have stumbled on the truth of the cyclical nature of the universe. Although where they have ended up may be the result of a truth that has been twisted, many ancient peoples, philosophies, and religions have taken note of this principal.

Traditional Native American beliefs include that "*The Creator designed the universe and our Mother Earth to function as a system of circles and cycles." Therefore, to heal we must understand and live by the cycle and circle system in every area of our lives".*[46]

Various Eastern religions are religions of "wheels" and cycles. Buddhists and Hindus have their reincarnation and Karma; "what goes around, comes around." All forms of astrology run rampant with cycles. Chinese Astrology cycles through ten various animal years before it repeats itself.

Like our own calendar, and the Sothic cycle found in the Egyptian calendar, the Mayans took note of the solar, lunar, and seasonal cycles of the earth. However, the Mayan calendar contains far more than yearly reoccurring cycles. They note cycles at 28, 65, 280, 819, 2200, 3120, 4680, and more days. Each period brought its own religious significance to the Mayans.

Cycles in the Bible

I am sure that this "cycle talk," sounds "spooky," or mystical, to mainstream or classically trained Christians, who have been taught or at least heard that these types of things are "evil" and originate from eastern mysticism religions. However, I would argue that God created cycles before the eastern mystics. Then, the "eastern mystical" religions took this component of God's operating system, twisted it, and turned it into what some would indeed call "evil." That is a common tactic of the deceiver, Satan.

Although I am not aware of other interpreters pointing to the Beast of Revelation as being a prophetic visual model of Satan's cycle-based failure of a plan, I am not the first one to point out "cycles" in prophecy. Charles Cooper writes the following:

> *...A prophecy can form a pattern that may repeat itself more than once... This is called "pattern fulfillment by some.* [47]

The Bible tells us of many cycles, the first being the seven-day week that God established (Genesis 1:1- 2:3). Jewish sages and early Christians believed that the seven-day week established the pattern of a larger seven thousand-year period of time. Day seven would be a thousand years of the Messiah ruling the earth. This period of time would end with what they called the "eighth day," when God would make all things new again. [48]

The prophet Isaiah tells us that God made the end known from the beginning (Isa. 46:9-10). God dictated several important days to be recognized weekly and annually, establishing cycles of worship, atonement, forgiveness, rest and renewal.

There are seven high holidays, or "feasts" that were established by God; the Feast of the Passover, the Feast of Unleavened Bread, Shavout (The Feast of Weeks or Pentecost), Rosh Hashanah (The Feast of Trumpets), Yom Kippur (The Day of

Atonement), and Sukkot (the Feast of Booths or Tabernacles). You can read about the establishment of these feasts in Leviticus chapter 23.

In Leviticus chapter 25 you can read about God establishing a 50-year cycle known as the year of "Jubilee," in which debts were forgiven, property went back to its original owner, and slaves were freed. Exodus 23: 10-11 establishes a farming cycle; farm your land for six years and on the seventh, let it rest.

Near and Far applications of Prophecy

One way cycles have been commonly recognized in the Bible is by observing "near" and "far" applications of many prophecies. In his book The Sign, the late Robert VanKampen states that one of his guiding principles of biblical interpretation is to recognize that "*many passages of Scripture, in both Testaments, have both near and far implications and applications.*" He goes on to state, *"in other words, prophecy often operates on two levels of fulfillment.*"[49]

Having both a near and far application means that a divine predictive utterance that was given through a prophet may have had immediate (near) importance and relevance for the contemporaries of the prophet. At the same time the same prophecy was also for the purpose of foretelling an event "far" off in the future. My argument is, because of the way God's operating system works, it can also sometimes mean that the prophecy concerns a reoccurring, cyclical event. Ultimately ending with the "final" event.

There Is an End to All Cycles

Failure to recognize that God works through cycles can lead to a great deal of confusion and misinterpretation of prophetic scripture. However, one needs to be very careful when applying this principal and note that while many things in God's universe work in cycles, all cycles appear to have an end or ultimate fulfillment.

"The circle of life," for example, occurs only when one is speaking of birth, living, dying, and then the one that is gone is replaced by a descendant who is born, lives, and dies. Individual people are not recycled, as many in the world believe. The author of the book of Hebrews writes:

And as it is appointed unto men once to die, but after this the judgment: Heb 9:27 (KJV)

Biblical cycles seem to have ultimate fulfillment's associated with them. For example, like the Passover, they occur and occur, year after year, and then Jesus comes along and fulfills the meaning of the Passover, by becoming the ultimate Passover sacrifice. Although the Passover celebration continues, it now has new meaning for the follower of Christ.

Examples

An example of the cyclical nature of prophecy is found in the book of Zechariah. The prophecy written by Zechariah (9:13-17) in about 480 BC:

When I have bent Judah for me, filled the bow with Ephraim, and raised up thy sons, O Zion, against thy sons, O Greece, and made thee as the sword of a mighty man. And the Lord shall be seen over them, and his arrow shall go forth as the lightning: and the Lord God shall blow the trumpet, and shall go with whirlwinds of the south. The Lord of hosts shall defend them; and they shall devour, and subdue with sling stones; and they shall drink, and make a noise as through wine; and they shall be filled like bowls, and as the corners of the altar. And the Lord their God shall save them in that day as the flock of his people: for they shall be as the stones of a crown, lifted up as an ensign upon his land. For how great is his goodness, and how great is his beauty! corn shall make the young men cheerful, and new wine the maids. Zech 9:13-17 (KJV)

This prophecy was perfectly fulfilled over three hundred years later, in 165 BC when the Jews rose up and defeated the evil Greek king Antiochus Epiphanes IV. However, God will ultimately fulfill this prophecy, for the last time, yet in the future when he again defends the nation of Israel from the Antichrist.

There are many other places in scripture that we can find examples of more than one fulfillment of prophecy. In the book of Malachi, we read about the Prophet Elijah, who is sometimes referred to as "Elias." Elijah had already clearly been around and done His time on the earth once, but as it turns out he had a mission left undone. A mission he would need to complete *two* times.

Behold, I will send you Elijah the prophet before the coming of the great and dreadful day of the Lord: And he shall turn the heart of the fathers to the children, and the heart of the children to their fathers, lest I come and smite the earth with a curse. Mal 4:5-6 (KJV)

For thousands of years, because of this prophecy, Jews have set an extra place at their Passover tables in anticipation of Elijah one day showing up. It is taught that Elijah will precede the Messiah, and as written in Malachi, he will precede the Day of the Lord. Yet, there is an easy case to be made that Elijah already has preceded the coming of the Messiah. It was 2,000 years ago when John the Baptist came "in the spirit of Elijah" turning people towards God just prior to Jesus beginning his ministry. Jesus says in regards to this:

And from the days of John the Baptist until now the kingdom of heaven suffereth violence, and the violent take it by force. For all the prophets and the law prophesied until John. And if ye will receive it, this is Elias, which was for to come. Matt 11:12-14 (KJV) (Also see Matthew 17:10-13)

Even though Jesus himself tells us that this prophecy concerning Elijah has been at least partially fulfilled, it is yet to be ultimately fulfilled since the world has not yet seen the great and terrible "Day of the Lord" that Malachi refers to in his prophecy.

Either Elijah or someone coming in the spirit of Elijah is predicted to come again prior to the return of Jesus and the pouring out of God's wrath. This is what we have an indication of happening in the book of Revelation, chapter 11, where we see "Two Witnesses" "prophesying" or proclaiming the word of God in Jerusalem, no doubt turning people's hearts back to the beliefs of their fathers Abraham, Isaac, and Jacob (Revelation 11:3-6).

Maybe the simplest examples of double or reoccurring prophecies in the Bible are those which relate to the coming of the Messiah, Jesus. He came once just as predicted in the Old Testament. Who would have ever thought before He came the first time that the Messiah was actually being predicted to come twice to this earth?

The Cyclical Nature of the Beast

In the Olivet Discourse Jesus refers to an event called the "abomination of desolation," spoken of by the Prophet Daniel. By doing so, he introduces the topic of the one that commits this Abomination of Desolation: The Antichrist. The Antichrist is referred to as "the Beast" in the Book of Revelation. I would argue that the Antichrist is really only depicted as being a part of the Beast in Revelation. The Beast is really a symbol for Satan's entire plan to control the world and destroy God's people. This plan has included several past iterations of antichrist "kings" or rulers. However, since "the Beast" is a commonly accepted term for the Antichrist that will arise at the end of the age, I will play along.

The important prophecy related grand cycle we are focusing on, is the cyclical nature of "the Beast." The "Beast" as seen in Revelation is a complex symbol that represents more than just an evil world leader of the future. The Beast is also a symbol representing specific historical kingdoms, or leaders of those kingdoms that have previously greatly oppressed, enslaved, and figuratively "had their way with," the nation of Israel. The Beast of Revelation, as previously stated, is best described as being a prophetic visualization of Satan's plan to come against God, and His chosen people, through the use of seven different earthly "kingdoms" and "kings."

Consider what the Apostle John documented regarding His unique experience. In the passage below, John has a fantastic vision from his vantage point on the island of Patmos, off the coast of what we now know as the nation of Turkey.

In Revelation, chapter 12 it is recorded that John had a vision of a "dragon." The book of Revelation often defines its own symbolism. In Revelation 12:9 the "dragon" is defined as being a symbol which stands for, "Satan." John then sees another "beast" described here:

And I stood upon the sand of the sea, and saw a beast rise up out of the sea, having seven heads and ten horns, and upon his horns ten crowns, and upon his heads the name of blasphemy. And the beast which I saw was like unto a leopard, and his feet were as the feet of a bear, and his mouth as the mouth of a lion: and the dragon (Satan) *gave him his power, and his seat, and great authority. And I saw one of his heads as it were wounded to death; and his deadly wound was healed: and all the world wondered after the beast. And they worshipped the dragon* (Satan) *which gave power unto the beast: and they worshipped the beast, saying, who is like unto the beast? Who is able to make war with him? Rev 13:1-4 (KJV)* (My character identification in parentheses added).

Later, we see a "woman" riding on this same beast described in Revelation 13:1-4.

So he (an angel) *carried me* (John) *away in the spirit into the wilderness: and I saw a woman sit upon a scarlet coloured beast, full of names of blasphemy, having seven heads and ten horns. Rev 17:3 (KJV)* (My character identification added)

Everything contained in these passages is symbolic for something. We know to take the characters in this scripture as symbolism and not literally, because these symbols are defined for us in what John wrote.

Prophetic symbolism, contrary to popular belief is *sometimes* easy to figure out in scripture. In this case, let's set aside the "woman," and the "leopard body," "bear feet," "lion mouth," and "10 horns" of the beast, and concentrate specifically on the "seven heads" of this particular beast. A couple of verses later, the symbolism of the seven heads is explained:

And here is the mind which hath wisdom. The seven heads are seven mountains, on which the woman sitteth. And there are seven kings: five are fallen, and one is, and the other is not yet come; and when he cometh, he must continue a short space. Rev 17:9-10 (KJV)

The heads of the beast symbolize two different things; "seven mountains" on which the "woman" sits, and seven "kings." Further, from the Apostle John's historical perspective in approximately 97 AD, it is explained to him that five of the kings or kingdoms represented "have fallen" already. They are dead historical figures from John's point of view; kings or kingdoms that no longer held power and political influence over Israel as of 97 AD.

A sixth king, the one who "is" was currently in power in John's day, that was the Roman Empire. The seventh of the seven kings or kingdoms from John's point in time had not yet come. John's vision was of a "beast," representing seven separate kings or kingdoms, yet all wrapped up into one.

The kings or kingdoms would likely have many things in common, in spite of the fact that they all reign at different points in history or the future. It is because of the seven-in-one Beast, that there is a cycle suggested. Because they are of the same beast, as kingdoms come and go, they will all have similar manners of operating. They may try to obtain similar results and hold similar goals and have a common purpose. They therefor may take similar actions. In fact, this is what we see occurring in the Bible when we identify the six different heads, or kingdoms of the beast.

There is an "eighth beast" (kingdom or ruler) that will have many similarities to the first seven beasts. In fact, unusual and unnatural as it may be, the eighth beast, as described, will actually be one of the original seven who previously died from a mortal head wound and comes back to life! Read what John recorded in the Book of Revelation regarding this bizarre situation:

And I saw one of his heads as it were wounded to death; and his deadly wound was healed: and all the world wondered after the beast. Rev 13:3 (KJV)

And the beast that was, and is not, even he is the eighth, and is of the seven, and goeth into perdition. Rev 17:11 (KJV)

And the angel said unto me, wherefore didst thou marvel? I will tell thee the mystery of the woman, and of the beast that carrieth her, which hath the seven heads and ten horns. The beast that thou sawest was, and is not; and shall ascend out of the bottomless pit, and go into perdition: and they that dwell on the earth shall wonder, whose names were not written in the book of life from the foundation of the world, when they behold the beast that was, and is not, and yet is. Rev 17:7-8 (KJV)

The angel tells John that this "eighth beast" he saw, once "was," or once did exist in the past. Then, the angel says that from the future point in time that John is prophetically viewing, the beast does not exist (He is dead). Finally, the angel says that the "eighth beast" is going to exist again one day by coming "up out of the abyss." That is to say he will "live again."

The eighth beast is the future Antichrist and his kingdom. He will have originally been one of the first seven "kings" or kingdoms that make up the overall beast. History does not get much more recycled than that!

Why doesn't John describe an eight-headed beast when he says that there is an eighth beast? After all, a separate head represents each of the seven preceding beast empires. It is because the "head" of the eighth beast empire will be represented by one of the original seven heads, because *it is* one of the original seven beast empires that has been revived and has come back to life.

To sum this up, this seven-headed beast vision that John had, represents eight cycles of Satan's puppet governments, the Beast Empires. The eighth and final cycle will be that of the future Antichrist's Empire. Five cycles had occurred before John's time, John found himself in the middle of the sixth cycle, and two cycles would come in the future from John's first century perspective in time.

Conflict Resolution: Preterism vs. Futurism

Understanding the principal of cycles could resolve some of the biggest points of contention in prophetic study circles. Preterists see most of the prophecies of the Olivet Discourse and of Revelation as having already occurred relatively soon after they were first uttered. This view largely depends on an authorship date of 64 AD for the book of Revelation. They say the events that the Apostle John wrote about would have mostly been fulfilled around 70 AD with the destruction of Jerusalem and partial destruction of the Jewish Temple Mount complex.

The Preterist approach fails to recognize that the entire scope of the book of Revelation and the Olivet Discourse is the end of the age, the return of Christ, the establishment of the Kingdom of Heaven on Earth, and the Day of the Lord. The book of Revelation and the Olivet Discourse involve far more than only the siege of Jerusalem and partial Diaspora of the Jews from Israel in the first century.

Yet, the Preterists are absolutely correct in some of their observations; they observed a fulfillment of prophecy when the Beast (the Roman iteration of the antichrist beast), acting like the beast he is, took over Jerusalem and the Temple…again. However, just as this was not the first time the Beast had done this, it was also not the last.

"Futurists," so far as prophetic studies are concerned, are those that believe that most end times prophecies are yet to be fulfilled. The fatal error that the typical end times Futurist makes, is that he or she fails to recognize and acknowledge that some biblical prophetic events *have* occurred or have been "fulfilled" at least once in the past. This is a denial of history and puts Futurists at automatic odds with Preterists.

The Preterist makes his or her mistake by trying to cram most prophecy into a historical box, saying that with little exception, it has all already been fulfilled. Both philosophies run into problems when dealing with a passage such as the Olivet Discourse. Obviously, some things Jesus was talking about have occurred in history, but just as obvious we can see Jesus is talking about His Second Coming and the "end of the age," a time yet to come.

There is no question that it appears that some of what was prophesied about by Jesus in Matthew 24, Mark 13, and Luke 21 *looks* like it already occurred, almost 2,000 years ago. Many of the prophecies could even be considered ultimately "fulfilled" if not for one main reason. All of the prophecies in the Olivet Discourse are tied to the Second Coming of Christ, the rapture of the Church, the Day of the Lord, and the establishment of His Kingdom, and none of those events have taken place.

The persecution mentioned in the Olivet Discourse, as well as the Antichrist and the destruction of the temple are without purpose, if they do not lead to the return of Jesus, His rescue of Israel, the rapture of His Church, and the beginning of the Day of the Lord.

The Cycle of the Abomination of Desolation

What happened in 70 AD with the destruction of the Jewish temple was the result of a beast acting like a beast. In other words, the Roman Empire, the kingdom, or the sixth "head" of the beast that was in existence during the time of John, was operating according to the typical way the beast operates and always has operated. A lion has typical predatory patterns as does a bear, a leopard, or any other animal that hunts. Man is also a creature of habit, ranging from people who need their first cup of coffee in the morning, to those with pathological, social deviant, predatory behaviors such as pedophiles and serial killers.

To illustrate this point, let's look at this specific prophetic event that Jesus spoke of during His Olivet Discourse:

When ye therefore shall see the abomination of desolation, spoken of by Daniel the prophet, stand in the holy place, (whoso readeth, let him understand:) Then let them which be in Judaea flee into the mountains: Let him which is on the housetop not come down to take any thing out of his house: Neither let him which is in the field return back to take his clothes. And woe unto them that are with child, and to them that give suck in those days! Matt 24:15-19 (KJV)

This is the prophecy Jesus was referring to in the book of Daniel:

And arms shall stand on his part, and they shall pollute the sanctuary of strength, and shall take away the daily sacrifice, and they shall place the abomination that maketh desolate. Dan 11:31 (KJV)

Jesus was speaking of an event that Daniel had prophesied about hundreds of years earlier. Jesus was saying that this event was in the future from the time He was speaking. How confusing His statement must have been to His disciples! No doubt they would have already thought that Daniel's prophecy had been fulfilled when the Greeks sacked Jerusalem hundreds of years earlier and King Antiochus Epiphanes IV caused pigs to be sacrificed to pagan gods on the Temple Mount in Jerusalem. Pigs are considered "unclean" animals according to Jewish law. Was Jesus saying that this prophecy had not yet been fulfilled, or was He saying it would be fulfilled again?

First century historian Josephus confirms the belief of his contemporaries that this prophecy had already been fulfilled. Concerning Daniel's Abomination of Desolation prophecy, Josephus wrote:

> *…and that from among them there should arise a certain king that should overcome our nation and their laws, and should take away their political government, and should spoil the temple, and forbid the sacrifices to be offered for three years' time. And indeed it so came to pass, that our nation suffered these things under Antiochus Epiphanes,*

according to Daniel's vision, and what he wrote many years before they came to pass.

-Antiquities of the Jews, Book X chapter 11:7

This event appeared to have been fulfilled again in 70 AD, when the Romans both destroyed the Temple in Jerusalem and again made sacrifices to Roman gods on the Temple Mount. That was truly an abomination of desolation. The Roman, sixth "head" of the beast seemed to be acting just like the Greek, fifth "head" of the beast. Even so, the eighth and final beast will again commit something like this act before Jesus will return and establish His Kingdom.

In addition to the desecrations taking place under the Greeks (5th beast empire) and once under the Romans (6th beast empire) one can see several instances of different types of desecrations and abominations occurring in Solomon's Temple, even before and during Daniel's day. The temple was also desecrated under King Nebuchadnezzar's reign.

Josephus tells us that Nebuchadnezzar's general, Nebuzara-dan, was ordered to plunder and set fire to the temple in Jerusalem. He robbed all of the gold and silver from the temple as well as the holy implements and vessels found there and took them back to Babylon, where Nebuchadnezzar dedicated them to his own gods. [50] The Babylonian "head" of the beast (3rd Beast Empire), was acting like the other beasts would in the future.

What happened in the Old Testament days and what happened under General Titus in 70 AD was all a type of evil that will have its final fulfillment under the "anti-Christ" man of "lawlessness" of the future. They all share the same type of evil in common. They were anti-Jehovah, anti-Israel, anti-Jew, and became anti-Messiah (Christ), and anti-Christian. How this evil plays out will apparently include the desecration of a future temple in Jerusalem one day, just as it has previously taken place in history.

The Apostle Paul tells us that the future "Antichrist" or "Beast" or who he refers to as the "man of lawlessness" will in fact do business in the same way as the past "heads" of the beast. Paul sent the following scripture to believers who seemed to be worried that the Lord had already returned and they had somehow missed it:

Now we beseech you, brethren, by the coming of our Lord Jesus Christ, and by our gathering together unto him, that ye be not soon shaken in mind, or be troubled, neither by spirit, nor by word, nor by letter as from us, as that the day of Christ is at hand. Let no man deceive you by any means: for that day shall not come, except there come a falling away first, and that man of sin be revealed, the son of perdition; Who **opposeth and exalteth himself above all that is called God, or that is worshipped; so that he as God sitteth in the temple of God, shewing himself that he is God.** *2 Thess 2:1-4 (KJV)* (Emphasis added)

Paul is warning of the act of the Abomination of Desolation. Clearly, the final act the "man of sin and lawlessness" (the Antichrist) is going to commit, is the act of the Abomination of Desolation by seating himself in the temple of God and displaying himself as God. This will be the final time that this will happen and the ultimate fulfillment of both Daniel and Jesus' prophecies.

Summary

There are many principles involved in a sound approach to the interpretation of prophetic scripture. Among them, must be an understanding of how God's universe works. Cycles are unavoidably observed all around us in every field of science and in every form of art.

History records how God has been telling His story through utilizing cycles. To ignore this principle is to ignore the fact that the sun will rise tomorrow like it has, according to its cycle, many times before.

Scripture deals with many events that appear to have repeated themselves in the past. Scripture oftentimes ties the events of the past to what will happen in the future. Just as we cannot ignore the rest of reality, it is only through understanding that God's universe works according to many types of cycles that we can accurately approach the study of end times prophecy.

Understanding that God's universe works in cycles, clears up confusion and provides an explanation of how both Preterists and Futurists may be right about how to interpret Jesus' statements during His Olivet Discourse; many of these things have indeed already occurred one or more times in the past. Yet, they will occur for the last and final time in the future.

There are definite cycles that can be identified in Bible prophecy such as the cycle indicated in the symbolism of the beast depicted in the book of Revelation. The value of identifying cyclical prophecies in history, such as the events of 70 AD, in Jerusalem, is to better understand what the future holds for the world in the final days before our Messiah returns. The future Antichrist will likely operate in a similar manner as he has in the past. What happened in 70 AD qualifies for being one of several "abominations of desolations," but not *The* Abomination of Desolation, Jesus was referring to during the Olivet Discourse.

Bottom line? When someone tells me that some of the prophesies in the Olivet Discourse appear to have been fulfilled in 70 AD, my response could be (if I spoke in such a direct way), "So what? God's universe operates in cycles and the ultimate fulfillment is yet to come."

11. The Foul and Detestable Thing

If worry is on one end of the spectrum, watchfulness is on the opposite end. Yet, many Christians today are worried about events that are taking place in the world around us. They wonder if things like wars, famines, Ebola, loss of morality in our nation, earthquakes, floods, fires, the effects of global warming, and the Islamic "radicalized" militant terrorists that fill our headlines daily, are signs that the end of the world is coming soon. Many worry unnecessarily about the end of the world, while they interpret tragic, yet normal world events as "signs;" Yet, how many Christians are watchful for the few signs Jesus gave us to indicate that the end of the age is near?

Jesus warned that a world full of false prophets, war and famines does not necessarily indicate that it's the end of the world. Such things have been occurring since the first time Jesus came.

Then, Jesus warned about the persecution of the Church. He stated prior to His coming, to expect to be hated for His namesake, and possibly suffer persecution, even resulting in death.

Now, in the Olivet Discourse, Jesus gives His disciples a very specific, recognizable sign to watch for, which will indicate His impending coming. This sign will be unmistakable. It will consist of a series of acts carried out by the Antichrist. It will begin with the confirming of a "covenant," and end with what is called the "Abomination of Desolation" 1,260 days later.

<u>Matthew 24:15</u>

When ye therefore shall see the abomination of desolation, spoken of by Daniel the prophet, stand in the holy place, (whoso readeth, let him understand:) Matt 24:15 (KJV)

So when you see the foul and detestable thing that causes desolation, set up in the holy place, spoken of by the Prophet Daniel, (let the one reviewing it understand) (DHT)

Mark 13:14a

But when ye shall see the abomination of desolation, spoken of by Daniel the prophet, standing where it ought not, (let him that readeth understand,) (KJV)

Now, when you see the foul and detestable thing that causes desolation, set up where it should not be, spoken of by the Prophet Daniel, (let the one reviewing it understand) (DHT)

In order to fully understand what Jesus is talking about in this passage, we will spend some time on three background topics; 1. the time period related to the Abomination of Desolation referred to in prophecy circles as the "seventieth week of Daniel." 2. We will also need to understand whom the person known as the "Antichrist" is. Finally, 3. we will need to know what he does which would be considered the Abomination of Desolation, or what I have translated as the "foul and detestable thing that causes desolation."

The Abomination of Desolation

The Abomination of Desolation will be a future event involving a reestablished, Jewish Temple, or holy place, in Jerusalem. Similar to the nation of Israel which had ceased to exist until 1948, that Jewish Temple does not exist today. If the prophecies in the Bible can be trusted to literally come true as they always have in the past, the temple will exist again one day.

The act of the Abomination of Desolation will be so terrible and repulsive in God's eyes that it will leave the holy place (the Jewish Temple) unsuitable and unusable for its intended purpose (making sacrifices to and worshiping the one true God). The foul and detestable act will leave the temple "desolate," or "empty." [51]

To understand the "Abomination of Desolation," Jesus said one must consider what the Old Testament Prophet Daniel, had to say on the subject. The term "Abomination of Desolation" is a quote from Daniel 11:31 and 12:11. As you read below, you will notice that the words used in Daniel are "abomination that makes desolate."

And arms shall stand on his part, and they shall pollute the sanctuary of strength, and shall take away the daily sacrifice, and they shall place the

abomination that maketh desolate. *Dan 11:31 (KJV)* (Emphasis added)

And from the time that the daily sacrifice shall be taken away, and the ***abomination that maketh desolate*** *set up, there shall be a thousand two hundred and ninety days. Dan 12:11 (KJV)* (Emphasis added)

According to traditional Christian and Jewish views, the book of Daniel was written in the sixth century BC by the Prophet Daniel.

From the first century Jew's perspective, they were looking at the sign spoken of by Daniel as though it had already occurred in 168 BC, when Antiochus IV built an altar to Jupiter on the sacred Hebrew altar of burnt offering, and then offered swine's flesh upon it.[52] This was a well-known historical event which records the presence of the Seleucid Empire ejected from the Temple, and a lamp containing only a single days' worth of oil, miraculously burning for eight days, ultimately bringing about the Jewish celebration of Hanukkah. Hanukkah was celebrated as a major holiday in Jesus' day and his disciples would have been very familiar with the story behind the holiday.

Daniel's prophecy was never *completely* fulfilled. The prophecy in Daniel, like Jesus' prophecy on the Mount of Olives, was associated with the coming and anointing of the Messiah as King forever. One can say that the prophecy was "partially fulfilled," but a partially fulfilled prophecy, is ultimately an unfulfilled prophecy.

"Reconsider What You Think You Know"

Jesus knew that this surprising statement about Daniel's Abomination of Desolation prophecy might lead some into confusion since this event seemed to have already taken place in history from the disciple's perspective. That is why He must have added the words, *"Let the reader understand,"* as translated in the King James Version of the Bible.

The phrase "*let the reader understand*," as it has been translated, once puzzled me. As you are reading through the Olivet Discourse and come across this statement, it sounds like Jesus pauses and makes an out of place editorial comment. People just don't normally speak in such a way. The other possibility that I considered was that maybe those who wrote down this version of the Olivet Discourse later (both Matthew and Mark) added this comment to stress how important it is to understand what Jesus said. Such an editorial comment would also be very unique. I no longer believe either of those things to be the case.

What I do believe is that the English word, "reader," is a completely inadequate translation from the original language. This phrase is not only for the benefit of future "readers," but also for those who were hearing it directly from Jesus on the Mount of Olives. These are Jesus' words that were recorded, and the disciples He was speaking to, were not "readers" of what He was telling them.

The statement is directed at anyone (His disciples and future readers or hearers of scripture) who may have some prior knowledge or understanding of Daniel's prophecy and may have already reached some conclusions about it. Jesus is telling them that they should think about, or reconsider what they think they know… again.

The Greek word, "ἀναγινώσκω," transliterated as "anaginosko" (an-ag-in-oce'-ko) [53] has been interpreted here as "read," or "reader." Anaginosko is made up of two words, one, transliterated as "ana," which means "again," and "ginosko," meaning "to know." The word can be translated, "knowing something certainly," "knowing something again," or "recognizing something." By extension it can also mean, "to read." [54]

In the New Testament, anaginosko is commonly translated into English as the word, "read." "Reading" is one of the main forms of media that allow us "to know again" information that has previously been given. It is one way we review information that has been stored for us. If you are forgetful of information, you can write it down, so you can "know it again," or review what you knew before, at a later time. Watching a video or listening to an audio recording is another modern way to "know" something "again."

The second important Greek word Jesus used in this parenthetical statement was, "νοιέω," transliterated as "noeo" (no-eh'-o). It means to "consider," "think about," "perceive," or "understand."[55]

"Ana-ginosko" in combination with "noeo," can mean to "think again about," or "reconsider" something. By using these words, Jesus is very likely saying, to "*review* what you already believe about the Abomination of Desolation spoken of through the Prophet Daniel, and *understand* it in light of what I am telling you now."

Again, He may have said this, because He knew that people had preconceived ideas that Daniel's prophecies had already been fulfilled. He wanted to make sure His followers understood that Daniel's prophecies are associated with the end of the age, and His return.

What Jesus said would not have made sense to His disciples present for the Olivet Discourse if He had thrown in a parenthetical phrase such as "let the reader understand." Why would He be singling out this passage to future "readers," and telling them to "understand" it more than any other part of the Olivet Discourse? Wouldn't He have been making an assumption that someone was going to be writing this down for people to read later? It makes far more sense that Jesus was telling the four disciples listening to Him to review the Daniel passages that He was referring to and reconsider its meaning in light of the rest of what Jesus was telling them.

What Form Will the Abomination Take?

Jesus gave almost no details about what would constitute the Abomination of Desolation. We have to look elsewhere for that information. Part of the answer comes from understanding the individual that will facilitate the abomination; the Antichrist. One specific thing that the Antichrist will cause to happen that Jesus does mention is found in Mark 13:13. There it says that the abomination is "standing where it ought not." Matthew adds the significant detail that it will be "standing in the holy place." An alternative way to translate these words is "set up" in the holy place, or "set up" where it should not be.

Daniel also uses words regarding "setting up" the abomination in the Temple. This very likely may be referring to a likeness, image, or "idol" of the Antichrist. An image of the Antichrist standing in a place devoted to the God of the Universe would definitely qualify as an abomination, or a "foul and detestable" thing.

The Apostle Paul gives us the most likely answer to what form the abomination will take in the following passage:

Let no man deceive you by any means: for that day shall not come, except there come a falling away first, and that man of sin be revealed, the son of perdition; Who opposeth and exalteth himself above all that is called God, or that is worshipped; ***so that he as God sitteth in the temple of God, shewing himself that he is God.*** *2 Thess 2:3-4 (KJV)* (My emphasis Added)

The book of Revelation gives some possible details regarding the "image" or idol that is "set up" in the temple:

And deceiveth them that dwell on the earth by the means of those miracles which he (the False Prophet) *had power to do in the sight of the beast* (Antichrist); *saying to them that dwell on the earth, that they should make an image to the beast* (Antichrist), *which had the wound by a sword, and did live. And he* (the False Prophet) *had power to give life unto the image of the beast* (Antichrist), *that the image of the beast* (Antichrist) *should both speak, and cause that as many as would not worship the image of the beast* (Antichrist) *should be killed. Rev 13:14-15 (KJV)* (My character identifications added).

These two passages together seem to indicate that the "False Prophet," the Antichrist's evil partner in crime, who act like the spiritual or religious "salesperson" for the Antichrist, is going to cause an image of the Antichrist to be erected in the "holy place," the Jewish Temple. The False Prophet will appear to give this image of the Antichrist "life." Magic, miracle, or technology, this is not that difficult to accomplish in this age of computer generated images, holographic projections, and animatronics.

Josephus, tells us what Antiochus IV did to constitute an abomination of desolation: He carried away the golden vessels and treasures of the temple, stopped the sacrifices, offered swine on the altar, and compelled people to stop worshiping God and to stop the act of circumcision. Those who refused to stop worshipping God were mutilated, strangled or crucified along with their children.[56]

It is likely that the Abomination of Desolation of the future will also involve defiling implements used in the holy place, as well as the holy place itself. This will be accomplished at the very least by the image of the Antichrist being "set up" there to be worshiped as god. Additionally, the Antichrist will halt the daily sacrifices to the one true God, which will have been reinstituted.

The Timing of the Abomination of Desolation

By going back to the book of Daniel we can know exactly when in the context of end times events, the Abomination of Desolation that Jesus warns His followers about, will take place. It will be precisely in the middle of a seven-year (360 day years based on the Hebrew calendar) period known as the "seventieth week of Daniel."

And he shall confirm the covenant with many for one week: and in the midst of the week he shall cause the sacrifice and the oblation to cease, and for the overspreading of abominations he shall make it desolate, even until the consummation, and that determined shall be poured upon the desolate. Dan 9:27 (KJV)

The Abomination of Desolation takes place "in the middle" of a period of time referred to as one "seven," or one "week." A covenant (discussed below) will be "confirmed" that lasts for this period of "seven." Many translations, such as the English Standard Version, interpret the word "seven" as "week." However, in context here, because of how it is used in the related Daniel passages, and how it is defined in surrounding scripture, this word literally means a period of "seven."

To begin to understand the answer to the question of a "*period of seven whats,*" we need to go back to the book of Daniel, chapter nine. Daniel tells us in that chapter that in the first year of the reign of King Darius (a Mede), Daniel studied the scriptures and came to find out that Jerusalem had to lie desolate for seventy years due to the sin of the people (Dan 9:1-2).

This study inspired Daniel to go to God in prayer and plead to the Almighty to set his people free from captivity (Dan 9:3-19). Because of this prayer, the Angel Gabriel, who Daniel recognized from an earlier vision, was sent to him to help him understand God's plans. Gabriel started by telling Daniel that he, Daniel, was considered "much esteemed" (Dan 9:20-23). The following is what Gabriel said to Daniel after that;

Seventy weeks are determined upon thy people and upon thy holy city, to finish the transgression, and to make an end of sins, and to make reconciliation for iniquity, and to bring in everlasting righteousness, and to seal up the vision and prophecy, and to anoint the most Holy. Know therefore and understand, that from the going forth of the commandment to restore and to build Jerusalem unto the Messiah the Prince shall be seven weeks, and threescore and two weeks: the street shall be built again, and the wall, even in troublous times. And after threescore and two weeks shall Messiah be cut off, but not for himself: and the people of the prince that shall come shall destroy the city and the sanctuary; and the end thereof shall be with a flood, and unto the end of the war desolations are determined. Dan 9:24-26 (KJV)

Daniel writes that the Angel Gabriel gave him information about a period of time that would last "seventy weeks" or more literally, "seventy sevens."

When dealing with prophecy related numbers, when the normal "literal" meaning of a number does not make sense, you need to determine the length of time represented by the number in some other way. Ideally we let scripture define scripture. In this case we are considering the meaning of the numbers "seventy" and "seven" in context to the surrounding scripture. Here we will be able to let scripture that follows in Daniel define what the period of "seven" means. We can verify the definition in light of our knowledge of what has taken place in history, after this prophecy was given.

What this passage is referring to, is the period of time between when the decree to rebuild the 'holy city' (Jerusalem) went out, until the "Most Holy" was "cut off." Looking back at history from our perspective, we know that the "Most Holy" that was to be anointed as King, but was "cut off" prior to that, is Jesus. So for us, because of when Jesus finally showed up hundreds of years later after Daniel gave the prophecy, we know that the length of time that the numbers in this case represent could not be literal days or weeks, but that they represented 70 "sevens" of *years*. Seventy times seven years equals 490 years.

To paraphrase the above passage in light of this definition; "*Daniel, your people have 490 years to get their act together before the Messiah comes to rule over Israel.*"

One "Seven" Short

Know therefore and understand, that from the going forth of the commandment to restore and to build Jerusalem unto the Messiah the Prince shall be seven weeks (49 years), *and threescore and two* weeks (62 "weeks" or

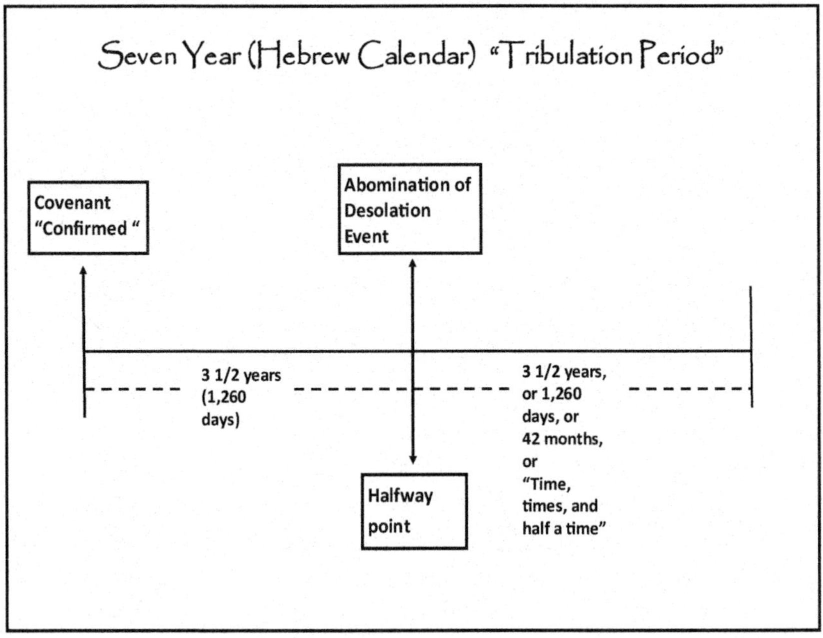

literally 434 years)*: the street shall be built again, and the wall, even in troublous times. And after threescore and two weeks* (62 "weeks" or 434 years) *shall Messiah be cut off, but not for himself: and the people of the prince that shall come shall destroy the city and the sanctuary; and the end thereof shall be with a flood, and unto the end of the war desolations are determined. Dan 9:25-26 (KJV)* (My interpretations and math added)

"Seven-sevens" (49) and "sixty-two sevens" (434) equals sixty-nine sevens (7+62=69). This represents 483 years (69x7=483). It is another discussion as to why seven-sevens has been separated out from sixty-two sevens. That is a topic for the study of the book of Daniel. For now, for our purposes, suffice it to say, there is a reason.

What concerns us here is Gabriel only accounted for 69 sevens; there is a "missing" seven. Gabriel first said there would be 70-sevens, or 490 years from the decree to rebuild the city until the 'Most Holy' would be anointed. We find only one verse later that the last seven years has been separated out. It was separated out, because after 69 "sevens" had elapsed, just as Daniel wrote and history records, the Messiah, Jesus, was "cut off" by being rejected by Israel and crucified.

The remaining, or missing "seven," is the seven years that is associated with the Abomination of Desolation and the end of the age. This seven-year period must take place in order for Daniel's prophecy to be completely fulfilled. It isn't until the end of this seven-year period that Jesus, will be "anointed" King and Messiah once and for always.

To sum up this prophecy in Daniel so far: Gabriel has informed Daniel that 1. There will be a decree to rebuild Jerusalem. 2. The Messiah would be "cut off" 483 years after that decree to rebuild goes out. 3. During that period of time, Daniel's people, the descendants of the tribes of Israel, needed to turn back to God and observe His commandments.

The Decree: The Event That Started the Clock

Historically there were three separate decrees by earthly Kings that might fit Daniel's vision. Because of several different calendars that have been used through history that utilize differing numbers of days that make up a year, the following dates are up for debate. In his book, *God's Elect and the Great Tribulation*, author and Pastor Charles Cooper, puts together a complicated, yet sound case for the following dates to be off by a number of years.[57] However, using the currently widely accepted dates, there are three possible start dates of the decree; the first by King Cyrus in 538 BC (see Ezra 1:1-4), the second by King Darius in 457 BC (see Ezra 6:6-7) and finally by King Artaxerxes in 445 BC (see Neh 2:5).

There is a difference of opinion among scholars as to whether it was the second or third decree to rebuild the temple that Gabriel had in mind when he spoke to Daniel. Some even think that Gabriel may have been referring to a "heavenly decree." If so, scripture and history are silent on when that would have occurred. I personally do not believe that God would have sent an angel to deliver such a message to Daniel only to have it be impossible to know when a heavenly decree would be announced outside of the earshot of mere mortals.

When 483 years is added to the King Darius decree, the date comes out to be 26 AD. That means if Jesus was 33 when he was crucified, or as the Daniel prophecy puts it, "cut off," He would have been born in about 6 BC. The best case I am aware of sets the birth of Jesus somewhere between 6 and 4 BC.

When the Artaxerxes decree date is used, 483 years later comes to 38 AD. Whether it was Darius or Artaxerxes that made the proclamation to rebuild Jerusalem, we can have confidence that 483 years after *the* decree went out, one of the decrees hit the Messiah being "cut off," right on the money according to God's plan, and in spite of our calendar guess work.

An Alternative Theory

Charles Cooper presents an alternative theory regarding this period of time. It is worth considering. To greatly sum up the several chapters in his book in which he lays out his case, Cooper believes that 483 years after King Cyrus decreed that the temple should be rebuilt, the year was 70 AD.[58] That was the year that the rebuilt temple was destroyed by the Romans and the Jewish leadership was exiled from Jerusalem. He then proposes that the current time period we are living in, rather than being referred to as "the Church Age," which began circa 33 AD, would be more appropriately called the period of "Jewish Desolation." There are several reasons that I consider Cooper's theory a viable alternative to the traditional. My suggestion is to read his book and decide for yourself.

Whether or not the well thought out case that Cooper makes is correct, or the traditionally accepted theory is, which states the 483 years ended with the crucifixion of Jesus, both theories agree that there is a missing seven-year period that is still in the future. That is what is important to what we are considering.

What Happens During the Missing Seven?

In chapter 12 of the book of Daniel, we read that after the Abomination of Desolation occurs "in the middle of the seven" until "the end" there will be a period of 1,290 days. As if to confirm that these periods of sevens are actually talking about periods of 7 *years*, the Daniel chapter 12 passage provides us with a definition by recording how many days are left until the end of the age from the time of the Abomination of Desolation.

Hebrew calendar years are based on 360-day years. 1,290 days is 3 ½ Hebrew calendar years, with thirty days left over. This scripture refers to the second half of the seven-year period spoken of in Daniel chapter 9 (the missing period of seven).

Why the additional period of thirty days beyond the end of the seven-year period? The answer to this requires an entirely different discussion that is more appropriately found in a study of the events found in the book of Revelation. According to Revelation, there are important events that take place after the seven-year period in question. However, for our purposes in this chapter, suffice it to say that the Abomination of Desolation will occur exactly 1,260 days or 3 ½ years, after the final "seven" begins.

How will we know when the final "seven" has begun? There is an event that Daniel tells us about that will start the seven-year clock ticking; the Antichrist will "confirm" a "covenant" with "many."

The Covenant

One of the few hard signs that will allow those followers of Christ who are alive at the time to identify the "end of the age" will be the Antichrist entering into or confirming a "covenant" with "many." Since all of the prophecies in the Book of Daniel concern Israel, the covenant will likewise concern the nation of Israel. During modern times, Israel has entered into several "covenants." If we want to be able to identify *the* covenant from the rest, there are several important questions that need to be answered.

We learn of the covenant in Daniel, Chapter 9, verse 27 where the angel tells Daniel that "he" the Antichrist, will make a strong covenant with "many" for one "seven." The "seven" Daniel wrote of in this passage, is the missing or 70th period of seven years that is yet to take place.

What Is the Covenant About?

Ultimately, the covenant will be about the nation of Israel putting their trust in some human being or outside government, rather than the Almighty God. This is a mistake that they have made before that can be read about in a number of Old Testament stories. This ill-founded trust always backfires on Israel.

The "peace process" in Israel is *always* in the news. Israel has been persecuted and hated since the children of Abraham born through his wife, Sarah, went on to become a nation. The covenant most likely will be "about" Israel seeking peace and security, by relying on someone's promises other than the Almighty God's. God, "chose" Israel as His people. It is through His people that He would reveal himself as the one true God of the universe. When Israel "chooses" another besides God to put their trust in, it never goes well for them. In the future covenant with the Antichrist, Israel will be choosing a "*covenant with death.*"

The following scripture, although it may have had relevance for the immediate future of Israel when it was written thousands of years ago, also is a prophetic passage ultimately speaking of the covenant that Israel will one day enter:

> *Wherefore hear the word of the Lord, ye scornful men, that rule this people which is in Jerusalem. Because ye have said,* ***we have made a covenant with death, and with hell are we at agreement;*** *when the overflowing scourge shall pass through, it shall not come unto us: for we have made lies our refuge, and under falsehood have we hid ourselves: Therefore, thus saith the Lord God, Behold, I lay in Zion for a foundation, a stone, a tried stone, a precious corner stone, a sure foundation: he that believeth shall not make haste. Judgment also will I lay to the line, and righteousness to the plummet: and the hail shall sweep away the refuge of lies, and the waters shall overflow the hiding place.* ***And your covenant with death shall be disannulled, and your agreement with hell shall not stand;*** *when the overflowing scourge shall pass through, then ye shall be trodden down by it. Isa 28:14-18 (KJV)* (Emphasis added)

This passage of scripture is a warning to the leaders of Israel, who rule over Jerusalem, that choose to enter into the covenant with the Antichrist. In the hopes that they will be spared great calamity (the "overwhelming scourge") they enter into the covenant, which is based on "lies." Because they chose to do so, God will "sweep away" the "refuge" of lies, leaving them subject to the very calamities they were trying to avoid. However, because of a "cornerstone" that God lays in Jerusalem, the covenant with death will be cancelled and God will save Israel. This costly "cornerstone" that is spoken of, is Jesus (see Matt 21:42, Mark 12:10, Luke 20:17, Acts 4:11, Eph 2:20, 1 Peter 2:6-7). Ultimately those that turn to their Messiah, Jesus, will be saved. This is precisely what we see the end time prophecy speak of in reference to Israel.

Beyond knowing the covenant will involve Israel, it is difficult to nail down additional details. Is it a peace treaty? Does it exchange land for peace? Does it speak of who controls the Temple Mount in Jerusalem? It is difficult to say. However, we may have a clue in that currently, there is no "sacrifice" taking place in Israel that is spoken of in Daniel and likewise there is no "temple" in Jerusalem.

Beyond peace and security, rebuilding the holy temple on the Temple Mount and reinstating the sacrifice are two things that many Jews in Israel would like to have. However, today, the Palestinians are in control of the Temple Mount on which the Temple must sit. Could it be that in partnership with the False Prophet, a part of this covenant will be to make provisions for a temple to be built and sacrifices to take place on a Temple Mount that is currently controlled by the Islamic community? Maybe, but as we remain watchful, we should not allow this speculation to distract us into ruling out any other possibilities.

Who Besides Israel Enters into The Covenant?

The "he" who makes firm the covenant in Daniel 9:27 is the Antichrist. However, some believe the "he" that makes the covenant, was Jesus when He died on the cross. According to their theory, Jesus, after all, did make a covenant with "the many," by providing a way to salvation not only for the Jew, but also for the "gentile." By dying on the cross and becoming the ultimate sacrifice needed, He made animal sacrifice unnecessary, thereby doing away with at least the need for it.

There is a reason that we can clearly know that the "he who makes firm the covenant" is not Jesus, but rather is the Antichrist. We see in Daniel 9:27 that the "he" being referred to puts an end to sacrifice and *then* engages in the activity labeled as the "Abomination of Desolation." Jesus neither entered into a covenant with "the many" that would only last seven years, nor did He cause an abomination of desolation in the temple. If He had done either one of these things, then three and a half years later, He would have started ruling the earth as its anointed Messiah. None of this occurred or makes sense.

Concerning "the many" who the covenant will be "made firm" with, along with Israel, when we look elsewhere in scripture we note that the Antichrist will wield a significant amount of power on the world scene. In the book of Revelation, where the Antichrist is referred to as "The Beast," we note that he will be a world leader of unparalleled proportion. He will be given power over all "peoples, tongues, and nations," (see Revelation 13:5-8). Based on this, it appears that the covenant that the Antichrist confirms is between those countries in the world that the Antichrist has influence over (all or a majority of them), and Israel. That will certainly involve "many."

How can we tell this final "covenant" from all of the rest Israel has been or will be involved in? The only sure way, is to see what happens 1,260 days after such a covenant has been entered into. We have already noted several activities that the Antichrist will engage in when he initiates the Abomination of Desolation half way into the seven-year period. Daniel has additional information to add:

And arms shall stand on his part, and they shall pollute the sanctuary of strength, and shall take away the daily sacrifice, and they shall place the abomination that maketh desolate. Dan 11:31 (KJV)

This passage of scripture was recorded after Daniel received a second visit from an angel who further explained the information Daniel received during his first angelic visitation. This angel explained to Daniel that because the Antichrist will have great military strength ("arms"), he will have the ability to "confirm," or make sure the conditions of the covenant are met. But, then he will also have the military strength to break the covenant and do the unthinkable.

Our composite picture now looks like the Antichrist is in control of armed forces. He will command them to rise up and desecrate "the temple fortress." He will cause the Jews to put an end to a daily sacrifice that is going to again be taking place at that time. He is going to proclaim that he is some sort of god and have an image of himself "placed," or "set up" in the Temple. It is these acts, that take place precisely in the middle of "the seven" that will confirm that it is *the* covenant that was entered into 3 ½ years (1,260 days) earlier between Israel and "the many" (all the nations the Antichrist has influence over).

When will *the* covenant of the Antichrist and "the many" be confirmed or entered into? No one knows. What if the public doesn't know the duration of the covenant? No problem, the important thing to know is that if it is *the* covenant, then it will be broken 1,260 days after it is entered into. If it is *the* covenant, it has a God ordained time frame of seven years.

Exactly in the "middle of the seven" (Daniel 9:27), or "1260 days" (Rev 12:6), or "42 months" (Rev 13:5), or "times, time, and half a time" (Rev 12:14) after the covenant is confirmed, the Abomination of Desolation will take place. In other words, we will only know with certainty the answer to the question, "*when will the covenant be signed*," 1260 days or 3 ½ years *after* it is signed. From our perspective now all I can say is that it is some time in the future.

Modern Day Covenants with Israel

Since I have been *watchful* for such things, I have seen Israel enter into several large covenants and I have watched the three-and-a-half-year mark come and go without incident. *Major* agreements do not occur regularly. They are significant and stand out in the news. They are relatively easy to "watch."

The Israel Ministry of Foreign Affairs lists fifteen key treaties and agreements entered into since 1978, starting with the Camp David Accords on September 17, 1978, and ending with a free trade agreement on December 18, 2007. These fifteen agreements also include peace agreements between Israel and Egypt, Israel and Jordan, agreements with the U.S., the Palestinians and others. A database that contains bilateral treaties and multilateral agreements with Israel is maintained by the Israel Ministry of Foreign Affairs and can be searched on-line at:

http://mfa.gov.il/MFA/AboutTheMinistry/LegalTreaties/Pages/Bilateral-Treaties.aspx

As of late summer 2015, the following was the most recent posting regarding the "peace process" between Israel, and the Palestinians:

> *On July 28, 2013 the Israeli Cabinet approved the opening of diplomatic negotiations between the State of Israel and the Palestinians, with US support, with the objective of achieving a final status agreement over the course of the next nine months.* [59]

As you can see, as of the time of writing this book, we know that Israel and the Palestinians, "with US support," has not achieved a "final status agreement." We also know there are no key covenants that have been entered into within the past three-and-a-half years. So, there are none that can currently be broken that would count as *the* covenant.

A Future Temple?

If this prophecy concerning a covenant, the Abomination of Desolation, and the return of Jesus is to take place yet in the future, there is a problem; there is not currently a Hebrew temple or "holy place" on the Temple Mount in Jerusalem. There is however, an Islamic Mosque. For this prophecy to literally occur in our future, a temple or tabernacle would need to be rebuilt in the spot that the mosque now sits.

Some would explain the lack of a physical temple away with saying that the future temple is not really a physical place. They would say that any reference to a temple is metaphoric in nature. How interesting that prior to 1948 many said there was even a larger problem; Israel was not even a nation! What a miracle it was for Israel, after more than 1900 years, to again be recognized as a nation! This was a fulfillment of a prophecy made by the Prophet Ezekiel (Ezekiel chapter 37). In the same way, it will be equally miraculous when the literal, physical temple in Jerusalem will be built.

There are organizations in existence today, such as the Temple Institute,[60] and the Temple Mount Faithful, [61] led by Gershon Salomon, one of the 1967 liberators of the Temple Mount, that are devoted to the construction of a new Temple on the Temple Mount in Jerusalem.

Since the destruction of the temple in 70 AD, Jews have been praying for the temple's restoration on the same spot that it has stood before. Ezekiel wrote of a temple that to date, has not yet ever existed in Jerusalem. The temple plans as outlined in the book of Ezekiel have been used as a guide by temple restoration groups such as the Temple Mount Faithful organization.

Amazingly, the Temple Mount Faithful organization already has the necessary implements ready to begin sacrificing on the Temple Mount in Jerusalem. The corner stones for the new temple have been cut and are ready to place. This group is actively raising red heifers to be the sacrifice, as required by the Old Testament, for the cleansing of the temple implements. This ceremony is mentioned in the book of Numbers chapter 19. Here is the stated goal of the Temple Mount Faithful Organization:

…the building of the Third Temple on the Temple Mount in Jerusalem in our lifetime in accordance with the Word of G-d and all the Hebrew prophets, and the liberation of the Temple Mount from Arab/Islamic occupation so that it may be consecrated to the Name of G-d.[62]

There is evidence that early Christians believed that the Antichrist would be the one responsible for rebuilding the Hebrew Temple in Israel.

The prophet sets forth these things concerning the Antichrist, who will be shameless, a war-monger, and a despot. Exalting himself above all kings and above every god, he will build the city of Jerusalem and restore the sanctuary. Hippolytus (c. 205 AD)[63]

Restoring the Hebrew Temple in Jerusalem would surely gain the Antichrist favor and trust with the Jews. There are many wealthy people who would sympathize with this cause. Money would not stand in the way of the third temple. The problem is control of the real estate that the temple needs to stand on.

In 2014, the *Temple Institute* in Israel underwent a funding campaign on the crowd-funding website called, INDIEGOGO, to raise $100,000 in order to have a functional set of blueprints drawn up for the construction of the third temple in Israel. They raised over $105,000. It is said this funding only took three days to be raised. You can still go to the INDIEGOGO web-site and take a virtual tour of the temple. [64]

The Holy Place

Scripture does not specify that a brick and mortar temple must be rebuilt in order for the Abomination of Desolation to take place. The only requirements are that burnt offerings and sacrifices will be occurring at the "holy place."

The "holy place" clearly is on the Temple Mount where the Hebrew Temple once stood. Traditionally, it is the same place where Abraham offered up his son Isaac as an offering. However, beginning with Moses and up to the time of Solomon, sacrifices were conducted in a temporary, portable tabernacle. These tent structures contained the Ark of the Covenant and other Holy implements. There is no reason a similar tabernacle could not be very quickly set up, on the Temple Mount in the future.

Implications of The Abomination of Desolation as a Sign

Jesus clearly gave His disciples a sign to watch for that would signal His coming. It is a sign, which will directly involve the Jews in Israel, but that will serve as a signal to all that have been called to "watch." Although His disciples are long gone, the implications are that His followers *will be* on the earth to see this sign and not safely tucked away in Heaven after they have been raptured.

Have you seen anything thus far in Jesus' words to indicate that His followers, Christians, would not be present to observe this sign? Did the Apostle Paul not clearly reinforce this fact to the Church in Thessalonica, who had become confused on this issue? Telling them that Jesus won't return and His followers won't be "gathered to Him" until they first see the Abomination of Desolation take place? (II Thess. 2:1-12).

Clearly, the followers of Jesus will be around to witness the sign of the covenant being broken and the "man of sin and lawlessness" declaring himself to be god. This act of the Abomination of Desolation will not occur for 3 ½ years into the seven-year period known as the seventieth week of Daniel or otherwise known as the "tribulation period."

Also important for you to note is that nowhere has Jesus mentioned anything about God's judgment being poured out up to this time. Although His disciples are told they will suffer for the cause of Christ, followers of Jesus are not appointed to suffer the wrath of God that will take place during the future period of time known as the "Day of the Lord." So far, all we have seen in Jesus' warning is the suffering of the first kind.

Jesus is clearly telling His followers that are alive during this future period of time, and Jews who will listen to Him, that they will "see" the Abomination of Desolation occur. There has been no indication that He is speaking to any special group of His followers that have been "left behind."

You may find yourself now saying, or someone else is saying it to you, "the Bible must say somewhere else that the Christians will be raptured by this point." However, if you take scripture as it comes, as we are doing here, I argue that you will never find a pretribulation rapture regardless of where you are looking in the Bible. You certainly have not seen a rapture take place yet in the Olivet Discourse. However, that will soon change.

Summary

The "Abomination of Desolation" is a specific sign associated with the return of Jesus. This foul and detestable act of desecration that is associated with the Hebrew holy place of sacrifice in Jerusalem has occurred in history on more than one occasion.

By Jesus citing Daniel's prophecy as a sign of the end of the age, He provided a time framework around the events of the end. The future and ultimate desecration of the Jewish temple will involve the setting up of an image of the Antichrist in the holy place. This will happen precisely 1,260 days after a "covenant" with "many" has been "confirmed." It will be necessary for a future holy place to be reestablished in Jerusalem if this prophecy is to be literally fulfilled. There is an effort to do just that in Israel today.

Jesus encouraged His disciples to reconsider or "think again" about what they thought they knew about the Abomination of Desolation, since from their perspective, they must have thought it was a prophecy that was already fulfilled. The ultimate fulfillment of the prophecies concerning the Abomination of Desolation could not have possibly occurred in the past since it is associated with the end of the age, the return of Jesus, the beginning of the Day of the Lord, and the resurrection of the dead.

The Church will clearly be present for this event, as there has been no evidence in the Olivet Discourse (or anywhere else in scripture) that any supernatural rescue will have taken place prior to this event.

Persecution of the Church will take place at the hands of the Antichrist. However, Jesus' return and the rescue of His Church, once the Abomination of Desolation has occurred, will soon follow so that the elect of God that remain on earth, will be saved from having to endure the wrath of God.

12. What To Do When the Antichrist Shows Up

"Well, when it all goes down, we need to go park our trucks at the end of the road, under the train trestle and keep everyone in town from coming out here and robbing us blind…"

To my shame, after living where I do for twenty-eight years, I had never met the nice neighbor lady who said this, even though she had also lived up the road from our house for just as long.

"Some of us are talking about getting organized…"

I smiled and nodded while inside my head I couldn't help but think that there are way too many zombie apocalypse movies available. However, my observations of this lady were that she was anything but crazy. She was quite rational and appeared normal.

After being involved in law enforcement for twenty-six years, I have known many people that were *not* "normal." At most, this lady just seemed a little worried about some safety and security aspects of her life based on what she has observed going on in the world around her. Like many, she had made a little bit of a logic leap in assuming that world events were all leading to some sort of apocalyptic ending.

Growing up in the 60's and 70's it was hard to miss the cold war. In the early stages of the cold war in the 1950's many people built fallout shelters and stocked them with food, water, first aid kits, and flashlights. A really deluxe model shelter, complete with a telephone, could be installed for you for around $5,000. My question: who is it they intended to make a telephone call to after the bomb went off?

A lot of people took steps in the years preceding December 31, 1999 to avoid being overcome by the "Y2K bug." The world was supposed to shut down and anarchy would rule because of a computer programming glitch. The Y2K bug became a regular topic at the church my family was attending at the time. Steps were taken to prepare for the worst. But, as many wrote books on the subject, and profited from the threat, my wife and I bought a few extra pounds of rice and beans and then ate them over the next few months while the lights remained on, and the water continued to flow.

People are still moving to remote areas, building underground shelters and stockpiling food and weapons in preparation for what they believe will be anarchy as a result of economic and government meltdown. They are doing everything they can in order to survive the calamity that they believe will come one day. An estimated 14.8 million Mormons in the world, to different degrees, follow the teachings of their apostles and prophets that have said making such preparations is the wise thing to do. [65]

The Bible contains many words of wisdom regarding preparing for what may come in the future. Especially when it comes to preparing for one's eternal future. Jesus left us with some specific instructions regarding what to do if you happen to be living in the region of Judea during the last days.

The book of Luke records additional details given during the Olivet Discourse, which add to the picture of what will occur during the Abomination of Desolation: Jerusalem will be surrounded by the armies of the Antichrist.

Luke 21:20

And when ye shall see Jerusalem compassed with armies, then know that the desolation thereof is nigh. (KJV)

Now, when you see Jerusalem surrounded by armies, then know that it's desolation is near. (DHT)

The act of the Abomination of Desolation will be accompanied by Jerusalem being surrounded by "armies." These armies will be under the control of the Antichrist who will cause the Abomination of Desolation to occur. An overwhelming outside military presence in Israel would be necessary in order to control that nation. They are a nuclear capable nation with a world class military force and would never willingly allow something like the events of the Abomination of Desolation without first being completely taken over. They have positioned themselves to "never again" allow a Masada-like situation.

Masada was a mountain top fortress constructed by Herod the Great in Israel between 37 and 31 BC. In 73 AD, Roman armies surrounded Masada. 960 members of a zealous Jewish splinter group known as the Sicarii, and their families, had taken refuge there. In the end, these last inhabitants of Masada chose the path of murder and suicide rather than being taken by the Romans. This event gave birth to a saying in Israel, "Never again Masada." They will never again willingly allow themselves to be put in a position where this type of situation could occur. It would take a very deceptive covenant, along with overwhelming military strength, to ever allow something like this to again take place.

The Daniel passages that are associated with the Abomination of Desolation strongly indicate that the Antichrist will be a military man. Daniel chapter 11 is for the most part a prophecy concerning several military campaigns. However, although most of these military campaigns were in Daniel's future, and because of the cyclical nature of prophecy they "may" be in ours, they are now historical events, belonging to the second century BC. In Daniel 11:36 however, the period of time being referred to, clearly changes to the end of the age. When those who are alive during the time of the end of the age, see the armies of the Antichrist surrounding Jerusalem, they need to recognize that "desolation is at hand."

Make no mistake, this is not a sign that will be difficult to confuse with other events, which have happened throughout history if one is "watching." That is why Jesus, in the Olivet Discourse, is about to give specific direction to His disciples as to what to do about it when it occurs.

What should the people who are in "Judea" do when they see or hear of this sign? It is clear in all three gospels:

<u>Matthew 24:16</u>

Then let them which be in Judaea flee into the mountains: (KJV)

Then let those who are in Judea, flee to the mountains. (DHT)

<u>Mark 13:14b</u>

then let them that be in Judaea flee to the mountains: (KJV)

Then let those who are in Judea flee to the mountains. (DHT)

Luke 21:21a

Then let them which are in Judaea flee to the mountains. (KJV)

Then let those who are in Judea flee to the mountains. (DHT)

This is a geographically specific statement. It is specific instructions for those living in Judea, not anywhere else, and for the time when they are specifically surrounded by the armies of the Antichrist.

Judea covers an area of about 2,000 square miles in the southernmost region of Palestine. It is about fifty-five miles long, from Bethlehem to Beersheba, and from twenty to thirty miles broad.[66] Judea includes Jerusalem, the city that will be surrounded by the armies of the Antichrist. Much of Judea sits in what is currently known as the Palestinian controlled West Bank.

This passage is not intended to mean that when the Antichrist surrounds Jerusalem, everyone else around the world should "head for the hills." Jerusalem is the city under attack and is the focus of the Antichrist at this point in time. This passage does not mean, "and let those who are in Los Angeles, flee to your bunker you have prepared in the Rocky Mountains of Montana."

Being watchful may one-day cause followers of Jesus to "run away." It may require others to stay put. Some will be called to survive until they see the Lord return in splendor. Others will meet Him in the air anyway, after they spring out of their newly dug graves in their resurrected eternal bodies.

If you were in Jerusalem right now and looked around, and only knew of Jesus' instructions to "flee" to the mountains, it might not be obvious which way to go. Jerusalem sits at a high point in Israel. Yet, there are mountains all over Israel. A great deal of them are in remote and desolate regions, away from population.

Jerusalem will be surrounded. According to prophecy, the Antichrist's armies will be mainly camped on the coastal plains to the west. The Judean mountains encompass Jerusalem, Hebron, Bethlehem, and Ramallah. They are mainly in Palestinian controlled territory of the West Bank. On the east side of the mountains is the Dead Sea. To the south of the Dead Sea lies the ancient city of Petra. A city carved in stone. It is not specifically mentioned in the Bible, but Petra is a place, often thought of, as where a remnant of Israel will flee.

Time will tell where those that heed Jesus' instructions will go. It will largely depend on which route is clear of enemies, and what type of transportation they have available to them at the time.

The instructions of Jesus become more detailed for those living in Judea. All of the following passages are stressing how important it is to act extremely quickly.

Matthew 24:17-20

Let him which is on the housetop not come down to take any thing out of his house: Neither let him which is in the field return back to take his clothes. And woe unto them that are with child, and to them that give suck in those days! But pray ye that your flight be not in the winter, neither on the sabbath day: (KJV)

Let him who is on the housetop not come down to take anything out of his house. Neither let the one in the field return back to take his clothes. And how awful for pregnant women and nursing mothers in those days! And pray that your flight not be in the winter or on the Sabbath. (DHT)

Mark 13:15-18

And let him that is on the housetop not go down into the house, neither enter therein, to take anything out of his house: And let him that is in the field not turn back again for to take up his garment. But woe to them that are with child, and to them that give suck in those days! And pray ye that your flight be not in the winter. (KJV)

And let the one who is on the housetop not go down to either enter or take anything out of his house. And let the one who is in the field not go back to take his clothes. And how awful it will be for pregnant women and nursing mothers in those days. And pray that it doesn't happen in the winter. (DHT)

<u>Luke 21:21b-23a</u>

and let them which are in the midst of it depart out; and let not them that are in the countries enter thereinto. For these be the days of vengeance, that all things which are written may be fulfilled. But woe unto them that are with child, and to them that give suck, in those days! for there shall be great distress in the land, and wrath upon this people. (KJV)

And let those who are in the middle of it, leave. And let the ones who are out in the country, not go in. For these are the days of vengeance, that all that is written may be fulfilled. And how awful for pregnant women and those who are nursing in those days! For there will be great distress in the land and punishment upon its people. (DHT)

To state the obvious; this is not a call by Jesus for people to stand their ground and be martyred for His namesake. Jesus stresses urgency and danger in order to motivate people to act quickly to save their physical lives. Jesus, loving His followers, would naturally want them to avoid the calamity that is to follow.

The reference to roof tops is not only giving advice to those who are in the roofing business, but in the days that this was written, people spent a lot of time on their roofs. They were flat and can be compared to what we now know as a deck or patio. People would use them as kitchens and cook on them and spend a good deal of their time interacting on them in the open air.

Fleeing in The Winter and Leaving Possessions

The importance of fleeing quickly is stressed when Jesus instructs those fleeing to leave all of their possessions behind, even those possessions as important and basic as their clothing that can protect from the elements. Extra clothes or a coat would be especially important in "the winter," which is why Jesus would advise the one fleeing to "pray that your flight not take place in the winter." The simple reason for not wanting to flee in winter is because one may find themselves fighting hypothermia as they try to survive in the cold desolate mountains without shelter or the clothing they have been forced to leave behind.

Jesus appears to be prioritizing for His followers and asking those that will heed His warning to have a little faith. He is saying two things; "the most important thing is to get out of Jerusalem," and, "get out of Jerusalem, and leave your survival after that to me."

It should be clear that Jesus is not giving any indication of when this event will take place. According to the words He chose, it appears He did not know.

Fleeing On the Sabbath

Why would Jesus also instruct the one fleeing to pray that their "flight not take place on the Sabbath?" First, this is a good indication that primarily Jews will still inhabit Judea during this prophetic future time. The Sabbath is *still* very different for Jews and the Judaism that drives the culture in Israel.

What is important that takes place on the Sabbath in Judea, is what does not take place on the Sabbath in Judea; transportation and commerce. To this day, Jerusalem all but shuts down except for emergency services on the seventh day of the week, which is still, at least technically, set apart for God. With a population of over three-quarters of a million people in Jerusalem, [67] it would be very difficult to "flee" even on a day when all basic services were operating. How much more difficult would it be when surrounded by enemy armies and with no public transportation or other services?

Pregnant and Nursing Mothers

Jesus points out how difficult it will be for nursing mothers and pregnant women during this time. Although He does not mention the group, I imagine the same could be said for the elderly, disabled, and those who are taking care of the elderly and disabled. It is not difficult to see why it will be difficult for pregnant and nursing mothers to leave home without stopping to pack clothes or food.

It was not so long ago that I cannot remember how long it took to leave the house when preparing to go somewhere for even a few hours with our kids when they were very small. How much more difficult it would be to leave your home for good, with no sure destination in mind.

When my wife and I have went camping in remote areas in the mountains for only a few days, even without small children, we have sometimes spent weeks and hundreds of dollars in preparation;

making sure we had the proper equipment, food, and supplies; being ready for any kind of weather, planning for shelter, sanitation, and toilet needs being able to navigate and communicate in unfamiliar country, having tires that will withstand unforgiving roads. So, adding in taking care of a baby or small child creates many other layers of preparation.

A mother leaving home with their small children unprepared is enough to consider, but Jesus has something more in mind here. The "dreadfulness" He is referring to has far more meaning to it than simply being unprepared to take on the elements and cope with hunger and dirty diapers. He reemphasized this warning to mothers again as He was on His way to die on the cross:

And there followed him a great company of people, and of women, which also bewailed and lamented him. But Jesus turning unto them said, Daughters of Jerusalem, weep not for me, but weep for yourselves, and for your children. For, behold, the days are coming, in the which they shall say, Blessed are the barren, and the wombs that never bare, and the paps (breasts) *which never gave suck. Then shall they begin to say to the mountains, fall on us; and to the hills, Cover us. Luke 23:27-30 (KJV)* (My definition added)

Jesus was referring to Old Testament prophecy. Prophecy that was fulfilled before, but due to the cyclical nature of things, Jesus was referring to what would be fulfilled again, perhaps more than once.

The Old Testament is full of documentation that records God's disappointment with Israel when they turn away from God to others. Because of the "covenant of death" Israel will enter into in the end of days with the Antichrist, God will again allow them to fall into the hands of the enemy. The words of the Old Testament prophecy will again be fulfilled: What was Jesus referring to when He said, "*For these are days of vengeance, that all things which are written may be fulfilled*"? The books of Isaiah and Hosea hold some of the answer to this question.

And your ***covenant with death*** *shall be disannulled, and your agreement with hell shall not stand; when the overflowing scourge shall pass through, then ye shall be trodden down by it. Isa 28:18 (KJV)* (Emphasis added)

Samaria shall become desolate; for she hath rebelled against her God: they shall fall by the sword: their infants shall be dashed in pieces, and their women with child shall be ripped up. Hos 13:16 (KJV)

Hosea contains a gruesome prophecy that has been fulfilled several times in history as documented in the Old Testament. Jesus again ties this type of unspeakable event to the time of the end. How important this makes it to "flee" without hesitation once those in Judea witness this sign.

Such horrific acts such as pregnant women being "ripped open" and children being "dashed in pieces" are very illustrative of why Jesus goes on to say the following:

Matthew 24:21

For then shall be great tribulation, such as was not since the beginning of the world to this time, no, nor ever shall be. (KJV)

For then there will be such exceedingly great anguish, such has not been since the beginning of the world, or will ever be. (DHT)

Mark 13:19

For in those days shall be affliction, such as was not from the beginning of the creation which God created unto this time, neither shall be. (KJV)

For in those days there will be such anguish, such as was not from the beginning of the creation, which God created until now, or ever will be. (DHT)

Luke 21:23b

for there shall be great distress in the land, and wrath upon this people. (KJV)

for there shall be great distress in the land, and passionate violence on this people. (DHT)

For those who would say that the gruesome and violent prophecies of the Old Testament have been fulfilled, I would say in light of this scripture, it doesn't matter. Whatever terrible things took place in history, it is still not as bad as what will take place during the period of time Jesus is talking about in the future.

Think briefly about all of the terrible things that have occurred in history. Pick a war. Choose a holocaust. The period of time Jesus is referring to will be worse. It will come at the hand of the Antichrist who becomes enraged and "turns himself against the covenant."

It is at this point, 1,260 days after entering into the covenant (the midpoint of the seven-year period) that the Antichrist very purposefully begins persecuting Jews and Christians. The book of Revelation speaks about this specific event. It appears that the Antichrist becomes a direct tool or puppet of Satan. Please read Revelation 12:9-17 and notice that when Satan is hurled down to the earth, he is given 1,260 days to go after, and persecute the Jews (the woman) and Christians (the ones who "hold to the testimony of Jesus"). This persecution takes place during the second half of the seven-year period. This is the time known as the "Great Tribulation" or as some call it, "the time of Jacob's trouble."

The good news in all of this, is that even though God allows Israel to be punished for their unfaithfulness, He will eventually rescue them, once and for all.

And these are the words that the Lord spake concerning Israel and concerning Judah. For thus saith the Lord; We have heard a voice of trembling, of fear, and not of peace. Ask ye now, and see whether a man doth travail with child? wherefore do I see every man with his hands on his loins, as a woman in travail, and all faces are turned into paleness? Alas! for that day is great, so that none is like it: it is even ***the time of Jacob's trouble; but he shall be saved out of it.*** *Jer 30:4-7 (KJV)* (Emphasis added)

Please read all of Jeremiah chapter 30, which talks about the, "time of Jacob's trouble (or distress)," and note that the closing words (verse 24) are "in the latter times, you will understand this." This statement indicates that this passage was written for "the latter times," and although something like the events mentioned may have occurred in history, the ultimate cycle is yet to take place.

Luke 21:24

And they shall fall by the edge of the sword, and shall be led away captive into all nations: and Jerusalem shall be trodden down of the Gentiles, until the times of the Gentiles be fulfilled. (KJV)

And they shall fall by the edge of the sword, and will be led away captive into all the nations. And Jerusalem will be crushed under foot by the nations until the times of the Gentiles is fulfilled. (DHT)

According to this prophecy, anyone not taking the advice of Jesus to quickly flee, but instead remains in Jerusalem, will either be killed or taken captive and deported to "all nations." Jerusalem will remain under the control of the Antichrist until the "times of the Gentiles are fulfilled."

The times of the Gentiles being fulfilled may be referring to the time that Jerusalem is occupied by Gentiles, but it is also referring to the same thing discussed in chapter nine, regarding "the mystery," and the "fullness of the Gentiles." The "seventh angel" talked about in Revelation will blow his trumpet 1,260 days (3 ½ years) after the Abomination of Desolation has taken place, the time of the Gentiles will be ended, and the Kingdom of Heaven will be established on the earth.

And the seventh angel sounded; and there were great voices in heaven, saying, the kingdoms of this world are become the kingdoms of our Lord, and of his Christ; and he shall reign for ever and ever. Rev 11:15 (KJV)

Matthew 24:22

And except those days should be shortened, there should no flesh be saved: but for the elect's sake those days shall be shortened. (KJV)

And except those days be cut short, no one would be saved. But for the sake of the chosen, those days will be cut short. (DHT)

<u>Mark 13:20</u>

And except that the Lord had shortened those days, no flesh should be saved: but for the elect's sake, whom he hath chosen, he hath shortened the days. (KJV)

And except that the Lord cuts short those days, no one will be saved. But for the elect's sake, who He has chosen, He has cut short those days. (DHT)

So terrible are the days predicted by Jesus to come, that He says that *no one* would survive, except those days be "cut short" or "shortened," for the sake of those who have been chosen by God; the ones Jesus calls the "elect."

"Those days" that Jesus is referring to are the ones written about in Revelation chapter 12 where a specific number of days are given to the "serpent," Satan, to do his worst, "*knowing that he has only a short time.*" "Cutting short" those days for the sake of the "elect," means that the "elect" or "chosen" of God will not have to endure the full length of "those days."

Prior to the end of the 1,260 days that remain until the end of the age, after the mid-point of the seven-year period, God will rescue those He has set apart or chosen for Himself. That "rescue" is what we soon will see in the next verses that follow and is what is commonly referred to as the "rapture." It will occur simultaneously with the Second Coming of Jesus, the Messiah.

Summary

Half way through the tribulation period, the Antichrist will surround Jerusalem with a great military presence and break the covenant he has made. He will commit the act of the Abomination of Desolation spoken of by the Prophet Daniel, Jesus, and the Apostle Paul. When this occurs, those living in the region of Judea should take it as a hard sign to leave that area immediately, leaving all possessions behind, and flee to the "mountains."

What follows this event will be the most horrific time in all history. So terrible will be the persecution and death of those future days, that "no one" would survive if not for God intervening directly for the sake of those He has called to Himself. Although the Antichrist will have been given a set amount of time (1,260 days) to rule over the earth by force, those days of persecution will be "cut short" for the sake of those whom God has chosen.

Enough already with the Antichrist and persecution! The next three chapters are devoted to the glorious event of Jesus' return and the rescue of His followers.

Notes

13.The Return of Jesus Will be No Secret

In spite of their utterly spent energy, and broken bodies, the two "Halflings" continued their attempt to make it up the ominous black and gray volcano, Mount Doom. The two had already suffered the loss of dear friends to violent deaths at the hands of the evil forces of darkness. They themselves had narrowly escaped numerous life threatening and injurious trials, including evading the Dark Lord, Sauron's, gaze, as well as his evil armies.

As their mission was not yet complete; starving, bleeding, and exhausted, they paused a moment on the side of the mountain among the jagged and sharp volcanic rocks to rest. Evil was about to declare victory on their world the situation seemed completely hopeless. The only light by which to see was provided by the molten lava of an unstable mountain.

Sam looked up into the dark, cloud shrouded sky as he held on to the broken body of his lifelong friend and companion, Mr. Frodo. The clouds parted ever so slightly, revealing a clear and deep sliver of sky, and in it, a bright star.

"Mr. Frodo," Sam said, *"look, there is light, and beauty up there, that no shadow can touch."*

Many will recognize this scene from J.R.R. Tolkien's *The Lord of the Rings, Return of the King*, directed by Peter Jackson. It is a scene that is close to the end of the movie, that comes just before the "end of the age," in Sam and Mr. Frodo's fictional world, "Middle Earth."

It is powerful and moving when you grasp the parallels between what is going on in that fictional world, and what is in the world's very real future. It is a scene conveying hope in the middle of the worst kinds of trials and tribulations. For the follower of Jesus, who is waiting on His return, the parallel is clear: no matter how bad the world may get, no matter how broken, beaten, and persecuted by the forces of evil we become, the Kingdom of Heaven lies just on the other side of the shroud of our ability to see. And, King Jesus will soon be bringing that kingdom to this world.

The common understanding of the word "hope" in our day, means little more than to "wish" for something. However, that is not the hope of the follower of Jesus. The hope found in the Bible for God's elect, is a hope that means we are waiting on something and fully expecting it to happen! As illustrative as J.R.R. Tolkien's novel is, we don't have to watch nine hours of *The Lord of the Rings* trilogy to understand the real hope that awaits us. Our hope is found in scripture. Our hope regarding the end of the age, is found in the *return of the real king*, Jesus!

According to the words Jesus has just spoken to His disciples on the Mount of Olives, things will look pretty bleak just prior to the "end of the age." Yet, things are about to get a whole lot better! Jesus moves on to talk about what He just referred to as "cutting short the days for the sake of the elect;" His return.

He starts by emphasizing that His return will *not* be a secret. His followers will not have to go looking for Him. He will find them.

Matthew 24:23-26

Then if any man shall say unto you, Lo, here is Christ, or there; believe it not. For there shall arise false Christs, and false prophets, and shall shew great signs and wonders; insomuch that, if it were possible, they shall deceive the very elect. Behold, I have told you before. Wherefore if they shall say unto you, Behold, he is in the desert; go not forth: behold, he is in the secret chambers; believe it not. (KJV)

At that time, if anyone says to you, look, here or there is the messiah, don't believe it. For there will arise false messiahs and false prophets and they will show great signs and wonders, so much so that they will deceive, if it's possible, even the elect. Pay attention, I have told you before, so if anyone says to you, look, he is in the desert, don't go out, or see, he is in a secret room, don't believe it! (DHT)

Mark 13:21-23

And then if any man shall say to you, Lo, here is Christ; or, lo, he is there; believe him not: For false Christs and false prophets shall rise, and shall shew signs and wonders, to seduce, if it were possible, even the elect. But take ye heed: behold, I have foretold you all things. (KJV)

And then if anyone says to you, look there is the messiah, or look, there he is, don't believe them. For false messiahs and false prophets will arise and will show signs and wonders to seduce, if it is possible, even the elect. So you watch out! Look, I have told you everything ahead of time. (DHT)

In the coming verses, Jesus will describe the final sign of His return. These signs will be unmistakable. Although many who "walk in the dark," may not know what to make of them, no one can miss them. Jesus is giving His followers, "those who walk in the light," all the information they need in order to avoid the deception of "false Christs" or "messiahs" and "false prophets." These deceivers will have the ability to perform "miracles" of a caliber that may fool "even the elect." However, His coming will not occur in a manner that could simply be validated by someone performing what appear to be miracles.

If we hear of someone claiming to be "the Christ" and backing it up with miracles, or someone claiming to be "a prophet of God," who is performing miracles and claiming that they know where and when Jesus will return, we are *not* to trust them. As we have seen in the preceding chapters, the "False Prophet," the Antichrist's religious right hand man, will have the ability to perform signs and wonders. Even calling down "fire from heaven," (See Revelation 13:13-14).

With the times as terrible as they will be during the last days, many will be looking for something or someone to save them. Those who are awaiting a messiah will be eager to see Him. Some, tired of suffering, may be too eager, and end up falling victim to the deception of a false messiah.

There are some who say (or at least think), people who study scripture concerning end times events are more likely to be deceived and end up "selling their possessions and sitting on a mountain top to await the Lords return." It is true that over-zealous watching, sans knowledge of the truth, can lead to a bad ending. However, knowing what Jesus said regarding His return and being watchful is the best protection from being fooled into "selling your possessions and sitting on a mountain top."

It will be those that are ignorant of scriptures pertaining to the end of the age who will be most easily fooled. Perhaps those who will be caught off guard, not watching, who don't think they will even be around for any signs to take place, will be the most susceptible.

Jesus is very clear that the false prophets and false messiahs of the end of the age will be quite skilled in the art of deception, even possessing the abilities in some cases to perform "signs and wonders." This is critical information to have in order to avoid falling into a trap. Even those who have been elected to salvation may be fooled! As if to say He won't accept any excuses, Jesus says, "*look, I have told you ahead of time.*"

A Case of Being "Fooled"

In 1904, the Watchtower Society (The Jehovah's Witnesses Organization), said, "*The stress of the great time of trouble will be on us soon, somewhere between 1910 and 1912 culminating with the end of the 'times of the Gentiles,' in October 1914.*"[68] Later the same group declared that Jesus had in fact come back in secret in 1914 to the "temple," where He "cleansed" it. Jesus was done with this work by 1918. However, since no one actually having seen Jesus, they claimed that it was not a physical return, but rather a spiritual return. [69]

As of August 2005, there were 6,613,829 Jehovah's Witnesses that hold this belief. [70] That makes at least 6.5 million people that are not listening to the commands and warnings that Jesus gave His followers on the Mount of Olives. *"If someone says, look he is in the secret inner room, don't believe it!"*

After making His point that His return will not be a secret event, Jesus next emphasizes just how public it will be.

<u>Matthew 24:27</u>

For as the lightning cometh out of the east, and shineth even unto the west; so shall also the coming of the Son of man be. (KJV)

For as lightning comes from the east and shines to the west, so shall also be the coming of the Son of Man. (DHT)

Like a bolt of lightning that flashes in one specific place and yet can still be seen and heard beyond the horizon, so will be the return of Jesus.

Why don't you need to worry about missing the return of the Messiah? Because it will be a spectacle for the entire world to see! This is the Son of God's return to the earth to rescue His people and establish His Kingdom. There will be no mistaking it. Matthew 24:27 indicates, like several verses to follow, that the signs accompanying this event will be easily seen. This is because, for the most part, the events will take place in the sky.

A Bizarre Saying

<u>Matthew 24:28</u>

For wheresoever the carcase is, there will the eagles be gathered together. (KJV)

For wherever the corpse is, there the eagles will gather. (DHT)

From our 21st century perspective, "*wherever the corpse is, there the vultures will gather*," is a bizarre statement. Jesus has said this same thing before. It may have been a common "saying" during the time of Jesus. Something like, "you catch more flies with honey." What would this saying about corpses and vultures have meant to the first century inhabitants of Judea? The people that Jesus was originally speaking to?

One Theory

In his book, *The Prewrath Rapture of the Church*, Messianic Jew and end times book author and publisher Marvin Rosenthal says that this statement by Jesus was "*a familiar Hebraic expression*." Rosenthal states that the meaning of this expression is that "*moral corruption requires divine judgment*." Carcasses in this case represent moral decay, and the eagles gathering implies divine judgment.[71]

Pastor and longtime "Through The Bible," radio commentator, Dr. J. Vernon McGee agrees with Rosenthal's assessment. Dr. McGee states that "*the birds that feed on carrion seem to be agents of divine judgment*." [72]

Preterist commentator, David Chilton, wrote this scripture is consistent with other prophetic warnings regarding Israel's destruction. That such warnings are "*often couched in terms of eagles descending upon carrion.*" [73]

There is a very similar saying found in a very similar end times passage in the book of Luke chapter 17. To set up the statement, please read the following passage that leads up to it. Some of this should sound familiar:

Even thus shall it be in the day when the Son of man is revealed. In that day, he which shall be upon the housetop, and his stuff in the house, let him not come down to take it away: and he that is in the field, let him likewise not return back. Remember Lot's wife. Whosoever shall seek to save his life shall lose it; and whosoever shall lose his life shall preserve it. I tell you, in that night there shall be two men in one bed; the one shall be taken, and the other shall be left. Two women shall be grinding together; the one shall be taken, and the other left. Two men shall be in the field; the one shall be taken, and the other left. Luke 17:30-36 (KJV)

Jesus is talking about the end of the age. In response to His statements about "one being taken and the other left," His disciples have a question for Him; taken where?

And they answered and said unto him, Where, Lord? And he said unto them, Wheresoever the body is, thither will the eagles be gathered together. Luke 17:37 (KJV)

In *The Interpreter's One-Volume Commentary on the Bible*, author William Baird says that this verse means, "*wherever men refuse to be alert and ready for the Son of man in faith, there will be the judgment.*" [74]

I don't know if Mr. Baird took into consideration the question that was asked of Jesus or not, but it doesn't seem to have much to do with his interpretation. The disciples are asking where the people in his parable will be "taken." They are not asking anything about "judgment." This explanation of what this phrase means just doesn't seem to fit, given the question the disciples asked Jesus.

On both sides of this statement in the Olivet discourse, Jesus is talking about His return, which seems out of place with *all* of the above interpretations. Jesus has gone from talking about trials, persecution and tribulations at the hand of the Antichrist, to not being fooled by false saviors and prophets. He turns to what His return will be like; It will be like lightning flashing from the east to west; powerful, irresistible, unmistakable. Something we won't have to go looking for or need to worry about missing. Why would He now throw in an out of context, a cryptic statement about judging the unrighteous? The current topic He is addressing is that of recognizing His coming. After this statement about the "gathering of the eagles," (or vultures in some translations) He will continue to describe the sign of His coming, which includes the "gathering of the elect."

Another Theory

18th Century Bible Commentator, Matthew Henry, has a different theory about Jesus' answer to His disciples concerning what "where" means. He says that this verse is communicating that wherever Jesus is, believers in him will instinctively find him. [75]

Henry may be hitting a little closer to being in line with what Jesus is talking about here; the "eagles" or Christians, according to his interpretation, are irresistibly gathered to the "carcass" or "body." The "body" being Jesus. In the same manner vultures always seem to somehow find the carcass of an animal in the middle of nowhere, so will the followers of Jesus be gathered to him. This is an especially interesting interpretation of this scripture

In just a couple of nights from when the disciples sat with Jesus on the Mount of Olives, Jesus would be telling his disciples that the bread they ate at the Passover meal represented His body that would be broken. Many Christians come together to this day to partake in the eating of the "body of Christ." Jesus may well have been adding to the meaning of what He would tell them at the Passover meal in this statement. Still, something just doesn't seem to flow with this interpretation…

A Third Interpretation

Both Matthew 24:27 that mentions "lightning" and verse 28, which talks about "eagles" or "vultures" gathering, are verses that primarily utilize symbolism to make a point. Symbolism is when one thing stands for something else. Symbols need to be defined to be understood or they are meaningless. Most of the time the symbolism found in prophecy is defined nearby in the passage. The lightning symbolism is easy. The lightning flashing across the sky stands for what the return of Jesus will be like.

When the definition of symbols is not found near to where the symbols are used, we can carefully expand our search outward to look for definitions. I believe the above interpretations of this scripture (Rosenthal, McGee, Chilton) that speak of judgment came about as a result of looking too "far away" in scripture in an attempt to define the symbolism represented in these verses. They took the passages from elsewhere in the Bible that deal with predatory birds, which for the most part have to do with God's judgment, and inferred that this passage had to do with judgment. However, I believe the definition of this symbolism is found much closer to home.

There is a third interpretation of this scripture that seems to fit the best. This interpretation relies mostly on defining the symbolism used by examining the context of the surrounding verses. The event that Jesus is describing is His coming and the "gathering" of the elect of God.

Compare the following verse of the coming of Christ to the symbolic verse describing His coming being like lightning:

- Symbolic lightning flash verse (Matthew 24:27)

For as the lightning cometh out of the east, and shineth even unto the west; so shall also the coming of the Son of man be. (KJV)

- Three verses later the lightning symbolism is defined (Matthew 24:30)

And then shall appear the sign of the Son of man in heaven: and then shall all the tribes of the earth mourn, and they shall see the Son of man coming in the clouds of heaven with power and great glory. (KJV)

Now compare the verse about bodies (corpse or carcass) and eagles (vultures) gathering, to the next verse in Matthew 24:

- Symbolic vulture, gathering verse (Matthew 24:28)

For wheresoever the carcase is, there will the eagles be gathered together. (KJV)

- Three verses later the vulture/ gathering symbolism is defined (Matthew 24:31)

And he shall send his angels with a great sound of a trumpet, and they shall gather together his elect from the four winds, from one end of heaven to the other. (KJV)

The word that has been translated as "carcass," can also be translated as "body." In a parallel scripture that describes this same event, Paul tells us that the "dead in Christ" shall rise and those who are alive, will be caught up with them together.

For the Lord himself shall descend from heaven with a shout, with the voice of the archangel, and with the trump of God: and the dead in Christ shall rise first: Then we which are alive and remain shall be caught up together with them in the clouds, to meet the Lord in the air: and so shall we ever be with the Lord. 1 Thess 4:16-17 (KJV)

The angels Jesus brings with Him, not literal birds, will be the ones that will "gather" the elect of God from one "end of the sky to the other." It is not the elect that will gather to Jesus, it is the elect that are gathered to Jesus by His angels.

It will be the bodies of the elect who are alive, and the "carcasses" or dead bodies of the elect who are no longer alive that will be gathered by the angels to Jesus. Jesus' answer to His disciple's question of "where" will the believers be taken, was essentially, "don't worry about where to go, I will provide the transportation, and you will be brought to me." Perhaps another way of looking at Matthew 24:28 would be to say, "regardless of where the elect are located on the earth, the angels will find and collect them all."

Summary

The message of Jesus is clear in regards to His return; We do not need to worry that we will miss it. It will not take place in secret. It will shake the world like a bolt of lightning for all to see. If you are one of the elect, you won't need to worry about finding your way to Jesus. Once He comes, He will arrange transportation for you, whether you are dead or alive at the time of His return.

Notes

14. This Looks Familiar

(Similarities Between the Olivet Discourse and Revelation Chapter Six)

At this point in the Olivet Discourse, Jesus relays more details of his Second Coming. One would expect that what Jesus had to say about end times events on the Mount of Olives would match up well with what the rest of the Bible has to say. That is indeed the case!

There are interesting parallel scriptures found in the book of Revelation chapter 6 that aid in better understanding the portions of the Olivet Discourse. This should be no surprise since it was Jesus who spoke to His disciples on the Mount of Olives, and it was Jesus who revealed further details regarding the end of the age to the Apostle John on the Island of Patmos.

It was on the Island of Patmos that John received the vision from Jesus recorded in the book of "Revelation." The Apostle John was present on the Mount of Olives with Jesus during the Olivet Discourse. He was one of the four Disciples that approached Jesus "privately" that Tuesday evening. (Mark 13:3).

In this chapter we will compare the teaching of Jesus as He spoke to His disciples on the Mount of Olives, with what takes place in Revelation chapter 6:1-11 as the first five "seals" of a very special scroll are loosed. We will see that the two passages lineup somewhat sequentially.

The Scene Found in Revelation Chapter Six

To catch you up on what is going on in the passage we will be reviewing in the Book of Revelation, we need to first look at chapter 6, which describes a scene playing out in the throne room of Heaven. There, we find four fantastic winged creatures around the throne of God. The Apostle John has been taken to Heaven and is the one who is witnessing and writing down what is taking place before him. There is a "scroll" that John wrote about which contains the will of God pertaining to His final judgment of the earth.

The scroll is sealed with seven seals. Each and every seal needs to be broken before the scroll can be opened and God's judgment can take place. Jesus, who appears as a "lamb" that has been slain in this vision, is the only one to have been found worthy to take the scroll from the hand of the Almighty God, who is sitting on the throne, and break the seven seals. This is what the apostle John wrote down;

Revelation 6:1-8

And I saw when the Lamb opened one of the seals, and I heard, as it were the noise of thunder, one of the four beasts saying, Come and see. And I saw, and behold a white horse: and he that sat on him had a bow; and a crown was given unto him: and he went forth conquering, and to conquer.

And when he had opened the second seal, I heard the second beast say, Come and see. And there went out another horse that was red: and power was given to him that sat thereon to take peace from the earth, and that they should kill one another: and there was given unto him a great sword.

And when he had opened the third seal, I heard the third beast say, Come and see. And I beheld, and lo a black horse; and he that sat on him had a pair of balances in his hand. And I heard a voice in the midst of the four beasts say, a measure of wheat for a penny, and three measures of barley for a penny; and see thou hurt not the oil and the wine.

And when he had opened the fourth seal, I heard the voice of the fourth beast say, Come and see. And I looked, and behold a pale horse: and his name that sat on him was Death, and Hell followed with him. And power was given unto them over the fourth part of the earth, to kill with sword, and with hunger, and with death, and with the beasts of the earth. (KJV)

The First Seal Opened: Deception

When the first seal in Revelation chapter six is broken a rider on a "white horse" appears. The rider is interpreted by some to be Jesus. Jesus is seen later in Revelation riding on a white horse in white robes (Rev 19:11-16). Believing this rider to be Jesus is the case with commentators such as Kuyper, Ladd, and Morris. [76] Although there is nothing indicating this will occur in scripture, they see this rider, "Jesus," as victoriously proclaiming the gospel throughout the world. However, casting Jesus in this role causes "story line" confusion. The rider is holding a weapon (a "bow") and is bent on "conquest." It also seems out of place to think this rider is Jesus, considering everything else associated with the loosing of the seals of the scroll is catastrophic in nature and represents "trials and tribulations."

This crown-wearing rider of the white horse, has also been called by other commentators such as Walvoord, Ryrie, Lindsey, and others to be an "imitator" of Christ. Some would even say he is, *the Antichrist.* [77] The Antichrist is thought to have been awarded his crown through conquest and deception. This is consistent with what we know of the Antichrist and his activities.

When we only consider the scripture in Revelation regarding the first horse that rides out, there is not a strong case supporting that this horse and rider represents the Antichrist or spirit of the Antichrist. Nor is a strong case made that this character is anything of a deceiver. However, when we compare the entire sequence of events in the Olivet Discourse with the sequence of events of the seals of the scroll of Revelation being opened, a stronger case is made.

If this rider does indeed represent false Christs, the Antichrist, or spirit of deception, it is interesting that even some Bible scholars are fooled by the symbolism. Some commentators have already seemingly become "deceived," as they confuse this character sitting on the white horse, with the real Messiah who rides a white horse in Revelation chapter 19.

What is it we see Jesus warning about first in the Olivet Discourse? We see many are coming as imitators of Christ, false messiahs, false saviors, deceivers. They will be successful in deceiving "many." Indeed, many have been deceived throughout the centuries. Many are now being deceived, and many will continue to be.

Each of the four horse riders that ride out as a result of a seal being broken, are associated with activities that have been going on since the world began; deception, death, famine, etc. This goes hand in hand with what Jesus has said thus far during the Olivet discourse. Now, we see in the book of Revelation that the horsemen are given something they didn't have up until the time when the seals of the scroll containing God's judgments for the earth are opened.

The Riders Are Given New Tools

Each rider is given something different; The rider of the white horse is now seen holding a bow and he is given a crown. The rider of the red horse will be given "power to take peace from the earth" and a "large sword," literally in the original language, a "mega-weapon." The rider of the black horse will be given a "pair of scales." The rider of the pale horse is "given power over a fourth of the earth to kill by the sword, famine and plague, and by the wild beasts of the earth." Although these symbolic "riders" have been through many cycles before, the things that they are "given" are unique to the last ultimate "cycle" associated with the end of the age.

Even though Jesus starts out in the Olivet Discourse warning about deception in general, the kind of deception there always has been, He eventually talks about a type of deception that is intense enough to fool even those who have been elected. A spirit of deception has existed in the world since Satan deceived Eve into taking a bite of the forbidden fruit. However, if the riders of the four horses in the Book of Revelation are given "extra tools" to work with in the time immediately preceding the Second Coming of Christ, then we are looking at unparalleled deception during the End of Days. Deception that "*may even fool the elect, if that were possible.*"

The spirits of antichrist and deception have been "riding" throughout the world long since before Jesus was born, but in the end as seen in Revelation chapter six, the rider of the white horse will be given a "crown." A crown is a sign of authority, and he will be "bent on conquest." The first warning that Jesus gives on the Mount of Olives was in regards to deception.

Because of the rest of the sequential similarities between the Olivet Discourse and Revelation chapter 6 that follow, I believe the white horse and its rider, a Jesus look-alike imitator, represents the false prophets and deception Jesus warned of on the Mount of Olives. These false prophets will be working in conjunction with the Antichrist. If the Antichrist will do anything, it will be to appear to "save the world," while in fact he is conquering it through deception and force.

The Second Seal: War

Following the mention of coming deception in the Olivet Discourse, Jesus speaks of war (Matt 24:6-7). Parallel to this in the Book of Revelation, the Apostle John documents that when the second seal of the scroll was broken, a rider appears on a red horse who has power to take peace from the earth. To him was given a "mega-weapon" (Rev 6:3-4).

Again, as Jesus points out wars have been around for a long time and don't necessarily indicate that it is the end of the world. However, as this rider of Revelation rides out, who is associated with "war," he is given a "mega-weapon" to utilize. Like the rider of the white horse who has been riding throughout time deceiving people, it appears that just prior to the end of the age, this rider representing war is given the ability to "kick it up" a bit.

If the events that are associated with the return of Christ are the ultimate fulfillment of all of the cycles of wars that have previously occurred, can you imagine what is in store for the end of the age?

The Third Seal: Economic Collapse

When the third seal of the Revelation chapter 6 scroll is broken, we see a rider appear that is associated with economic collapse. A quart of wheat will cost a person an entire day's wages. Back then a "denarius" was a full day's wages. A full day's wages were a "penny" in the days that the King James Version of the Bible was being translated. Paying a full day's wages for basic food is exactly what one might expect in the midst of a severe famine. Famine is the next thing that was spoken of by Jesus on the Mount of Olives (Matt 24:7b).

"Hunger" is a word that can be used in place of "famines." "Pestilence" is something that causes famines. Famines are synonymous with the kind of inflation related scarcity of food we see in the parallel Revelation passage (Revelation 6:5-6).

The Fourth Seal: Death

Upon opening the fourth seal of the scroll, a rider named "Death" appears. People have been doomed to die since the fall of Adam. However, "Death," is mentioned here due to the unparalleled death rate associated with the end of the age. The rider named Death, appears to use the same tools as previously mentioned when the first three seals were opened; war, famine, etc. However, upon the opening of the fourth seal, "Death" is given permission to "rule over a fourth part of the earth" (Revelation 6:7-8). Additionally, the rider named Death will utilize persecution when the next seal of Revelation chapter 6 is opened to claim "his" victims.

The Fifth Seal: Persecution

Beyond the wars, earthquakes, famines, and pestilence, associated with the Second Coming, will be the persecution of the Church and all of those who do not align themselves with the Antichrist. The next issue in sequence in the Book of Revelation (Rev 6:9-11), and what we have seen thus far in the Olivet Discourse (Matthew 24:9-22) is the persecution of the Jews and the Church. Again, as discussed in previous chapters, persecution is not unique to the "End Times."

The similarities between Revelation Chapter six and the events of the Olivet Discourse don't "make or break" any particular prophetic Second Coming "model" that I am seeking to demonstrate. Few would argue against both passages speaking of the end of the age. The two parallel passages serve to complement one another. Where Jesus warns of events in one passage, the other passage provides more details. The Apostle John was present for both "uncoverings," or "revelations" of end times prophetic events; on the Mount of Olives, circa 30 AD, and the Island of Patmos, circa 97 AD.

The sequence observed in both passages and the similarities continue throughout a significant portion of the Olivet Discourse. This allows us to overlay the events of Revelation chapter six on top of the events of the Olivet Discourse, and gives us the opportunity to "fill in some blanks" and put together a more complete composite picture of the Second Coming using scripture and not speculation.

The next extremely strong similarity that we will observe in both passages, which follows the persecution of God's chosen people, will be the event that will "shorten the days" for the "sake of the elect." It is the anchor event that ties the passages unmistakably together. It is *The* sign of the return of Jesus.

Timing

Of course everyone is always interested in timing. When will the events associated with each of these broken seals take place? The Bible does not provide enough details to give a clear answer. However, there are some things we do know. For example, the events are given in a specific numerological order. Our first face value assumption should be that this order was for a reason. Jesus could have revealed the events to John in some way other than the order they are revealed: one comes before two, two before three, etc. This being said except for the sixth seal, which is associated with a specific event, there is nothing to indicate that the events corresponding with each seal will not take place concurrently rather than consecutively. They will likely overlap. For example, the deception represented by the white horse rider in the first seal, will likely take place throughout the entire tribulation period.

The sixth seal, discussed in the next chapter is unquestionably tied to the Second Coming of Jesus and the rapture of the Church. The totality of scripture suggests that this will take place sometime during the second half of the seven-year tribulation period.

The fifth seal is associated with the souls of martyrs in heaven. We know that there will be a great persecution which takes place following the unveiling of the Antichrist and the Abomination of Desolation. The unresurrected souls seen under the altar in Heaven are given "white robes to wear," suggesting that their resurrection will happen very soon. Both of these things suggest that the fifth seal is opened earlier in the second half of the tribulation period than the sixth seal.

The timing of the first four seals is not as easy to determine. They stand out from the last three seals in that they are associated with four "horsemen." Although a case can be made that these horsemen have been riding throughout history, each of them is given something new as they ride out during the end of the age.

The first seal, likely representing the Antichrist and his deceptive work, suggests a timing sometime prior to the initiation of the covenant being confirmed. The breaking of the first seal may even be associated with the Antichrist's rise to power before the covenant is confirmed. That could mean it is opened years before the seven-year period begins.

Logically, the next three seals would follow the first seal and take place before the fifth seal is opened.

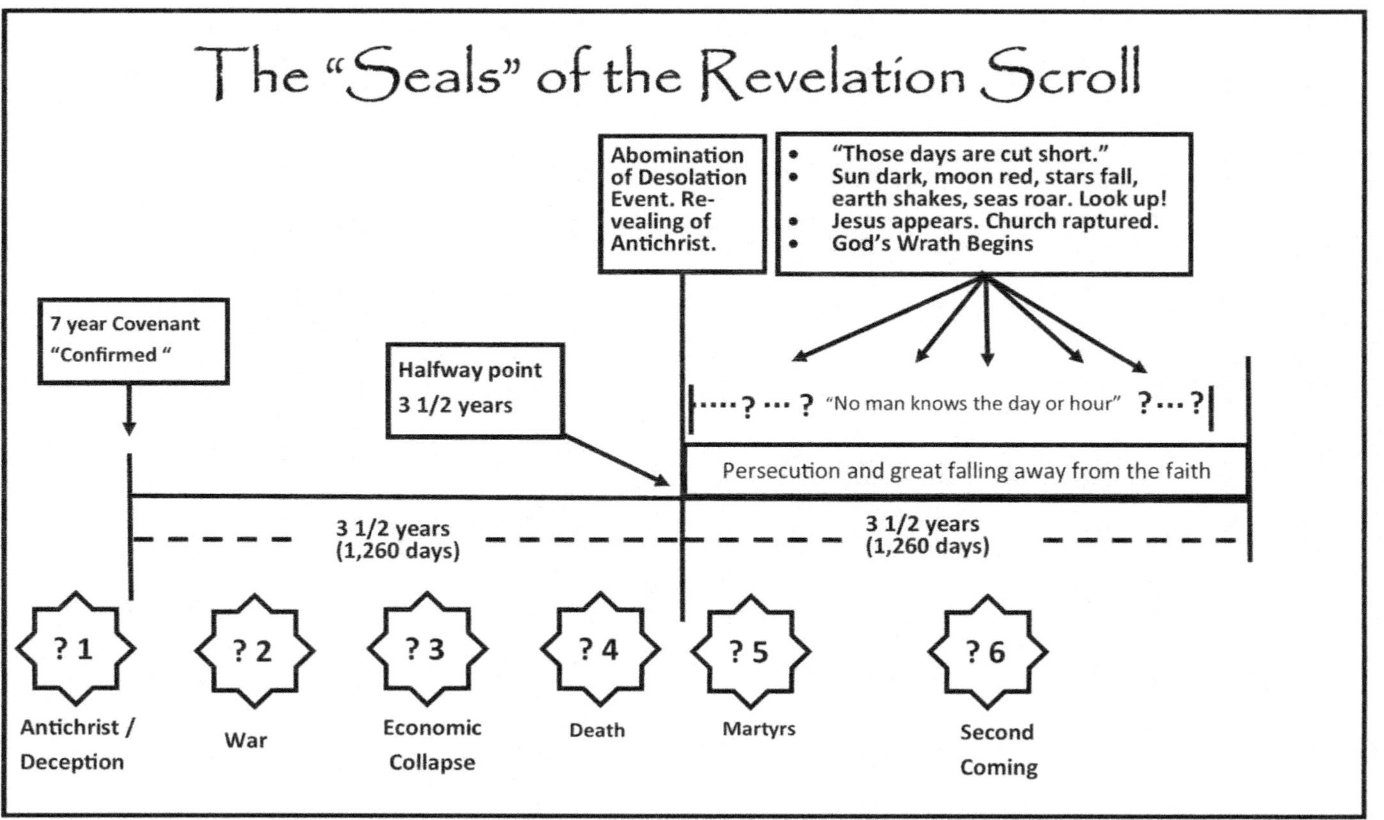
The "Seals" of the Revelation Scroll
7 year Covenant "Confirmed "
Halfway point
3 1/2 years
Abomination of Desolation Event. Re-vealing of Antichrist.
"Those days are cut short."
Sun dark, moon red, stars fall, earth shakes, seas roar. Look up!
Jesus appears. Church raptured.
God's Wrath Begins
....? ... ? "No man knows the day or hour" ?...?
Persecution and great falling away from the faith
3 1/2 years (1,260 days)
3 1/2 years (1,260 days)
? 1
Antichrist / Deception
? 2
War
? 3
Economic Collapse
? 4
Death
? 5
Martyrs
? 6
Second Coming

Summary

There are many passages in the Bible that speak of the same End of the Age that Jesus was speaking about to his disciples on the Mount of Olives. Since they all deal with the same period of time, it makes sense that there will be similarities. By overlaying the passages where it is safe to say they are referring to the same events, we can fill in a great deal of detail.

During His Mount of Olives talk to His disciples prior to His crucifixion, Jesus gave them an idea what the End of the Age will look like from an earthly perspective. During Jesus' later revelation to the Apostle John, who was also present for the first talk on the Mount of Olives, Jesus revealed details regarding the End of the Age from the unique and awe inspiring perspective of being in the throne room of God. Two different perspectives same events. Those events are:

1) Deception at the hand of the Antichrist
2) An increase in war
3) An increase in famine and outrageous inflation
4) An increase in the death rate
5) Unprecedented persecution

As we have previously learned, since deception, war, famine, death, and persecution have always been a part of history, even though these things will greatly increase at the end of the age, they can only be looked at as "soft" signs. The exception is the persecution associated with the Antichrist after he is revealed by means of committing the act of the Abomination of Desolation.

The persecution under the Antichrist's reign of terror will be so bad, that no human being would survive. However, for the sake of the elect of God, He will intervene and save His people. That is what we will see happen next in both Jesus' Olivet Discourse, and in His Revelation to John.

Notes

15. The Final Sign

Perfect submission, perfect delight
Visions of rapture now, burst on my sight…

Blessed Assurance, Jesus is Mine
Words by Fanny J Crosby 1873[78]

Forty days after Jesus rose from the dead in His new glorified body, He stood before His followers on the Mount of Olives, ready to ascend to Heaven and take His place next to His Heavenly Father (Acts 1:6-12). Five days before His resurrection, on the same mountain, Jesus gave His disciples the information He thought they needed to know about His return.

The Mount of Olives seemed to be the place to ask Jesus about the future. The last thing they asked Him before He started His ascent to Heaven was if He was now going to restore the Kingdom to Israel. Nothing had changed since the last time this topic came up on the Mount of Olives. Jesus told them that it was not for them to know.

Instead of Jesus telling them when the Kingdom of Heaven would be brought to this world, Jesus told them that the Holy Spirit would come upon them and give them "power." They were to use that power to be His "witnesses" in Jerusalem and throughout the entire world (Acts 1:6-8).

After Jesus gave His servants their final assignment, He defied nature as "He was lifted," up into the clouds. Afterwards, an angel satisfied a little of their curiosity and informed the awestruck disciples that Jesus would be returning to earth in much the same way as He just left it (Acts 1:11). He will be in the sky and in plain sight.

All of the events we have looked at so far will serve as signs that the return of Jesus is imminent and require foreknowledge in order to have the ability to recognize them. However, the next sign that Jesus spoke of on the Mount of Olives will be unmistakable. It won't matter if a believer was ever aware of it beforehand, because it will result in every elected follower of Christ, awake, sleeping, or dead, being "collected" or "gathered" to Jesus.

The Church Will Not Suffer the Wrath of God

The gathering of believers to Jesus at His Coming is the event commonly referred to as the "rapture" of the Church. Although many traumatic and catastrophic events have been mentioned by Jesus, nowhere up to this point in His Olivet Discourse has there been any mention of the "wrath of God" being poured out on the earth. This is consistent with what we know from elsewhere in scripture: The Church will not suffer the wrath of God.

Those who support the pretribulation rapture position say the Church will not suffer God's wrath. They use this as one of their chief arguments. However, they associate all of the events within the seven-year tribulation period with the Day of the Lord, and the wrath of God. Since they do so, they are led to the conclusion that the Church will be raptured some time prior to the tribulation period beginning.

If there is one key point of failure in the pretribulation rapture point of view, it is that they fail to recognize the difference between the "tribulation period," and the "Day of the Lord." Although the Day of the Lord (God's Wrath) begins sometime within the second half of the tribulation period, the two terms are not synonymous.

The "Pre-Wrath" rapture theory, says that the Church will be rescued from this earth (raptured) just before the Day of the Lord begins and the wrath of God is poured out on the earth. The Pre-Wrath rapture position recognizes that deceptive teaching, the coming of false messiahs, persecution of Jews and Christians at the hand of the Antichrist, wars, famines, disease, economic collapse, and widespread death *are not* what should be considered a part of the Day of the Lord. Rather, those things are part of living in a world that is groaning and travailing and being run by an evil tyrant.

Both the Pre-Wrath rapture and the Pretribulation rapture positions agree that the Church will not suffer God's wrath for very sound reasons found in scripture.

And to wait for his Son from heaven, whom he raised from the dead, even Jesus, which delivered us from the wrath to come. 1 Thess 1:10 (KJV)

For God hath not appointed us to wrath, but to obtain salvation by our Lord Jesus Christ, 1 Thess 5:9 (KJV)

If we were to discard any theories pertaining to the rapture of the Church that we have previously been taught (like the pretribulation rapture theory), we would have no reason to believe from scripture that a rapture has previously taken place up to this point in the Olivet Discourse.

The scriptures below describe the final signs prior to the Second Coming of Christ. They describe the point at which the elect of God are rescued, and the Day of the Lord, which has been foretold by both Old Testament and New Testament prophets, will be announced. The Day of the Lord is a time directly associated with the pouring out of God's wrath. God's wrath eventually destroys almost every recognizable geological feature of the earth and most of its inhabitants.

We can now conclude anything prior to the Second Coming event cannot be considered a part of the Day of the Lord and God's wrath. Consequently, any event prior to this point in the Olivet Discourse does not qualify the Church as suffering God's wrath.

The Most Spectacular Event Ever to Be

Jesus had just finished speaking of the persecution and death of His followers, the Abomination of Desolation, and fleeing when he said the following:

Matthew 24:29-31

Immediately after the tribulation of those days shall the sun be darkened, and the moon shall not give her light, and the stars shall fall from heaven, and the powers of the heavens shall be shaken: And then shall appear the sign of the Son of man in heaven: and then shall all the tribes of the earth mourn, and they shall see the Son of man coming in the clouds of heaven with power and great glory. And he shall send his angels with a great sound of a trumpet, and they shall gather together his elect from the four winds, from one end of heaven to the other. (KJV)

Immediately after the persecution of those days, the sun will be darkened and the moon will not yield its light, and the stars shall fall from heaven, and the powers of the heavens shall be

shaken. And then the sign of the Son of Man shall be seen in heaven. And then all the tribes of the earth will mourn and they will see the Son of Man coming on the clouds of heaven with power and great glory. And He will send His angels with the sounding of a great trumpet, and they will gather together His elect from the four winds, from one end of the heavens to the other. (DHT)

Mark 13:24-27

But in those days, after that tribulation, the sun shall be darkened, and the moon shall not give her light, And the stars of heaven shall fall, and the powers that are in heaven shall be shaken. And then shall they see the Son of man coming in the clouds with great power and glory. And then shall he send his angels, and shall gather together his elect from the four winds, from the uttermost part of the earth to the uttermost part of heaven. (KJV)

But in those days after the persecution, the sun will be darkened and the moon will not yield its light. And the stars shall fall out of the heavens and the powers that are in heaven shall be shaken. And then the Son of Man will appear coming in the clouds with power and great glory. And then He will send angels and they will gather together His elect from the four winds, from the uttermost part of the earth to the uttermost part of heaven. (DHT)

Luke 21:25-28

And there shall be signs in the sun, and in the moon, and in the stars; and upon the earth distress of nations, with perplexity; the sea and the waves roaring; Men's hearts failing them for fear, and for looking after those things which are coming on the earth: for the powers of heaven shall be shaken. And then shall they see the Son of man coming in a cloud with power and great glory. And when these things begin to come to pass, then look up, and lift up your heads; for your redemption draweth nigh. (KJV)

And there will be signs in the sun, and the moon, and the stars. The nations of the earth will be distressed and perplexed. The waves of the sea will roar. Men's hearts will fail them out of fear. And looking forward with expectation to what is coming on the earth, the powers of heaven shall be shaken. And then they will see the Son of Man coming in a cloud with power and great glory. And when these things begin to happen, lift your heads and look up, for your deliverance and redemption is drawing near. (DHT)

According to some, there will be no warnings prior to the Second Coming of Christ. They claim that there will be two Second Comings of Christ; The first one will be in secret. That is when, they say, that Christ will return to rapture (gather) His Church. All of those who are "saved," will simply vanish from the earth and be taken away. Then later, the second, Second Coming of Christ will be for all to see. Those who hold to this theory dissect the available prophetic scriptures pertaining to Christ's coming; devoting some of them to a secret coming and some to a coming of Jesus for all to see.

There are many problems with the secret rapture theory, but the largest, as we will see, is that once one compares all of the scriptures with each other pertaining to the Second Coming of Christ, the scriptures are all "used up." There are none left to support two different Second Comings.

The coming of the Messiah will clearly not be in secret. Jesus goes from talking about the persecution of those that believe in Him, right into the sign of His coming. Even going so far as to say "*immediately* after the distress of those days…"

There are two hints that such an event would take place prior to this in the Olivet Discourse:

And except those days should be shortened, there should no flesh be saved: but for the elect's sake those days shall be shortened. Matt 24:22 (KJV)

For wheresoever the carcase is, there will the eagles be gathered together. Matt 24:28 (KJV)

The rapture event we are now looking at, is the "shortening" of "those days." What we now see, is the "eagles" (angels) gathering the "carcasses," (the elect).

The following is a composite of the final signs that will accompany the Second Coming of Christ as recorded in three synoptic gospels (Matthew, Mark, & Luke) quoted above.

- **The Sun appears to "go black."**
- **The moon loses its light.**
- **The stars appear to "fall from the sky."**
- **The "powers of the heavens" will be "shaken."**
- **The waves of the seas become very violent and "roar."**
- **People experience great fear (they are anguished and perplexed) because of "what is coming" on the world.**
- **Jesus then appears in "power and glory."**
- **There is a loud "trumpet call."**
- **The "elect" are gathered from every corner of the world.**

A Confession

I held the view for many years that Jesus would originally come in secret simply because that is what I had been taught my entire life. Before my intensive study of the scriptures, I whole-heartedly bought in to the pretribulation rapture theory. I believed Jesus' return would happen without warning and could literally happen at any minute of any day. I have been in many church services on Sunday morning that ended with the pastor inviting people back for the Sunday evening service, "unless Christ would return that afternoon."

What a happy, twenty-first century, American, worry free, responsibility free, night-before-Christmas-like-anticipation thing to have believed in. I did not trade this theory for what I now believe to be the truth easily. I would love to say that I still think Jesus will suddenly show up and quietly catch us away without any warning, and before anything bad happens. However, decades of study, prayer, seeking others opinions, and meditation have lead me to a different conclusion. My hope is no less great, just more biblically based.

It is a complicated house of cards that makes the pretribulation rapture theory work, but for a number of reasons, *most* modern day Evangelical Christians still believe in that house of cards. Statistically, most who are reading this book still believe it. The theory is commonly taught from the pulpit by those pastors who at least have enough courage to talk about the end of the age at all. Pastors are still taught this theory in most conservative Christian seminaries, and few have the courage to rock the boat.

Thank God, Disciples of Christ can still learn about the Second Coming and the end of the age from Jesus' own words, rather than from a seminary.

Why Is the Pretribulation Theory Accepted as True by Most Christians If It Is Not True?

It is my own opinion most pastors believe that the study of the end of the age (eschatology) is too complicated and controversial to attempt to gain a more in-depth understanding. How much more difficult would it be then to teach this topic to others once a week in under an hour and fifteen minutes, including worship music, offering, and prayer? Like college professors with break through ideas in their field of expertise who don't want to take on the world of academia, only to be branded a fool, most pastors don't want to go out on their own and differ with their seminary, conference, and elders. Nor do they want to upset their congregation by teaching them something other than a pain free, End of the Age theory.

Like so many other aspects of Christian doctrine, we want to make people "feel good," so we sugar coat things. We can all be "healthy, wealthy, and happy in Christ." "If we follow God's plan our lives here on earth will go great for us." We don't like plainly presenting things that are difficult to hear because we think we will lose our audience or at the very least make someone sad or worried.

It is difficult to risk offending people with a blunt presentation of the truth. A God that would never allow me, or anyone else to suffer, is a much easier God to "sell." So, when the details of the pretribulation rapture theory don't really feel right or make total sense, pastors and teachers engage in cognitive dissonance and attempt to place their faith in something unworthy of it.

A Thief in The Night

Many (not all) Pre-tribulation rapturists say Christ's return will be imminent and they talk of His "secret coming," a coming other than the famous "Second Coming." The secret coming is a main part of what they refer to as the "Blessed Hope." It is this "secret coming" in which Christ will rapture His Church. Pretribulationists rely on scriptures that say that Jesus will return as a "thief in the night," normally failing to point out the second part of the scripture;

For yourselves know perfectly that the day of the Lord so cometh as a thief in the night. For when they shall say, Peace and safety; then sudden destruction cometh upon them, as travail upon a woman with child; and they shall not escape. ***But ye, brethren, are not in darkness, that that day should overtake you as a thief.*** *Ye are all the children of light, and the children of the day: we are not of the night, nor of darkness. 1 Thess 5:2-5 (KJV)* (Emphasis added).

The group of Christians that the Apostle Paul is addressing in his letter are being told that unlike non-believers, they do not have to be caught off guard and surprised by the Day of the Lord. As we have seen, there will be signs that precede it.

Likewise, those that hold the pretribulation rapture view are quick to point out the following verse about Christ's return, implying that it means Christ's return will be a total surprise.

But of that day and hour knoweth no man, no, not the angels of heaven, but my Father only. Matt 24:36 (KJV)

Those who believe in the imminent, no warning return of Christ do sometimes admit that we can recognize the general "season" that Christ will return, but not the day or hour. This is in fact very biblically based truth. However, the signs that they cite as indicators of the "season" of Christ's return, being very subjective, have almost always indicated that the season of the Messiah's return must be "now."

If we can determine where in sequence the rapture of the Church takes place in relation to the prophetic events that will actually be significant, such as the Abomination of Desolation, we will want to watch for those significant events that precede the rapture. Logically, if we have the ability to recognize those events, and are watching for them, we will "not be caught sleeping" like the rest of the world. Like Paul said, there is no need to be caught off guard if one truly is a child "of the light." Children of the light will be able to recognize the season, guard against deception, and while not knowing the "day or hour," we will know that Christ's return will be very soon.

The Imminent Return of Jesus

The doctrine of the imminent return of Christ is very important to many modern day evangelicals. I have had my eternal standing with Christ called to question over the issue by those that passionately hold to that belief. I do completely agree that you could be meeting Jesus face to face in the next few hours. However, unless you are reading this after the Antichrist has committed the Abomination of Desolation I believe that it will only mean that you have dropped over dead. It will not mean Jesus has raptured His Church. Either way, I hope to see you at the rapture!

Staunch defenders of the Pretribulation Rapture Theory base much of their defense of that theory on the doctrine of the imminent return of Jesus. They tend to place that doctrine higher in importance than what scripture plainly says. In other words, scripture cannot say that there will be any signs prior to the coming of Jesus because of the doctrine of His imminent return.

The return of Jesus will be imminent for everyone, in that no one knows when the future seven-year tribulation period will begin. Then, once it does begin and the Abomination of Desolation takes place, not even those who are watching will know when, in the next three and a half years Jesus will return.

Certainly those not watching for the return of the Lord will be overtaken by Jesus like He is a "thief in the night." The doctrine of the imminent return of Jesus will hold true for them. That group will unfortunately include many Christians who are not looking for the hard signs Jesus gave, because they have been taught there will not be any.

The bottom line is that we should not hold scripture accountable to fit into doctrines, such as the doctrine of the imminent return of Jesus. We should hold doctrines accountable to fit in to scripture.

"Children of the light," do not need to be caught off guard. Although we won't know the "day or hour," because we have been given signs, we will know when the time is near.

The Second Coming and The Rapture Are the Same

In the Olivet Discourse, the Second Coming of Christ is tied directly to the "gathering of the elect," which immediately follows the signs in the heavens. Specific, unmistakable, and awesome signs and events like this that makes it easy to compare scripture with scripture and sometimes determine that they are talking about the same event.

See if you find any similarities between the Olivet Discourse passage concerning the signs in the heavens, and the following scripture from Revelation chapter six, when the sixth seal of the scroll of God's Judgment is loosed;

And I beheld when he had opened the sixth seal, and, lo, there was a great earthquake; and the sun became black as sackcloth of hair, and the moon became as blood; And the stars of heaven fell unto the earth, even as a fig tree casteth her untimely figs, when she is shaken of a mighty wind. And the heaven departed as a scroll when it is rolled together; and every mountain and island were moved out of their places. And the kings of the earth, and the great men, and the rich men, and the chief captains, and the mighty men, and every bondman, and every free man, hid themselves in the dens and in the rocks of the mountains; And said to the mountains and rocks, fall on us, and hide us from the face of him that sitteth on the throne, and from the wrath of the Lamb: For the great day of his wrath is come; and who shall be able to stand? Rev 6:12-17 (KJV)

Here the Apostle John was having a vision of very similar signs Jesus said would take place immediately preceding His coming:

- The sun goes black.
- The moon turns red (loses its light in the Olivet Discourse).
- The stars appear to fall from the sky.

Several things happen next in John's vision; the commoners, the rich, and rulers of nations hide in caves and among the rocks out of fear of what God will do to them. Recognizing that this is a supernatural sign they announce "*the great day of the Lord has come*!"

After the announcement that the Day of the Lord has come, 144,000 descendants of the tribes of Israel, who are to remain on the earth, are "sealed." Since they, unlike the Church, will remain on the earth throughout the "Day of the Lord," in which God's wrath will be poured out, they are given God's seal of supernatural protection (Rev. 7:1-8). After this, with John's perspective being in Heaven, he witnesses the following;

After this I beheld, and, lo, a great multitude, which no man could number, of all nations, and kindreds, and people, and tongues, stood before the throne, and before the Lamb, clothed with white robes, and palms in their hands; Rev 7:9 (KJV)

Who are these people who suddenly show up in Heaven after the sun appears to go black, the moon appears to turn red, and the stars appear to fall from the sky? From earlier descriptions in Revelation of the scene in Heaven, we know that this group was not previously present. They have only shown up after the "sixth seal" was broken and before the seventh and final seal was loosed. They have suddenly appeared.

It is clearly not the group of 144,000 descendants of the tribes of Israel that suddenly shows up in Heaven. This group is a multitude that "no one could count." They were not from only one people, such as the Hebrews, but from "every nation, tribe, and people." If you don't know who this group is, don't feel bad. John didn't know who they were either, until an "Elder" told him.

And one of the elders answered, saying unto me, what are these which are arrayed in white robes? and whence came they? And I said unto him, Sir, thou knowest. And he said to me, these are they which came out of great tribulation, and have washed their robes, and made them white in the blood of the Lamb. Rev 7:13-14 (KJV)

These people had just come "out of" the tribulation. Apparently they showed up as one big group and are people who have had their robes made "white" by what Jesus did for them at the cross. These people didn't trickle into heaven as they died over a period of thousands of years. They were suddenly present and came "out of the great tribulation." Do you see the similarity here and what happened as described by Jesus on the Mount of Olives?

Comparison:
Olivet Discourse

- Sign of The Sun Moon and Stars
- The Heavens Are Shaken
- Gathering of Gods Elect from The Entire Earth
- Great Fear by Those Remaining On Earth of What Is Coming

Revelation 6 & 7

- Sign of The Sun, Moon, And Stars
- A Great Earthquake Takes Place
- God's Elect Show Up in Heaven
- Great Fear of the Day of the Lord from Those Remaining On Earth
- Day of The Lord Is Declared to Have Now Come

I have greatly boiled down the passages in the above comparison, but it does accurately show the essence of the events that take place.

Other Scripture Passages

There are several other passages of scripture that talk about the above specific end times events mentioned in the Olivet Discourse and Revelation chapters six and seven.

I Thessalonians 4:16-17

For the Lord himself shall descend from heaven with a shout, with the voice of the archangel, and with the trump of God: and the dead in Christ shall rise first: Then we which are alive and remain shall be caught up together with them in the clouds, to meet the Lord in the air: and so shall we ever be with the Lord. 1 Thess 4:16-17 (KJV)

Absent from this passage is the mention of the sign of the sun, moon, and stars, but let's again compare this scripture with the Matthew 24 passage listed earlier.

Comparison:
1 Thessalonians 4:13-17

- Lord Returns with The Voice of The "Archangel" And with A Loud Trumpet Call
- The Dead and Alive in Christ Are "Caught Up" To Be with The Lord

Olivet Discourse

- Christ Returns with His Angels and A Trumpet Call
- The Elect of God Are Gathered from Throughout the Earth

We are either talking about the same very similar event or there have been three raptures described in all of the above very similar passages.

Here is another:

<u>II Thessalonians 2:1-4</u>

Now we beseech you, brethren, by the coming of our Lord Jesus Christ, and by our gathering together unto him, that ye be not soon shaken in mind, or be troubled, neither by spirit, nor by word, nor by letter as from us, as that the day of Christ is at hand. Let no man deceive you by any means: for that day shall not come, except there come a falling away first, and that man of sin be revealed, the son of perdition; Who opposeth and exalteth himself above all that is called God, or that is worshipped; so that he as God sitteth in the temple of God, shewing himself that he is God. 2 Thess 2:1-4 (KJV)

The topic that Paul is concerned with in II Thessalonians 2 is the coming of our Lord Jesus Christ, and the Church being gathered together to Him. Paul pairs the Second Coming and the rapture together. He also associates those two things with yet another event; the Day of the Lord. Paul explains that the Day of the Lord, will not occur until after a "falling away" takes place, and that the "man of sin" (the Antichrist) has been revealed. This "man of sin," will be revealed by "proclaiming himself to be God" (committing the Abomination of Desolation).

Comparison:
II Thessalonians 2

- A "Falling Away" Takes Place

- The Antichrist Commits the Abomination of Desolation
- Jesus Returns
- The Church Is Gathered to Jesus
- The Day of the Lord Begins

Olivet Discourse

- Many Will "Fall Away"
- The Antichrist Commits the Abomination of Desolation
- Jesus Returns
- The Church Is Gathered to Jesus

I Corinthians 15:51-52

Behold, I shew you a mystery; We shall not all sleep, but we shall all be changed, in a moment, in the twinkling of an eye, at the last trump: for the trumpet shall sound, and the dead shall be raised incorruptible, and we shall be changed. 1 Cor 15:51-52 (KJV)

Comparison:
1 Corinthians 15:51-52

- Trumpet Sounds
- The Dead and Alive in Christ Are All "Changed"

Olivet Discourse

- Trumpet Sounds
- The Elect Are Gathered

Revelation Chapter 14

In the Book of Revelation, chapter 14, several events take place. We have already looked at one of those events involving the "eternal gospel" (Revelation 14:6-7). A little later in Revelation chapter 14 we see the following "harvest" take place:

And I looked, and behold a white cloud, and upon the cloud one sat like unto the Son of man, having on his head a golden crown, and in his hand a sharp sickle. And another angel came out of the temple, crying with a loud voice to him that sat on the cloud, thrust in thy sickle, and reap: for the time is come for thee to reap; for the harvest of the earth is ripe. And he that sat on the cloud thrust in his sickle on the earth; and the earth was reaped. Rev 14:14-16 (KJV)

Jesus, is the "one like a son of man." The "Son of Man" is the phrase often used to address Jesus (about twenty-nine times in the Gospel of Matthew alone). Jesus is given the go ahead to harvest the earth. This harvest is quite different than the one that immediately follows in Revelation in which the wicked of the earth are harvested and thrown into the "great winepress of God's wrath." Assuming that those that Jesus is harvesting are the righteous, as opposed to the wicked, which are "harvested separately," this passage also matches up nicely with the Olivet Discourse.

Comparison:
Revelation 14

- The "Eternal Gospel" is spread through the entire world
- Jesus harvests the earth.

Olivet Discourse

- The gospel is spread through the entire world
- Jesus sends forth His angels to harvest the elect.

To paint an even more complete picture of this cosmic event of the sign of the Sun, Moon, and Stars, let's look into the Old Testament.

Joel 2:30-32

And I will shew wonders in the heavens and in the earth, blood, and fire, and pillars of smoke. The sun shall be turned into darkness, and the moon into blood, before the great and the terrible day of the Lord come. And it shall come to pass, that whosoever shall call on the name of the Lord shall be delivered: for in mount Zion and in Jerusalem shall be deliverance, as the Lord hath said, and in the remnant whom the Lord shall call. Joel 2:30-32 (KJV)

Recognize the events again? Wonders in the heavens, a red moon, and a darkened sun. Did you get the part about everyone, not just the Jewish nation, who calls on the name of the Lord, "*whom the Lord calls,*" will be saved? Most importantly, did you notice that this event, the same event Jesus spoke of in Matthew 24 and revealed to the Apostle John in Revelation 6, comes "***before*** *the coming of the great and dreadful day of the Lord?*"

Comparison;
Joel 2:30-32

- Sign in The Heavens, Sun, And Moon.
- Those whom the "Lord Calls" (His Elect) Are Saved *Before* the Day of the Lord.

Olivet Discourse

- Sign of The Sun Moon and Stars.
- Gathering of Gods Elect Are Saved

Acts Chapter 2

In the book of Acts, on the day of Pentecost, we find the Apostle Peter quoting the Book of Joel. Please notice the New Testament verification that this sign comes *before* the "Day of the Lord."

And I will shew wonders in heaven above, and signs in the earth beneath; blood, and fire, and vapour of smoke: The sun shall be turned into darkness, and the moon into blood, ***before that great and notable day of the Lord come:*** *And it shall come to pass, that whosoever shall call on the name of the Lord shall be saved. Acts 2:19-21 (KJV)* (Emphasis added)

Other Passages

Daniel, the very book that Jesus cites in the Olivet Discourse, adds consistent detail to what we have put together here. Daniel chapter 12 contains one of the Old Testament's best descriptions of the rapture. There we see the following sequence of events: 1. The Archangel Michael (the restrainer) stands back and allows Satan to do His worst (This happens at the mid-point of the seven-year period). 2. There is an unprecedented time of trouble for Israel. 3. Those whose names are found written in the book of life are saved. 4. There is a resurrection of the dead.

Isaiah chapter 13 speaks of the initiation of the Day of the Lord with consistency to the rest of the passages: the sun, moon, and stars lose their light, and heaven and earth are shaken.

The Coming of God's Wrath Announced After the Rapture

Just as we have not seen any indication of God's Wrath up to this point in the Olivet Discourse or any of the scriptures, it is very significant that the word "wrath" has not even been used up to the parallel point in the Book of Revelation (the sixth seal is broken). After this, the word for wrath is used several times (thirteen times total in the KJV) in the book of Revelation, and always in connection with *God's* wrath.

And said to the mountains and rocks, fall on us, and hide us from the face of him that sitteth on the throne, and from the wrath of the Lamb: ***For the great day of his wrath is come****; and who shall be able to stand? Rev 6:16-17 (KJV)* (Emphasis added)

God's wrath will not begin until we are well inside of the seven-year (seventieth week of Daniel) period, and only after the rapture occurs. The event of the sun, moon, and stars does more than accompany the rapture of the Church, and more than signal the return of Christ. This sign declares the Day of the Lord; the outpouring of God's wrath is about to start.

The sign of the sun, moon, and stars marks the end of act one. The curtains draw closed, and the stage is reset. The message is, "look out world," you have a much different situation on your hands as Jesus breaks the seventh and final seal on the scroll that contains God's judgment!

Although the Olivet Discourse does not directly address all of the events that take place in association with the Day of the Lord, the Revelation passage that is tied to the events of the Olivet Discourse does (See Revelation chapters 8 & 9).

After the Church has been rescued from the earth and the heavenly announcement is made that the great Day of God's wrath has come, with the opening of the seventh seal, seven trumpet-playing angels step forward in Heaven (Revelation chapter 8). As each angel plays their prophetic melody, a judgment from God is unleashed on the earth.

Before the angels start to play their trumpets, there is a "silence in Heaven" that seems to last for "a half hour" (Rev 8:1). This sober break in the action separates the prior tribulation related events of Revelation from the wrath of God, which is about to be poured out. It will be an awesome time for all that are witnessing this event from a heavenly vantage point to stop and revere.

Summary

Several passages of scripture throughout the Bible that are associated with the Second Coming of Christ tie into the framework of the Olivet Discourse. As we look at these passages together we can gain an increasingly clear and complete picture. It is a picture of one Second Coming of Christ and not two. It is not a picture of a "secret coming" and a separate Second Coming. All of the passages of His return and the gathering of His elect are referring to the same event.

The distinct similarities of the events described in these related scriptures bear witness to one, cohesive, composite picture of the rapture of the Church and Second Coming. These two events are inseparable. As we look at this picture, we see clearly that God's wrath starts immediately after the Church has been rescued away from the earth.

There are many more scriptures that pertain to the end of the age than we have considered in this chapter. What we have focused on here are only those that pertain to the specific signs that immediately precede the Second Coming of Christ and the rapture of the Church.

The chart on the following page uses only the scriptures cited in this chapter that directly deal with the Second Coming.

*See end note 79	Olivet Discourse	Revelation Ch. 6&7	Joel Chapter 2	I COR 15:51-52	I Thess 4:16-17	Acts Ch. 2:12	Revelation Ch. 14	II Thess 2:1-4	Isaiah Chapter 13
Gospel spread to entire earth	X						X		
Sign of Sun, moon, stars	X	X	X			X			X
Earth/ Heaven shaken	X	X	X						X
Trumpet / Shout	X		X	X	X				
Gather Elect	X	X	***X	X	X	***X	X	X	
Day of the Lord Preceded by the Antichrist	X	*X						X	
Resurrection of the Dead	** X			X	X				
Day of the Lord Begins		X	X			X		X	X

As you can see by the chart on the preceding page; although not one scripture passage contains all of the events, all of the scriptures are united by two or more significant events. By tying the scriptures together, we gain a more complete idea of what the Lords return will be like.

Composite Sequential Picture of the Second Coming of Jesus to This Earth

1. The Second Coming, rapture of the church, and Day of the Lord is preceded by the revealing of the Antichrist.
2. The gospel is spread to the entire earth.
3. The sign of the Sun, Moon and Stars occurs.
4. A great earthquake takes place. The "heavens" are shaken.
5. The seas become very violent and "roar."
6. The Lord appears to descend from the sky, coming on a cloud.
7. Jesus is accompanied by His holy angels.
8. There is a loud shout and a trumpet blast.
9. The dead who know Jesus as savior rise from the grave in their new bodies. They are gathered by angels to meet the Lord in the air.
10. Those who are alive at the time and know Jesus as savior change into imperishable bodies, and are gathered by His angels to meet the Lord in the air.
11. Jesus takes the elect back to heaven where they proclaim praises to god.
12. The Wrath of God (Day of the Lord) begins.

16. Something is Wrong With the Lights

Signs

One day a man was driving along a four-lane highway in a small city in Oregon and missed a traffic signal. A few months later the District Attorney put out a statement regarding the opinion of Oregon courts.

> "*Mere inadvertence, brief inattention, or errors in judgment*" (now to paraphrase), "*have been found to not be good enough reasons to charge someone with running a red light and killing three children all under the age of nine, and critically injuring their mother.*"

On that February day, the traffic signal failed to adequately warn the driver of the car that he needed to take action and stop. The investigation revealed the man wasn't under the influence of any intoxicants, wasn't speeding, wasn't texting or on the phone, wasn't distracted by any activity or sleepy, and didn't have any medical issues. The sun wasn't in his eyes and the traffic signal was functioning as designed. In his humanness, the driver just missed the signal. I can only imagine how much he regrets doing so.

The world is full of signs and signals that provide information, make recommendations, signal warnings, or tell us what to do. When you see a sign, generally you have a decision to make and then you either take action or ignore the sign.

Some people look for "signs" to help guide them through life. Several people in history have been attributed with saying, "*we don't see things as they are, we see things as we are.*" Whoever first said it, these are words to listen to when one is looking for "signs" in their life.

One who looks through the lens of "hating" their job may look at it as a "sign" if they find their car battery dead in the morning that they should not go to work that day. Another person who loves their job (*yes, this happens*), when they discover their battery is dead in the morning, will look at the same event as a sign that they should replace their battery.

How can we know if we are really being given a sign or not? If I have to ask that question, the answer I always go back to is, it probably was not a sign. God is not a poor communicator.

God installed signs into His creation. We all pick up on things in nature when there are changes in the air. God made it so that communication from one person to another is primarily (93%) made up of non-verbal cues and signals.[80] Failing to recognize signals in creation, especially where it involves interpersonal relationships, can result in all sorts of calamity.

God provided many signs that we can read about in the Bible. They established the authority of His Son and the Prophets. Unlike a stoplight, they cannot be missed. However, in cases like Moses and Pharaoh, these signs were still often ignored.

People's lives are full of "signs" pointing the way to God. The heavens declare who He is. All of His wondrous creation stands as a complex sign pointing the way to the Creator. God puts people and situations in our lives that serve as signs pointing to the reality of who He is and what we need to do to have a relationship with Him. Yet, just like Pharaoh, people choose to ignore the signs.

One Sign, Two Meanings

No one will miss the signal indicating the return of Jesus to this earth. There need be no confusion about what it will look like. It will not be subtle or quiet. However, the final sign God provides will be different. God's unmistakable signal, which indicates His Son's return, will mean two different things to two different groups of people.

If you are a follower of Christ, when the earth starts to violently shake and you see the sun and moon go dark, and the stars appear to fall from the sky, it means the wait for your rescue is over. It means you are about to be given an immortal body and go into the presence of, and be accepted by the Almighty God.

If you are not a follower of Christ, and you see the same sign in the sun, moon and stars, it means you have ignored all previous signs and waited too long to take action. It means you are appointed to suffer the wrath of God. Any action taken, must be taken before this final signal occurs and not after. To one group, the sign means "*congratulations.*" To the other group, it means, "*you are too late.*"

What Form Will the Sign Actually Take?

The preceding chapter looked at how several passages of scripture document the future prophetic event of the sun going black, the moon also not giving its light, or turning "blood red," the stars appearing to fall from the sky, and the entire earth being shaken. A face value read of those events sounds dramatic, ominous, and awe inspiring to say the least.

In this chapter, we will look deeper into this final sign. We will attempt to arrive at a conclusion as to the form of this sign. This will be based on what the Bible has to say, rather than what Hollywood has, or what the latest alarmist, Pop-Christian book has tried to sell as possible truth.

The sign in the Sun, Moon, and Stars, that accompany a worldwide earthquake sound like they will work together to be an unmistakable sign that the Lord's return is imminent. However, on the surface, scripture appears to be silent as to exactly what causes the sun to go black, the moon to turn red, and the stars appear to fall from the sky. It is also silent as to what extent these things occur. Further, there is little if any information as to the timing and sequence of these events. Because of this, I am forced to admit that my belief that this sign will be unmistakable is based on logic and not a quote from a biblical prophet. It is therefore a worthy issue to look into further.

The Moon Loses its Light and Turns Red

On the explain-it-away-by-natural-phenomenon end of the spectrum, we know that a natural phenomenon known as a lunar eclipse can result in a moon that appears to be red in color. During a full eclipse of the moon, the earth lies directly between the sun and the moon. The earth blocks the sun's light from the moon, thereby causing the moon to "lose its light." What we see going across the face of the moon is the earth's shadow. When the moon is centered in the earth's shadow, the sun's light passes around the earth in earth's atmosphere. If the earth had no atmosphere, the moon would just appear black when the sun's light was blocked from it. As light bends around the earth in its atmosphere, all of the light except that of the red portion of the light spectrum is filtered out. This is due to a scientific principle known as the "Rayleigh scattering." [81]

The light from the red portion of the spectrum is cast on the moon, causing it to appear red to humans here on planet earth. The amount of dust in the atmosphere dictates the intensity of this phenomenon. Years where there is volcanic activity, the red moon during lunar eclipses is most pronounced.[82]

There is a rare lunar eclipse known as a "tetrad." A tetrad is when you have four total lunar eclipses six months apart from each other, without any partial eclipses in between. [83] That is a pretty specific series of events. A tetrad was completed as recently as the September of 2015. The first lunar eclipse took place April, 2014, the second, was on October 8, 2014, while I was in the Hells Canyon National Recreation area hunting for deer. The moon was so bright that night, everyone said you could read by its light. The next two full eclipses took place on April 4, 2015 and September 28, 2015.

Because of this most recent tetrad, and what has occurred in regard to Israel during the past three tetrads, Pastor and Author John Haggee, wrote a book called *Blood Moons*. "Blood Moon" is the name that Pastor Haggee gives the tetrad phenomenon. Several other authors also wrote books on the subject.

Quoting Luke 21 regarding the same sign of the sun, moon and stars, we are concerned with here, the Amazon.com advertisement for *Blood Moons* clearly attempts to imply that the recent tetrad possibly played an important part in that sign. [84]

The moon turning blood red is a specific sign that is revealed in conjunction with other signs (the sun going black, stars appearing to fall, and a great earthquake). As we have seen in the Olivet Discourse, that astro-phenomenon will take place after the Antichrist is revealed. On its own, without the other components of the final sign, I am not sure why a tetrad would be significant.

According to Hagee, tetrads have taken place in the past during significant times in Israel's history. The Bible does clearly tell us that the heavenly bodies will serve as signs and to mark days, years, and seasons (Genesis 1:14). There have been eight tetrads since the first century and only three out of four lunar eclipses during the current tetrad have been or will be visible in Israel, where Jesus was speaking.

We do know a specific detail from scripture that does give a full lunar eclipse a possible measure of merit. Revelation 6:12 says that the "full," or "whole" moon in some translations, appeared to turn blood red.

When he opened the sixth seal, I looked, and behold, there was a great earthquake, and the sun became black as sackcloth, ***the full moon*** *became like blood,* Revelation 6:12 (ESV) (Emphasis added).

This verse indicates that the entire moon, not a partial or crescent moon, appears to turn red in the sky. We can assume from this, that this sign will take place during a full moon as viewed from Israel. The Hebrew calendar is based on cycles of the moon. The moon is full in the middle of the Hebrew month. If the moon is "full," as stated in Revelation 6:12, when it appears to turn to blood, this sign will take place in the middle of one of the Hebrew months.

Is Jesus, in His Olivet Discourse, talking about a natural phenomenon such as the Rayleigh scattering during a full lunar eclipse?

My logic tells me that something, which happens on a regular and predictable basis, would not serve as much of a sign by its self. How many times has there been a red moon in the sky, explainable by natural phenomenon, and Jesus has not returned? By itself, a red moon seems pretty to look at, but too easy to miss to serve as a sign.

It is possible that one day a full lunar eclipse may serve as one of the components of the final signal that Jesus is returning. Whether or not this most recent tetrad serves to "signal" any significant future events that are about to take place (I will reserve judgment), it *should not* be confused with the specific sign that immediately precedes the coming of Jesus. To tie the event spoken of in the Olivet Discourse to the most recent tetrad was a misuse of scripture.

The Sun Grows Darker

Within every twenty-four-hour period, unless you live close to the North or South Pole during the summer months, the sun disappears from the sky as the earth rotates every twenty-four hours. Additionally, the sun occasionally goes black during a solar eclipse when the moon moves between the earth and the sun. Living in Oregon, sometimes the clouds cover the sun for days and you would hardly know it is there. In May of 1980, the volcanic ash from Mount St. Helens, in the State of Washington, totally blocked the sun as far as 930 miles away. Although not totally blocking the sun everywhere, the ash had completely encircled the globe within fifteen days. [85]

The original passage of Revelation 6 in the Greek indicates that the most literal translation pertaining to the sun going dark would be, "*the sun became black, like sackloth made of mohair.*" Sackcloth was made of goat's hair and commonly worn when someone was in mourning. It was also used as material for grain sacks. The imagery according to Revelation six would be like suddenly throwing this goat hair material over the sun.

The literal translation of the Matthew 24 passage would be that "the sun will be darkened" or "obscured." The Greek word for "darken," σκοτίζω, is transliterated at "skotizo." It means to "deprive of light, to make dark." The root of "skotizo" is transliterated into English as the word "ska" meaning "to cover."[86] Put these things together and we can say with certainty that the sun doesn't burn out. Its light is merely covered up and obscured by something.

The peak of solar eclipses, when the sun is fully darkened, only last about seven minutes and there is only a swath of the earth a few degrees wide in latitude that can see the eclipse. From any point on earth there is a solar eclipse only about once every 300 years.[87]

If, in Jerusalem, there would be complete solar and lunar eclipses within a short period of time of each other, they could possibly qualify as part of the final "sign." A quick check of on-line eclipse calculators doesn't show any total solar eclipses up through 2024 in that region of the world and there are only two total lunar eclipses in Israel between now and then. [88] This is not to say that the Lord's return must take place by 2024! It is only to say such occurrences are extremely rare. I am not sure solar and lunar eclipses will ever occur close together from a Jerusalem vantage-point. Even if it did, there is also the matter of the stars appearing to fall from the sky, and the world-wide earthquake that would also need to occur.

How much of a sign would it be if Jesus was merely referring to the sunset or an eclipse when he said, "immediately following those days the sun will be darkened?" I don't think this would be much of a sign:

> *"So when you see the sunset in the west, as it always has done since the first day of creation, and then a lunar eclipse occurs sometime within the next few months, like they do several times a year, then know that my return will happen at any time."*

The logic of these regular and natural occurrences serving as signs for the most significant event the universe will ever see, just doesn't seem to flow and make sense. I don't see people becoming "anxious" or "perplexed" as scripture puts it, as a result of such normal and natural occurrences.

Given the literal translations of the Matthew and Revelation passages pertaining to the darkening of the sun, the most likely scenario is that something covers up the sun besides the moon, which occurs every now and then. Given the rareness of lunar eclipses in Jerusalem, the extremely short time period involved, and the very limited amount of geographic space affected, it is likely that "something" that covers up the sun is not the moon.

We would have to speculate in order to say what will cover up the sun. Will it be something to do with the earthquake that is also mentioned? Volcanic dust? Dust from an asteroid that hits the earth? Clouds? Something entirely supernatural? No one knows.

A final indication that we are neither looking at a sunset or eclipse explanation of the sun being darkened is the additional language used in the Revelation six passage:

> *And the heavens departed as a scroll when it is rolled together; and every mountain and island were moved out of their places.* Revelation 6:14 (KJV)

In order for the sky to appear to "depart" or be "rolled up," as other translations put it, something is occurring that is way beyond an eclipse or sunset! Although pyroclastic flows from volcanic eruptions normally move along the ground at about 450 miles per hour, it could be something similar moving across the sky.

The Stars Appear to Fall from The Sky

Every year as Planet Earth passes through the same spots in the galaxy that it did the year before, regular predictable meteor showers take place. This is caused by cosmic dust left from a comet's tail as it burns up in our planet's atmosphere.

Every year in August on my wife's birthday, as we all pass through the same spot we did the year before, the Perseid meteor shower takes place. This is perhaps one of the best meteor showers to view from the Northern Hemisphere. It produces fifty to 100 meteors per hour that can be observed streaking across the sky. There are nine such major meteor showers that take place throughout the year. They are predictable because as the earth makes its laps around the sun, we annually pass through the same spots in the galaxy each year containing the cosmic dust.

A regular meteor shower, even when one or two "falling stars" are observed each minute, does not seem to fit the description given in Revelation chapter 6:

And the stars of heaven fell unto the earth, even as a fig tree casteth her untimely figs, when she is shaken of a mighty wind. Rev 6:13 (KJV)

Fig trees produced two crops in Israel. The early harvest, called the "bikkore" was harvested in June. The second crop, called the "kermouse" was harvested beginning in August and continuing through the winter into March.[89] The "kermouse" crop of figs would be the "winter fruit" that John refers to. It is likely that the Apostle John, the one who recorded the Revelation given to him by Jesus, used imagery that was familiar to him such as a fig tree being blown by a winter gale force wind. He would have likely been thinking that the reader of his letter to the seven churches in Asia (the Book of Revelation) would have had a good mental picture from the imagery he used.

Even those living in a non-fig tree region of the world, two thousand years after the Book of Revelation was written, can still relate to this imagery. Just today, the remnants of an October, Pacific Ocean, hurricane sent its winds inland to the Willamette Valley of Oregon where I live. The beautiful multicolored leaves were giving up their grip on the oak, ash, and maple trees and flying everywhere, providing quite the spectacle. It could not be missed and it had my wife's and I's complete attention.

Both Israel and the modern day coast of Turkey, where John was living at the time he wrote the book of Revelation, actually have higher average wind speeds in the summer time than winter. However, I am sure in John's ninety plus years on the planet, he, and many others, had witnessed figs flying out of the trees during especially large winter storms.

I have never seen a fig tree's winter fruit get shaken loose by a strong wind, but I have witnessed modern fruit tree harvesting devices that shake trees in order to get the ripe fruit to fall. When the machine is activated, the fruit does not come off one piece at a time. It happens quickly and in large numbers. This is what I would expect to see if a tree was being "buffeted" by "gale force winds." I would not expect to see one or two pieces per minute falling to the ground. Likewise, based on John's description of the "falling stars," I would not expect to see only one or two meteors per minute enter the earth's atmosphere like they do during a regular meteor shower.

Timing

Since there is no time frame specifically mentioned regarding these three signs, if we set logic aside, the signs could theoretically take place over a period of days, weeks, or even months. However, I do not believe this to be the case for several reasons:

1) The signs are mentioned in the scriptures as if they are one sign or a group of signs occurring in rapid succession.
2) Besides the necessity of the sun being darkened during the day and stars appearing to fall at night, there is nothing specifically raising the possibility that the three signs take place over an extended period of time,
3) The "immediate" language used in Matthew 24 seems to include all three phenomenon taking place "immediately" (Matt 24:29),
4) The reaction of those remaining on the earth is that of being "anguished" and "perplexed," as if completely overwhelmed,
5) Jesus said when these things begin to take place to "lift your head" and "look up" as if the next thing you will see is Him coming in the clouds.
6) The upcoming language we will see in Matthew 24 indicates people (both believers and non-believers) are going about their normal business when Jesus suddenly returns following these signs.

One thing we do know for sure from scripture regarding the timing of these fantastic things occurring in the sky, is that they follow the event of the "Abomination of Desolation." If we would see something like these astronomical events occur before the Abomination of Desolation takes place, even in the form of four "Blood Moons," over a period of two years, it would only be a "sign" that someone may be profiting from book and video sales, but nothing more.

It makes sense that the return of Jesus would occur immediately after this large, unmistakable worldwide sign in the heavens. After all Jesus said when you see this sign take place, "look up." I don't believe Jesus would tell His people to do something like "look up," if His return were beyond the normal period of time a human being could hold such a pose and stay awake! I personally think there will be just enough time to "look up," before we are gathered to Jesus and see Him in person. If Jesus were to delay beyond a very short period of time, my guess is that His instructions would have been more along the lines of "keep about my business." However, Jesus' command here to "look up," is as if to say, "your work on earth is done."

We know based on Matthew 24:36-44 that up until this sign people will be going about their relatively normal business. This sign is a game changer. If I, being watchful, after I had witnessed the Abomination of Desolation taking place, and my brothers and sisters in Christ subsequently being persecuted, then saw the Sign of the Sun, Moon, and Stars, along with a worldwide earthquake, I would not be going about my normal business any longer. I would be confidently searching the sky for my King and Savior.

We do not know when the covenant spoken of by the Prophet Daniel will be "confirmed" by the Antichrist, so we don't know what year in the future the seven-year tribulation period will begin. Because of the sign of the Abomination of Desolation, those alive at that time who are watching and recognize that sign will know that they are within three and a half years of the return of Christ. However, they still will have no way of knowing what day or hour His Coming will occur. Since this sign is so closely tied to the return of Jesus, no one will know the day or hour that these events will occur either.

Location

Based on scripture we don't know for sure the location where these signs will all be seen. It makes sense that they would be viewable from the region of the world that these prophecies were all given; the Middle East; specifically, Jerusalem. However, it also makes sense, especially in our day and age of digital and, almost instant knowledge of the news, the entire world will be aware that the signs in the heavens are occurring. At least while digital communication still exists.

When such events as these take place, it is very likely that our fragile digital communication infrastructure will be damaged to the point of uselessness. Watching events on television after this point, like some rapture books and movies have portrayed, will be very unlikely.

It is interesting that the three signs in the heavens include one that would only be evident during the day; the sun being darkened, and one that could only be seen at night; the stars falling from the sky, and one that could be seen during either time; the moon turning red. If God uses natural phenomenon to bring about these three signs, and if the intentions of the scriptures is that these three signs will be observable from one geographic location on the earth, it would mean that these three signs would have to span a period of time of at least several hours.

With the above discussion in mind, there is nothing in scripture indicating that all three signs must be observed from a single location on the earth. For example, the sun could be blotted out on one side of the earth where it is daylight hours. Whatever is blotting out the sun (dust, ash, etc.) could cause the sign of the full moon turning red, while an especially active meteor shower takes place in the night time sky elsewhere on the planet.

Supernatural Sign for A Supernatural Event

Finally, regarding what form this sign may take, God may not have it in His plan to use natural phenomenon to bring it about. He may cause all three things to appear in the same sky within a matter of seconds through supernatural means. This is after all the return of Jesus to the planet to establish His Kingdom.

It will be an event that will be worthy of the most supernatural of occurrences ever! Jesus, is going to appear from nowhere, riding on the clouds of the sky, in "power and great glory." Is it really a stretch to think that the sign in the sun, moon, and stars may occur supernaturally? The sign coming about in a supernatural way would seem to "perplex" people the most.

Ramifications of Not Getting It Exactly Right Ahead of Time

The final sign in the Sun, Moon, and Stars will indicate that the return of Lord Jesus is imminent. My hope is that the above discussion of what form this final sign may take, has shown you that there are several logical possible scenarios that could in the most literal sense fulfill the prophecies. Since we cannot narrow down and be dogmatic about exactly what this prophecy will look like, should we discard it and say it cannot be relied upon to provide an unmistakable sign? Absolutely not!

To review; one of the main reasons we are given prophecies like this is so we can recognize a legitimate sign *after or when it happens.* We are not given prophecy in order to make educated guesses about all of the "who, what, where, when, and how" details beforehand. Even this sign, as unmistakable as it seems it will be, has proven to be a perfect example of this point. The important thing is that the follower of Jesus is watchful for such things, is able to recognize them once they have occurred, and is not blinded by preconceived notions of how things might play out.

When this final astronomical sign occurs, what would it matter if we missed it or got what we were watching for wrong? It won't! All that will be left to do is leave this present world behind, because our "blessed hope" is at hand. Jesus said when you see this sign take place, "look up for your redemption draws near" (Luke 21:28).

The elect of God will be gathered to Jesus whether they observe the sign or not. I imagine those followers of Jesus left on the earth, when this sign occurs, who have somehow managed to escape the persecution of the Antichrist with their lives (and probably little more), will be very excited, relieved, and overcome with joy that they are about to be rescued by the Messiah. What a day that will be.

Christians Disappearing in The Rapture? No Big Deal at This Point

One of the things that has always troubled me, even when I thought the pretribulation rapture theory was correct, was that life would seemingly go on as usual after tens of millions of Christians would suddenly, without explanation, vanish from the face of the earth.

There have been a number of theories that would explain the mass disappearances. Mostly ones that Hollywood has attempted to fabricate. One explanation is that the remaining citizens of the world would demand some dynamic political figure, like the Antichrist, to put the world back together. With the Church out of the way, this would be more easily accomplished for such an evil based person.

Perhaps hundreds of millions of people would suddenly lose their loved ones. Can anyone really think that the world would just continue without them? Even the "wicked" left on the earth after such an event would demand answers in the aftermath for years. People would be so "freaked out" by the vanishing that they would likely not be able to function.

The prophecies regarding economic collapse we find in the Bible don't even come close to the kind of economic chaos that would ensue. With millions of people suddenly disappearing and the physical damage that would take place to infrastructure around the world as a result, the world would barely function at a level that the Antichrist would need to pull off a plan; his plan.

The only explanation that could possibly make sense to those that remained on the earth after the rapture is that the Christians must have been right all along about Jesus. It makes sense that there would be a great turning to God after such an event. Yet, that is not what we see occur in the Bible. People continue to reject God.

There is a much better logical fit for the timing of such an event as the rapture. A plausible explanation that would not cause these kind of concerns.

Post Abomination of Desolation Rapture Scenario

Following the midpoint of the tribulation period, just after the Abomination of Desolation takes place, we are told that the Antichrist will cause everyone to take his mark if they wish to buy or sell. Not taking the mark carries the death penalty. If you are a true follower of Christ or Jew at this point in the future and refuse the "mark" of the Antichrist, you will either be put to death, be put in prison, or go into hiding.

A few short months after the Antichrist has had an opportunity to execute his holocaust-like plans, there will not be many Christians or Jews left on the streets, or in their former homes.

Just as was the case in Nazi Germany only a few decades ago, it will again be in the future under the rule of the Antichrist.

Then, with Christians and Jews already scarce, add in a world-wide earthquake that will undoubtedly bury many people alive, wash them out to sea, and destroy most of the world's communication infrastructure. Information will be hard to come by. Tens or hundreds of millions of people, not just Christians, will suddenly disappear or be displaced from their homes because of this catastrophic event. Millions of nameless refugees will wander the countryside.

Because of persecution, most Christians will already be absent from people's everyday lives. What happened to the few that remained after the worldwide earthquake and subsequent tsunamis will seem obvious to the remaining inhabitants of the earth; they perished. This scenario, as opposed to millions of people suddenly disappearing without warning or natural explanation, leaving only a pile of neatly folded clothes or ashes behind, is much more plausible.

Summary

The envelope of how the prophecies of the Olivet Discourse, Joel chapter two, and Revelation chapter six concerning the sun, moon, and stars will play out is large. The range of what could take place within the parameters of the details recorded in scripture includes the possibility of God using natural phenomenon that take place now, to God accomplishing these signs totally through supernatural means.

This sign will most likely occur immediately preceding the Second Coming of Jesus and the Church's gathering to Him. Logic dictates that the sign will be recognizable apart from routine natural events that take place such as the sun setting, regular annual meteor showers or solar and lunar eclipses.

Although we don't know exactly how God will pull it off, the sign preceding the return of the Lord Jesus to this earth as its King, the coming of the Day of the Lord, the outpouring of the Almighty's wrath on this earth, and the end of this world as we know it is worthy of miraculous, never seen before, supernatural splendor.

This final sign that will take place in the heavens serves as a great reminder to the purpose of biblical prophecy of this type. It was not given to us so we can know all of the details beforehand of exactly what is going to happen. It was given so that after something happens we will recognize it for what it was. What a relief it will be for those Christians in the future who are around to see it happen. What a dreaded thing it will be for those who failed to heed the signs and act beforehand and come to know Jesus as their King and Savior.

Notes

17. Fig Trees and Mountains

The Mayan culture was thriving as early as 800 BC and its roots go all the way back to 2,000 BC. The Mayans had elaborate government systems, a communication and travel network, their own calendar, a system of writing and distinct religious practices that included human sacrifice. The total Mayan population could have been as high as 22 million, with up to 100,000 residents living in the ancient city of Tikal, alone. The last Mayan city fell in 1697, as a result of the Spanish colonization of Central America. The Mayans were as much of an established civilization as any in the Middle East at the time.

Perhaps some can remember back to the late 1940s, when the United Nations was clamoring to carve out a region in southern Mexico to create a new nation that would be the home of the ancient Mayan people? Or, maybe you remember hearing the headlines declaring how Mayans from around the world were moving back to their native lands 300 years after their once thriving civilization had disappeared? Mayans from around the globe were looking forward to restoring their ancient language and religious practices that included human sacrifice… No! Because none of this ever occurred.

How amazing and absurd would the above story be if it were true! Such an event of a lost civilization coming back together to become a modern, first-world power might be unknown to our planet if not for one such true story involving the nation of Israel. There are some important differences worth noting.

Israel fell out of existence for over 1,800 years, whereas it's only been 300 years that the Mayan's culture ceased to exist. Also, the Jewish residents of Israel were scattered throughout the world, where several purposeful attempts were made to erase them from history. Yet, in spite of the anti-Semitic efforts of Rome, the Inquisition, the Russian Czars, Hitler, and many others, in 1948 Israel again became a nation. It's rebirth, and subsequent survival has been nothing short of an epic miracle.

Around 2,500 years before Israel came back together as a nation, the Prophet Ezekiel was told by God that first the nation of Israel would cease to exist and be dispersed. This occurred, just as prophesied. Ezekiel was also given a vision from God that the nation of Israel would live again one day. Using a couple well-known symbols, Jesus also spoke about this event.

The Fig Tree

While speaking to His disciples on the Mount of Olives, Jesus moved from the topic of specific signs that will occur at His coming to speaking of recognition of the general season. Jesus often spoke in parables to illustrate concepts. Such is the case here.

Matthew 24:32-33

Now learn a parable of the fig tree; When his branch is yet tender, and putteth forth leaves, ye know that summer is nigh: So likewise ye, when ye shall see all these things, know that it is near, even at the doors. (KJV)

Now learn a parable of the fig tree. When his branch is still tender and it puts forth leaves, you know that summer is near. So likewise, when you shall see all these things, know that it is near; right at the door. (DHT)

Mark 13:28-29

Now learn a parable of the fig tree; When her branch is yet tender, and putteth forth leaves, ye know that summer is near: So ye in like manner, when ye shall see these things come to pass, know that it is nigh, even at the doors. (KJV)

Now learn a parable of the fig tree. When her branch is still tender and puts forth its leaves. You know that summer is near. In the same way, when you see these things happen, know that it is near; right at the doors. (DHT)

Luke 21:29-31

And he spake to them a parable; Behold the fig tree, and all the trees; When they now shoot forth, ye see and know of your own selves that summer is now nigh at hand. So likewise ye, when

ye see these things come to pass, know ye that the kingdom of God is nigh at hand. (KJV)

And He told them a parable. Consider the fig tree and all the trees. When they now shoot forth, you yourselves know that summer is now close at hand. So also you, when you see these things happen, you know that the Kingdom of God is close at hand. (DHT)

A "parable" is a short allegorical story that is used to illustrate a principle. The story is generally com- "parable" to, or like something else. We know this fig tree illustration is a parable and not a lesson on fig trees, because Jesus called it a parable.

In order to understand this parable, we need to recognize what are we comparing to the fig tree, what does it mean that the "twigs get tender," and what does "summer" represent?

Fig Tree = "These Things"

The simplest explanation of what the symbolic "fig tree" represents is found within the immediate context, just a couple sentences after the term "fig tree" is used. The "fig tree" represents "these things." The simplest understanding of what "these things" are would be to understand them as the "things" that Jesus spoke of immediately prior to His telling this parable. Those "things" include false prophets, persecution, a great falling away from the faith, the Abomination of Desolation, more persecution, and finally a worldwide earthquake and the sign in the sun, moon, and stars.

Putting Forth Its Leaves (Shoots) = "Happen"

"When you see the fig tree *putting forth its leaves*" (shoots), is the same as saying, "when you see these things (the signs), *happen*."

Summer = Kingdom of God

The phrase, "you know that summer is near," is essentially the same in all three gospel accounts. However, the gospel of Luke is the only account that gives us a clear definition. "Summer," being close at hand, represents, the "Kingdom of God," being close at hand. That is to say that the return of Jesus, and His bringing the Kingdom of God with Him, is close at hand.

Reading The Signs

Inhabitants of ancient Israel, just like people of the current time we live in, were able to read the seasons by observing signs such as spring time buds putting forth leaves. This type of sign, although not being accurate to the "day or hour," has always served as a reliable approximation of what general seasonal change people can expect.

Jesus is telling His disciples that by observing the signs, although they won't know the exact day or hour, they can recognize the general season of His return.

The above interpretation of the meaning of the *Parable of the Fig Tree* is great and works by itself without further analysis. However, there may be more to what Jesus was talking about.

A Possible Deeper Meaning of The "Fig Tree" Parable

Certainly the most important thing to glean from this parable is that the signs Jesus has just described will be recognizable indicators of His imminent return and the establishment of the Kingdom of God on earth. However, earlier the same day Jesus gave His talk atop the Mount of Olives, there was a famous encounter with a fig tree. Because that miraculous encounter was still fresh in the minds of the disciples, it is possible that the "fig tree bringing forth its leaves," may symbolize more than what first comes to our minds.

Given their recent experiences, how would the disciples have looked at this parable? Here is the story of the fig tree that took place just before the Olivet Discourse, as found in the Book of Mark, chapter 11:

And on the morrow, when they were come from Bethany, he (Jesus) *was hungry: And seeing a fig tree afar off having leaves, he came, if haply he might find any thing thereon: and when he came to it, he found nothing but leaves; for the time of figs was not yet. And Jesus answered and said unto it, no man eat fruit of thee hereafter for ever. And his disciples heard it. Mark 11:12-14 (KJV)* (My character identification added)

Jesus and His disciples went on to the Temple in Jerusalem that day, then returned to where they were staying in Bethany that Monday night. The next day, Tuesday, the day Jesus gave the Olivet

Discourse, as they walked along the same route as the day before, this happened:

And in the morning, as they passed by, they saw the fig tree dried up from the roots. And Peter calling to remembrance saith unto him, Master, behold, the fig tree which thou cursedst is withered away. And Jesus answering saith unto them, Have faith in God. For verily I say unto you, that whosoever shall say unto this mountain, be thou removed, and be thou cast into the sea; and shall not doubt in his heart, but shall believe that those things which he saith shall come to pass; he shall have whatsoever he saith. Therefore, I say unto you, What things soever ye desire, when ye pray, believe that ye receive them, and ye shall have them. Mark 11:20-24 (KJV)

Jesus cursed the fig tree for not bearing fruit. The very next day it had noticeably withered up and died. The same day the disciples took note that the fig tree was dead after Jesus had cursed it, they also watched Jesus "curse" the leaders of Israel and Jerusalem because that establishment was also not bearing fruit.

Jesus demonstrated with the fig tree what would happen to Israel. He was showing the disciples the authority that He possessed, through what happened when He cursed the fig tree. Using nothing more than His words, Jesus condemned the fig tree to its destruction. He did this in order to demonstrate what would happen to Israel when He used His words to pronounce judgment on its leaders.

Not Just Any Mountain

The passage found in Mark 11:20-24 was so much more than a lesson on how to put one's faith to work. That passage may contain a lesson on faith, but in the context of the important historical events that took place later that day, Jesus was first and foremost relaying an important prophecy. As He explained what had taken place with the fig tree, Jesus went on to hint to His disciples that He intended on cursing Israel.

"*This mountain*" that Jesus said could be "*taken up and cast into the sea*" was not just any mountain. The common Greek language of the first century did not utilize what we call in the English language, "indefinite articles." Indefinite articles are words such as "a" or "an." However, when it makes sense in English to do so, translators may insert those words when the "definite article" (like the word "the") is not connected to a noun.

The noun in this case is the word "mountain." It is clear that this is just not "any old" mountain. There is no room for a translator to slip in an indefinite article ("a" or "an"), since the original Greek uses the word "this" (τούτῳ), in referring to a *specific* mountain. This specific mountain was apparently in close proximity to Jesus and His disciples, when Jesus made the statement.

Jesus was traveling from Bethany, west to Jerusalem. Given where Jesus and His disciples likely were when Jesus spoke these words, and the direction they were going, He was speaking of "Mt. Zion," which lay ahead of Him.

There are a number of hills and "mountains," including the Mount of Olives, which make up the geography in and around Jerusalem. Mt. Zion is a literal mountain that sits close by the old city of Jerusalem. The reason Mount Zion stands out from the rest is because it is synonymous with the nation of Israel. This being the case, to paraphrase what Jesus was saying in Mark 11:20-24; *a word spoken in faith could result in the nation of Israel being cast into the "sea."*

Prophetically speaking, where "the land" oftentimes represented the nation of Israel, "the sea" oftentimes represents the gentile nations. Jesus' prophetic words of "this mountain," (Mt. Zion) or the nation of Israel, being cast into the sea, or into the gentile nations, were literally fulfilled between 70 and 132 AD.

Mt. Zion Cast into The "Sea"

After the destruction of Jerusalem and the Second Temple by the Romans in 70 AD, the Jewish Diaspora began as the Sanhedrin was disbanded and the Jewish leadership was all exiled. With a second revolt, known as the "Bar Kokhba rebellion" being put down by the Romans in 132 AD, Emperor Hadrian renamed the region of Judea, "Syria Palestine," and the City of Jerusalem, "Aelia Capitolia." Along with renaming the geography, Hadrian banished *all* remaining Jews from the city. [90] The inhabitants of "Mount Zion" had all been truly "cast into the sea" of gentile nations.

A Lesson On Faith?

This passage certainly contains information regarding the importance of faith. However, it is unlikely that Jesus was simply trying to teach His disciples (and us) a quick lesson in faith at the expense of the fig tree, and by specifically using the example of "this mountain" being thrown into the sea. However, Jesus did say, "*what ever things you desire, when you pray, believe that you receive them, and you shall have them* (Mark 11:24).

Praying in Line with God's Will Is the Key

The fact that "whosoever" or "anyone" could say to Israel (Mt. Zion) to be "cast into the sea," and that it would be done, is only because God had already determined that action would take place. Ezekiel prophesied about this event. Jesus sealed the deal. Obviously God would not act as anyone's genie in a bottle and cast out His chosen people from the land, if it were not already His own will to do so.

If there is a deeper lesson on praying in faith to be gained from this passage of scripture in light of the greater context, this is it; pray about whatever you want in faith according to what you know God's will to be, and it's going to happen. By doing so, one's faith becomes greatly simplified. One's faith is no longer about hoping that what it is you're praying about will happen, but rather one's faith is simply trusting that God is who He says He is and knowing that He will do what He says He will do.

I have faith one day Jesus will return to this earth and establish His Kingdom. However, it is not my faith that will bring about this event. My faith comes in the form of my belief in what God has told me would happen, will happen: *"Thy Kingdom come, they will be done…"*

The difficult part of all this is that we don't always know the will of God. But, rather than patient and prayerful study of the Bible in attempt to discover the will of God, we often resort to telling Him what "we" think His will should be.

Another Fig Tree Parable

In an earlier story Jesus told, He compared the action of a fig tree being "cut down," after not "bearing fruit," to people who do not "repent."

He spake also this parable; A certain man had a fig tree planted in his vineyard; and he came and sought fruit thereon, and found none. Then said he unto the dresser of his vineyard, Behold, these three years I come seeking fruit on this fig tree, and find none: cut it down; why cumbereth it the ground? And he answering said unto him, Lord, let it alone this year also, till I shall dig about it, and dung it: And if it bear fruit, well: and if not, then after that thou shalt cut it down. Luke 13:6-9 (KJV)

This parable must have still been fresh in the minds of the disciples as they watched an actual fig tree wither and die after Jesus had cursed it.

The Disciples may also have been familiar with Israel being symbolically represented by a fig tree. This occurs at least twice in the Old Testament (see Jeremiah chapter 24 and Hosea chapter 9).

Considering the fig tree parables, watching the fig tree wither after Jesus had cursed it, and knowing that Israel was symbolically represented as a fig tree, perhaps the conversation before the disciples bedded down for the night went something like this;

Peter: *"What's up with all the fig tree stuff, John? You saw that tree wither and die this morning too, right? Then, tonight Jesus compared a fig tree putting forth new leaves, to the signs He was talking about, which will indicate the Kingdom of Heaven is near."*

John: "*Oh yeah. I saw it too, Pete. And, wasn't the Master just telling a story a little while back about fig trees that don't produce fruit?*"

Peter: *"Yeah, that had something to do with those that don't repent. Based on Him chewing out the Pharisees today, I think He was mostly talking about Jerusalem. Remember how he cursed Jerusalem the same way he did the fig tree?"*

Jesus Curses Jerusalem

Was it a coincidence that Jesus was using a fig tree to make a point during the Olivet Discourse, or could He have known that the disciples would have associated what He was saying now, with the amazing thing that happened that morning? Luke's gospel weakens the case for this theory slightly by including the statement, "and all the trees" (not just the fig tree).

It is reasonable to conclude that Jesus' expected His "fig"-urative speech to be taken by His disciples as a whole and that they would pull all of the lessons of the fig tree they had personally witnessed together. The disciples could have understood that like a cursed and cut down fig tree sending forth new shoots, Jerusalem would be cursed, "cut down," and again come back to life one day. If this is true, then seeing Jerusalem showing signs of life again in the future after essentially dying could be considered a sign that precedes the Second Coming of Jesus.

The Death and Rebirth of Israel as a Nation

As stated above, the prophetic words of Jerusalem being "cut down" were fulfilled in 70 AD by Roman General Titus. Any signs of life that remained afterwards had been squashed by 135 AD when the Jewish population of Judea was dispersed from the land. There were no signs of national Israel left in the land. That is until a little over 1,800 years later, on May 14, 1948 when Israel again gained its independence and sprang back to life as a nation. In June of 1967, all of Jerusalem was reclaimed at the conclusion of the Six-Day-War. Seeing Israel again come to life, can be likened to what seems like a dead fig tree putting forth its new tender spring leaves.

Few people stop and ponder what an amazing prophetic fulfillment the descendants of Abraham, Isaac and Jacob returning to their Promised Land was in 1948. It was only by Israel returning to their native land that any of the other prophetic events Jesus, Paul, John, Ezekiel, Daniel, Isaiah, and all of the other prophets spoke of in regard to end times events, could be fulfilled in a truly literal way. It was plainly a miracle.

Which Generation Will Witnesses the Return of Christ?

<u>**Matthew 24:34**</u>

Verily I say unto you, this generation shall not pass, till all these things be fulfilled. (KJV)

I am telling you the truth; this same generation will not pass, until all of these things take place. (DHT)

<u>**Mark 13:30**</u>

Verily I say unto you, that this generation shall not pass, till all these things be done. (KJV)

I am telling you the truth; this same generation will not pass until all of these things happen (DHT)

<u>Luke 21:32</u>

Verily I say unto you, this generation shall not pass away, till all be fulfilled. (KJV)

I am telling you the truth; this generation shall not pass away, until all this happens. (DHT)

What "generation" is Jesus referring to? Is it the generation He was speaking to on the Mount of Olives or the generation that would witness the signs He was just speaking about?

"All these things" that Jesus spoke about include the Abomination of Desolation, the sign in the Sun, Moon, and Stars, the gathering of the elect from the four corners of the earth, and the Second Coming of Jesus. Since "this generation" would witness all of "these things," the first century "generation" Jesus was addressing in person on the Mount of Olives has to be eliminated from consideration.

By making this statement, Jesus was saying two different things: "all these things" will take place within one generation's worth of time. Secondly, the generation that sees these things occur, will also see the Second Coming of Christ and the end of the age.

History and time passing has answered the question of what generation will witness "all of these things." Since this statement is made immediately following the parable of the fig tree. It seems possible that the generation of the end will also witness the "fig tree" showing its new signs of life.

Conservatively this scripture is referring to the generation that is around that will witness the Abomination of Desolation occurring and the sign in the Sun, Moon and Stars. The broader interpretation is that it is the generation that sees national Israel starting to show signs of life again that will be around to see "all of these things" take place. If the second view is true, wouldn't that mean that we are living in that generation right now? Maybe, maybe not…

Has Ezekiel's Prophecy Been Completely Fulfilled?

If the second, more specific interpretation involving Israel again becoming a nation is true, there are still things to think about. Has Ezekiel's prophecy been completely fulfilled? Did Israel truly come back to life in the way prophesied about by Ezekiel, or would that require them to also completely turn to God? Just because man has recognized Israel's political borders, has this action fulfilled what God had in mind? Do the descendants of the tribes of Israel need to first rebuild the temple in Jerusalem and reinstitute the daily sacrifice? God only knows the answers to these questions.

Ezekiel's prophecy likens Israel becoming a nation again to bones, once scattered throughout the world, being rejoined, flesh being put back on the bones, and life breathed into the reconstituted body. I personally think of Israel today as having its "bones" back together after being scattered throughout the world, but those bones have not had flesh put back on them, nor life breathed into them (See Ezekiel 37:7-9). It is my opinion that life will be breathed into the Nation of Israel either when God causes the remnant of Israel to be sealed at the mid-point of the seven-year tribulation period, or at the Second Coming, when they recognize Jesus as their Messiah.

Our Current Heaven and Earth Are Temporary

Matthew 24:35

Heaven and earth shall pass away, but my words shall not pass away. (KJV)

Heaven and earth shall pass away, but my words shall not pass away. (DHT)

Mark 13:31

Heaven and earth shall pass away: but my words shall not pass away. (KJV)

Heaven and earth shall pass away, but my words shall not pass away. (DHT)
Luke 21:33

Heaven and earth shall pass away: but my words shall not pass away. (KJV)

Heaven and earth shall pass away, but my words shall not pass away. (DHT)

Jesus informs His disciples that even though He is talking about the end of one age, what He says (His word) will endure into the next age. He will be, after all, the King of that age.

Jesus has just warned of tremendous destruction where literally the foundations of the earth will be shaken. Every "mountain and island will be moved." His Coming will change everything …except His "word." This is consistent throughout scripture.

Of old hast thou laid the foundation of the earth: and the heavens are the work of thy hands. They shall perish, but thou shalt endure: yea, all of them shall wax old like a garment; as a vesture shalt thou change them, and they shall be changed: ***But thou art the same, and thy years shall have no end.*** *Ps 102:25-27 (KJV)* (Emphasis added)

The grass withereth, the flower fadeth: but ***the word of our God shall stand for ever.*** *Isa 40:8 (KJV)* (Emphasis added)

Lift up your eyes to the heavens, and look upon the earth beneath: for the heavens shall vanish away like smoke, and the earth shall wax old like a garment, and they that dwell therein shall die in like manner: ***but my salvation shall be for ever, and my righteousness shall not be abolished.*** *Hearken unto me, ye that know righteousness, the people in whose heart is my law; fear ye not the reproach of men, neither be ye afraid of their revilings. For the moth shall eat them up like a garment, and the worm shall eat them like wool:* ***but my righteousness shall be for ever, and my salvation from generation to generation.*** *Isa 51:6-8 (KJV)* (Emphasis added)

Being born again, not of corruptible seed, but of incorruptible, ***by the word of God, which liveth and abideth for ever.*** *For all flesh is as grass, and all the glory of man as the flower of grass. The grass withereth, and the flower thereof falleth away:* ***But the word of the Lord endureth for***

ever. *And this is the word which by the gospel is preached unto you. 1 Peter 1:23-25 (KJV)* (Emphasis added)

Jesus, and His Word, will be around forever. With this short sentence, Jesus summed up the last eleven chapters of Revelation. The passing of this current planet as we know it is no small matter. Yet, Jesus' statement is simple regarding the final results of the signs.

Much to Look Forward To

Every physical thing we are familiar with will pass, but Jesus will go on. The framework of our reality and all of what we have experienced will be no more, except for Jesus and those that have placed their trust in His reality. That is where all of the signs He spoke of are finally leading.

We will not need to take any of man's discoveries with us. Man simply discovers what God has already "invented" or created. Man manipulates and rearranges the elements. God creates the elements out of nothing, and then commands them. Having been gathered to Him, we will be face to face not with a "discoverer," but with the actual Creator of everything that currently is, and that will be.

There will be no need or lack of anything, since we will be living with the God of fulfillment. This will not be a temporary situation. It won't be like going on vacation where the thought of returning to work is always looming overhead. Nor will it be like retirement, where although the idea sounds great, almost every day there is some kind of reminder of how temporary and limited are our capabilities and resources.

Summary

Jesus used the imagery in the *Parable of the Fig Tree*, to bring home His point that those who are watching for the signs will be able to recognize His return is close at hand. Further, this parable *may* also represent Israel coming together again as a nation in their original homeland. Ezekiel wrote of national Israel's death and rebirth. This prophecy was fulfilled, at least in part, as Israel once again became a nation in May of 1948. God had preserved a remnant of His chosen people for over 1800 years in spite of several great efforts of attempted genocide.

Israel coming back together as a nation is not comparable to anything else known to history. There are no cases of other peoples such as the Assyrians, Hittites, Babylonians, Persians, Mayans, Inca, or any other ancient group, returning to their lands and within a few decades becoming a first-world nation, complete with nuclear capabilities.

Jesus stated the signs would occur within one generation. Secondly, the generation that sees all of the signs take place, will also be around to witness His Coming.

Although events have taken place in history that may resemble, at least in part, the prophecies of the Olivet Discourse, none of them have ultimately qualified as having fulfilled the prophecies. We know this for sure, because many generations have passed and Jesus has not returned. The generation that sees the actual signs take place will also see the return of Jesus to this earth.

The Almighty God is the ultimate recycler. Plunging this present earth into His divine wash tub, and wringing it out like a wet towel, He will make all things new again. Jesus' words and His Kingdom will outlast the current terrestrial sphere that we inhabit. Those who He has set apart for Himself and purchased with His own blood will endure with Him for all time and eternity. That is the believer's "blessed hope."

18. Two "Harvests"

For our citizenship is in heaven from where also we await our savior, the Lord Jesus Christ, who will transform our lowly body to be like his glorious body, through the power that He is able to make all things subject to Himself.

-Phil 3:20-21 (DHT)

In the late 1990's, Angela and I had an idea that would allow our three children to earn some money during the summer months; we would plant a half-acre of blueberries for our kids to pick and sell. Blueberry bushes take up to eight years to mature and can last for longer than thirty years. seventeen years later, the kids have all moved away from home, leaving Angela and I to take care of the 500 blueberry plants. Now that was some fine planning on our part!

As poor of a plan as it may have been, there is a lot of time to think when one performs repetitive tasks in the blueberry field, like picking, weeding, and pruning. I think a lot about the agricultural imagery that the Bible uses when I am working in the field. Jesus told parables about sowing seeds, planting vineyards, and harvesting.

Each year, we have two kinds of harvests on our micro-farm. There is the one that we look forward to; the harvesting of the blueberries, which usually starts in early July and lasts for about a month. Then there is the "harvest" of the weeds, which I try to accomplish about once a month throughout much of the year.

Last year we decided to go "organic" with our blueberries. What "going organic" mostly means to me, is that rather than spraying an herbicide to control weeds, I now spend up to eight hours per month moving down about two miles of rows, bent over with a hoe in my hands, manually removing the weeds from around the base of the plants. It is physically demanding and monotonous, but it is also very necessary to maximize the quantity and quality of the blueberry harvest. Two harvests; one that we look forward to makes all the previous work and expense worthwhile, and one that is dreaded but necessary.

The Bible speaks of "harvests" in association with the return of the Messiah. We will see that like in our blueberry field, scripture reveals there is actually more than one harvest associated with the end of the age. There is the rapture or "harvest" of the Church, which will occur in conjunction with the return of Jesus, and there is a second harvest; a harvest of the "wicked."

Without close study and comparison of the various passages of scriptures that clarify the two harvests, a person may become confused, think the Bible contradicts itself, or arrive at false conclusions while trying to pound a square peg of interpretation into a round hole of truth. Understanding the two different harvests and more specifically who is involved in them is important to understanding a parable that Jesus will relay a little later on in the Olivet Discourse.

The Harvest of Matthew 13

The Gospel of Matthew chapter 13, tells us that one-day Jesus was sitting by a lake and a large crowd of people started to gather around Him. He began teaching them by telling them stories. On this particular day His stories started off with a farming theme. There was a lot of agricultural work going on in the area, and Jesus knew it was the best way to relate to the people. Jesus first told them the story already discussed in chapter seven of this book regarding seeds that were planted; some fell by the wayside, some had no root, etc. (Matt 13:3-8). Following the *Parable of the Seeds*, Jesus told His disciples exactly what this story meant.

After Jesus told how "seed" (the gospel) is planted with various levels of success, He moved on to a story about "weeds" or "tares," as they are called in the King James Version of the Bible. Jesus explained that weed seed can get mixed in with the good seed and sprout alongside the intended crop. He goes on to lay out what His method of dealing with those weeds, or tares, would be.

Another parable put he forth unto them, saying, the kingdom of heaven is likened unto a man which sowed good seed in his field: But while men slept, his enemy came and sowed tares among the wheat, and went his way. But when the blade was sprung up, and brought forth fruit, then appeared the tares also. So the servants of the householder came and said unto him, Sir, didst not thou sow good seed in thy field? from whence then hath it tares? He said unto them, an enemy hath done this. The servants said unto him, wilt thou then that we go and gather them up? But he said, Nay; lest while ye gather up the tares, ye root up also the wheat with them. Let both grow together until the harvest: and in the time of harvest I will say to the reapers, gather ye together first the tares, and bind them in bundles to burn them: but gather the wheat into my barn. Matt 13:24-30 (KJV)

Later Jesus clearly explains this parable. In the following passage, Jesus is "the Son of Man":

He answered and said unto them, He that soweth the good seed is the Son of man (Jesus)*; The field is the world; the good seed are the* ***children of the kingdom****; but the tares* (weeds) *are the children of the wicked one; The enemy that sowed them is the devil; the harvest is the end of the world; and the reapers are the angels. As therefore the tares are gathered and burned in the fire; so shall it be in the end of this world. The Son of man shall send forth his angels, and they shall gather out of his kingdom all things that offend, and them which do iniquity; And shall cast them into a furnace of fire: there shall be wailing and gnashing of teeth. Then shall the righteous shine forth as the sun in the kingdom of their Father. Who hath ears to hear, let him hear. Matt 13:37-43 (KJV)* (My Character identification and definitions added)

The "*children of the kingdom*" obviously belong to God and will be saved for Him and by Him. The "*children of the wicked one,*" the weeds (tares), are those who are of the world who don't know God. They are harvested, or removed from the earth by angels. Unlike my "harvesting" of weeds throughout the year in the blueberry patch, this harvest of "the children of the wicked one," will happen only once, at the end of the age.

The essence of this harvest story Jesus told concerns what will happen with two groups of people that are alive at the time of Christ's return. Jesus will use His angels to:

1. Gather the "Sons of Satan" (the weeds or tares) and throw them into the "fiery furnace." So the:
2. "Children of the Kingdom" (The wheat) will shine like the sun in their Father's Kingdom.

Notice: There is no mention of the "Children of the Kingdom" being "harvested" or taken away in this story. It appears they are left on the earth.

It is very important to notice the sequence that occurs in this parable. It is because of the sequence that many that read this harvest story then misapply it to the Olivet Discourse and reach various erroneous conclusions.

Is this a "rapture" of the wicked that takes place prior to the Church being raptured? Is the gathering that follows the signs Jesus gave (sun, moon, stars, earthquake) the rapture of the wicked, leaving the followers of Christ on earth? Are the scriptures found later in the Olivet Discourse that talk about two "working in the field" or "at the mill" saying that the "one that is taken" is evil, and the one that is left is a Christian?

To understand the answers to these questions, we must first answer yet another question; Who are the "Sons of the Kingdom" in this story? What leads anyone to believe they represent the Church?

There is a group that qualifies to be called the "Sons of the Kingdom" left on the earth *after* the Church has been raptured.

Let's look at another scriptural account of a different harvest of the end:

The Harvest of Revelation 14

And I looked, and behold a white cloud, and upon the cloud one sat like unto the Son of man, having on his head a golden crown, and in his hand a sharp sickle. And another angel came out of the temple, crying with a loud voice to him that sat on the cloud, thrust in thy sickle, and reap: for the time is come for thee to reap; for the harvest of the earth is ripe. And he that sat on the cloud thrust in his sickle on the earth; and the earth was reaped. Rev 14:14-16 (KJV)

The Apostle John, author of the book of Revelation, describes the one "sitting on the cloud" as looking "like a son of man." As we have previously noted, this is an expression used for the identification of Jesus several places in scripture (Rev 1:13, Dan 7:13, Matt 13:37). John most likely would not use the same "Son of Man" terminology on just any angel, after first using it for his Lord at the beginning of the book of Revelation.

The wearing of a crown by itself in no way proves or disproves this angel is Jesus. We do see other characters, including the white horse rider of chapter 6 of Revelation, who is likely not Jesus, wearing a crown. However, to further the case that this angel, is most likely Jesus, the angel who is sitting on the cloud is wearing a crown. A crown is a sign of power and authority. The wearing of a crown, along with being referred to as "the Son of Man," makes a very strong case that this "angel" is actually Jesus.

This angel, if not Jesus, is clearly at least acting on Jesus' behalf. The identification of this Revelation chapter 14 angel is not as important as what the angel does. The harvest this angel accomplishes fits amazingly well with what Christ will be doing at the end of the age; gathering the elect.

God's Wrath Comes After the Revelation 14 Harvest

If the harvest of Revelation 14:14, does represent the rapture of the Church, the next event we should expect to see in Revelation (if it continues sequentially) is evidence of God's Wrath.

What we have already established by comparing scripture with scripture is that the Day of the Lord and the outpouring of God's wrath follows the rapture of the Church. That is in fact what we also see take place next in the Revelation 14 passage:

And another angel came out of the temple which is in heaven, he also having a sharp sickle. And another angel came out from the altar, which had power over fire; and cried with a loud cry to him that had the sharp sickle, saying, thrust in thy sharp sickle, and gather the clusters of the vine of the earth; for her grapes are fully ripe. And the angel thrust in his sickle into the earth, and gathered the vine of the earth, and cast it into ***the great winepress of the wrath of God****. And the winepress was trodden without the city, and blood came out of the winepress, even unto the horse bridles, by the space of a thousand and six hundred furlongs. Rev 14:17-20 (KJV)* (Emphasis added)

No one should be looking for a giant Angel one day towering above the earth with an enormous cutting tool in his hand. This passage is not talking about God taking out his frustrations by making up a batch of earth-vino. In this passage, just about everything is symbolic.

The meaning of the symbolism must be defined by comparing scripture with scripture. First, when we look within the passage itself, we will find that the "wine," actually symbolically stands for blood.

"*…They were trampled in the winepress outside the city, and* ***blood*** *flowed out of the press.*"

We know that the "winepress" is "outside the city." "The city" is generally thought to be Jerusalem since that is the city in which the book of Revelation revolves.

When we look at several different passages it is imperative that you notice the similar language that ties this symbolism of God's wrath and the winepress all together. Later on in Revelation we see Jesus:

And he (Jesus) *was clothed with a vesture* ***dipped in blood:*** *and his name is called The Word of God. And the armies which were in heaven followed him upon white horses, clothed in fine linen, white and clean. And out of his mouth goeth a sharp sword, that with it he should smite the nations: and he shall rule them with a rod of iron:* ***and he treadeth the winepress of the fierceness and wrath of Almighty God.*** *And he hath on his vesture and on his thigh a name written, King of Kings, and Lord of Lords. Rev 19:13-16 (KJV)* (My interpretation and added)

Jesus alone will tread the "grapes" that will be gathered, or harvested, and thrown into the winepress of God's wrath. The battle that is mentioned in relationship to this winepress of chapter 19 is none other than the future infamous battle of Armageddon.

The armies of the world will be "gathered" to the place called Armageddon by the divine will of God.

And I saw the beast, and the kings of the earth, and their armies, gathered together to make war against him that sat on the horse, and against his army. Rev 19:19 (KJV)

Even though the Antichrist and the rulers of the earth think it is their own decision to come together to make war against Israel and their Messiah, it is by the will of God that they will be gathered.

One of the last things that we see happen as God pours out His judgment on the earth are demonic spirits that are loosed specifically to entice and "gather" the kings of the earth to the place of the final "battle."

And I saw three unclean spirits like frogs come out of the mouth of the dragon, and out of the mouth of the beast, and out of the mouth of the false prophet. For they are the spirits of devils, working miracles, which go forth unto the kings of the earth and of the whole world, to gather them to the battle of that great day of God Almighty. Rev 16:13-14 (KJV)

And he gathered them together into a place called in the Hebrew tongue Armageddon. Rev 16:16 (KJV)

As a side note in regard to the battle of Armageddon and the role of the follower of Jesus, one should not worry about not having the stomach for war. It is controversial whether or not the army that accompanies the Lord will be the Church or His Angels. But even if the Lord does decide to take His "Bride," the Church, along with Him into battle, there is nothing to dread. As written, the Lord Himself will tread the "grapes" of God's wrath.

Read this awe-inspiring passage from Isaiah. As you do, realize that the Lord himself provides the answers to the two questions that are asked.

Who is this that cometh from Edom, with dyed garments from Bozrah? this that is glorious in his apparel, travelling in the greatness of his strength?

(Jesus Answers) *I that speak in righteousness, mighty to save.*

Wherefore art thou red in thine apparel, and thy garments like him that treadeth in the winefat?

(Jesus Answers) *I have trodden the winepress alone; and of the people there was none with me: for I will tread them in mine anger, and trample them in my fury; and their blood shall be sprinkled upon my garments, and I will stain all my raiment. For the day of vengeance is in mine heart, and the year of my redeemed is come. And I looked, and there was none to help; and I wondered that there was none to uphold: therefore, mine own arm brought salvation unto me; and my fury, it upheld me. And I will tread down the people in mine anger, and make them drunk in my fury, and I will bring down their strength to the earth. Isa 63:1-6 (KJV)* (My character identification added)

Jesus is the only one who will have blood stained garments. All of His follower's robes are "white and clean" (Rev 19:13-14). The battle of Armageddon will be somewhat anticlimactic for those who have come for a good fight. It will be over in an instant. Jesus will accomplish this by simply speaking it into being.

And out of his mouth goeth a sharp sword, that with it he should smite the nations: and he shall rule them with a rod of iron: and he treadeth the winepress of the fierceness and wrath of Almighty God. Rev 19:15 (KJV)

The "sword" of His mouth is the same sword we see in John's description of Jesus in Revelation 1:16. This sword that comes out of Jesus' mouth is "the Word of God." It is the same Word of God that caused worlds to leap into existence at the time of creation. It will be this same sword that makes swift work of those who oppose Jesus at Armageddon. When God speaks, things happen. In reference to this battle we read the following:

And the remnant were slain with the sword of him that sat upon the horse, which sword proceeded out of his mouth: and all the fowls were filled with their flesh. Rev 19:21 (KJV)

The only ones at this battle not "killed with the sword" are the Antichrist and False Prophet, who are cast directly into the lake of fire (Rev 19:20).

The "word of God" that comes out of the mouth of Jesus either itself causes His enemies to be slain, or it causes His angelic warriors to act as His agents and carry out His will. Either way, Jesus "owns" what occurs as a result.

By making all of the above comparisons, we are led to the conclusion that the "blood" coming out of the "winepress" is the blood of the ungodly people of the world who have been gathered and thrown into God's "winepress;" Armageddon. What about the "ungodly" people of the world who were not "gathered" to Armageddon? Are they off the hook? The answer follows.

The Connection

The similarities and the connection between the Matthew 13 passage regarding the harvest of "wheat and tares" (The Children of the Kingdom and Children of Satan), and the Revelation 14 passage having to do with two separate harvests are strong. However, trouble begins when we try to say that the "Children" or "Sons of the Kingdom" in the Matthew 13 passage are the same as those apparently "raptured" by the angel (Jesus) sitting on the white cloud (Rev 14).

In Matthew 13, the ungodly (weeds) are harvested *first.* In Revelation 14, the ungodly (grapes) are harvested second.

Matthew 13

1) The wicked (weeds) are gathered and destroyed
2) The Sons of the Kingdom are left

Revelation 14

1) The Righteous are gathered
2) The Wicked (grapes) are gathered and destroyed

Which is it, are the ungodly "harvested" first or second? On the surface if we try to force the events of the two passages together, we run into a sequential problem. Did God not intend us to pay attention to this detail, or is it simply unimportant? How do we fit this all together?

"Post-Tribulational" rapturists are those who say that the Church will go through the entire tribulation period, God's wrath and all. Some who hold to this theory may point to the Matthew 13 passage as being one that defends their position. They view the harvest of the "wheat" as the rapture of the church that takes place at the very end of the tribulation period, only after the Wrath of God has occurred, and the "weeds" have been removed. If you hold to this theory, you still need to deal with the sequence conflict between Matthew 13 and Revelation 14.

The true solution is clear when we realize that we are not talking about the same groups of people in the two different passages. At least partially anyway.

The ungodly people who are harvested and destroyed in both passages are the same. The harvest of the Matthew 13 "weeds" and the Revelation 14 "grapes" that are thrown into the "winepress" are referring to the same event; the judgment of the wicked.

The leaving of the "wheat" (Children of the Kingdom) in Matthew 13, and the "rapture" as seen in Revelation 14:14 and Olivet Discourse, are dealing with two different events and groups of people.

In Revelation 14:14, the harvest, or rapture, takes place before the wicked have been gathered. In Matthew 13, the "wheat" (Children of the Kingdom) are left *after* the wicked have been gathered. Who are these "Children of the Kingdom" if the Church is already gone?

Notice again the language of the Matthew 13 passage. Jesus said:

The field is the world; the good seed are the children of the kingdom; but the tares are the children of the wicked one; Matt 13:38 (KJV)

The Son of man shall send forth his angels, and they shall gather out of his kingdom all things that offend, and them which do iniquity; Matt 13:41 (KJV)

These passages are talking about a future time when God will establish His "Kingdom" on the earth. This "weeding of the field" or, cleansing the earth of the "sons of the evil one," will come at a time when Jesus has brought His "Kingdom" to this world, which in this parable is called "the field."

Jesus' Kingdom does not come to this world, until Jesus returns. Who will be left on the earth after the Church has been raptured and all of the ungodly people have been gathered and "thrown into the fiery furnace?" Besides some "lucky" souls who never took the mark of the Beast and somehow escaped all of the fatal portions of the Wrath of God, there will be a group left on the earth to which this scripture refers. They will be the "seed stock" of the millennial kingdom. This is the group the scripture is referring to as the "Children of the Kingdom."

And I looked, and, lo, a Lamb stood on the mount Sion, and with him an hundred forty and four thousand, having his Father's name written in their foreheads. Rev 14:1 (KJV)

These are they which were not defiled with women; for they are virgins. These are they which follow the Lamb whithersoever he goeth. These were redeemed from among men, being the firstfruits unto God and to the Lamb. And in their mouth was found no guile: for they are without fault before the throne of God. Rev 14:4-5 (KJV)

How is it this group of 144,000 "children of the Kingdom," made it through the tribulation period on the earth to be able to stand with Jesus on Mount Zion? It is because they were divinely sealed prior to the beginning of God's wrath.

And I saw another angel ascending from the east, having the seal of the living God: and he cried with a loud voice to the four angels, to whom it was given

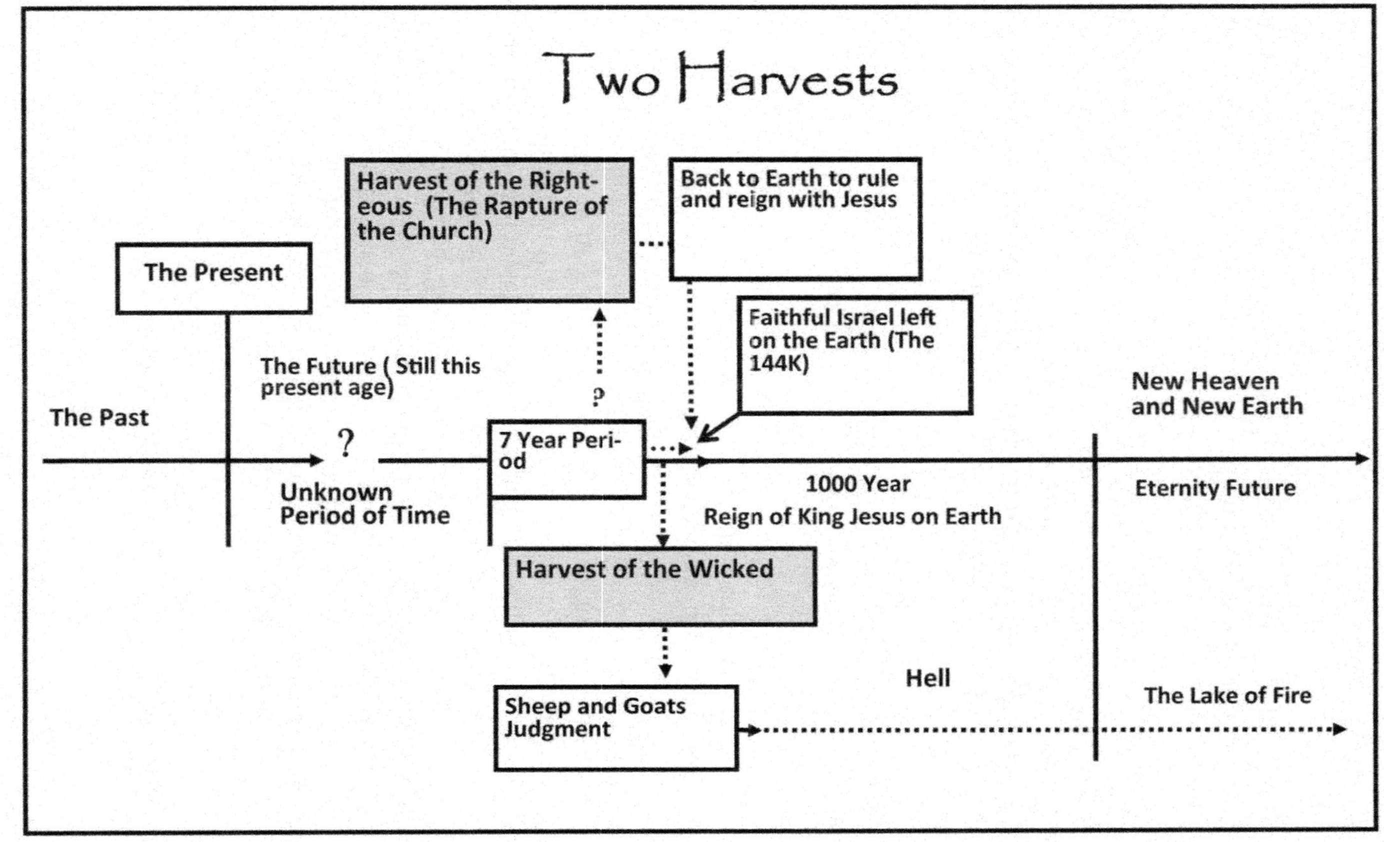
Two Harvests
The Present
Harvest of the Righteous (The Rapture of the Church)
Back to Earth to rule and reign with Jesus
Faithful Israel left on the Earth (The 144K)
The Future (Still this present age)
?
The Past
?
Unknown Period of Time
7 Year Period
1000 Year
Reign of King Jesus on Earth
New Heaven and New Earth
Eternity Future
Harvest of the Wicked
Sheep and Goats Judgment
Hell
The Lake of Fire

to hurt the earth and the sea, Saying, hurt not the earth, neither the sea, nor the trees, till we have sealed the servants of our God in their foreheads. And I heard the number of them which were sealed: and there were sealed an hundred and forty and four thousand of all the tribes of the children of Israel. Rev 7:2-4 (KJV)

These 144,000, "male, virgins" are supernaturally "sealed" about the same time we see the Church standing before the throne in Heaven just after the "sixth seal" of the scroll of Revelation was broken. Both the Church being gathered to Heaven, and the protective sealing of the 144,000 "Children of the Kingdom," occurs before God's wrath begins.

Putting It Together

Tying all of the harvest and rapture passages together:

- The Elect of God (the Church) are gathered together by His angels into the presence of God. (Rev 14:14-16, Rev 7:9-15, Matthew 24:31)
- The ungodly ("weeds" or "children of the evil one") are gathered together and thrown into the fiery furnace and God's "winepress". (Matt 13:40-42 & Rev 14:17-20)
- The "Children of the Kingdom" (144,000 descendants of the tribes of Israel) are *left* on the Earth to live in the Kingdom of Heaven that has been brought to the Earth by King Jesus (Matt 13:43, Rev. 14:1-5).

Another Point of View

Some who hold the pretribulation rapture point of view, don't believe that the Church is even mentioned in the Book of Revelation after chapter three. They believe that the first angel mentioned in Revelation 14 represents a harvest of a different kind. Remember, the "pre-trib" view is the point of view that says the church will be "caught up" or "snatched away" (raptured) prior to any end times events, without any sign or warning. What this Revelation 14 angel does, in this theory, represents a great harvest of souls that takes place *after* the rapture of the Church.

The pretribulation rapture theory secondary harvest is due to a large-scale revival of mankind turning to God during the great tribulation. This, some think is as a result of "144,000 Jewish witnesses" and the "gospel angel" who proclaims the "eternal gospel." This all takes place, after the Church is no longer found on the earth. This same theory argues that the Holy Spirit will have left the earth with the Church at the rapture and won't be present on the earth during this time of "great revival."

Wrong On All Counts

There are many problems with the pretribulation rapture theory. Some of these problems are discussed below.

What 144K Jewish Witnesses?

The Bible does not even hint that the 144,000 descendants of the tribes of Israel mentioned in Revelation chapter seven have anything to do with witnessing to anyone. In fact, during the second half of the tribulation period, they will be in hiding in the wilderness. We discuss the roll of the 144,000 descendants of the tribes of Israel later on in this book.

What Post Rapture Revival?

Secondly, we find overwhelming scriptural evidence that there will not be a turning towards God during this period of time, but a great falling away. There will be anything but a revival. The following scriptures dealing with "the end" do not support people turning towards God after the Church is raptured, as the pretribulation rapture theory suggests.

Let no man deceive you by any means: for that day shall not come, except there come ***a falling away*** *first, and that man of sin be revealed, the son of perdition;* II Thess 2:3 (KJV) (Emphasis added)

And with all deceivableness of unrighteousness in them that perish; because they received not the love of the truth, that they might be saved. ***And for this cause God shall send them strong delusion, that they should believe a lie: That they all might be damned who believed not the truth, but had pleasure in unrighteousness.*** *2 Thess 2:10-12 (KJV)* (Emphasis added)

This know also, that in the last days perilous times shall come. ***For men shall be lovers of their own selves, covetous, boasters,***

proud, blasphemers, disobedient to parents, unthankful, unholy, without natural affection, trucebreakers, false accusers, incontinent, fierce, despisers of those that are good, Traitors, heady, highminded, lovers of pleasures more than lovers of God; *Having a form of godliness, but denying the power thereof: from such turn away. 2 Tim 3:1-5 (KJV)* (Emphasis added)

For the time will come when they will not endure sound doctrine; but after their own lusts shall they heap to themselves teachers, having itching ears; ***And they shall turn away their ears from the truth, and shall be turned unto fables.*** *2 Tim 4:3-4 (KJV)* (Emphasis added)

And the rest of the men which were not killed by these plagues yet repented not of the works of their hands, that they should not worship devils, and idols of gold, and silver, and brass, and stone, and of wood: which neither can see, nor hear, nor walk: ***Neither repented they*** *of their murders, nor of their sorceries, nor of their fornication, nor of their thefts. Rev 9:20-21 (KJV)* (Emphasis added)

And the fifth angel poured out his vial upon the seat of the beast; and his kingdom was full of darkness; and they gnawed their tongues for pain, and blasphemed the God of heaven because of their pains and their sores, ***and repented not of their deeds.*** *Rev 16:10-11 (KJV)* (Emphasis added)

In his book, *Antichrist Before the Day of the Lord*, author Alan Kurschner writes, "*Any repentance by Gentiles and Jews during the day of the Lord's wrath will occur through God's gracious exception; it will not be the rule.*"[91] I completely concur with Kurschner.

Who Does the Convicting and "Saving" Apart from God's Holy Spirit?

There is a third problem with the Revelation 14 angel representing a "great harvest of souls" during a post rapture revival. If the Holy Spirit has "left the earth" as the pretribulation rapture theory says He does, who does the calling and saving of souls? Are these post rapture Christians not called by the Holy Spirit and not indwelled by Him upon their salvation? Will they be Christians in head knowledge and name only? What scripture in the Bible supports being spiritually reborn and saved apart from the work of the Holy Spirit?

Saying that there will be a "great revival" during the tribulation period where there is according to the same theory no Holy Spirit present is clearly not consistent with the rest of the Word of God. However, saying the Revelation 14 angel passage represents the rapture of the Church, harmonizes perfectly with the rest of scripture.

Why Do They Think the Holy Spirit Is Gone?

Believing that the Holy Spirit will not be present on the earth after the pretribulation rapture is a widespread belief among pretribulation rapturists. That theory is included in the *Ryrie Study Bible.* [92] People that believe this theory do so for a couple of reasons. First they believe that the Church is the entity that the Holy Spirit accomplishes His purposes through. Without the Church present on the earth, the Holy Spirit will essentially be "taken out of the way" of Satan. There will be no one left on earth to put into action the will of the Holy Spirit. Second, they base this component of the pretribulation rapture theory on the following passage of scripture that we have seen before:

> *And now ye know what withholdeth that he might be revealed in his time. For the mystery of iniquity doth already work: only he who now letteth will let, until he be taken out of the way. And then shall that Wicked be revealed, whom the Lord shall consume with the spirit of his mouth, and shall destroy with the brightness of his coming: 2 Thess 2:6-8 (KJV)*

The pretribulation rapture theory says that the one who is currently restraining or "withholding" the "the mystery of lawlessness" and the Antichrist in the future, is the Holy Spirit. That much is correct. However, they also say the Holy Spirit will withdraw and be absent from the earth along with the Church and therefore be powerless to restrain evil.

This interpretation, where our omnipresent God is somehow absent, is unlikely. A more likely scenario is that the Almighty Holy Spirit of God will simply allow Satan to act, while still being present. This is how our all-powerful, omnipotent and omnipresent God has always operated. How He accomplishes this, is the subject of a different book. Never-the-less, it is only by the will of God that Satan is allowed to do anything.

There is nowhere one cannot find God. God, by His very nature is present everywhere and is all-powerful with, or without human beings in the form of His Church, to carry out His will. He did pretty good creating the heavens and the earth without us…

No one, no place, and no thing, will ever be out of the reach of God and His Holy Spirit or out of His control. Satan will run unbridled in the world only because God will allow it for an "appointed time." It is also God, who will "cut short" those days, when Satan will be unrestrained, for the "sake of the elect."

No Follower of Christ is Appointed to Suffer the Wrath of God

The final major problem with a great revival taking place after the elect of God have been rescued, is that immediately after the rapture of the Church, the Day of the Lord begins. The Day of the Lord is that future period of time when God will pour out His wrath on the earth. As seen in Revelation chapters 8, 9, and 16, the wrath of God will include:

Trumpet Judgment Wrath (Revelation 8 & 9)

- Hail and fire, mixed with blood.
- A third of the earth, trees and grass will be burned up.
- Something like a great mountain, burning with fire, will be thrown into the sea.
- A third of the sea will become like blood.
- A third of the living creatures in the sea will die, and a third of the ships will be destroyed.
- A great star will fall from heaven, blazing like a torch, and fall on a third of the rivers and on the springs of water. Many people die from the polluted water.
- A third of the sun will be "struck," and a third of the moon, and a third of the stars, so that a third of their light might be darkened, and a third of the day might be kept from shining, and likewise a third of the night.
- From smoke will come stinging locusts on the earth, and they will have power to sting like scorpions. They will be allowed to torment people for five months, but not to kill them.

- Four Angels who have been "bound" will be released to kill a third of mankind.

Bowl Judgment Wrath (Revelation 16)

- Harmful and painful sores will come upon the people who bear the mark of the beast and worship its image.
- The sea will become like the blood of a corpse, and every living thing in the sea will die.
- All rivers and the springs of water will become like blood.
- The sun will scorch people with fire.
- The Antichrist's kingdom will be plunged into darkness. People will gnaw their tongues in anguish and curse the God of heaven for their pain and sores.
- A great earthquake such as there has never been since man was on the earth will take place. The great city (Jerusalem) will be split into three parts, and the cities of the nations will fall.
- Every island will sink and every mountain will collapse.
- Great hailstones, about one hundred pounds each, will fall from heaven on the people of the earth.

The above is a list of all of the things followers of Christ are promised to not endure in association with the end of the age. I personally am very happy about that!

Christians have clearly been promised that they will not have to suffer God's wrath.

For God hath not appointed us to wrath, but to obtain salvation by our Lord Jesus Christ, 1 Thess 5:9 (KJV)

If there is a "great revival" after the Church has been raptured, and people are becoming Christians during the Day of the Lord when God's wrath is being poured out on the earth, how is it these new "Christians" have to endure God's wrath? Is there such a thing as being a second class Christian that will have to go through God's wrath? Will I Thessalonians 5:9 not apply to them?

As terrible as the persecution at the hands of the Antichrist might be, it pales in comparison to what will happen on the earth when God's wrath is poured out. God's elect are not appointed to suffer that wrath, so they will not be present during that time. Therefore, there cannot be a "great revival" after the rapture of the Church.

Summary

There are several different groups of people that help make up the cast of characters found in Biblical prophecy pertaining to the end of the age. Many people trip up when they attempt to superimpose the Church into every prophecy or take the Church out and say that the prophecies only deal with Israel. In fact, both the Church and Israel play important independent supporting roles in God's end time production in which Jesus is clearly the star.

In regard to the prophecies concerning "harvests" studied in this chapter, there are two different harvests, and three different groups of people involved;

1) The Church, who we see raptured, or harvested (Revelation 14:14-16, Revelation 7:9-15, Matthew 24:31).
2) The "son's" or "Children of Satan" (the non-believing unsaved), who we see "harvested" and thrown into the winepress of God's wrath (Matt 13:40-42 & Rev 14:17-20), and
3) The "children of the Kingdom, who are considered the "first fruits" that are left to live in the new Kingdom Jesus will establish (Matt 13:43, Rev. 14:1-5). This is the group referred to as 144,000 individuals made up of all the tribes of Israel. We will see more of this group as we continue to study what Jesus said during His Olivet Discourse.

19. And Jesus Answered, "I Don't Know"

He which testifieth these things saith, Surely I come quickly. Amen. Even so, come, Lord Jesus.

-Revelation 2:20

Many can clearly remember "Operation Desert Storm," the code name for the combat portion of the Persian Gulf war that took place in January and February of 1991. The full fury of conventional weaponry of 34 coalition nations, including the United States, in the lead role, showered down on the nation of Iraq for over a month and a half. Iraq's entire infrastructure was destroyed; roads, reliable water and food supplies, and utilities. Homes were erased from the earth. Many people were annihilated. There was nowhere safe to hide.

Angela and I spent a great deal of time watching the war unfold on television. For the first time ever, the United States Department of Defense was supplying first hand video footage of battle events only hours after they had taken place. This included videos from recognizance drones that were searching for targets, along with cruise missiles in which the video would turn to static after the missiles had hit their targets.

I doubt that I will ever forget the surveillance drone footage of a wedding taking place somewhere outside of Baghdad after several days of destruction had already occurred. In the middle of the chaos, people were still eating, drinking, and getting married and celebrating.

Seeing events of normal life take place in the middle of extreme difficulty helped me to relate to the next thing Jesus spoke of during the Olivet Discourse. In spite of extreme hardships and challenges that will arise during the end of the age, life will go on. Some will be faithful and watching for the return of Jesus, others will not.

The Original Questions

Remember the four questions that brought about the Olivet Discourse?

1. When will "these things" happen?
2. What will be the sign that "these things" are about to happen?
3. What will be the sign of your coming and presence back on the earth?
4. What will be the sign of the end of the age?

So far during the Olivet Discourse, Jesus has spent a few minutes giving great answers for questions three through four. One question remains to be answered. That is the "when" question. When will the destruction of the temple take place? The "when question" also concerns when the return of Jesus will occur.

To sum up Jesus' answer as to when all of these things would take place; *He didn't know.* That is correct, at least prior to His death, burial, and resurrection, the Son of God, in His humanness, had not been given the answer to that question by His Heavenly Father.

<u>**Matthew 24:36**</u>

But of that day and hour knoweth no man, no, not the angels of heaven, but my Father only. (KJV)

But no man knows the day and hour. Not the angels of heaven, nor the Son, but my Father only. (DHT)[93]

<u>**Mark 13:32**</u>

But of that day and that hour knoweth no man, no, not the angels which are in heaven, neither the Son, but the Father. (KJV)

But no man knows the day and hour. Not the angels which are in heaven, nor the Son, but the Father. (DHT)

Those that ask questions such as, "since Jesus is God, did He know… (fill in the blank), when He was on the earth?" There are several scriptures that inform us that the human, Jesus, only knew what God the Father revealed to Him. God came to earth in the un-enhanced form of a human, named Jesus. He had all of our human limitations, including being subject to the will and revelations of

Father God. Why didn't the universe spin out of control during the thirty-three or so years Jesus was limited to human form? Because God the Father was not in human form. He had it all under control.

Of course Jesus had the advantage of experiencing very real and personal communion with God the Father, which would have given Him quite a leg up on other humans, to say the least. He unquestionably recognized the voice of the Father. He also knew that to know Himself, was to know God the Father (John 14:8-11).

God the Father did reveal a great deal to His Son while He was on the earth, but like other humans, Jesus had a finite amount of knowledge about the world we live in and its history. He also only knew what His Father supernaturally revealed to Him about the future.

Jesus' answer regarding "when these things" would take place, was a two-fold, "I don't know" answer. Part number one, is that even though we can recognize the signs of His coming, no one knows when those signs will begin, not even Jesus, but only "the Father."

The second "fold" of Jesus' "I don't know" answer, is that Jesus is saying that even when we see the signs indicating His return will be soon, all we know is that His return is imminent, but we still won't know the "day or hour" it will take place.

The sign of the Antichrist committing the Abomination of Desolation will signal that the world is exactly in the middle of a seven-year tribulation period. However, although many like to guess and try to come up with formulas, no one has a clue when that seven-year period may begin. Then, even when the sign of the Abomination of Desolation takes place, no one will know when the final sign of the sun, moon, and stars will occur that will accompany the return of Jesus. Those who are alive and watchful at the time will know that once the Abomination of Desolation occurs, Jesus' return will happen sometime within the next three and a half years.

The Parable of Noah

Next, Jesus makes a statement that almost seems contrary to what He just said. Having just said that "no one knows" when His return will be, Jesus goes on to say how it is both *not good*, and *unnecessary* to be caught off guard by His return. He gave a couple of illustrations to make His point, comparing those who are watchful, with those who are not. First comes an example using a well-known character from the Old Testament; A righteous zookeeper and mariner named Noah.

<u>**Matthew 24:37-39**</u>

But as the days of Noe were, so shall also the coming of the Son of man be. For as in the days that were before the flood they were eating and drinking, marrying and giving in marriage, until the day that Noe entered into the ark, and knew not until the flood came, and took them all away; so shall also the coming of the Son of man be. (KJV)

But like the days of Noah, so will also be the coming of the Son of man. For like in the days before the flood, they were eating, and drinking, and marrying, and giving in marriage until the day Noah entered the ark, and didn't know until the flood came and took everyone away. So shall also be the coming of the Son of Man. (DHT)

The Olivet Discourse comparison of the story of Noah to the end of the age is only found in the book of Matthew, although the same comparison is found elsewhere in the gospel of Luke (Luke 17:26-28).

In the Luke account, it looks like Jesus was on His way to Jerusalem for the Passover when He used the Noah illustration (Luke 17:11). This was the same journey that eventually will find Jesus in Jerusalem for the last time. He and His disciples had not yet even reached Jericho when He was asked by some Pharisees when the Kingdom of God will come (Luke 17:20). Jesus gave the Pharisees a brief answer. However, scripture says that Jesus continued His answer concerning His Second Coming with His disciples later (Luke 17:22).

If this passage in the book of Luke was indeed properly placed in chronological order, this conversation regarding His coming came several days, perhaps even up to a week before the Olivet Discourse. Much of what Jesus told them in the Luke account is repeated in the Olivet Discourse. You can read what Jesus told His disciples regarding His coming in Luke 17:22-37.

When we find nearly identical passages in two different gospels that don't appear to be in the same chronological order, some jump to the conclusion that at least one of the gospel writers must have gotten their story wrong. However, there are several reasonable and likely explanations for this. I resonate with one particular explanation.

Typically, when I am trying to teach a principle, and I find an example that works, I will use it over again. I will even use them over again with the same group of people. I will do this for several different reasons. I may use the same story as a reminder of a principle previously taught. If I want to stress that a point is really important I may repeat myself. I may do this if I want to make sure they remember what I am talking about. I may retell a story if I think the principle can better be understood in light of new information. It is very reasonable to conclude that Jesus, when speaking of His return, would use the same illustrations to teach important points.

It would have probably been very meaningful for the four disciples present for the Olivet Discourse to hear things like the Noah parable *again,* in light of what Jesus just told them regarding the signs of His coming.

There is documentation in scripture that the disciples did not understand what Jesus was talking about the first time they heard Jesus use the Noah story.

And they understood none of these things: and this saying was hid from them, neither knew they the things which were spoken. Luke 18:34 (KJV)

Jesus would have recognized this lack of understanding. It would make perfect sense for Him to repeat the information that evening on the Mount of Olives. Given the new information Jesus had just revealed during the Olivet Discourse regarding His coming, what He had previously said on the way to Jerusalem would have been better understood by the curious disciples.

The Luke version of the Noah story being compared to the return of Jesus goes like this:

And as it was in the days of Noe, so shall it be also in the days of the Son of man. They did eat, they drank, they married wives, they were given in marriage, until the day that Noe entered into the ark, and the flood came, and destroyed them all. Luke 17:26-27 (KJV)

The Noah story in the book of Luke is immediately followed by a short summary of the story of the Old Testament character, Lot:

Likewise also as it was in the days of Lot; they did eat, they drank, they bought, they sold, they planted, they builded; But the same day that Lot went out of Sodom it rained fire and brimstone from heaven, and destroyed them all. Even thus shall it be in the day when the Son of man is revealed. Luke 17:28-30 (KJV)

The original story of Noah is found in the books of Genesis, chapters 6 to 9. Noah was said to be a righteous man in the eyes of God. God told Noah to build a large floating vessel in a place where there was no sea and told him He was going to destroy the earth with water. Noah did as God asked and he and his family were saved because of it. The flood destroyed the rest of the world's population.

The main message derived from the story of Noah as compared to the return of Jesus is that there will be people caught off guard by His return. These people will be going about their lives like always, oblivious to the signs that Jesus' return is imminent. However, we need to adequately absorb a key point; Noah *was not* caught off guard. He was prepared, watchful, and ready when the flood came. He was following the plan given to him. He was prepared for the flood through His attentiveness, obedience and devotion to God. This is the point Jesus, Peter, and Paul want us to understand; we do not need to be caught off guard.

Another thing we can take away from both the story of Noah and the story of Lot, is that once God had seen to the protection of Noah and Lot by taking them out of the way, the judgment of those that remained behind was immediate. So it will be after Jesus gathers His Church to Himself.

A Different Looking Life

A day in the life of Noah looked very different than other people's lives. After receiving his calling from God, by faith he worked diligently day after day in order to be obedient and please

God. This different lifestyle undoubtedly came with a high social price tag.

Noah was going against the "science" of his day. No one had ever observed rain, and there was not a body of water close enough for Noah to have taken his ship. Noah lived by faith. Decades came and went with no indication of rain, and Noah persisted.

Although, being a righteous man would have had its benefits, the fact that Noah was so different, had to cost him some social relationships. He may even have been thought of as a little crazy, or a fool. Yet, because of Noah's faith in something that he could not see, based on only a promise from God that it would happen, Noah and his family were saved. Noah lived with *certainty* and *expectancy* of what God told him would come to pass.

The comparison is obvious; the watchful elect of God will live in a manner that reflects their belief that what Jesus said is going to happen *will* come to pass in a very real way. They will work diligently, daily to please their Master so that they will be found ready to meet Him when He returns. Others, who have their own priorities in life, who look at the promises of Jesus as foolishness, will be counted among the lost.

One Taken, the Other Left

Jesus went on to give another example to His disciples regarding the coming "harvest."

Matt 24:40-41

Then shall two be in the field; the one shall be taken, and the other left. Two women shall be grinding at the mill; the one shall be taken, and the other left. (KJV)

At that time, two will be in the field; one will be taken and the other left. Two will be grinding at the mill; one will be taken, and the other left. (DHT)

Luke records Jesus saying much the same thing to His disciples in an earlier passage.

I tell you, in that night there shall be two men in one bed; the one shall be taken, and the other shall be left. Two women shall be grinding together; the one shall be taken, and the other left. Two men shall be in the field; the one shall be taken, and the other left. Luke 17:34-36 (KJV)

Who Are Those Taken, And Who Are Those Left?

The classic interpretation of this passage states the ones being suddenly taken, are the righteous and the ones who are left behind are the unrighteous. This illustration Jesus is using represents the rapture of the church. [94] Those who hold to the pretribulation rapture prefer this interpretation, although it is strange they do, since many of them don't believe the Olivet Discourse applies to the Church!

A second interpretation of this passage says it is the wicked who are suddenly taken, and the righteous are those who are left. That theory says Jesus is talking about a time when the earth is cleansed of the wicked. They are suddenly taken away and "thrown into the winepress of God's wrath" (See the previous chapter). [95] Those that hold to this theory typically use this interpretation against those who believe in a pretribulation rapture.

After years of studying this topic, the conclusion I have reached is based on the understanding that there are two harvests, as also discussed in the previous chapter. My supposition is that most who attempt to interpret this passage of scripture get too bogged down in attempting to fit this story into one harvest or the other. In my opinion, this passage of scripture fits nicely with both harvests.

The general intention of the passage, is to convey the importance of being watchful and about the business of the Master until His return. We are to do so with endurance and in faith. I am not sure that it is necessary to force a more specific interpretation.

Both the Church and those that inhabit the coming Kingdom of Jesus on this earth will be supernaturally protected from God's judgment which will be poured out on the wicked. Both groups will also be going about the business of living a human existence right up until the events of the end of the age occur.

The idea is people will be caught away while engaging in day to day activities. The fact that some are "in bed" and some are in "the field" merely speaks to the fact that this is a world-wide event, where both night and day exist at the same time. The people represented in this passage are engaging in activities which would indicate what Jesus just said is true: "no one knows the day or hour."

Even though followers of Christ living in close proximity to the end of the age may be "watchful," "awake" and know they are close to the return of Christ, they will still have to eat. They will need to sleep. They will need to support their families. They will still fall in love and want to get married. They will be doing all of these things when the angels are sent to "gather the elect from the four winds."

Surviving The End

You may notice all of the following statements are absent from Jesus' words:

- "Two shall be sitting in their fallout shelter because they know the end is near, one will be taken, and the other left."
- "Two shall be selling all their possessions, giving the money to the poor, and preaching the gospel on the street corner. Both shall be taken because they are such good Christians."
- "Two shall be stock piling food and weapons, because that is what will be needed to survive. One shall be taken, and the other left with an outrageous credit card balance."
- "Two shall be sitting on their roof tops watching for Jesus to appear in the sky. One shall be taken, and the other left, because the one misunderstood the Olivet Discourse."

There is absolutely nothing wrong with preparing for emergencies. It is a wise thing to do as God gives us the ability. However, followers of Christ preparing their way out of trials and tribulation is not the message of the Olivet Discourse or any other end times related scripture. Jesus told us that there would be suffering for His namesake. There is no preparation that you can do that will circumvent the plan God has in store for you.

Although I did not manage it directly, as Chief Deputy of the Sheriff's Office, one of the areas I had administrative responsibility for was the Emergency Management Section. I know that for any given emergency, there are steps you can take to prepare in order to mitigate the outcome. I also know there are things that you can do to eliminate certain degrees of risk. My training included the survival philosophy that "if it is predictable, it is preventable." If you don't want your house to be flooded, live above the flood plain. If you don't want a forest fire to burn your house down, create a defensible space around it by removing easily combustible vegetation.

What the Olivet Discourse tells us is that although the Second Coming of Christ is predictable, it is not preventable! The way to be prepared for the Second Coming of Christ is to be counted amongst those that know Jesus as their Lord and to be "watchful."

The most important survival advice which can be given in regard to the end of the age is to abide in Christ, watch for His Coming and be found His faithful servant when He returns! Outside of fleeing to the hills if you live in Jerusalem when you see the Abomination of Desolation take place, believers are given little instruction on survival.

The elect of God will need to use their God given wisdom when it comes to practical physical matters such as when to stay and when and where to go, how much food to store, or how ready you need to be to flee. The end of the age will be a time, like many other times in history, when followers of Jesus will need to rely first on God, secondly on their wisdom and on each other, and lastly on their stockpile of food.

The idea that people will be going about their regular business gives a lot of credibility to the idea that the final sign of a great, world-wide earthquake, the sun going black, the moon turning red, and the stars falling from the sky will happen suddenly, and immediately before the elect are gathered to Jesus.

I believe that the type of "watchfulness" that Jesus is talking about next in the Olivet Discourse has to do more with abiding in Christ and less to do with knowing exactly the signs of His coming. No one, who is elect of God, will be "left behind" for not having their eschatology correct. They may become confused, disillusioned, imprisoned, or put to death, but God won't leave them behind because they fail to recognize the final signs.

An observation about this scripture that I find very comforting, is that even though the Church is in the midst of great persecution and tribulation at the hand of the Antichrist, life, at least for some, will be somewhat normal.

It is estimated that today, almost 22% of the world's GDP is driven by a shadow economy, or "black market."[96] Just because an identification "mark" will be required by the Antichrist in order to buy or sell, doesn't mean those who don't take it will starve to death. The world has always been full of people that are skilled in circumventing the "system." Christians that refuse to abide by the Antichrist's rules, will be no different.

Matthew 24:42

Watch therefore: for ye know not what hour your Lord doth come. (KJV)

Therefore, be vigilant; because you don't know what hour your Lord will come. (DHT)

Mark 13:33

Take ye heed, watch and pray: for ye know not when the time is. (KJV)

Pay attention, stay awake, and pray; for you don't know when the time is. (DHT)

Luke 21:34-36

And take heed to yourselves, lest at any time your hearts be overcharged with surfeiting, and drunkenness, and cares of this life, and so that day come upon you unawares. For as a snare shall it come on all them that dwell on the face of the whole earth. Watch ye therefore, and pray always, that ye may be accounted worthy to escape all these things that shall come to pass, and to stand before the Son of man. (KJV)

And pay attention to yourselves, lest at any time your hearts be overcome by revelry, and drunkenness, and distractions of this life, so that day catches you off guard. For that day will come like a trap on everyone that dwells on the face of the entire earth. Stay awake therefore, and always pray that you might prevail and escape all of these things that are going to happen, and to stand before the Son of man. (DHT)

Because we can't know exactly when it will take place, Jesus strongly commands that His disciples be sober and watchful. While they pay attention to what is going on in their own lives, they are also to actively perceive what is going on in the world around them.

We don't need to "watch" in order to take some action when Jesus shows up that will allow us to go with Him. He will take care of everything. We also know that we don't need to "watch" because Jesus' coming will be a secret and only those who are watching closely will see it. Jesus' coming will be no secret. "Watchfulness" *is* important for all of the reasons stated in chapter three of this book.

Staying Undistracted

Luke 21:34 gives us some further specifics on what it means to be watchful; paying attention to ourselves that we don't become distracted by the cares of this life. Jesus seems to be focusing on the kind of watchfulness that has to do with how we conduct our lives, while we are waiting for His return. We need to behave in a manner in which we would not be ashamed if the Master were to return today.

Included in Jesus' "list of distractions" is being drunk and engaging in "surfeiting," which literally means to experience giddiness and have a headache that is typically associated with being drunk. Surfeiting seems to include everything in the drinking experience from the point of becoming "giddy" or having a heavy buzz through the point of the subsequent hangover.

For those legalistic minded, anti-fermentation types who are leaning back in their chairs with a smirk now and thinking to themselves, "See I told you so. Drinking is a sin!" I would point out that surfeiting and drunkenness have to do with over indulgence and not what liquid you drink.

I am not advocating for consuming alcohol, but some who have never drank alcohol honestly don't know this; drinking a beverage containing alcohol does not make you drunk, giddy, or give you a hangover, unless you overindulge. Overindulging is different for everyone, based on their body mass and chemistry.

The things of this life, both pleasures and troubles, can be distracting and can easily take our focus off of God. Those that are heavily engaged with the world, are those who will be caught off guard by the return of Christ. This portion of the Olivet Discourse is focusing on not only people being caught off guard and surprised by

His return, but being caught off guard in a way that finds them ashamed when the Master returns.

Those who are caught off guard are the ones who are overtaken like when a thief breaks into someone's home in the middle of the night. This is what the Apostle Paul wrote about being caught off guard.

But of the times and the seasons, brethren, ye have no need that I write unto you. For yourselves know perfectly that the day of the Lord so cometh as a thief in the night. For when they shall say, Peace and safety; then sudden destruction cometh upon them, as travail upon a woman with child; and they shall not escape. 1 Thess 5:1-3 (KJV)

The group of people that Paul is talking about are those that are so unaware, that they have bought into the idea that the world, most likely due to the efforts of the Antichrist, is a place of "peace and safety." No worries; "eat, drink, and be merry." This is the same group of people the Apostle Peter wrote about:

Knowing this first, that there shall come in the last days scoffers, walking after their own lusts, and saying, where is the promise of his coming? for since the fathers fell asleep, all things continue as they were from the beginning of the creation. 2 Peter 3:3-4 (KJV)

This group of unwatchful mockers, confident that life will go on as usual forever, are those that will be caught off guard. They will be leading their lives according to their own self determined plans, instead of according to the wisdom of God.

These scriptures serve as warnings. Peter and Paul are not saying that this will be the case for everyone. The message is that it is *unnecessary* to be overtaken like a "thief in the night." Remember, Paul continued in the same passage:

But ye, brethren, are not in darkness, that that day should overtake you as a thief. Ye are all the children of light, and the children of the day: we are not of the night, nor of darkness. Therefore let us not sleep, as do others; but let us watch and be sober. 1 Thess 5:4-6 (KJV)

In order to drive home the idea of not being caught off guard even further, Jesus continues with the following illustration:

<u>**Matt 24:43-44**</u>

But know this, that if the goodman of the house had known in what watch the thief would come, he would have watched, and would not have suffered his house to be broken up. Therefore be ye also ready: for in such an hour as ye think not the Son of man cometh. (KJV)

But understand this, that if the head of the household would have known at what time the thief would come, he would have watched and not had his house broken into. The same goes for you; be ready; for at such a time when you don't think, the Son of Man will come. (DHT)

The Gospel of Luke records that Jesus made this same statement to His disciples some time earlier.

And this know, that if the goodman of the house had known what hour the thief would come, he would have watched, and not have suffered his house to be broken through. Be ye therefore ready also: for the Son of man cometh at an hour when ye think not. Luke 12:39-40 (KJV)

This imagery of the "thief," the same as used later by the Apostle Paul (1 Thes 5:2-6) and the Apostle Peter (2 Peter 3:10-11), is intended to convey the idea of un-expectancy to those who are not watchful and prepared. Matthew 24:43 also conveys the idea that those who are not watchful will regret it. Those that believe that they can go through life without being good and faithful servants of God, may want to take note of this scripture and what Jesus says next.

A Personal Note

As a personal side note, this particular scripture played a part in my being led to engage in the study of end times to the extent that I have in the past decades.

The Bible records that God used the dreams of people on several occasions to foretell the future or guide people's lives. I would always be extremely skeptical if someone were trying to impart some sort of advice to me that they had received in a dream. However, I have had a few very powerful and vivid dreams that have impacted my own life. One of them contained this scripture.

In early 1997 experienced increasing conviction to share with others the things that I had been discovering through my intense study regarding the Second Coming of Christ. These discoveries were not new "revelations" or unique "personal interpretations" I was experiencing. They were only the result of following a systematic approach to studying the Bible.

During the preceding few years of study I had found several things that did not match up with what I knew was being taught in most evangelical circles. At the time I was also observing that many Christians were beginning to become distracted with "Y2K" fear. The year 2000 computer date interpretation issue was commonly being related to possible end time scenarios. I mostly ignored the conviction to share what I had learned with others, thinking, "who am I to talk to anyone about this stuff." Then one night I had the dream.

In my dream, it was the middle of the night. I was in my underwear, asleep in my bed when someone who was beating on the back door of our house suddenly awakened me. I jumped out of bed and rushed to the door and looked through the peephole. I saw a very large, hairy, Neanderthal-like human being, with bad teeth. I can still clearly see him in my mind's eye today. No words were exchanged with this threatening looking individual.

As I was standing there in my underwear, unarmed, thinking about how I would address this situation, the large "man" effortlessly kicked in my door. As I aggressively lunged at him in an effort to protect my sleeping wife and three children, he grabbed me by the throat, picked me up and hurled me against the wall, fifteen feet away. I melted to the floor like a limp noodle.

As I tried to make my way to my feet, the "man" quickly closed the distance and picked me up again by my neck before I could know or react to what was going on. He again slammed my body against the wall.

As my broken, barely conscious body slumped to the floor, I heard a voice. The voice did not come from the man. It very clearly and authoritatively said to me, *"If the owner of the house would have known what time of night the thief was coming, he would have kept watch and would not have let his house be broken into.*"

I woke up breathing hard, shaking, and in a cold sweat. Soon after I started a five-year run of intensive study and published a monthly research and teaching publication called, "*The Watchful Watchman.*" It is the thousands of hours of study, and hundreds of pages of notes taken during that period of time, that have served as a basis for much of this book.

Summary

As we have seen in preceding chapters of this book, Jesus gave several signs that will occur very soon before His coming. Among those signs are the coming of the Antichrist who commits the act of the Abomination of Desolation in the temple in Jerusalem. This will be followed by severe persecution of the Jews and the Church. Finally, there will be a signs in the heavens that will take the form of the sun going black, the moon turning red, the stars appearing to fall from the sky, and a great world-wide earth quake. In spite of these signs, *no one* will know the day or hour of Jesus' return, until it happens.

The illustrations Jesus used, regarding some who were watchful and others who were caught off guard, seem to work with both harvests that will take place at the end of the age. However, the most important thing to glean from the illustrations Jesus used is that His followers need to be faithfully and diligently about their Masters business until He returns.

Believers and non-believers alike will be engaging in normal day to day activities up until Jesus' return. As in the times of Noah, before a flood wiped out the world's population, people will be going about their business. They will still need to eat during the tribulation period. They will still be getting married. They will still need money. Most will not recognize the signs that are occurring around them, but the faithful servant of God will remain watchful and not be caught off guard.

20. The Faithful and the Naughty
(Parable of the Servants)

On one particular slow news day, I watched a feature story on a local station that was inspired by a group of astronomers. They were putting on a symposium in the city close to where I live. The topic of the news story was, "Just where is the center of the universe?" Quickly taking the philosophical fork in the road, leaving science behind, the reporter put this question to random citizens on the street.

The answers varied a little, but one seemed to be dominating the others. It was in fact the reporter's own answer. From his perspective, the center of the Universe is *wherever he is.*

I wonder how a true follower of Jesus would answer that question? A follower of Jesus that understands the master-servant relationship we have with Him. A servant that understands who their Master is; the one who created the universe.

While maintaining a theme of watchfulness, Jesus addresses the master and servant relationship. He points out both the pitfalls of not being watchful, and the benefits of being watchful through the telling of a story about a servant who has been put in charge of his master's household, while the master is away.

Matt 24:45-51

Who then is a faithful and wise servant, whom his lord hath made ruler over his household, to give them meat in due season? Blessed is that servant, whom his lord when he cometh shall find so doing. Verily I say unto you, that he shall make him ruler over all his goods. But and if that evil servant shall say in his heart, my lord delayeth his coming; And shall begin to smite his fellow servants, and to eat and drink with the drunken; The lord of that servant shall come in a day when he looketh not for him, and in an hour that he is not aware of, and shall cut him asunder, and appoint him his portion with the hypocrites: there shall be weeping and gnashing of teeth. (KJV)

Who then is a faithful and wise servant who the Lord has made ruler over his household, to give them food at the proper time?

Fortunate is the servant who is found doing so when the lord comes. I am telling you the truth; he will give him authority over all of his possessions. But if the evil servant says in his heart that the master is delayed, and he begins to beat his fellow servants, and begins to eat and drink with the drunken, the lord of that servant will come in a day that he is not looking for him and at an hour that he is not aware of, and will cut him in two, and assign him his portion with the hypocrites: there will be wailing and grating of teeth. (DHT)

This story casts Jesus in the role of the "master" who goes away. The true and faithful disciple of Jesus plays the role of the good "servant." The bad servant represents one who is a Christian in name only.

You will find a very similar parable found in Luke 12:42-48. In regard to where the bad servant will be sent, the Luke account says that the servant will be assigned to the same place as "unbelievers," rather than the Matthew passage which says with "hypocrites." The servant, representing his or herself as a believer, and not really being one, is both a "hypocrite" and an "unbeliever."

Whereas many stories and parables that Jesus told use symbolism, the "servants" in this story are really intended to represent literal servants. I have discovered that there are those within the Church, who don't particularly like to be thought of as servants. Some are more comfortable with thinking of themselves as a "child of God," or a "joint heir with Jesus," or other such titles that convey more of a sense of freedom and authority than the title "servant" does.

The New Testament is rich in scripture pointing out that those of us who have been purchased by Jesus, through the shedding of His blood on the cross, are indeed His "bond servants."

Bought and Paid For

Many, who choose to accept Jesus as their Savior have tragically missed or don't understand a major part of the transaction that took place when Jesus shed His blood for them on the cross. They know with His blood Jesus "redeemed" them, by "paying the price" or penalty, or making atonement for their sin. However, they have neglected, although probably unintentionally, an entire component of what the blood of Christ did.

What the shedding of Jesus' blood accomplished is of such importance that it *cannot* be missed if Christians are going to even begin to understand our roles and our very purpose as followers of Christ. It is only through having the knowledge of this particular essentiality that we should approach our God in prayer in the name of our "Master," Jesus. We have to grasp this principle in order to try to understand His word, or even understand how we as Christians should do our business and live in this world while we await Jesus' coming.

The Lamb That Was Slain

A lamb, in the fifth chapter of Revelation, looking as though it had been butchered or slain is seen by the Apostle John, as he entered the throne room of Heaven in his vision. An unquestionable case is made by the immediate and greater context that this Lamb represents Jesus.

God chose to use the imagery of a slain Lamb to represent Jesus rather than the familiar form of a man. Jesus is referred to as "the Lamb" twenty-nine times in the book of Revelation alone. God often uses symbols in prophecy, like this lamb, as a means of communicating a complex message or concept across time and culture.

The answer as to why Jesus is seen as a Lamb starts to unfold as we listen to the words of those that are also seen gathered around the throne, along with the Apostle John, in the Revelation chapter 5 scene in Heaven as they sing a "new song."

In that "song" the "singers" give praise to Jesus for what He did when He, like a sacrificial lamb of the Old Testament or "Old Covenant," paid the price for and made atonement for sin. The difference between the routinely made Old Covenant sacrifices, and Jesus' sacrifice is that Jesus paid this price once and for all for all mankind. This sacrifice was for all who ever had and ever would exist. The Apostle Peter put it this way:

Forasmuch as ye know that ye were not redeemed with corruptible things, as silver and gold, from your vain conversation received by tradition from your fathers; But with the precious blood of Christ, as of a lamb without blemish and without spot: 1 Peter 1:18-19 (KJV)

The sinner's redemption was not paid for with normal currency or worldly goods, but with the "precious blood of Christ."

It is what Jesus did in the role of a sacrificial Lamb that makes being a "Christian" possible. It is only because He redeems one from one's sins that they are able to be spiritually reborn and enter the Kingdom of God. However, when Jesus steps in and pays off someone's debt with His blood, redemption from sin is only part of what happens during the miraculous transaction. With His blood, He also "purchases" the person that accepts Him as his or her redeemer.

And they sung a new song, saying, Thou art worthy to take the book, and to open the seals thereof: for thou wast slain, and hast redeemed us to God ***by thy blood*** *out of every kindred, and tongue, and people, and nation; And hast made us unto our God kings and priests: and we shall reign on the earth.* Rev 5:9-10 (KJV) (Emphasis added)

The word translated in the King James Version of the Bible as "ransomed," is the Greek word, ἀγοράζω, transliterated as "agarazo," meaning to "buy" or "purchase." [97]

A one-time, everlasting transaction took place as Jesus traded His life's blood for the eternal souls of those that would follow after Him. Those souls, by the grace of God, were chosen from a time before the foundations of the earth were set in place. With His blood they were not only saved from eternal damnation, but they were also *purchased* from among mankind to become a special people of God.

Looking for that blessed hope, and the glorious appearing of the great God and our Saviour Jesus Christ; Who gave himself for us, that ***he might redeem us*** *from all iniquity, and purify unto himself a peculiar people, zealous of good works. Titus 2:13-14 (KJV) (Emphasis added)*

Take heed therefore unto yourselves, and to all the flock, over the which the Holy Ghost hath made you overseers, to feed the church of God, ***which he hath purchased*** *with his own blood. Acts 20:28 (KJV)* (Emphasis added)

It is hard to miss the fact in the New Testament that Jesus not only paid the price for redeeming His servants in full, but He also purchased them in the transaction as His own *possessions*. He didn't pay for our sins only to turn us out as free agents to be victimized by our own flesh again, but so that we may serve Him as "bond servants," just as those closest to Jesus did.

Like the Apostle **Paul**: *Paul, a* ***servant*** (Transliterated from the Greek as "doulos") *of Jesus Christ, called to be an apostle, separated unto the gospel of God,* Romans 1:1 (KJV) (Emphasis and transliteration added)

And like **Peter***: Simon Peter, a* ***servant*** (doulos*) and an apostle of Jesus Christ, to them that have obtained like precious faith with us through the righteousness of God and our Saviour Jesus Christ: 2 Peter 1:1 (KJV)* (Emphasis and "doulos" added)

And **James**: *James, a* ***servant*** (doulos) *of God and of the Lord Jesus Christ, to the twelve tribes which are scattered abroad, greeting. James 1:1 (KJV)* (Emphasis and "doulos" added)

And **John**: *The Revelation of Jesus Christ, which God gave unto him, to shew unto his* ***servants*** (doulos) *things which must shortly come to pass; and he sent and signified it by his angel unto his* ***servant*** (doulos) *John: Rev 1:1 (KJV)* (Emphasis and "doulos" added)

And like **Jude**: *Jude, the* ***servant*** (doulos) *of Jesus Christ, and brother of James, to them that are sanctified by God the Father, and preserved in Jesus Christ, and called: Jude 1:1 (KJV)* (Emphasis and "doulos" added)

Bond-Servants of Christ

The Greek word for "bond-servant" is "δοῦλοζ," transliterated into English as "*doulos*" (doo'-los), which is an adjective meaning "servant" or to be "in bondage."[98]

The book of Revelation is addressed to the "bond-servants" of Christ also identified later in the book as the "Church." The way we see *doulos* used in the New Testament is in the usual way you would think of a "slave;" as if the person called a slave was owned by another and completely subject to their will.

The apostles of Jesus in their New Testament writings refer to the followers of Christ as "bond-servants" and instructs them (us) how to act accordingly in this role.

But now being made free from sin, and become ***servants*** *to God, ye have your fruit unto holiness, and the end everlasting life. Rom 6:22 (KJV)*

As free, and not using your liberty for a cloke of maliciousness, but as the ***servants*** *of God. 1 Peter 2:16 (KJV)*

Any truly born again Christian, voluntarily became a slave and possession, when they allowed Jesus to purchase them. They belong to and are "owned" by Jesus.

Our reward is secure and lasts forever because of what our Master and Owner, Jesus, has done for us. Our reward is that we have been saved from the eternal damnation that we deserve. It is only through God's grace and by His mercy that He has rescued us, allowing us to dwell with Him and to serve Him throughout all of eternity (see Rev 7:14-17).

We did nothing to gain favor with God or did nothing to deserve to be ransomed. He was, or is in no way obligated to pay for our sins that condemned us to eternal death. It is because of the ransom that was paid that the born again Christian is a *possession,* or a bondservant of Christ.

Bond Servant Explained

Understanding the practices of slavery in ancient Israel, helps to further understand the kind of "bondage" involved with being a bondservant.

And if a sojourner or stranger wax rich by thee, and thy brother that dwelleth by him wax poor, and sell himself unto the stranger or sojourner by thee, or to the stock of the stranger's family: After that he is sold he may be redeemed again; one of his brethren may redeem him: Lev 25:47-48 (KJV)

In ancient Israel, if one had incurred a debt in which they could not pay, they could *voluntarily* sell themselves into slavery. There was no forced slavery in Israel. However, debts needed to be paid. Similarly, when human beings sin, they incur a debt that they cannot pay themselves. The penalty for that debt is death. In ancient Israel, one could voluntarily allow another to pay their debt for them in exchange for becoming their bondservant. Jesus is the only one who has the "bank" to be able to pay our debt and redeem us. Once we voluntarily allow this to happen and accept Him as our Master, our debt is paid, and we become His bondservants.

Joint Heirs with Jesus?

How do we reconcile being both "free," and a "slave" at the same time (1 Peter 2:16)? How does a slave become a "joint heir" with Jesus (Romans 8:17)? How can we, a group of bondservants be considered to be a "royal priesthood" (1 Peter 2:9)?

Slavery has taken on many forms in history. Becoming a bondservant specifically in Israel, subject to Hebrew laws, was nothing like how we might picture someone becoming enslaved; chased down, captured, beaten, chained up, thrown on a ship, starved, humiliated, striped of all dignity and identity and then sold, only to be treated like a beast of burden.

In Israel a slave became a member of the slave owner's family, just as if they were adopted. He or she enjoyed all of the same rights as the rest of the family, with the exception of inheritance. Additionally, every seven years, all slave contracts were considered cancelled and the slave could go free.

If thou buy an Hebrew servant, six years he shall serve: and in the seventh he shall go out free for nothing. Ex 21:2 (KJV)

On the surface, the Hebrew slave-master relationship comparison to the follower of Christ's relationship with Jesus looks like it starts to break down for a couple of reasons: Although treated like a family member, a Hebrew slave does not receive inheritance as a family member, while the elect of God are considered "joint heirs" with Jesus. Secondly, unlike Hebrew slaves, there is no seven-year clause that gets us out of our sin debt and cancels our slave contract.

The interesting thing is that although a slave had the option to go free after six years, they also had the option of voluntarily staying and becoming a slave "forever."

And if the servant shall plainly say, I love my master, my wife, and my children; I will not go out free: Then his master shall bring him unto the judges; he shall also bring him to the door, or unto the door post; and his master shall bore his ear through with an aul; and he shall serve him for ever. Ex 21:5-6 (KJV)

If one understands what it means to become a bondservant, and accepts Jesus' offer to pay off her or his debt, and he or she plainly declares, I "love my Master" and "will not go out free on my own," Jesus will mark him or her as His own possession, and she or he will become His servant for all eternity.

Inheritance as a Slave?

As previously stated, in ancient Israel, even though a slave was treated as a part of the family as though he or she was adopted, they would not ever be in line to inherit anything. How does this reconcile with being a "joint heir with Jesus?"

Wherefore thou art no more a servant, but a son; and if a son, then an heir of God through Christ. Gal 4:7 (KJV)

After Jesus' human flesh died on the cross, He rose to eternal life and was given all power and authority. Everything that is, is His. When you accept His offer of redemption and become His possession, it is as if you are adopted into His eternal family. It is not necessary to be an "heir" in the normal sense. Usually descendants only receive an inheritance if someone dies. However, Jesus will never die again. By being purchased and adopted by Him, those that belong to Him will enjoy the benefits of being in His eternal family, where Jesus has possession of, and authority over everything!

Will Jesus be Your Master or Judge?

To leave anyone with the impression that a true follower of Christ is only a "slave" of God in the sense that we would normally think of slaves, would be an oversimplification causing an inaccurate image in most people's minds. One would understandably feel uncomfortable as a slave if their master were evil. That is not the case when Jesus is the Master. With Jesus as our Master, we need not ever fear the task that He gives us:

Come unto me, all ye that labour and are heavy laden, and I will give you rest. Take my yoke upon you, and learn of me; for I am meek and lowly in heart: and ye shall find rest unto your souls. For my yoke is easy, and my burden is light. Matt 11:28-30 (KJV)

Prior to being a slave or possession of God, we were "slaves to sin" (Romans 6:15-19). Our old master was Satan (II Timothy 2:26). In order to attempt to break the bondage of sin, outside of belonging to Christ, people enslave themselves to the law. Being adopted into Jesus' family, you are no longer in bondage to Satan, sin or the law. Belonging now to our Master, Jesus, we are absolutely free from our old master.

Our position as slaves to Christ in this physical world is voluntary (as far as our free will goes). If you choose not to become a bondservant of Jesus, no one on this earth will hunt you down or beat you. However, after living a life in bondage to sin and Satan, you will ultimately be subject to Jesus, and know Him as your Judge.

The Parable of the Pearl

There is a famous parable in the New Testament about a man who secretly finds a pearl he feels is so valuable that he sells everything else he owns in order to buy it.

Again, the kingdom of heaven is like unto a merchant man, seeking goodly pearls: Who, when he had found one pearl of great price, went and sold all that he had, and bought it. Matt 13:45-46 (KJV)

If you are familiar with this parable, you may have been taught that the "pearl" in this passage represents Jesus, and that the one who finds the pearl is the one who chooses to follow Jesus. Those that choose Jesus are to go and sell, or in other words leave everything else behind, give up their personal dreams, etc., in order to gain salvation and follow Jesus. This explanation seems to work until we pay attention to what else we know about salvation; that it is a gift from God and that there is nothing we can give or do to earn it, and it is God that does the choosing, not us.

We could sell everything we own, leave everything and everybody behind and still fall miserably short of the purchase price of salvation. There is but one who gave up everything in order to purchase from among men, the "pearls" that are to make up the special people of God, and that is Jesus. Jesus is the merchant of the parable, that gave His very life in order to *purchase* us.

What Then Are We to Do About It?

With an understanding of our relationship as bondservants to Christ, what then should be our attitude towards our needs, comforts, and affairs of this world? How should we approach God in prayer? Does our Master, who owns us free and clear, owe us anything more than He already has paid for us? If we do an especially good job for Him, can we expect a bonus? Here is a little story straight from the mouth of Jesus that gives us some answers:

But which of you, having a servant plowing or feeding cattle, will say unto him by and by, when he is come from the field, Go and sit down to meat? And will not rather say unto him, make ready wherewith I may sup, and gird thyself, and serve me, till I have eaten and drunken; and afterward thou shalt eat and drink? Doth he thank that servant because he did the things that were commanded him? I trow not. So likewise ye, when ye shall have done all those things which are commanded you, say, we are unprofitable servants: we have done that which was our duty to do. Luke 17:7-10 (KJV)

In this parable Jesus is in the role of the master and those who He has purchased with His blood are His servants. The point of the parable is slaves are supposed to do what they are told, and not expect anything more than they already have in return. The master always comes first. When you consider what we already have by being adopted into God's family, is there really anything more you need?

When you study the life of Jesus, do you find an individual who is seeking comfort and pleasure in this world? What then do we do with those preachers and teachers who teach doctrines contrary to the life of Christ while He dwelled on the earth? Jesus said:

The disciple is not above his master, nor the servant above his lord. Matt 10:24 (KJV)

If you are a human being, you will likely wrestle with the wants and desires of your flesh until the day you die. As for me, as I struggle with these things, I need to continually consider the following "code of conduct" in regards to my relationship with my Master, Jesus.

A Servants Code of Conduct

I am not trying to add to what the Bible has to say about how the elect of God should conduct themselves. However, the term "bondservant," brings with it an implied meaning. As though we should already have some idea as to what it means to be one.

How is a "bondservant" expected to conduct his or her self? Does a slave order around His master? Of course not: good and wise slaves approach their master humbly and realize that their purpose is to please Him. A good slave does everything with his master in mind.

The slave owns nothing. Everything they have, including their very lives, belongs to their master. They don't spend the money their master has entrusted to them unwisely. Although they may seek wise counsel, they also don't let others besides their master tell them how to spend what has been entrusted to them.

Every activity the slave takes on is only done after they consider if it benefits the master's household or something the master would want the slave to be doing if the He were to show up. As they walk through their community conducting their master's business, they realize they represent their master's household and conduct themselves accordingly.

The slave is accountable only to the master for their actions. However, the master expects his slaves to remind each other of that accountability. The master also expects them to love one another and treat one another as they would want to be treated.

Motivations

Argue all you like about the "law vs. grace," or "faith vs. works." Try to come up with motivations on why not to sin after the sin has all been paid for by Jesus on the cross. I will listen and continue to learn, but for me, my motivation for trying to please Jesus is as simple as understanding that I am no longer my own. After dying to myself and being reborn a new creature, I have a new identity; I am a bondservant of my Lord, Jesus Christ.

I belong to a master whom I want to please. Not because I'm trying to pay Him back, that's not possible, but because I love my Master. I may mess up all the time, but He is forgiving and knows that I am trying.

My Master knows me very well. In fact, He created me. He does not hold who He created me to be against me. He knows I am flawed, that I am subject to battling my flesh continually, and that I am still learning.

I don't obey my Master out of fear that I might break a law and be found guilty or think my salvation is in jeopardy, I want to be obedient to Him because I love Him and don't want to hurt Him. I am a willing slave who has been won over by a loving master. Through the faith He gave me, I love Him because I understand who He is and what He has already done for me. My love is not dependent on what He *could* do for me.

A slave never takes center stage, even in their own life. Their life is not their own to control. Most of us cannot come close to relating to what it means to be a slave. How different the slave's life is compared to what we see around us in our culture.

Me Centered Teaching

The most important thing for a disciple of Christ to learn in regards to how to follow Jesus, is to understand who they are in Christ. To embrace being a bondservant and desire to please the Master is life changing. It causes one to set their affections "on things above," where the Master currently resides, and not on their own temporary situation.

Today, Christians are bombarded with teaching that tells them how to become the center of their universe. Of course you probably have not seen any sermon titles like "how to really become the center of the universe," but the message is preached regularly on how to get things to go your way. How to be "victorious" in this present age. How to be healthy, wealthy, popular, and happy. The materialistic pleasures of this world are all under the control of our God who owns the "cattle on a thousand hills," and because we are "joint heirs with Jesus," it is all ours for the asking!

We hear teaching on how to be in dominion over this earth and manipulate the powers of the universe through leading the right kind of life and praying the right and effective prayer. We are taught that we can move the hand of God by holding Him accountable to the universal rules or "promises" that He put into place. We are told that in prayer we may march "boldly into the throne room" of the Almighty God and demand Him to give us what He said he would.

We are told to memorize scriptures, as though they are magical spells, in order to speak God's own words back to Him, as if God should have been warned, "anything you say can and will be held against you."

We are told to pray the prayer of Jabez or trust in the latest "Biblical" formula for success in order to get what we want. If we do absolutely everything right and still don't see results for our efforts, we are told we either have "hidden sin in our lives," we are "not tithing," or we "don't have enough faith."

The sad fact is that what many of the above "me centered" teachings within the modern Church have done, is to aid believers in their selfish pursuits. These doctrines are "equipping the saints" to be the center of their own universe and not to be good servants of Christ.

For the Christian and non-Christian alike, putting ourselves at the center of the universe sums up the root of all sin: being self-centered, instead of God-centered. It's the difference in thinking that it is all about me, as opposed to it is all about the Master, Jesus.

We are taught to read through the Bible and see how it *all* relates and applies to our lives, rather than seeing that the Bible is all about the life of our Master, Jesus.

It is a gross understatement to say that there is still plenty of room for meeting our own needs and experiencing great pleasure on this earth when God *is* the center of our universe.

What a relief it is for the bondservant when he or she comes to realize that her or his Sovereign Master knows everything, is everywhere, has everything under control, and has the best interests of His servants in mind. Until that realization occurs many spend their prayer time making requests to God about things that they believe would be good from their limited, human, self-centered, tiny corner of the world, 21st century, middle-class, three dimensional, carbon based, limited-self-control, perspective.

The follower of Christ, who has been purchased with His blood, *must* answer the question of where the center of the universe is by saying it is centered around God, and not themselves. Adam and

Eve in the Garden wanted to follow their own plan and not God's. Everyone, save one (Jesus), since that time has committed and now commits the same act of self-centered rebellion repeatedly. As long as one lives in their physical body, Christian or not, they are subject to committing these non-God-centered acts.

The Bondservant's Struggle

In spite of being purchased with the "blood of the Lamb," my body continues to pay attention to its five senses. Even though I am a servant of Jesus, I still have a brain that has been "hard wired" with certain behaviors and memories. My brain still seeks to be comfortable and experience pleasure. My physical body is acting consistent with the way it was created. I constantly seek to satisfy my "needs."

The world around me that God also created is full of opportunities to feed needs and desires. Never the less, as a servant of Jesus I need to endeavor to not misuse His creation by engaging in selfish pursuits. I must not use His creation in a manner that it was not designed for or intended to be. Realizing that my good Master wants happy, healthy slaves, I need to endeavor to avoid any activities that are not glorifying or profitable to my Master. Above all, I must remember that I have been *bought* with a high price and am a *possession* of Christ.

What? know ye not that your body is the temple of the Holy Ghost which is in you, which ye have of God, and ye are not your own? ***For ye are bought with a price:*** *therefore glorify God in your body, and in your spirit, which are God's. 1 Cor 6:19-20 (KJV)* (Emphasis added)

A follower of Christ's outlook and perspective on life is to be that of a slave or bondservant that puts their own life and desires aside and lives to please their Master.

For he that is called in the Lord, being a servant, is the Lord's freeman: likewise also he that is called, being free, is Christ's servant. ***Ye are bought with a price;*** *be not ye the servants of men. 1 Cor 7:22-23 (KJV) (Emphasis added)*

Those of us who have been bought and paid for by Jesus, should not put ourselves back in a position of serving the world from which we have been ransomed.

No servant can serve two masters: for either he will hate the one, and love the other; or else he will hold to the one, and despise the other. Ye cannot serve God and mammon. Luke 16:13 (KJV)

What does one *do* in order to be a "good and faithful" servant until the Master returns? Simply stated, they will *do* what their Master told them to do as recorded in His Word. The Master also set a good example for His servants. A good servant will live a life patterned after his or her Master. Jesus said:

And why call ye me, Lord, Lord, and do not the things which I say? Luke 6:46 (KJV)

Ye call me Master and Lord: and ye say well; for so I am. If I then, your Lord and Master, have washed your feet; ye also ought to wash one another's feet. For I have given you an example, that ye should do as I have done to you. Verily, verily, I say unto you, the servant is not greater than his lord; neither he that is sent greater than he that sent him. If ye know these things, happy are ye if ye do them. John 13:13-17 (KJV)

The Penalty of the Unbelievers and Bad Servants

The parable of the servant found in Matthew 24 and Luke 12:42-48 indicates that those who believe themselves to be bondservants of Jesus, but are not living their lives in such a way to give meaning to that belief, are fooling themselves. They appear to be no better off than the "hypocrite" or "unbeliever" in the end, being "assigned" a place with them.

The Luke account of the *Parable of the Servants*, clearly says that those who have knowledge of what Jesus expects of them, but don't do it, will be worse off than those who don't know what Jesus expects of them (the unbeliever).

And that servant, which knew his lord's will, and prepared not himself, neither did according to his will, shall be beaten with many stripes. But he that knew not, and did commit things worthy of stripes, shall be beaten with few stripes. For unto whomsoever much is given, of him shall be much required: and to whom men have committed much, of him they will ask the more. Luke 12:47-48 (KJV)

More is expected from those whom have been given more. That includes knowledge of the gospel. In this way it is better to be a non-believer than a false one.

The Place of the Unbelievers and Hypocrites

The words "*weeping and gnashing of teeth*" are used several times by Jesus. These words are typically associated with also being "cast into outer darkness" and into a "furnace of fire." Matthew 8:12, 13:42, 13:50, 22:13, and 25:30 all use this same imagery. These are common images of what we normally associate with "Hell," the place assigned to the hypocrite and unbeliever. Hell is the holding place for the unbeliever. It is a place of "torment."

Is Hell Real?

Jesus' parables were all based on situations that would be commonly understood by those He was addressing. He did not engage in speaking in the realm of science fiction, fantasy or unrealistic or unreasonable scenarios when teaching. Because of this, we can learn about what Jesus, and those He was speaking to in the first century, generally thought to be true.

Since Jesus is my master, 21st century philosophy and "science" be damned, I trust what He believed and taught to be true. One parable Jesus taught had to do with the place of unbelievers. Here is that parable:

There was a certain rich man, which was clothed in purple and fine linen, and fared sumptuously every day: And there was a certain beggar named Lazarus, which was laid at his gate, full of sores, and desiring to be fed with the crumbs which fell from the rich man's table: moreover the dogs came and licked his sores.

And it came to pass, that the beggar died, and was carried by the angels into Abraham's bosom: the rich man also died, and was buried; And in hell he lift up his eyes, being in torments, and seeth Abraham afar off, and Lazarus in his bosom. And he cried and said, Father Abraham, have mercy on me, and send Lazarus, that he may dip the tip of his finger in water, and cool my tongue; for I am tormented in this flame. But Abraham said, Son, remember that thou in thy lifetime receivedst thy good things, and likewise Lazarus evil things: but now he is comforted, and thou art tormented. And beside all this, between us and you there is a great gulf fixed: so that they which would pass from hence to you cannot; neither can they pass to us, that would come from thence.

Then he said, I pray thee therefore, father, that thou wouldest send him to my father's house: For I have five brethren; that he may testify unto them, lest they also come into this place of torment. Abraham saith unto him, they have Moses and the prophets; let them hear them. And he said, Nay, father Abraham: but if one went unto them from the dead, they will repent. And he said unto him, if they hear not Moses and the prophets, neither will they be persuaded, though one rose from the dead. Luke 16:19-31 (KJV)

There are many points to be made from this story, but here are the observations I would like to make in regards to the "place of the unbeliever." Hell is a real place or Jesus would not have told a story like this. The souls of unbelievers go there when they die and will remain there until their final judgment. While those souls are in Hell, they have consciousness and are aware of their surroundings. They are not "asleep."

Hell is an unpleasant place of torment. Those who have died and reside there, have deep regrets. There are "flames" and great thirst in Hell. It appears that even though the souls in Hell have left their physical bodies behind, they can still recognize other souls. It also appears that they can communicate. They will remember the things of this life and the living they left behind.

If Hell were simply the "grave," meaning the cold ground that we place bodies in, and if people were simply unconscious and only experienced silent blackness until the final judgment, as some believe, Jesus' parable would be pointless and based on fantasy and falsehood. That would make this parable unique to all others.

One day, after the judgment of the dead has taken place, according to the Book of Revelation, both "hell and death" will be destroyed in a "lake of fire."

And the sea gave up the dead which were in it; and death and hell delivered up the dead which were in them: and they were judged every man according to their works. And death and hell were cast into the lake of fire. This is the second death. Rev 20:13-14 (KJV)

A Place of Torment Before Judgment?

One may ask how it is that a person can be "sentenced" to suffer torment prior to being put on trial and judged. After all, aren't we "innocent until proven guilty?"

Confusion is generated when we mistake human governments and judicial systems for God's sovereign judgment. Besides personally witnessing the transgressions of the unbelievers throughout their entire lives, God already knows who will be declared "innocent" by means of redemption; it will be only those that belong to His Son.

Just as there is a difference between a jail, where people are held pending their trial, and prison, where people with felonies are sentenced to go, there is a difference between being held in Hell and ultimately being sentenced by God and cast into the lake of fire.

As an inmate in jail, you may have not yet been found guilty while awaiting your trial. However, like hell, jail is generally not a nice place to spend your time.

<u>Mark 13: 34-37</u>

For the Son of man is as a man taking a far journey, who left his house, and gave authority to his servants, and to every man his work, and commanded the porter to watch. Watch ye therefore: for ye know not when the master of the house cometh, at even, or at midnight, or at the cockcrowing, or in the morning: Lest coming suddenly he find you sleeping. And what I say unto you I say unto all, Watch. (KJV)

It is like a man taking a far journey, who left his house and gave his servants authority and told every man what to do and told the gatekeeper to watch. So likewise you watch, because you don't know what time the master will come; in the evening, or at midnight, or when the rooster crows, or in the morning. God forbid he comes suddenly and finds you sleeping. And what I say to you, I say to everyone; watch! (DHT)

Although the watchful message is consistent, the gospel of Mark's version of this parable contains a little bit of a variation from what we find in the Matthew account. Here we see a similar story in which the master of a house goes on a journey and puts his servants in charge.

In the Mark account, we see a "gate keeper," or "porter," with the specific duty of watching. Yet, what Jesus says to one, He ultimately says to all; "*watch.*" Every one of Jesus' followers share this responsibility. No one should be caught sleeping and relying on others to be watchful.

The key message in the Gospel of Mark account is watchfulness, and all that implies. The secondary message is that no one will know exactly when the master will return.

Summary

If you have been purchased by the blood of Jesus, He has paid a great price for you. Being a bondservant of Christ also means that you have been adopted into His eternal family, with all rights and privileges of being a member of that family.

Jesus' bondservants are to keep watch and faithfully take care of their Masters business while He is away. It will not be good for those servants who are not doing so. In fact, it may be an indication that they were never a servant of Jesus' at all, but rather a "hypocrite and unbeliever."

Hell is a real place where hypocrites and unbelievers go after they die while they await their final judgment.

Jesus has given His followers a strong imperative command in regards to His Coming: stay awake and be watchful! Few places in the gospels contain such strong and repetitious commands from Jesus.

Notes

21. What's A Wedding Without Extra Virgin Oil? (The Parable of Ten Virgins)

The Book of Matthew is the only one of the three synoptic gospels that records what Jesus went on to say next on the Mount of Olives.

After the final admonition to be watchful, the Gospel of Mark moves on to talk about the plot to kill Jesus in Mark chapter 14. The book of Luke ends chapter 21 by saying that Jesus continued to teach in the temple by day, and take lodging (likely camp) on the Mount of Olives at night (Luke 21:37).

Matthew 25:1

Then shall the kingdom of heaven be likened unto ten virgins, which took their lamps, and went forth to meet the bridegroom. (KJV)

At that time the kingdom of heaven will be like ten virgins, which took their lamps and went out to meet the bridegroom. (DHT)

"At that time," or "then," is referring to the specific time in the future that Jesus has been talking about His return to earth: the end of this current age, the time that He is bringing His Kingdom of Heaven to this earth.

The "Kingdom of Heaven" Jesus referred to is not how the Kingdom of Heaven always will be, but is meant to illustrate what it will be like "at that time," meaning at the time the Kingdom of Heaven comes to this earth.

We know that this is a parable containing symbolism and not to be taken literally because Jesus says the Kingdom of Heaven will be "like" ten virgins.

In order to properly understand this parable, it is necessary to define who all of the characters are in the implied "wedding:" the "virgins" and the "bridegroom." Then, although the parable does not directly say, who might the "bridegroom" be marrying?

Matthew 25:2

And five of them were wise, and five were foolish. (KJV)

And five of them were foolish and five were wise. (DHT)

Jesus had just told a similar parable where the Master, Jesus, had returned to His servants. He found some that were wise, and some that had been foolish (see the previous chapter). That theme seems to continue here as He relays that the virgins in this parable, yet to be identified by us, are made up of two groups: the wise and the foolish.

Matthew 25:3-5

They that were foolish took their lamps, and took no oil with them: But the wise took oil in their vessels with their lamps. While the bridegroom tarried, they all slumbered and slept. (KJV)

Those that were foolish took their lamps, but didn't take any oil with them. But the wise took oil in their containers with their lamps. While the bridegroom took his time, they all laid down and fell asleep. (DHT)

The simplest way to look at this statement is that the "wise" are prepared and have made themselves ready for the return of the bridegroom. The foolish, although they had lamps, took no fuel for them and were not prepared for the coming of the bridegroom. Both the foolish and the wise "fell asleep."

"Falling asleep" could imply that some time passes before the bridegroom returns. People fall into routines, life goes on, and they grow weary watching for an event that they are unsure will occur. This may be especially true after 2,000 years have passed and the "bridegroom" or "master" has still not come.

Matthew 25:6-10

And at midnight there was a cry made, Behold, the bridegroom cometh; go ye out to meet him. Then all those virgins arose, and trimmed their lamps. And the foolish said unto the wise, give us of your oil; for our lamps are gone out. But the wise answered, saying, not so; lest there be not enough for us and you: but go ye rather to them that sell, and buy for yourselves. And while they went to buy, the bridegroom came; and they that were ready went in with him to the marriage: and the door was shut. (KJV)

And halfway through the night a cry went out, "look, the bridegroom is coming. Go out and meet him!" Then all the virgins got up and trimmed their lamps. Then the foolish said to the wise, "give us some of your oil, for our lamps have gone out." But the wise answered, saying, "no, there might not be enough for you and us. Better that you go and buy some for yourselves from those that sell." And when they left to make their purchase, the bridegroom came. And those that were prepared went in with him to the wedding and the door was shut. (DHT)

Upon the return of the one they had been waiting for, the wise "virgins" seem unwilling to give up what will allow them to go out and meet the bridegroom: their "oil." Unless each individual is prepared *on their own*, they will not be able to meet the one they are waiting on. There will be no sharing of "lamps" or "oil."

"The door was shut," implies that there is a finite period of time to make it into the "wedding feast." There will come a day when it is too late to prepare, and the unprepared will not make it in. There will not be a second chance for anyone "left behind." As we see in the next verse, if you are not ready when the "bridegroom" returns, you are just out of luck.

Matthew 25:11-13

Afterward came also the other virgins, saying, Lord, Lord, open to us. But he answered and said, Verily I say unto you, I know

you not. Watch therefore, for ye know neither the day nor the hour wherein the Son of man cometh. (KJV)

Afterwards the other virgins also came, saying, "Lord, Lord, open to us." But he answered and said, "believe it when I tell you, I don't know you." Watch therefore, because you don't know the day nor the hour when the Son of man will come. (DHT)

Those who were not prepared to meet the bridegroom were left out in the cold. The strong and clear command to be watchful and prepared concludes the parable.

Interpretations

Some have assumed that this parable is talking about Jesus, the bridegroom, coming to claim his future wives (virgins), as though he intends on marrying a harem. This interpretation would seem at least partially consistent with imagery found elsewhere in the Bible where Jesus is the groom, and the Church, made up of many people, is the "Bride." This parable then would represent Jesus returning to earth for His Bride, the Church, and taking "her" away (i.e. The rapture). However, as we have seen, not all of the "virgins" are ready when the groom comes for them. Some get "left behind."

Spirit Filled Christians Vs. Not So Spirit Filled Interpretation

If you are drawn to the more Pentecostal beliefs, then you may be sure that the five virgins who have oil for their lamps are born again, "Spirit filled" believers who have all given evidence that they are "saved" by speaking in tongues. Jesus, of course is the bridegroom and the five virgins, whom He takes away, rescuing them from the tribulation to come, corporately make up His "bride." The "oil" mentioned is symbolic for the Holy Spirit of God. Having their lamps "full" of oil is symbolic for being full of the Holy Spirit.

Continuing with this interpretation, the five foolish "virgins," who are left behind, are those people who are perhaps Christian in name only. Or, maybe they are even those who have prayed the sinner's prayer and accepted Jesus as their Savior, but they have not been "filled with the Spirit." This group qualifies as being set apart as "virgins," but not being "spirit filled," they have left their "vessel" empty of "oil" and are just not *ready* to meet the bridegroom.

If you do not consider yourself a Pentecostal, but do believe that there are those people in the world who are Christian in name only, you may favor the next theory…

True Christians Vs. In Name Only

Some think that the five virgins who get taken by the bridegroom are actual born again followers of Christ who truly know Him as their Lord. The other five virgins, who have no oil, are only Christians in the sense that the United States is a "Christian nation." If this is your interpretation of this parable, you will probably still interpret the "oil" as representing the Holy Spirit of God, but would say that anyone who truly is a Christian has the Holy Spirit inside them whether or not they are emotional and animated in their worship style or speak in tongues.

Active Christians vs. Backsliding Christians

The next interpretation of this parable is a hybrid version of the above theories, which says that all of the virgins actually are Christians, but the ones who are without oil are in a state of "back-sliding." The foolish virgins, according to this theory, would include "Sunday morning saints, Saturday night sinners."

Being a Christian worthy of being taken by the bridegroom would largely be works or behavior based. The "foolish virgins" in this theory are not watching for the Lord's return. They are the ones who are not "walking with God." When Jesus returns, He will rescue those who are serious about their relationship with Him and will leave those other "poor excuses of Christians" behind in order to discipline them. He will sort of "whip them into shape," so they too will be worthy *after* they have been "tried by fire." Hopefully, during the period of time that God pours out His wrath on the earth, according to this theory, these second-class Christians will come to their senses and turn towards God. This theory and the one before it, reads like a very popular series of end times fiction books and movies.

Temporary Salvation Theory

Of course there are any number of other versions of this parable that fall in between the ones I mentioned above, but there are some who would be disappointed if I didn't mention one more. There are those that believe that this parable is complete proof that Christians can lose their salvation. "Eternal" life according to this school of thought is actually a "temporary" life for those who don't continue to meet up to God's standards. Eternal life then, is based on a set of conditions. Although Jesus saves you, once you're "saved," retaining your salvation is highly dependent on your actions. The five virgins, whose lamps have gone out according to this theory, are those Christians who once knew salvation, but have lost it because they just are not "good enough." Jesus didn't leave them, they left Jesus, or so the theory goes.

One Important Thing

Halley's Bible commentary on this passage cuts through all of the details and simply states that "*we should keep our minds on the Lord, and be ready when he comes.*" [99]

Although I think Halley over simplifies when he says "this parable means just one thing," I completely agree with the principle he states here; we should keep our minds on the Lord, and be ready when He comes.

I also agree for the most part with the concept mentioned in the theories above that there are many Christians, in name only. They will indeed be "left behind." However, I would stop short of agreeing that "bad" Christians will be "left behind." A "bad" Christian being a label that a legalistic and judgmental person would place on someone who is actually chosen by God for salvation, but that continues to struggle with behavioral issues (sin).

I do not agree at all that Christians can lose their salvation if they were elected by God for salvation in the first place. When God does "save," He really saves, regardless of our actions from moment to moment. The blood of Jesus does not wear off and He would never sell us back into slavery.

With the above being said, other than in the general sense that we all should be watchful for the return of Jesus, I am not convinced that the Church (the elect of God) has anything to do with any of the ten "virgins" mentioned in the parable.

In order to understand what this parable of the ten virgins is talking about, it is important to understand a few key things: 1. The term "virgin" as used in the parable, 2. the first century Jewish wedding ritual, and 3. who are the key characters represented in the story.

The Church is The Bride

Even though the versions of scripture translated from the Greek indicate that this parable doesn't mention a bride, that there is a bride is always implied in the case of a wedding. The *Peshitta*, which is the Aramaic Bible used by the Church of the East, actually says that the ten virgins go out to meet the bridegroom and "the Bride." [100]

The "Church" as we think of it today, did not exist when Jesus spoke this parable. Because of this it is not completely without controversy, that the Church may be the "Bride" in this parable. Paul indirectly refers to the Church as the "Bride of Christ," in II Corinthians 11:2. A strong scriptural case from elsewhere in the Bible can also be made supporting the idea that the Church is the bride.

And I John saw the holy city, new Jerusalem, coming down from God out of heaven, **prepared as a bride** *adorned for her husband. Rev 21:2 (KJV)* (Emphasis added)

And there came unto me one of the seven angels which had the seven vials full of the seven last plagues, and talked with me, saying, come hither, I will **shew thee the bride, the Lamb's wife**. *And he carried me away in the spirit to a great and high mountain, and shewed me that great city, the holy Jerusalem, descending out of heaven from God, Rev 21:9-10 (KJV)* (Emphasis added)

The above passage goes on to describe a beautiful and enormous, awe-inspiring city. On the surface, one may say "wait a minute, the bride is a city called the New Jerusalem," and that would be true. However, a city is so much more than brick and mortar, or in this case jasper and gold. A city is made up of inhabitants. It is the city's inhabitants, which are mentioned a few verses later:

And there shall be no more curse: but the throne of God and of the Lamb shall be in it; and ***his servants*** *shall serve him: And they shall see his face; and* ***his name shall be in their foreheads****. And there shall be no night there; and they need no candle, neither light of the sun; for the Lord God giveth them light: and they shall reign for ever and ever. Rev 22:3-5 (KJV)* (Emphasis added)

The city, referred to as "the bride of Christ" is made up of the servants of Jesus: the Church. The inhabitants of the city are referred to as an actual part of the city. In the following verse you will see that the name of the city will even be written on the followers of Christ:

Him that overcometh will I make a pillar in the temple of my God, and he shall go no more out: and I will write upon him the name of my God, and the name of the city of my God, which is new Jerusalem, which cometh down out of heaven from my God: and I will write upon him my new name. Rev 3:12 (KJV)

The elect of God (the Church), who dwell in the temple of God, which is in the "New Jerusalem," are said to be the "Bride" of Christ.

Jesus is the Bridegroom

There is no doubt that Christ *is* the bridegroom mentioned in the Revelation scripture and in the parable of the ten virgins. It could be no other. He is the "Son of Man," mentioned at the end of the parable.

John the Baptist referred to Jesus as the Bridegroom when he said:

Ye yourselves bear me witness, that I said, I am not the Christ, but that I am sent before him. He that hath the bride is the bridegroom: but the friend of the bridegroom, which standeth and heareth him, rejoiceth greatly because of the bridegroom's voice: this my joy therefore is fulfilled. John 3:28-29 (KJV)

We can also be fairly certain that the "Wedding Feast" referred to in the parable, is the "Marriage supper of the Lamb" that we read about in Revelation chapter 19. This "wedding feast" will take place shortly after the return of Jesus.

And I heard as it were the voice of a great multitude, and as the voice of many waters, and as the voice of mighty thunderings, saying, Alleluia: for the Lord God omnipotent reigneth. Let us be glad and rejoice, and give honour to him: ***for the marriage of the Lamb is come, and his wife hath made herself ready****. And to her was granted that she should be arrayed in fine linen, clean and white: for the fine linen is the righteousness of saints. And he saith unto me, Write, Blessed are they which are called unto the marriage supper of the Lamb. And he saith unto me, these are the true sayings of God. Rev 19:6-9 (KJV)* (Emphasis added)

Who Are the Ten Virgins?

So, if Christ is the bridegroom, and the Church is the bride, who are the virgins with lamps in Matthew chapter 25? Some would say that the Church plays the part of both bride and wedding guests in this parable. But why stop there? After all, it could be argued that the Church is the "body of Christ." Wouldn't that make the Church the bridegroom too? To see the Church as all (or more than one) character in this parable wouldn't make sense.

In his book entitled *End Times Events*, author Charles Capps, tries to argue just that. In one paragraph he makes the case that the Church is the "body of Christ," in the next paragraph he argues that the Church is the five virgins with oil in their lamps. The only character in the story he says the Church is not, is the Bride. [101]

Maybe the meaning of this parable was never meant to be taken this far. Maybe the simple message of being watchful *is* the only message for sure. But, if nothing else other than to show you that perhaps others are a bit off in their specific interpretations of who the virgins are, let's consider another interpretation.

Next time you hear someone matter-of-factly using the parable of the ten virgins to support their end time scenario, there are a few things you should consider.

"At That Time"

If we are to understand who the "virgins" are, the opening words of this parable cannot be overlooked. The phrase, "at that time" is talking about the future time of Jesus' return. It is the period of time on which almost His entire discourse has focused. Jesus did a lot of teaching about the Kingdom of Heaven. During Jesus' day, and still in our day, the Kingdom of Heaven, was and is still centered in heaven and not on this earth.

It is true followers of Jesus who can be considered citizens of the Kingdom of Heaven, but the status of those citizens is that they are currently aliens in a foreign land. Besides those of us who have been spiritually reborn into it, the Kingdom of Heaven currently is found in the spiritual realm, literally in Heaven, and not on this earth.

One day, the day that Jesus is referring to when He says "at that time," the Kingdom of Heaven will be physically expanded to this earth. It will be the literal answer to the prayer, "thy kingdom come, thy will be done on earth as it is in Heaven." "At that time," the Kingdom of Heaven will be undergoing rapid and drastic expansion related changes as its King comes to this planet in power and glory. Jesus' kingdom will then include a physical world, which will be in need of human beings worthy of inhabiting it.

An Alternative View of Who the Virgins Are

Nowhere in the parable does it state or even imply that any one, five, or ten virgins represents the "Bride of Christ." That is a major assumption made in some of the above theories. What kind of a wedding would that be? Can you imagine being one of the "lucky" five virgins on your wedding night? Yes, polygamy was allowed in the Jewish culture in Jesus' day, but it was frowned on and not commonly practiced.

It is very unlikely that Jesus would have been implying in this story that the bridegroom had the intentions of coming for ten "brides" and then settled for five. If that were the case, I think we would have read in the scripture something like; "*Master, five brides? This is a hard teaching to understand. What manner of man could accomplish this, or even want to?*" However, we don't read anything of the sort.

To understand the role of the different characters involved in this parable, we must understand that there are at least two story lines taking place in the New Testament. Jesus is the key character in both.

One story line concerns the fulfillment of promises God made to the natural line of descendants from Abraham, Isaac, and Jacob, commonly known as the Jews. The other story line involves the expansion of the Kingdom of Heaven to include the Church. Many times these stories are so intertwined that there is no difference. One story line is dependent on the other. Jesus is the central character that ultimately ties the story all together. However, sometimes there are two distinct story lines.

What we find in this parable is the interaction of characters from both story lines. This parable represents the coming together of what God is going to be doing with the Jews during the end of the age, and what will be occurring with the Church. They are both represented, although the Church or the "bride" is not the focus and is not specifically mentioned. The focus is clearly on those who will be physically inhabiting the Kingdom of Heaven "at that time" as it arrives to the earth.

The Teachings of Jesus Not for Christians?

Many dispensationalists demand that the Olivet Discourse was intended for the Jews. They believe that Jesus spoke the words recorded there only to his Jewish disciples to pass on to future generations of Jews. Since they would ultimately be the generation that would be around for His Second Coming. They believe that the message of the Olivet Discourse is specifically given to the Jews of the end of the age who will inherit the earthly kingdom of God. Further, they believe that the passage has nothing to do with the Church and is of little value to modern day disciples of Christ.

I will concede that Jesus was speaking to His disciples, and that they were all Jews when Jesus called them. At the point of following Christ, even though they may have continued on with many Jewish traditions, and even though they were still ethnically Jews, they by definition became the first Christians.

God did not rewrite the script for planet earth's past and future when he revealed His mystery that the gentile peoples could be saved. He only allowed us to see what he had planned all along. This revelation did not include God rewriting the future as was recorded in prophecy.

As for me, I will continue to apply a uniform set of hermeneutics. I will attempt to determine if Jesus is singling out and focusing on any group of people in the Scriptures. Although the Olivet Discourse has much to say to both Christians and Jews (if they were to listen to the words of Jesus), in the case of the parable of Ten Virgins, Jesus does appear to be getting specific about the righteous descendants of the nation of Israel.

The Church is Everywhere?

Some Christians try to see the Church in many places in scripture in which they just don't belong. This is almost the opposite of those who think much of what is written in the gospels is only intended for the Jews.

When interpreting the book of Revelation for example, some say John stands for the Church. Where John goes in the book is symbolic for where the Church goes in prophecy. They say John being called up to heaven in his Revelation vision is symbolic for the Church being raptured to heaven. Some say the "24 elders" seen in Revelation by John represent the Church. Others say that the "Two Witnesses" of Revelation chapter 11 represent the Church. Many believe that the "Holy Ones" who ride to Armageddon with Jesus to defeat the Antichrist's forces are the Church.

"Replacement Theology," is the theory that claims that the Church now inherits everything the Jews were promised in the Old Testament. According to this theory the Church is able to do so because the Jews "blew it" with God by continuing to turn their back on Him and ultimately rejecting their Messiah; Jesus.

An example of Replacement Theology in prophecy would be where some say the 144,000 descendants of Israel mentioned in Revelation are representative of the Church. Replacement Theology was an especially popular theory before the nation of Israel was reborn in 1948. Prior to that time many people could not imagine how the promises made by God to the Jews could ever possibly be literally realized. They decided that the Church must have taken national Israel's place.

The Church is Not There?

Still others have said they don't see the Church anywhere after the first three chapters in the book of Revelation. Many interpretations would have the Church playing two or more different parts at the same time.

There is indeed much confusion as to the role of the Church and Israel. What is essential to realize is that we need to be extremely careful not to superimpose the Church over the top of what God is really trying to tell us. Similarly, we need to be careful to understand when Jesus is speaking to His Church and not Jew's in scripture.

God's plan is complex and we need to recognize that there are more factors involved than just what is happening with the Church. God is dealing with several different groups: the elect, the world, the nation of Israel, Satan, the Antichrist. Remember, we, either as individuals, or as the corporate Church, are not the center of the universe. The Bible is not written about us. Jesus is the star of the show and there are many things going on around Him.

144,000

In the seventh chapter of the book of Revelation, at the same time we see the Church show up in Heaven, there is a separate group of 144,000 people that have descended from Abraham, Isaac, and Jacob that are mentioned. It names them specifically by their tribes. There are twelve thousand from each of the twelve tribes. This group's story line continues to play out on planet earth after the Church has been removed.

First Century Jewish Weddings

Another important factor in understanding the parable of the Ten Virgins is understanding a little bit about the Jewish culture of Jesus' day. A first century Jewish wedding is nothing like what we 21st century North Americans now think of as a wedding. However, they are not so different that the Jewish wedding included ten brides!

Several commentaries refer to the virgins in the parable as "maidens." Those commentaries suppose that the virgins are female bridesmaids whose job it is to attend to the bride and make sure she is ready for the wedding feast. However, unless the groom already had the bride with him, which would have been unusual, he would not have come to collect the bridesmaids. The groom coming to pick up ten female virgins, who were friends of his fiancé, would have been improper.

The Greek word used for "virgins" in this scripture is transliterated into English as "parthenoi." This word is used for "virgin" throughout the New Testament whether the person they are talking about is male or female. The 144,000 descendants of Israel that I referred to earlier are said to be "virgins."

It is these who have not defiled themselves with women, for they are virgins (parthenoi). *It is these who follow the Lamb wherever he goes. These have been redeemed from mankind as firstfruits for God and the Lamb, and in their mouth no lie was found, for they are blameless.* Rev 14:4

It is assumed that the "virgins," (parthenoi) in the above passage are males, since they have not "defiled themselves with women." Most of the usage of this word in the New Testament refers to female virgins. However, the exact same form of the word (parthenoi) is used in both the Revelation passage mentioned above, as it refers to males, and the Olivet Discourse passage we are looking at now. It is always necessary to look at factors such as culture and context to decide on how to properly understand this word.

Male "Virgins?"

There is a strong possibility that the ten "virgins" in this parable are males just like they are in the Revelation passage concerning the 144,000. The fact that there are ten of these special wedding guests described as virgins would be no surprise to a first century Jew. Anything important like a wedding that was done in "public," was done in the presence of at least ten people. In fact, many public matters had to be established in the presence of ten *male* witnesses. This is Jewish Talmudic oral tradition.

Talmudic tradition defined the culture of Jesus' day. There is a biblical example of this practice in the book of Ruth chapter four. In his book *The Essential Talmud*, Author Adin Steinsaltz, writes in regards to the first century Jewish marriage ceremony that a wedding involved two different stages as far as the legal procedure. First was the betrothal. Secondly, in the presence of ten male adults, the man would bring his wife under a canopy, which would symbolize his home. It is then that the bride would become his wife. [102]

It is expected that if the bridegroom was young, that his ten male guests, would be unwed virgins as was the bridegroom. However, beyond the commentaries, there are several translations of the Bible that unfortunately translate the word "virgin" as "maiden."

Like the commentaries, the study notes will go so far as to say these are "bride's maids."

I don't know of a Bible translation that calls the virgins in this parable, "groomsmen." However, when you consider the culture of the day, and how the disciples would have taken what Jesus was saying, with their knowledge of first century Jewish wedding practices, "groomsmen" is the most likely way to accurately translate the word.

The ten "virgins" are likely the traditional young unmarried male friends of the groom. The groom has no intention of marrying anyone of these ten. He intends on them being witnesses and guests of the wedding feast. This was the tradition in the day that Jesus relayed this story to His disciples.

The significance of determining the "sex" of the "virgins" is important when building a case for tying this scripture to scripture found elsewhere. Tying this scripture to other scripture is important in order to identify who the virgins in this parable symbolically represent. Hopefully now we can say who the virgins are not; they are not the future "bride(s)" of the groom.

Jesus' Friends: The Groomsmen

Why not just leave it simple and say that the virgins in this parable are the elect of God or "the Church?" Why not just say Jesus is using the word "virgins" in the same sense that Paul does in 2 Corinthians 11:2, when he is writing of the Church that has been set aside for Jesus?

In my opinion, Jesus is specifically using a parable involving a wedding because He knows there are several key characters involved, and that each one has their specific roles. When we consider the cultural practices of Jesus' day, He is being specific that the bridegroom is coming for His *friends* who are found ready and worthy to be a part of the wedding celebration.

Rapture Confusion

It is very understandable how confusion can arise over this parable given the context of what Jesus is talking about. Only a few sentences earlier He was talking about His Second Coming and the gathering of the elect from the "four-corners" of the earth. At first glance it would make sense that this parable has something to do with that event. It does have everything to do with His Second Coming, but nothing to do with the gathering of the elect.

As you will recall, Revelation 7:9-17 gives us the scene after the sign of the sun, moon, stars, and earthquake has just occurred. Jesus has sent His angels to gather those that belong to Him to His presence. His followers, those who have come out of the tribulation from "every nation, tribe, and people," now find themselves raptured, standing before the throne of God in Heaven singing praises to God. The title of this group, who stands before God in "white robes," as far as this parable goes, is the "Bride of Jesus."

Just before we see the Bride of Jesus show up in Heaven in Revelation chapter 7, we see a completely different group; 144,000 Jewish males that are going to be left on earth, but sealed and saved from the wrath of God.

And I saw another angel ascending from the east, having the seal of the living God: and he cried with a loud voice to the four angels, to whom it was given to hurt the earth and the sea, Saying, hurt not the earth, neither the sea, nor the trees, till ***we have sealed the servants of our God in their foreheads****. And I heard the number of them which were sealed: and there were sealed an hundred and forty and four thousand of all the tribes of the children of Israel. Rev 7:2-4 (KJV)* (Emphasis added).

These Jewish male "virgins" follow Jesus wherever He goes (Rev. 14:4). This is a distinct group apart from the Church in prophecy. At the same time, we see the Church raptured from the earth in Revelation chapters 6 and 7, we see this group of "virgins," "sealed" and left on the earth.

I believe it is no accident that both the Olivet Discourse and Revelation passages are referring to male "virgins," since in my opinion, both passages are talking about the same group of people. The sequence of events is too close in both passages to ignore. The sealing of these "virgins," comes at the same time that the "bridegroom" comes to earth.

Note in the Revelation passage that not every descendant of Israel is sealed at this future point in history, but only a finite group of 144,000. According to scripture (Romans 11:25-27), one day, all of Israel *will* be saved. As true as this is, God will ultimately define who "all of Israel" will include.

Old Testament Mention of This Group

The Old Testament book of Ezekiel is where I believe we first learn about how God will select the "144,000" "Virgins." In chapter eight of the Book of Ezekiel we read about God showing Ezekiel various abominations that were taking place in Jerusalem, and at the temple itself. Many of these detestable things were happening at the hands of seventy of those who were thought to be the most trustworthy elders in the land.

In chapter nine of Ezekiel we read about God sending out individuals to impose His judgment on Jerusalem. However, just as it occurs in the Book of Revelation when the 144,000 are sealed, God's judgment on Jerusalem only takes place after God sends out one individual, dressed in white linen, to place a "mark" on the foreheads of those who think the practices have been taking place are detestable. Those who receive this mark are to be left unharmed. The rest, young and old, are to be "slain" (Ezekiel 9:1-7).

From the Old Testament stories, we know that the Jews had somewhat of a habit of turning to the worship of false gods thereby engaging in the types of detestable activities described in Ezekiel chapter eight. Those that know history, also know that Jerusalem has fallen to foreigners on several occasions in the past. There have been many residents of that region who have been slain in association with those events. There appears to be several historical events that would qualify for "fulfilling" Ezekiel's prophecies. However, I again argue that the ultimate fulfillment of many of Ezekiel's prophecies are yet to take place in the future after the 144,000 descendants of the tribes of Israel have been sealed.

There is one thing that God considers detestable, which Ezekiel saw in his vision that is openly occurring today in Jerusalem. Anyone with access to the internet can see images of it taking place. This is how Ezekiel describes this detestable act:

Then said he unto me, Hast thou seen this, O son of man? turn thee yet again, and thou shalt see greater abominations than these. And he brought me into the inner court of the Lord's house, and, behold, ***at the door of the temple of the Lord, between the porch and the altar, were about five and twenty men, with their backs toward the temple of the Lord, and their faces toward the east;*** *and they worshipped the sun toward the east. Ezek 8:15-16 (KJV)* (Emphasis added)

If you Google images of "*Muslims worshiping on the Temple Mount in Jerusalem*," you will see pictures of far more than twenty-five men in the exact spot described by the above scripture engaging in worship. You will notice that all those engaged in worship are doing so with their back sides pointed at where the Holy of Holies traditionally once stood. To this day, where the temple stood is still considered to be the most holy site in the world by Jews. It is there where the one true God literally dwelled among men on this planet.

Today there is an Islamic Mosque standing where God's temple once stood. Each day, only a few feet away from that spot hundreds of Muslims turn their backs on where God once dwelled and bow to the east, worshiping a false god.

Although the glory of God currently does not reside on the Temple Mount as it once did, the significance of these disturbing actions are obvious. Also significant is that the nation of Israel, which is primarily made up of "God's chosen people," is allowing the worship of false gods to take place on the Temple Mount.

Just as in Ezekiel's day, there are those individual Jews in Israel that find these types of practices to be detestable, just as God does. They are those that "sigh and cry" because of the abominations that are taking place. Although they may not yet be followers of the Messiah, Jesus, they are passionately devoted to their faith in God.

It is these types of devout Jews that Ezekiel saw being "sealed" so as not to be harmed by the judgment of God. It is also likely that it will be this type of devout Jews that will make up the 144,000 "virgins" who receive God's seal of protection at the time of Jesus' return.

One Story, Two Groups, Two Story Lines

Two story lines come together at the Second Coming; the story line of the Jews and the story line of the Church. Romans 11:25-26 tells us that when the fullness of the Gentiles "comes in," then "all Israel will be saved." The fullness of the Gentiles coming in, will be complete with the rapture of the Church. "All of Israel" being saved will begin to be accomplished when God supernaturally seals and protects Israel from any further harm from the Antichrist, and from God's coming wrath on the earth. That "sealing" will occur at the mid-point of the tribulation period.

The 144,000 Jews, made up of twelve thousand from the twelve tribes of Israel, represents "all of Israel" that will be saved. The fact that the 144,000 descendants will be followers of Jesus, once He returns, indicates that these are Jews that will make Jesus their Messiah, Lord and King. This group of Jews would meet the necessary criteria of having "oil in their lamps." They are Jews that are "ready" to meet their Messiah and Master.

Is the number 144,000 to be taken literally or figuratively, indicating a number of completeness? Is this really only a group of males, or could it include females? Maybe, as in other places in scripture, only the males were counted because of the culture of that time, but it is assumed that females and children are to be included in addition to the number of males? Are we really talking about "virgins," in the normal sense (have never had sex), or are we talking about figurative virgins, meaning they have never worshipped false gods? These are all great questions that are worthy of a chapter or two in another future book!

This group of Jews that have kept themselves pure will accept Jesus as their Messiah at His return. Why wouldn't this group of newly converted Messianic Jews, which are just as "Christian" as any other believer at that point, not be raptured with the rest of the Church? After all there is no "Jew nor Greek," in Christ Jesus (Col 3:11). The answer is that this group is probably "saved," or become followers of Jesus, as a result of seeing their Messiah at His Second Coming, which occurs at the same time as the rapture. The Bible says that the Jews will "*look on the one whom they pierced*" and weep.

And I will pour upon the house of David, and upon the inhabitants of Jerusalem, the spirit of grace and of supplications: and ***they shall look upon me whom they have pierced****, and they shall mourn for him, as one mourneth for his only son, and shall be in bitterness for him, as one that is in bitterness for his firstborn. Zech 12:10 (KJV)* (Emphasis added)

Behold, he cometh with clouds; and every eye shall see him, and ***they also which pierced him****: and all kindreds of the earth shall wail because of him. Even so, Amen. Rev 1:7 (KJV)* (Emphasis added)

In other words, the 144,000 Jews will recognize who Jesus is, their Messiah, and what their ancestors did to Him. With this knowledge, they will repent and turn to Him.

This group will be kept on the earth because God has something special in mind for them. He made promises to their ancestors that must be kept. This is the remnant of Israel that is going to inherit all of the literal promises God made to the descendants of Abraham, Isaac, and Jacob that are documented in the Old Testament of the Bible.

The idea that the identification of the virgins in the *Parable of the Ten Virgins,* is actually referring to descendants of Israel, fits perfect with the idea that they once had oil in their lamps, but they let their lamps go out and that all of them "went to sleep." When you are a true follower of Christ, you cannot lose your salvation. However, if you are a Jew, you can be unprepared to receive your messiah and reject him.

This prophetic parable is a continuation of the Old Testament story line of what will happen with the descendants of Israel; God's chosen people. It informs them as to what their status will be if they are faithful or not to God, and do or do not accept Jesus as their Messiah.

What Does This Mean for The Church?

If the above is true, what is the significance of this parable for the Church? First, even though the Church may not be the "virgins" in the parable, we are still called to watch for Christ's return and be prepared just the same. This parable, like Old Testament stories, sets an example of correct behavior for the follower of Christ.

Second, it is so important for followers of Jesus to recognize the fact that the descendants of Israel play a major part in the end of the age, just as the Church does. However, they have a separate and distinct role, which interacts closely with the Church.

God made national Israel many specific promises that He intends on keeping with them. Because the story line of the Church is so closely intertwined with that of the Jews, the role of Israel in end times prophecy should be carefully studied for clues of what will happen to the Church.

Next, and perhaps most importantly, those who say that one can lose their salvation, will need to look elsewhere for proof, just as those who say that only "Spirit filled" Christians or "good" Christians will be raptured and the rest "left behind." This parable simply cannot be used for supporting those positions when properly understood.

A subtle significance of this parable is that the Church, though not mentioned here, is obviously present in the role of the Bride. This is an example of one of those times when God had revealed something ahead of time, in this case through Jesus during the Olivet Discourse, which would only be completely understood after the "mystery" was later revealed to the Church through the Apostle Paul.

Summary

The parable of the Ten Virgins mainly concerns the story line of the descendants of Israel. When Jesus returns to this earth, it will be as King. At that time, He will be annexing the earth as a part of the Kingdom of Heaven, which He will rule with a rod of iron. His kingdom on earth will include a group of people that have kept themselves pure for Him. They will be supernaturally protected from God's wrath that will be poured out on the earth.

A strong case has been made that the prophetic characters found in the Parable of the Ten Virgins represent the following:

- Jesus is the Bridegroom
- The Church is the Bride
- The "Virgins" or "Groomsmen" represent the saved portion of the descendants of Israel who accept Jesus as their Messiah at His coming. This is likely the same group as the 144,000 "virgins" mentioned in Revelation chapter 7 & 14.
- Having oil for their lamps likely represents being prepared for recognizing and receiving Jesus as their Messiah.

The Bridegroom's coming is synonymous with Christ's Second Coming. However, whereas the Church is raptured at that point, the group of 144,000 Jews who recognize Jesus as their Messiah, are left on the earth under God's supernatural protection. Unlike the Church, they will be a group of mortal human beings that will be Jesus' chosen followers on the earth. They will inhabit Israel during the millennial reign of Jesus.

Notes

22. Three Things That Transcend Time

The young, neatly groomed man sat across the table from me sipping his coffee. I didn't know him well, but I knew he took his coffee black. It was only our second meeting, and I wasn't there to judge him, but he appeared to me to be doing well in many aspects of his life; providing for his family, healthy, concerned about pleasing God. He told me about the several Bible study and Christian discussion and support groups he was a part of every week. He explained how busy his life was between doing a lot of overtime at work, having a growing family, and church related activities. From what I knew and what he was telling me, there were no outward signs or symptoms of anything wrong in this man's life. Why then was he experiencing confusion, anxiety and guilty feelings about not knowing what his "ministry" should be?

I felt the same way as this man for many years of my life. I had sat under teaching about what it was I should be doing as a Christian. This was not only in regard to my behavior, but also what I should be doing in order to "serve" God.

Sometimes I was told I should serve according to what my "gifts" and "talents" are, since they are from God and should be used first for His purposes. So, I was also told I needed to figure out what my talents and gifts might be. I was also taught that I was a "missionary," no matter if I went to a far off land, or if I never moved away from where I was born. And, if nothing else, I could serve and support others in their mission field by giving them money and of course praying for them.

In addition to figuring out my gifts, talents, ministry and mission field, it was always stressed to me that if my church was meeting, a part of serving God was to be in attendance. When you have a church that has Sunday school, Sunday morning service, Sunday and Wednesday evening services, along with a separate small group bible study, you better be there. And don't even think about not serving God by failing to show up at the potluck after Sunday morning service!

Wanting to please God, I always felt a great deal of pressure and guilt to figure out my gifts, talents, who I was supposed to be a missionary to, and what my "ministry" was.

There were so many more committees I could have served on, so many sound boards and projectors I could have operated, so many choirs I could have sang in for Jesus, and so many Bibles I could have handed out in order to relieve my conscience. I could have gone on mission trips with the youth group to Mexico. I could have altered my family's life even more in order to give more money while Angela and I raised our children on a single income. All of those things would have been so much more in line with what I was being taught. The possibilities were, and remain limitless. There is no shortage of ideas that people have about telling others what they should do in order to serve Jesus.

In the next parable that Jesus gave on the Mount of Olives, He informs His servants about the basic principle behind what it is that *He* believes they should be doing while they await His return.

Matthew 25:14-15

For the kingdom of heaven is as a man travelling into a far country, who called his own servants, and delivered unto them his goods. And unto one he gave five talents, to another two, and to another one; to every man according to his several ability; and straightway took his journey. (KJV)

It is just like a man travelling on a long journey who called his servants and entrusted to them his possessions. And to one he gave five talents, to another two, and to another one. Each according to his abilities. And then immediately took his journey. (DHT)

What Do the Talents Represent?

As in a previous parable Jesus has already relayed during the Olivet Discourse, we see a person who has "servants" who is going away on a journey. As we will see, this parable like the others, concerns what happens when the master returns. Because of the context of this story, we know that the Master in this story is Jesus.

One of the most important tasks we have to take care of with this parable, like the previous ones, is to define the symbols that are used. In this case it is important to define what the "talents" represent.

The "talent" was a unit of money in Jesus' day. A "talent" used by Jesus in its literal form would not have represented some sort of skill or ability, as the word means in the English language. It would have meant a monetary unit. However, we are dealing with symbolism, so it is not likely that we are simply talking about money, but rather something of value.

Spiritual Gifts?

Some have taken this parable to mean that we are to use whatever spiritual "gifts" God has given us to the best of our ability. The Apostle Paul in his letter to the Ephesians had some interesting things to say that parallel what is being said in this parable by Jesus. In the following passage, note how Paul points out that each of those who Jesus has taken "captive" has indeed been given a gift. Also note like in the parable, this passage is in reference to the Master going away, or "ascending."

But unto every one of us is given grace according to the measure of the gift of Christ. Wherefore he saith, when he ascended up on high, he led captivity captive, and gave gifts unto men. (Now that he ascended, what is it but that he also descended first into the lower parts of the earth? He that descended is the same also that ascended up far above all heavens, that he might fill all things.) And he gave some, apostles; and some, prophets; and some, evangelists; and some, pastors and teachers; For the perfecting of the saints, for the work of the ministry, for the edifying of the body of Christ: Eph 4:7-12 KJV

It is clear how some may believe the "talents" in the Parable of the Talents, are symbolic for the "gifts" Jesus gives His followers. Spiritual gifts after all, are something that can only be given to us by our Master. However, there is more to think about before making a final determination on what the talents represent.

Money

This parable has also been used by many to make a case for the biblical road to wealth. Give your money that God has given you to godly institutions, and you will get more money. You just need to have faith that God is true to his word… Or so the theory goes. I have no comment here on if that principle is true or not. My only comment is, if it is true, my studies have led me to the conclusion that those who teach the reciprocity principle need to look elsewhere for scriptural proof.

The talent is a symbol for a thing of value which is given to the servants by the Master, whom we have identified as Jesus. Further, as we will see, the talent not only has value when the Master leaves, but it still has value when the Master returns. That rules out money, property, or any material goods. Everything you can see is a material item subject to corruption and will pass away. When Jesus returns and you are raptured, your money will have no value. We must ask the question, what is it that Jesus left with us which will still have value when He returns and dwells among His servants?

Something You Can Hold in Your Hand?

This parable was not directed specifically at the contemporary disciples of Jesus, but was meant to transcend the centuries and speak to His followers until He returns. All of the original disciples have been dead and gone for over 1900 years. Since that is true, Jesus cannot be talking about something that He could physically give to anyone in person. What He is talking about has to be something that He can give to someone in the 21st century as easily as the first century.

In the parable, Jesus can give the "talents" to different people in different amounts, according to their abilities. Certainly through Jesus we have grace and mercy given to us. He gives us love and the ability to love others. He gives us faith. We may be able to make a case that He shows some more mercy than others, since some have transgressed more. Some may have been given more "faith" than others.

It is interesting that the Master knows the abilities of each of His servants, and gives to them accordingly. "Abilities" to do what? The ability to use the "talents" that He has given us. It is the ability to "deliver" or "invest" the talent. "Ability" is the way in which we are "able" to use the talent or the means in which we deliver or invest the talent. It is *not the talent* itself.

Possessions in Addition to Talents

It is important not to miss the fact that the "master" in the parable left his "possessions," or "goods," or "stuff," in the care of the three servants in addition to the various amounts of "talents."

Being good stewards of the master's possessions, besides the talents each were given, would have been of high importance to the master. The master would hardly want to come home and find all of his possessions had been lost, stolen, broken, sold off, or fallen into disrepair.

Certainly everything a servant owns belongs to their Master. Anything we possess, or have authority over, should be taken care of and stewarded with that in mind. Besides our physical possessions, that would include our families, and our job.

Most importantly, Jesus also left us with His "household" to take care of while He is gone. That includes, His word, the gospel, and His other servants. In other words, His household is His Church.

Matthew 25:16-18

Then he that had received the five talents went and traded with the same, and made them other five talents. And likewise he that had received two, he also gained other two. But he that had received one went and digged in the earth, and hid his lord's money. (KJV)

Then the one that received the five talents went and put them to work and made five more talents. In the same way, the one that had two, gained two more. But the one who had one went and dug a hole in the ground and hid his master's money in it. (DHT)

Whatever these "talents" represent, it must be something that can be "used" or put to work in some way. Secondly, these "talents" must have the ability to "grow." You can also have the option of not doing anything with whatever the "talents" represent. Finally, like money, there must be many different ways to use this commodity.

One way to attempt to identify what the talents represent is to engage in deductive reasoning. We will take the observations we have made about the parable and then ask questions to determine what fits and what doesn't.

What is it that Jesus gives us that:

1) Can be given to any of His servants throughout the ages?
2) Can be given to people in different measure according to their ability?
3) Will have lasting value in the next age as well as this one?
4) Can, by choice, be put to work by those it is given to?
5) As a result of being put to work, will actually increase?
6) Can be put to use in different ways?

Material Wealth

How does material wealth fit when we ask these questions?

- Can it be given to anyone throughout the ages? Yes.
- Can it be given to people in different measure? Definitely.
- Will it have lasting value in to the next age? No. Definitely not for those who have been raptured.
- Can it be put to work in our lives? Yes
- As a result of being put to work, will it actually increase? Sometimes.
- Can it be used in different ways? Yes

Material wealth gets five out of six matches. Not good enough. Additionally, even though we did not ask the question, it must be noted that according to the documentation found in the Bible, Jesus did not appear to be concerned with material wealth. It is very doubtful that some of Jesus' last counsel to His disciples would have been financial advice.

Spiritual Gifts

What about spiritual "gifts?" This is not meant to be an argument for or against what form spiritual gifts may take, or the role that they may play in the modern Church, but assuming for at least the moment they play some part in the modern day believer's life;

- Can they be given to anyone throughout the ages? I would argue, yes.
- Can they be given to people in different measure? Yes.
- Will they have lasting value in eternity? This is debatable. According to some, when Jesus returns, gifts will no longer be necessary and will pass away.

- Can they be put to work or use by us? Yes
- Can they be used in different ways? Yes
- As a result of being put to work, will they actually increase? This is debatable also. If it is actually God that gives a gift, in this case some sort of supernatural ability, can you cause your gift to "grow," or does God just give you more of the gift or perhaps another gift?

Four yes's and a couple maybes.

The Word of God

How about "the Word" of God? This is something that Jesus left for His servants and remember what Jesus just said:

Heaven and earth shall pass away, but my words shall not pass away. Matt 24:35 (KJV)

- Can the Word of God be given to anyone throughout the ages? Absolutely. Although up until the 20th century, much of the world's population was illiterate and dependent on receiving the word through others. Bibles were also not nearly as available as they are now.
- Can the Word of God be given to people in different measure? Maybe, if we are talking about understanding, but the entire Word of God is available in the form of the Bible, to all believers.
- Will the Word have lasting value in to eternity? Yes
- Can the Word be put to work in our lives? Yes
- As a result of being put to work, can the Word of God actually increase? No. Only one's knowledge of the Word can increase. As a result of putting the word of God to work in our lives, we grow in wisdom and understanding of God's word. If we seek the meaning of God's word, we find the meaning and grow in the knowledge of His word.
- Can it be used in different ways? Yes

The word of God is close, but not a perfect match.

Abilities

Everything we are comes from God. What about the "abilities" He gives to people?

- Can ability be given to anyone throughout the ages? Yes
- Can ability be given to people in different measure according to their ability? Yes, but this leads to a circular reasoning problem!
- Will ability have lasting value into eternity? It depends what the ability is. The ability needs to be defined more clearly. The ability to throw a Frisbee, for example, may or may not have a value in eternity. However, the ability to Love others, will never pass away.
- Can abilities be put to work in our lives? Yes
- As a result of being put to work, can our abilities actually increase? This depends on a number of factors such as the ability, our age, our resources, and our time to invest in developing the ability. According to the laws of thermodynamics and the curse of God in Genesis 3:19, all of my abilities will one-day fail.
- Can the ability be invested in a variety of ways? Probably.

Too many "depends" and circular reasoning problems to be the answer. Abilities seem to be more of a way to deliver talents, rather than being the talents themselves.

Wisdom, Faith and Love

What about God given wisdom, faith and love for others?

- Can wisdom, faith and the ability to show love to others be given to anyone throughout the ages by Jesus? Yes
- Can wisdom, faith and the ability to show love to others be given to people in different measure? Yes, some have more wisdom and faith than others and some have a greater capacity to show love than others.
- Will wisdom, faith and the ability to show love to others have lasting value in to eternity? Yes

Charity (love) *never faileth: but whether there be prophecies, they shall fail; whether there be tongues, they shall cease; whether there be knowledge, it shall vanish away. 1 Cor 13:8 (KJV)*

And now abideth faith, hope, charity (love), *these three; but the greatest of these is charity* (love). *1 Cor 13:13 (KJV)*

- Can wisdom, faith and the ability to show love to others be put to work in our lives? Absolutely.
- As a result of being put to work, can wisdom, faith and the ability to show love to others actually increase? Yes
- Can wisdom, the ability to show love to others, and faith be spent in various ways? Yes, millions of them.

Six out of six "yes" answers for wisdom, faith and the ability to show love to others.

The Winner: Faith, Wisdom, Love

As I began to review all that the Bible has to say about the kind of love, wisdom, and faith that only comes from God, I decided that perhaps volumes of books could be written on how those things can properly be related to the *Parable of the Talents*. For now, I need to sum it up by saying that I believe that those three things are all closely related, perhaps inseparable, and that they make up what is symbolically being represented in this parable as "talents."

To put it concisely, a "talent" is God given love, used according to God given wisdom, both of which are only made possible because of God given faith.

Remember that the talents symbolically stand for something else. That something else does not have to be boiled down to one word. That is the beauty of symbolism. If I had to come up with one Greek word that would adequately define what the "talent" in the parable represents, it would be a word that does not exist, which is made up of three words; faith, transliterated as "pistis," wisdom, transliterated as "sophia," and love, transliterated as "agapao." The word would be "pistisophiagapaho" (pis'-tis-sof-ee'-ahg-ah-pah-o).

God given love being put to work according to God given wisdom, because of our God given faith, can take on too many forms to list.

Remember the story of the wise servant Jesus told at the end of Matthew 24? In that story we see an example of a servant who puts wisdom and love to work by giving the other servants their "food at the proper time." Because the servant had been faithful and acted and put love for others to work, the master rewarded him by putting him over all of his (the master's) possessions. Contrast this to the unwise servant who does not put love to work; he beats his fellow servants. When the master returns the penalty for not putting love to work is severe:

And shall cut him asunder, and appoint him his portion with the hypocrites: there shall be weeping and gnashing of teeth. Matt 24:35 (KJV)

Later, in the *Parable of the Talents*, we see the unwise servant who did not put his talent to use receive a very similar penalty when the master returns.

And cast ye the unprofitable servant into outer darkness: there shall be weeping and gnashing of teeth. Matt 25:30 (KJV)

Loving others is important to Jesus. There are many scriptures dealing with just how important love is. The evidence is mountainous. When asked how one inherits eternal life, Jesus answered in the following way:

And, behold, a certain lawyer stood up, and tempted him, saying, Master, what shall I do to inherit eternal life? He said unto him, what is written in the law? how readest thou? And he answering said, thou shalt love the Lord thy God with all thy heart, and with all thy soul, and with all thy strength, and with all thy mind; and thy neighbour as thyself. And he said unto him, thou hast answered right: this do, and thou shalt live. Luke 10:25-28 (KJV)

Faith and love have an interesting relationship. The Apostle Paul wrote in the book of Galatians:

For we through the Spirit wait for the hope of righteousness ***by faith.*** *For in Jesus Christ neither circumcision availeth anything, nor uncircumcision;* ***but faith which worketh by love.*** *Gal 5:5-6 (KJV)* (Emphasis added)

For, brethren, ye have been called unto liberty; only use not liberty for an occasion to the flesh, but ***by love serve one another****. For all the law is fulfilled in one word, even in this; Thou shalt* ***love thy neighbour as thyself****. Gal 5:13-14 (KJV)* (Emphasis added)

Love

I am not a real "squishy" guy that would typically be the one to go around talking about the importance of love. I would even go so far as to say that if my personal preferences determined the rules of how the Bible should be interpreted, I would probably reach a different conclusion. However, I cannot deny that "love" makes up a large part of the definition of what "the talents" seem to represent in this parable.

I chose my wording carefully in my questions regarding if love would qualify as a "talent." I specifically stated, the "ability to show love to others." I did so in order to attempt to avoid some confusion. I wanted to separate out the "feelings" associated with love from actually showing love.

Love can be "felt" as an emotion, but it can be confused with so many other feelings such as pity, concern, guilt, and helplessness. Hormones can come into play when people "feel" love. There are various kinds of love described in the Bible. There is God given love, and there is love that is inherent to all mankind. The truth is, I don't know where one feeling and type of love starts, and the next feeling ends.

When I watch starving people in foreign countries on television, or images of a bald six-year-old that is dying of leukemia in a children's hospital, or see things like battered women's shelters on the news, I feel a number of emotions. I wish I could help every one of the victims of disease, poverty, starvation and abuse I see. Is it God given love, empathy, and compassion, which moves me to want to help these people, or is it pity and guilt? Where does one feeling start and the next one end? My point is that many different "feelings" can result in one being motivated to do something loving. Love is the action that can pick up, where guilt and pity leave off.

Acting in love towards one another, looks like *the* thing that our Master really expects of His Servants while He is away. It appears that anything done apart from the love of Christ ultimately has no value. The Apostle Paul put it this way:

If I speak in the tongues of men and of angels, but have not love, I am a noisy gong or a clanging cymbal. And if I have prophetic powers, and understand all mysteries and all knowledge, and if I have all faith, so as to remove mountains, but have not love, I am nothing. If I give away all I have, and if I deliver up my body to be burned, but have not love, I gain nothing.
1 Corinthians 13:1-3 (KJV)

How we act in love can take many different forms. There are millions of followers of Christ and probably millions of ways that love can be shown by them.

Those that have arrived at other conclusions as to what the "talents" represent are likely only taking a broader or narrower view than what I have done here. That is to say, they are putting into different words how and when Christ-like love is "spent," invested, or shown. They are talking about "ministries" or methods of how "love" is delivered.

For example, people often show love by giving money to support various efforts. Followers of Christ will use their spiritual gifts and abilities as they show love for others. In both of these cases, I argue that giving money, or using gifts and abilities are all simply delivery methods, and not the "talent" itself. *Love*, obtained through *faith*, used according to *wisdom*, is the God given commodity they are delivering.

Wisdom

God given wisdom and love must go hand in hand. How to spend the Master's "talents" or love He has given you, requires God given wisdom.

But the **wisdom** *that is from above is first pure, then peaceable, gentle, and easy to be intreated, full of mercy and good fruits, without partiality, and without hypocrisy. James 3:17 (KJV)* (Emphasis added)

Remember, each servant was given a finite amount of talents by the master. Although the talents can grow, they are not unlimited. Whereas God has an unlimited capacity to love, we as humans have a limited capacity to deliver love.

A man who spends his evening delivering food boxes to the poor after he has been at his job all day, may not be showing love to his children who hardly ever get to see him. That's okay… *the video games and television are there to take his place….*

The youth minister who is busy raising other people's kids, may be neglecting the needs of his wife. That's okay… *someone else will be willing to do that…*

Similarly, if I send my entire income to some "feed the children" type organization, I will be out on the street, making myself a liability and dependent on someone else for love. For many, that would put their families at risk, and they may even lose their job, leaving them with no money to feed anyone. That would be love spent sans wisdom. The two are inseparable.

Your Love, Wisdom, and Faith Wallet

Given your finite amount of talents you have to spend in your figurative "wallet," how will you spend them? As you answer this, first remember that they are the Master's talents, not yours. Secondly, before you go looking for "investment opportunities," remember that the Master left you all of His possessions to take care of. That means figuratively (and probably literally) making sure that you are paying the regular "bills" that come in. It means taking care of regular maintenance and running the household while the Master is away.

How does this translate to the real world? How should you wisely spend the love entrusted to you by your Master? How that is accomplished by many may appear to lack any form of sensationalism. Especially to others who don't know how much is in your "wallet," and how much your master has left in your care.

Spending your talents may mean that by the end of the day, you have spent the entire day working a job in order to lovingly put food on the table for your family and pay for sending your kids to a school that teaches about Jesus in addition to teaching about math.

Spending your love wisely, might mean that you take over for your wife or husband when you get home from work and supervise the kids, so he or she can take care of some of their basic needs. While they are doing that, you will share your love with your kids.

Spending love might mean that you are caring for an elderly parent who is ill and possibly dying. This act of love may be even causing you to temporarily go into "debt" and run a love deficit. In other words, you may need the love from others to make it through.

Maybe there are people at work that are very challenging to be around, or people who even anger us. People to whom showing love is tiring. After simply taking care of what it is that the Master has left you to routinely care take, by the end of the week, your faith-based-wise-love "wallet" may be pretty empty and you have very little "discretionary talents" left to invest.

There are those, that have a lighter burden when it comes to routine responsibilities. They may have more talents left in their wallet at the end of the week to invest. There are also those who have been given a greater capacity to show love. These are those who have been given more "talents," "according to their abilities."

Having "greater abilities" may come in the form of being more energetic, maybe they are better time managers, are more articulate, better educated, or maybe they have more financial resources. Maybe their genetics has brought about greater physical strength or organic intelligence. Maybe their life experience has given them the ability to communicate and relate better with youth or people from different lands. Maybe God has given them more ability to be empathetic with others than the average person. It could be that they have leadership skills that inspire people. Or, possibly it is indeed a spiritual gift that they have received that has given them a greater ability to show love. These are all "abilities" that may affect the number of "talents" that God gives to people.

People in full time ministries may have a greater capacity to show love, because that is what their job inherently involves. They may also have greater resources at their disposal devoted to showing love, which increases their ability to do so. Supporting those in full time ministry is often a great way for those that don't have as much time, or limited resources by themselves to show love. I am sure that our Master loves it when He sees us teaming up with our co-servants in order to show love in His name! That can be likened to pooling our talents in order to make a greater investment that none of us could make on our own.

What God has given you to deal with in your life, what God given abilities you have, and how much capacity to love God has given you based on your abilities and resources, is only truly known by you and God.

There is one thing we can know for sure, even if you only have "one talent" left over at the end of the week, it is better to invest it, than to "bury it in the ground," like the one servant did.

My "Mission" In Life

It is not my objective to undermine anyone's good intentions for the Kingdom of God. There are hundreds of great love based ministries in existence. However, this issue confuses, distracts, and depresses followers of Jesus who are trying to figure out how to best serve Him.

I have heard many, many sermons over five decades of man's ideas of how I should serve God in order to use my "talents." With the threat of what happens if we don't use our talents, like the wicked and lazy servant, hanging over my head, these sermons always used to leave me feeling guilty and inadequate, no matter what my life looked like at the time. I do not believe I am unique in experiencing those feelings.

These sermons have taken the form of encouragement to "discover my spiritual gift," to "determine my ministry," and to figure out "how to serve." Using the *Parable of the Talents*, some speakers have attempted to use guilt to attempt to get me to give more money.

Due to my sin nature, I admittedly can still get a little irritated when a co-bonded servant of Christ tries to tell me how to spend the Master's talents entrusted to me. I also admit that the same may be true when someone tries to compel me to take part in an organized effort in the name of Christ, which appears to only be for the sake of having an organized effort in the name of Christ. However, I generally no longer experience feelings of guilt, now that I have a clear understanding of the *Parable of the Talents*. In fact, I have come to view other Christian's ideas of how to spend the talents God has entrusted me with as "investment opportunities."

When I get up in the morning, I understand that I am 100% *owned* by my Lord Jesus. I am His bond-servant. I represent Him and His interests in my home and community. As I reach into my figurative pocket each day, I find that His Holy Spirit has refilled my wallet with His "talents" (love). He has put in just the right amount that He knows I can use on His behalf. It is always enough according to my abilities. It is up to me as I go through life each day "doing business" on behalf of the Master, to determine how to spend those talents. I am going to probably spend them differently each day as I come across different situations, people, needs and "investment opportunities."

I don't need to spend long hours determining my purpose or ministry. My purpose is to do business for My Master in His absence. I recognize that He has given each of His servants differing amounts of talents (love) according to their ability to use them (love). I also recognize My master has a large organization and He has millions of things that need to be taken care of each day.

In any given day, my Master's talents will be spent by millions of His different servants, in tens of millions of different ways. Arguably most of which were unplanned and unforeseen, requiring no formal "ministry," organized effort to "serve," or recognition ahead of time of gifts or abilities.

Some servants may spend all of their talents providing for their family today and raising their children to love God. Some will spend all of their talents on their spouse, and have none left to spend elsewhere today. Some, whom God has positioned in places of authority, will use their talents to make or influence decisions that will allow the love of Christ to impact their work place or community.

Some servants of the Master will have been given enough talents to take care of their family and still be able to fly off to Africa and help feed thousands. Some will prepare a Bible lesson. Others will talk about Jesus to strangers at a school. Servants will spend their talents comforting loved ones dying in the hospital, taking elderly parents to doctor's appointments, teaching a grandchild a song about Jesus, or making cookies for a Sunday morning Church service.

How servants of Jesus spend their talents today, may not be the same way they spend their talents (show Christ's love) tomorrow. Our situations all change as we grow older.

I have no idea how my fellow bondservants of my Master, Jesus, are spending the talents that He gave them. I don't know how many talents they were given. I don't know the depths of their abilities.

I am in no position to judge others as to how they are using their talents. Those that appear to have not been given many talents, may be out spending me at a rate of ten to one. As we see in the

Parable of the Talents, every servant is only responsible to the Master. Each must give an accounting of how they used their talents (love). Perhaps one way to spend the love that I have been given, is to understand this about my co-bondservants.

Digging A Hole

Angela and I have lived on the same three acres of property for coming up on 30 years. When we moved here, we saw the potential the property had, but the more immediate reason was because our financial situation was changing for the worse, and it was more affordable. There were sixty-some pickup loads of scrap metal that I pick-axed up out of the ground and hauled off the property, along with the top half of a school bus, most of a couple car bodies, and twenty-six rusty bed springs. There were sheds full of miscellaneous auto parts and logging paraphernalia. There was an open cesspit in the back yard and we had to go outside to answer the telephone. There was no insulation in the walls (or on many bare electrical wires in the attic!) and the only heat source in our then, 850 square foot home was a small wood stove.

There were thousands of hours of grueling labor involved in transforming our home into what it is today over the last thirty years. It is still far from a palace or even what some may consider "nice," but our home is drastically different than it once was. From being covered in sweat and insulation in a 120-degree attic, to digging out thirty yards of dirt from under the house by hand while laying on my back, I have to say my least favorite task has always been digging holes or ditches. Where we live, the unpleasant experience of digging in the rocky soil can be very physically demanding and frustrating.

Based on my personal digging experience, when I think of how much easier it would have been for the servant, who had been given one talent, to take it to the bank in order to earn interest, rather than digging a hole to hide it in, I have to ask a question; Was this guy an idiot? It took a great deal more effort on this servant's part to hide his talent, then to invest it.

<u>Matthew 25:19-23</u>

After a long time the lord of those servants cometh, and reckoneth with them. And so he that had received five talents

came and brought other five talents, saying, Lord, thou deliveredst unto me five talents: behold, I have gained beside them five talents more. His lord said unto him, well done, thou good and faithful servant: thou hast been faithful over a few things, I will make thee ruler over many things: enter thou into the joy of thy lord. He also that had received two talents came and said, Lord, thou deliveredst unto me two talents: behold, I have gained two other talents beside them. His lord said unto him, well done, good and faithful servant; thou hast been faithful over a few things, I will make thee ruler over many things: enter thou into the joy of thy lord. (KJV)

After a long time had passed, the master of those same servants returned and settled accounts with them. And so the one who had received five talents came and brought five additional talents saying, "master, you entrusted me with five talents and look, I have gained five more." His master replied to him, "well done good and faithful servant. You have been faithful over a few things. Over many things, I will make you a ruler. Enter into the joy of your lord." The one that had two talents also came and said, "master, you entrusted me with two talents and look, I have gained two more talents." His master replied to him, "well done good and faithful servant. You have been faithful over a few things. Over many things, I will make you a ruler. Enter into the joy of your lord." (DHT)

The theme of the return of the Master is repeated from an earlier parable. He has come to "settle accounts" with His servants. What have His servants done with what He left with them? It is interesting to note here that what the servants were "given," never really belonged to them. They were only stewards of the possessions and talents that were entrusted to them. The Master has come back to check on what clearly belongs to him.

Verses 19 to 23 tell a story of two servants who both did well with their talents. Because they had done so, they each received what appears to be the same reward, even though one had originally been given more than the other, and subsequently earned more with it.

Both servants received the reward of hearing the words, "well done good and faithful servant." Both received the reward of continuing to remain in fellowship or being associated with the Master. Both were put "in charge" of "many things." Both have been invited to "enter into the joy of their Lord," or as the New International Version translation puts it, "*come and share in your Master's happiness*."

Could there be any greater gift for a Christian who has never seen Jesus and yet has lived his or her entire life as His follower, than to one day meet Jesus face to face and hear the words, "well done good and faithful servant?"

Being Put "In Charge"

We have clues elsewhere in scripture regarding what it may mean to be "put in charge of many things." All of the following scriptures, like the parable we are examining, apply to a future time after the return of Jesus.

And he that overcometh, and keepeth my works unto the end, to him will I ***give power over the nations: And he shall rule them with a rod of iron****; as the vessels of a potter shall they be broken to shivers: even as I received of my Father. Rev 2:26-27 (KJV)* (Emphasis added)

Therefore I endure all things for the elect's sakes, that they may also obtain the salvation which is in Christ Jesus with eternal glory. It is a faithful saying: For if we be dead with him, we shall also live with him: If we suffer, ***we shall also reign with him****: if we deny him, he also will deny us: If we believe not, yet he abideth faithful: he cannot deny himself. 2 Tim 2:10-13 (KJV)* (Emphasis added)

Do ye not know that the saints shall judge the world? *and if the world shall be judged by you, are ye unworthy to judge the smallest matters?* ***Know ye not that we shall judge angels?*** *how much more things that pertain to this life? 1 Cor 6:2-3 (KJV)* (Emphasis added)

And hath made us ***kings and priests*** *unto God and his Father; to him be glory and dominion for ever and ever. Amen. Rev 1:6 (KJV)* (Emphasis added)

And hast made us unto our God ***kings and priests: and we shall reign on the earth****. Rev 5:8 (KJV)* (Emphasis added)

Blessed and holy is he that hath part in the first resurrection: on such the second death hath no power, ***but they shall be priests of God and of Christ, and shall reign with him a thousand years.*** *Rev 20:6 (KJV)* (Emphasis added)

The "faithful servant" of Jesus in this age, will be given a great deal of responsibility in the coming age. In the kingdom that Jesus brings to this earth and beyond, His faithful servants will act as His "deputies" in making decisions as they govern on His behalf in His Kingdom that will extend throughout the entire world. This is how we will "rule" with Jesus.

Under Jesus' authority, His faithful servants will have complete dominion, power, and authority to execute those decisions. That is how we will "reign," with Him.

The faithful servants of Jesus will act as magistrates and arbitrators among the inhabitants of the earth, wherever their Master has assigned them in His Kingdom. This will make us "judges," on Jesus' behalf.

Finally, the faithful servants of Jesus will make sure the physical needs of the people are being met and serve as ministers and teachers for the people regarding spiritual matters. This is one way that we will act in our role of "priests," on behalf of Jesus.

The Joy of the Lord

What does it mean to be given an invitation to take part in the "joy" or "happiness of the Lord?" God, literally only knows. Followers of Jesus cannot possibly imagine all of the joys that lay ahead of them. The mere concept of "eternity," is something that will take a while to sink in… in eternity. Our lives now are spent rushing about with a looming sense of urgency, as though the clock is always ticking, and our time is running out. Many look forward to life slowing down in retirement. I did. Now, I am retired and I still rush around with a sense of urgency as if time is running out.

How blissful it will be for the elect of God to have the dimension of time come to an end. What will it be like to have a body that is imperishable coupled with no time limitations? A body that does not know hunger, loneliness, sickness, soreness, tiredness, or sadness? A body that is no longer subject to death? And, no longer in bondage to hundreds of generations of genetic breakdown caused by the fall of man.

The joy of the Lord? One day I will not need a bungee in order to jump into a river that is 100 feet below, or an aircraft, wing suit or parachute to soar over the mountains. I, like my Master, will be able to walk across the top of a raging sea. If Mount Everest survives the Second Coming and my Master gives me any vacation time, I plan on climbing it without the aid of an oxygen tank or ropes. There are places that I would love to visit that I likely will never see in my mortal lifetime. If they still have any appeal to me after Jesus returns, there will be plenty of time to explore.

One day I won't have to feel bad about children around the world who don't have enough to eat, because my Master will stop hunger. I won't have to pray for cancer patients, because cancer will only be known to history since Jesus, the Great Healer, will be the King of the World. Hospitals will be empty. Crime, corruption and injustice will not fill the headlines. Jesus will abolish such things as He rules with a rod of iron.

Our God is a God of infinite wisdom and creativity. In addition to the responsibilities in the coming age already mentioned, one of the things the Bible tells us we will be doing in eternity is serving God in His Temple. While on "temple duty," we will never know who, or what will next come through the door of God's throne room.

Our physical universe is contained in three dimensions, yet goes on forever in all directions. Jesus demonstrated that His glorified body had the ability to travel in any one of those directions and even pass through matter. How long would it take to explore an infinite universe if we are allowed to do so? Is there an infinite amount of things we cannot even dream of left to discover? Will our glorified bodies have the ability to feel things our current bodies cannot? We cannot even begin to imagine the depth of the joy that lies ahead for the faithful servant of Jesus!

The Naughty Servant

What about the third "servant?" Like the other two, he was both called a "servant," and given the same thing of value by the master, although in a smaller quantity. Unlike the other two, this servant did not do anything with what he was given. What happened as a result?

<u>Matthew 25:24-25</u>

Then he which had received the one talent came and said, Lord, I knew thee that thou art an hard man, reaping where thou hast not sown, and gathering where thou hast not strawed: And I was afraid, and went and hid thy talent in the earth: lo, there thou hast that is thine. (KJV)

Then the one who had been entrusted with one talent came and said, "Lord, I know that you are a tough man, reaping where you have not planted, and gathering where you have not scattered, so I was afraid and went and hid your talent in the earth. Look, here is what is yours." (DHT)

The servant with one talent, like the other two, had been entrusted with the master's possessions. The master, knowing this servant, gave to him according to his "ability." Relative to the trust placed in the other two servants, the master didn't trust this servant's abilities very much. It turns out with good reason.

The master could have chosen to give the man's one talent to one of the other two servants before He went away on the journey, but he didn't. The master, knowing that the servant did indeed have some ability, decided to give this servant a chance. This servant simply made the choice not to put to work what the master had left him. He had the ability to do something constructive with what he was given, but instead chose to hide it away and do nothing with it.

This servant knew he had nothing to show for what had been entrusted to him. Yet, he seems to approach the master almost defiantly. He even appears to attack the master's character, calling him a "hard," or "tough" man.

The third servant had just witnessed the master hold the first two servants accountable for their actions while he was away. The servant assumed that his co-servants must have had to surrender not only the original talents they were given but the ones they had earned; five additional talents from the servant who was originally given five, and two additional from the servant who started with two.

In addressing the master, the third servant, later identified as "wicked and lazy," called attention to the fact that the master did not do the actual work to earn the additional talents he was collecting from his co-servants. In the wicked servant's mind, the master was not the one that did the work of "sowing," or "scattering" of "seed." Yet, here he was doing the "gathering" and "reaping" of the harvest that came about as a result of the labors of his servants.

The wicked and lazy servant must have thought the two servants before him were no better off than before they had gone to all the work of earning additional talents, since they had to give up what they had earned to the master. Further, in the mind of this third servant, if the master was willing to take everything from the first two servants, none of which the master had earned himself, he must also be the kind of "hard" man that would punish someone for not returning what they were originally given. So, at least he wasn't going to make that mistake…

Regardless of what the third servant may have been thinking, or the reasons behind his excuses, the third servant was too lazy to do anything with the talents he had been given. So, he buried the one talent he was given in the ground so he could return it as given to him by the master. His stated motivation for taking this approach was fear of the master. How clever this lazy servant must have thought himself to be, having not expended any energy on gaining "talents" only to have to give them up to this "hard" man he falsely called his "master."

This misjudgment of the master's character along with the wicked servant's laziness did not serve him well.

Matthew 25:26-28

His lord answered and said unto him, thou wicked and slothful servant, thou knewest that I reap where I sowed not, and gather where I have not strawed: Thou oughtest therefore to have put my money to the exchangers, and then at my coming I should have received mine own with usury. Take therefore the talent from him, and give it unto him which hath ten talents. (KJV)

His master answered and said to him, "you wicked and lazy servant. You knew that I reap where I have not planted and

gather where I have not scattered? Then you should have put my money on deposit with the bankers, so when I returned I would have received what belongs to me with interest. So take the talent from him and give it to the one who has ten talents." (DHT)

The Master first answers the servant by calling him a couple names; "wicked and slothful," or "lazy." The question on the part of the master, "*You knew that I reap where I have not sown and gather where I scattered no seed?*" is not an admission of anything regarding the master's character or business practices. The master is simply feeding back to the servant what he just heard the wicked servant say, and is confirming it with him. The master's statement appears to be a challenge of disbelief at the excuse the wicked servant had to offer.

The master also appears to be holding the servant accountable to his own beliefs about the master. To paraphrase the master's statement, "*If you think I am such a hard man, then you would have at least invested my money for me rather than doing nothing. Because you didn't, I don't believe your excuse. I think you are just wicked, lazy, and no servant at all.*"

The master knew the servant had the ability to at least invest the talent to earn interest and he failed to do so. It must have taken more of an effort for the servant to dig a hole, bury the talent, keep track of where he buried it, and then dig it up, than if he would have simply put the talent in the bank in order to earn interest. Perhaps, he could have "teamed up," and even invested it with one of the other servants.

As a result of misjudging the master, and his being wicked and lazy with what was entrusted to him, this servant had what was given to him taken away. The talent he had was given to the servant that proved to be faithful and turned his five talents into ten.

It is noteworthy that the master says "give it to him who *has* ten talents," as though that servant was still in possession of all of the ten talents. The master had indeed *not* taken the original talents, or the additional talents he had earned, away from the servant.

<u>Matthew 25:29-30</u>

For unto every one that hath shall be given, and he shall have abundance: but from him that hath not shall be taken away

even that which he hath. And cast ye the unprofitable servant into outer darkness: there shall be weeping and gnashing of teeth. (KJV)

For everyone that has, shall be given, and he shall have in excess. But the one who has nothing, even what he has will be taken away. And, expel the useless servant into outer darkness. In that place there will be weeping and grinding of teeth. (DHT)

Jesus ends this parable with a summary statement regarding those faithful servants who have been given much. They will be given more upon the return of the master. But He also said that those who have nothing or very little would even have that taken away from them. What does that mean?

Remember what the servants had been given quite possibly represent the ability to put God given love into action.

God given love in action could mean sharing the gospel, feeding the hungry, counseling the heavy of heart, praying for the sick, providing for your family, showing mercy or kindness, or thousands of other actions. No greater love will anyone ever receive than the servant of Jesus when she or he accepts the loving sacrifice that Jesus made for them.

Being purchased out of bondage to sin and given the assurance of spending eternity with Jesus, His servants have already truly been given much. How much more will Jesus' love for His servants be openly shown upon His return to this earth? I for one will enjoy my new eternal, glorified body, that will no longer only know things "in part," but rather in the presence of the King of Kings, know everything fully. That is a whole lot of love that my Master will bestow upon me.

Conversely, there are those who have heard the truth, or at least observed the reality of the existence of the Creator around them, but deny His existence. Maybe they have even demonstrated knowledge of the act of love carried out for them by Jesus in the Eternal Gospel, and maybe they have even declared that they believe it to be true, but they have done *nothing* with this knowledge. Even with this knowledge and confession, they failed to truly make Jesus their Lord.

It is those people who reject the love of Jesus that is freely offered to them, that have "nothing." It is through their own self-centered wickedness and laziness that they will even lose what they do have. They will be the ultimate losers.

A Loss of Salvation?

Will someone who will be considered by Jesus upon His return to be a "wicked servant," "lose his or her salvation?" We have visited this loss of salvation question before as we looked at previous parables in the Olivet Discourse. Again, in my opinion, people that fit this profile are servants in name only. Although maybe having a knowledge of who Jesus is and even believing what the gospel says, they never truly made Jesus their Master and Lord. They never got up off the throne of their life and invited Jesus to sit down in their place.

I don't believe the third "servant" was ever "saved." The servant was like one of the people in the parable of the sower who heard the gospel, but then falls away. In the *Parable of the Sower*, found in Matthew chapter 13, Jesus gives three examples of people who initially heard the gospel, yet are not saved by it (see chapter 18 of this book). Two out of three of the people in that parable apparently even understood the gospel and initially embraced it, yet still fell away. They had been "given" something by the master, yet ultimately failed to do anything with it.

Jesus has clearly told us that there are people who may originally profess to be Christians, may even have a "salvation experience," receiving what they heard "with joy," but the gospel never takes hold. This is likely the case with the wicked servant who was only given one talent.

Take Away Something from Nothing?

Jesus made the statement, "from the one who has not, even what he has will be taken away." How can you take away anything from someone who already has nothing? The answer is that even those people who walk the face of earth who call themselves atheists are still living under the influence of Christ's love.

It is the grace of God that is holding this universe together (Colossians 1:17). It is God's will that is restraining Satan. God is putting off the end of the world because it is His desire that not one should perish (2 Peter 3:9). Out of His love for us, God will continue to provide for the "just and the unjust" right up until they die or He returns. God created the universe in which we live, declared it good, and made our planet resilient in order that we might continue to live on it. Both the one who is in rebellion against God, and the devout follower of Jesus are the beneficiaries of all these things.

There are many who are not followers of Christ who have not been reborn to live forever. In that sense, they have "nothing." Yet, they are still living under the influence of, and receiving the benefits of God's love. Upon judgment day, that too will be taken away from them.

Parable of the Sower Sheds Additional Light

In Matthew chapter 13, we see that inbetween the time Jesus tells the *Parable of the Sower* and when he defines the symbolism found in it, He made the same statement that we find in the *Parable of the Talents*;

> *For whosoever hath, to him shall be given, and he shall have more abundance: but whosoever hath not, from him shall be taken away even that he hath. Matt 13:12 (KJV)*

When Jesus made this statement, He had just been addressing a "great multitude" as He sat by the sea. After He conveyed the *Parable of the Sower* to them, His disciples approached him with a question that led to the above statement.

> *And the disciples came, and said unto him* (Jesus), *Why speakest thou unto them in parables?* He (Jesus) *answered and said unto them, because it is given unto you to know the mysteries of the kingdom of heaven, but to them it is not given.* ***For whosoever hath, to him shall be given, and he shall have more abundance: but whosoever hath not, from him shall be taken away even that he hath.*** *Therefore speak I to them in parables: because they seeing see not; and hearing they hear not, neither do they understand. And in them is fulfilled the prophecy of Esaias, which saith, by hearing ye shall hear, and shall not understand; and seeing ye shall see, and shall not perceive: For this people's heart is waxed gross, and their ears are dull of hearing, and their eyes they have closed; lest at any time they should see with their eyes, and hear with their ears, and should understand with their heart, and should be converted, and I*

should heal them. But blessed are your eyes, for they see: and your ears, for they hear. Matt 13:10-16 (KJV) (Emphasis added)

The gospel has been "given" to many, yet not everyone has "eyes" to see the truth, or "ears" to understand it. As we have just read, Jesus has even personally delivered the message to those that are spiritually "blind" and "deaf." They have sat in the very presence of the Son of God and heard the gospel in His own words, yet they didn't "get it." They are examples of those who have been given to, yet have nothing, and even what they do have, will be taken away.

Weeping and Gnashing of Teeth

In the *Parable of the Talents* we find imagery associated with "going to hell." The disciples heard similar words used just a little earlier in another parable concerning wicked servants. "Wicked and lazy servants" will be sent into "the outer darkness," where there will be "weeping and gnashing of teeth." This same imagery is used often by Jesus in scripture (see Matt 8:12, Matt 13:42, Matt 13:50, Matt 22:13, Matt 24:51, Luke 13:28).

Those who are not true servants of the Master, will spend eternity apart from Him. They will be eternally separated from the love of God and left with absolutely nothing.

Summary

The *Parable of the Talents* doesn't have much to do with answering the disciple's original questions. Jesus is no longer only explaining when the things He spoke of will happen or what will be the sign of His coming and the end of the age. What He is talking about in the *Parable of the Talents* has everything to do with what His followers should be doing until such time as He returns. Jesus tells His parable towards the end of His discourse as if to say, "so when I do return, these are my expectations of what I will find…"

In the *Parable of the Talents*, we can identify Jesus as the Master who "goes away." The master in the parable says he is going away for a long time. Jesus did go away, and it has been a long time since He left. The "servants" in the parable are those who represent themselves to be the followers of Jesus. In the end, not all of these servants turn out to be "faithful" or actual servants.

Those that want to use this parable to support the somewhat shallow theory that it represents a formula for financial success will need to look elsewhere in scripture. The “talents” that the Master leaves with His servants may best be defined as a combination of God given love, faith, and wisdom. All three of those things can grow and can be utilized by the servants of Jesus in numerous ways.

Just as some in the parable are given more “talents” to use than others, some followers of Christ have been given a greater ability to show or deliver God’s love to others. God’s love can be shown in more ways than can be listed here. “Spending” love and wisdom can be subtle or overt, public or secret. It can involve praying. It can involve dying. It can involve how you use your money. Putting God given faith, wisdom and love to work can involve using one’s natural abilities or spiritual gifts.

Love, faith, and wisdom that is given by God will never pass away. Love is the essence of the top two commandments from God found in the New Testament. Without love, everything else is worth nothing. We obtain God’s love through God given faith, and effectively utilize it only through God given wisdom.

Those true servants that have “used” their “talents” wisely, that is to say, use their abilities to show Christ’s love to others, will bc rewarded upon the return of Jesus with eternal life. Those who are not actual servants of Christ, or who are servants in name only, are destined to spend eternity apart from the love of God. And “there will be weeping and gnashing of teeth.”

Notes

23. Better to Be a Sheep Than a Goat

My daughter Rachel, her husband, and my three beautiful grandchildren live in the house next door. Rachel is a health-minded, do-it-yourselfer, recovering 4H-club member. She ferments teas in closets, pickles things that once grew in the organic garden, and collects various amounts of eggs every day from her free-range chickens. If not for Rachel, there would be no sheep or goats in our field. If not for the sheep and goats in our field, I don't believe I would be as in touch with the numerous sheep and goat references found in the Bible.

Sheep and goats are different from one another. There are exceptions, but sheep like being a part of the flock. It is easier to keep them inside of a fence than it is to keep goats. Goats are the first ones to find a weak spot in the fence and escape. They are curious and independent thinkers. They can be a challenge to like, especially if it is you chasing them through your blueberry field trying to catch them after they have escaped their enclosure.

Sheep like lying about the field looking like a part of some 19th century, Romantic Period, pastoral painting. Goats like to climb on your neatly stacked woodpile, knock it over, and eat the tarp that was covering it. Sheep keep your grass neatly mowed and fertilized. Goats eat your wife's Gravenstien apple tree that you bought for Mother's day.

I believe Jesus well understood the differences between sheep and goats and that is why He used them as symbols while making His final comments to His Disciples during the Olivet Discourse. Jesus begins the Olivet Discourse speaking of watching and warnings, and ends it by speaking of judgment.

Jesus has already spoken of judging between "good and wicked servants," and sorting out wise and foolish "virgins." The servants in Jesus' parables represent these two categories: His true followers, and those who are Christian in name only. The *Parable of the Ten Virgins*, spoke about judging among the descendants of Israel who will be found ready to meet their Messiah.

The final parable is about judgment of yet another group. This last parable starts off more direct than the previous two;

Matthew 25:31

When the Son of man shall come in his glory, and all the holy angels with him, then shall he sit upon the throne of his glory: (KJV)

When the Son of Man shall come in his glory, and all the holy angels with Him, then He shall sit upon His throne of glory. (DHT)

Many passages describe the Second Coming of Jesus to be one of glory and judgment (Matthew 16:27, Matthew 26:64, Mark 8:38, Luke 9:26, II Thessalonians. 1:7, Jude 1:14-15, Revelation 1:7). There will be many things that take place when Jesus returns to the earth. One of the events that will take place is the judgment of those who are still alive on the earth just before the Millennial Kingdom of Jesus begins.

Earlier in the Olivet Discourse Jesus spoke of His glorious coming, which takes place just after the sign of the sun, moon, stars, and great earthquake. His coming will be like "lightning flashing from the east." He returns with His angels, who will be sent forth to gather the elect.

Now we see Jesus taking a seat on His throne. This is at a time when He has made His enemies His "footstool." The following Psalm is referred to several times in the New Testament as a prophecy that will one day be fulfilled at the Second Coming of the Messiah. It speaks of a coming time of judgment of all nations.

The Lord said unto my Lord, sit thou at my right hand, ***until I make thine enemies thy footstool.*** *The Lord shall send the rod of thy strength out of Zion: rule thou in the midst of thine enemies. Thy people shall be willing in the day of thy power, in the beauties of holiness from the womb of the morning: thou hast the dew of thy youth. The Lord hath sworn, and will not repent, Thou art a priest for ever after the order of Melchizedek. The Lord at thy right hand shall strike through kings in the day of his wrath.* ***He shall judge among the heathen, he shall fill the places with the dead bodies; he shall wound the heads over many countries.*** *He shall drink of the brook in the way: therefore shall he lift up the head. Ps 110 (KJV)* (Emphasis added)

The final event marking the nations becoming the "footstool" of Jesus is the Battle of Armageddon. This battle ends when the Antichrist and his chief false prophet are "thrown alive" into the "lake of fire" and when the rest of those who have gathered to meet Jesus in battle are killed by the very words of Jesus. (See Revelation 16:14-16 & Revelation 19:11-21)

Following this "battle," we see Satan bound and cast into hell for "a thousand years," where he will not be able to influence the nations during that period of time (Rev 20:1-3). Once the last enemy, Satan, has been bound and cast into hell, the "sheep and goats" judgment spoken of in this final Olivet Discourse prophecy will take place.

Several passages of scripture indicate that today, as I write this, Jesus is seated at the right hand of God the Father, until such time as the enemies of Jesus will be put down during the Day of the Lord (See Psalms 110: 1-7, Luke 20:43, Hebrews 1:13, Hebrews 10:12-13).

Once the Day of the Lord has come, the nations will be judged. This judgment is not to be confused with another judgment, which has been referred to as "The Great White Throne Judgment" (Revelation 20:11-15), which takes place at the end of the thousand-year reign of Christ, otherwise known as the "millennial period."

Millennial Period?

The millennial period is a 1000-year period that follows the great tribulation. It is a period of time during which Jesus will reign over this present planet earth from His temple in a newly rebuilt Jerusalem. It is during this period of time that many of the promises made to national Israel will come to be.

Eternity begins, and history "ends" at the end of the Millennial Kingdom of Christ. A thorough study of all that happens during the millennium is outside of the scope of this book. The 1000-year period of time is chiefly based on the following scripture:

And I saw an angel come down from heaven, having the key of the bottomless pit and a great chain in his hand. And he laid hold on the dragon, that old serpent, which is the Devil, and Satan, ***and bound him a thousand years****, and cast him into the bottomless pit, and shut him up, and set a seal upon him, that he should deceive the nations no more,* ***till the***

thousand years should be fulfilled: *and after that he must be loosed a little season. And I saw thrones, and they sat upon them,* ***and judgment was given unto them:*** *and I saw the souls of them that were beheaded for the witness of Jesus, and for the word of God, and which had not worshipped the beast, neither his image, neither had received his mark upon their foreheads, or in their hands; and* ***they lived and reigned with Christ a thousand years.*** *But the rest of the dead lived not again* ***until the thousand years were finished.*** *This is the first resurrection. Blessed and holy is he that hath part in the first resurrection: on such the second death hath no power, but they shall be priests of God and of Christ,* ***and shall reign with him a thousand years.*** *And when* ***the thousand years are expired,*** *Satan shall be loosed out of his prison, Rev 20:1-7 (KJV)* (Emphasis added)

Three Different Judgments?

A careful study of Revelation chapter 20 indicates that there will be two separate judgments in the future that concern unbelievers. There will also be a "judgment" of the righteous, sometimes referred to as the "Bema Seat Judgment."

Concerning the judgment of unbelievers, there is the judgment mentioned above in the Revelation 20:1-7 passage, and the Great White Throne Judgment. Those two judgments are separated by the 1000-year millennial reign of Christ. The Great White Throne Judgment (the second judgment) is described in the following passage.

And I saw ***a great white throne,*** *and him that sat on it, from whose face the earth and the heaven fled away; and there was found no place for them. And I saw the dead, small and great, stand before God; and the books were opened: and another book was opened, which is the book of life: and the dead were judged out of those things which were written in the books, according to their works. And the sea gave up the dead which were in it; and death and hell delivered up the dead which were in them: and they were judged every man according to their works. And death and hell were cast into the lake of fire. This is the second death. And whosoever was not found written in the book of life was cast into the lake of fire. Rev 20:11-15 (KJV)* (Emphasis added)

We see the first judgment, the one that we will call the "*Sheep and Goats Judgment*," occur at the end of the battle of Armageddon.

Then, at the end of the millennial period, the Great White Throne Judgment takes place.

With two exceptions, the Great White Throne Judgment is for all of those who have died ever since the beginning of time. That will include those who die during the future 1000-year reign of Christ. The two groups who will not be judged before the Great White Throne will be the elect of God who were raptured a thousand years earlier and already found to be worthy of eternal life by being redeemed by the blood of Jesus. The second group will be those who had already been judged at the "Sheep and Goats" judgment that takes place at the end of the tribulation period, just before the millennial reign of Jesus begins.

The Judgment of the Righteous

Scripture describes a third judgment for those who are "saved" through being purchased by the blood of Jesus. This group will have already been declared righteous and been granted eternal life. The thing in store for them that resembles a "judgment" will be what is described in Romans 14 and II Corinthians 5:

But why dost thou judge thy brother? or why dost thou set at nought thy brother? for we shall all stand before the judgment seat of Christ. For it is written, As I live, saith the Lord, every knee shall bow to me, and every tongue shall confess to God. So then every one of us shall give account of himself to God. Romans 14:10-12 (KJV)

For we must all appear before the judgment seat of Christ; that every one may receive the things done in his body, according to that he hath done, whether it be good or bad. 2 Cor 5:10 (KJV)

The above "judgment" is reflected in the Olivet Discourse parables concerning the "servants" of Jesus. For example, because one servant was faithful with "some," he was put in charge of "more" and invited to enter into the "joy of the Lord."

Although there is no way to earn your way in to Heaven, because of this judgment, we know that how you spend the "talents" Jesus has entrusted to you will follow you into the next age.

Matthew 25:32-33

And before him shall be gathered all nations: and he shall separate them one from another, as a shepherd divideth his sheep from the goats: And he shall set the sheep on his right hand, but the goats on the left. (KJV)

And all people will be gathered before him. And He shall separate them, one from another as a shepherd separates his sheep from the goats. And He shall place the sheep on His right side, but the goats on the left. (DHT)

The simplest interpretation of this passage might be to say that Christ will come in judgment and separate those who deserve eternal life from those who don't. That simple interpretation is not correct.

The Sheep and Goats judgment represented in this passage only involves the people who have survived the Day of the Lord judgments and remain alive on the earth at the end of the tribulation period, just before the millennial kingdom begins. Those that are found worthy during the Sheep and Goats judgment will remain alive as normal, human inhabitants of the earth during the 1000-year Kingdom of Jesus.

The second judgment (Great White Throne) will take place at the end of the 1000-year period. That judgment will involve the judgment of the dead who were not resurrected at the Second Coming (the unsaved), those who die during the Millennial Kingdom, and those who live until the end of the millennial kingdom. There will be new babies born during the Millennial Kingdom. Those people, along with the rest, will all be judged during the "Great White Throne" judgment.

In chapter 18 we examined "two harvests." The "gathering of the nations" for the Sheep and Goats judgment is separate and different than the gathering of the elect, which will have taken place just prior to the beginning of the Day of the Lord. The Sheep and Goats judgment will include a gathering that takes place just after "the kingdom of this world has become the Kingdom of our Lord:"

And the seventh angel sounded; and there were great voices in heaven, saying, the kingdoms of this world are become the kingdoms of our Lord, and of his Christ; and he shall reign for ever and ever. Rev 11:15 (KJV)

It would not make any sense for a king to take his throne in judgment prior to establishing His kingdom. The kingdoms of the world become the "kingdoms of our Lord" at the end of the seven-year tribulation period, just after God's Wrath has been poured out on the earth.

There is much that takes place on the earth in between the time Jesus rescues or raptures His followers and when His Kingdom on the earth is proclaimed. A third of the earth is burned, a giant mountain of fire plunges into the sea, a giant asteroid slams into the earth, and stinging locusts are released from the pits of Hell. The Day of the Lord judgments conclude with the infamous Battle of Armageddon during which Jesus puts the last of His enemies "under His feet."

Who Is Left On the Earth to Be Judged?

By the time the Battle of Armageddon takes place, who will be left on earth to be judged? The elect of God will have previously been gathered together and will be safely tucked away. The same will be true for the "Sons of the Kingdom," the 144,000 descendants of Israel who will have been miraculously protected by God through the Day of the Lord judgments. The prophet Isaiah says that during the time in question, God will make "*people rarer than fine gold*" (Isa. 13:12)

Most, who will have gathered on the plains of Armageddon, will have perished. The wrath of God being poured out on the earth will have ended the lives of the *majority* of its human population. Who besides the 144,000 descendants of the tribes of Israel will be left to judge?

Morbid Math

Conservatively using the "death toll" numbers provided in prophecy, as they would apply to today's population level, at least four and a half billion people will have died or been raptured in less than seven years.[103] That will leave approximately 2.5 billion inhabitants of the earth.

There is no way to know how many survivors there will be. This disturbing conservative estimate only serves to illustrate the likelihood that there will still be a significant number of survivors left on the earth following the outpouring of God's wrath. This large group of people are the ones that will be "sorted out" at the Sheep and Goats" judgment.

Survivors

Scripture strongly supports the idea that there will be mortal human beings walking the face of the earth after the Wrath of God has taken place and the Millennial Kingdom of Christ has been established. We already know that the 144,000 descendants of the tribes of Israel will inhabit Jesus' Kingdom. Additionally, there will still be many nations of Gentiles present on the earth after Jesus returns. These inhabitants will have survived the tribulation period, and the Sheep and Goats judgment, and will have been declared to be "sheep." That is to say they will be considered to be worthy enough to have not been thrown into the "lake of fire," with those determined to be considered "goats."

*And it shall come to pass in the last days, that the mountain of the Lord's house shall be established in the top of the mountains, and shall be exalted above the hills****; and all nations shall flow unto it. And many people shall go*** *and say, come ye, and let us go up to the mountain of the Lord, to the house of the God of Jacob; and he will teach us of his ways, and we will walk in his paths: for out of Zion shall go forth the law, and the word of the Lord from Jerusalem. And* ***he shall judge among the nations****, and shall rebuke many people: and they shall beat their swords into plowshares, and their spears into pruninghooks:* ***nation shall not lift up sword against nation****, neither shall they learn war any more. Isa 2:2-4 (KJV) (*Emphasis added)

Sheep or Goat?

Many of the Gentile people (non-Jews) who have survived the Great Tribulation will have identified themselves with the Antichrist by taking his "mark," which will be required to buy and sell (Rev. 13:16-18). Anyone depending on buying or selling anything: food, clothing, housing, etc. will be tempted to take this mark. For additional incentive, the penalty imposed by the government of the Antichrist for not taking the mark will be death.

Those that take this mark in order to save themselves, thereby identifying themselves with the Antichrist, will not do well at the Sheep and Goats judgment.

And the third angel followed them, saying with a loud voice, If any man worship the beast and his image, and receive his mark in his forehead, or in his hand, The same shall drink of the wine of the wrath of God, which is poured out without mixture into the cup of his indignation; and he shall be tormented with fire and brimstone in the presence of the holy angels, and in the presence of the Lamb: And the smoke of their torment ascendeth up for ever and ever: and they have no rest day nor night, who worship the beast and his image, and whosoever receiveth the mark of his name. Rev *14:9-11 (KJV)*

It is unknown how many will defy the Antichrist and will not take his mark. We cannot know how many will survive by defying such an evil character who controls the governments of the world.

Those that do survive and find themselves at the Sheep and Goats judgment, according to Matthew 25:32, will come from "all nations," or "all peoples." However, the word used here for "nations," transliterated from the Greek as "ethnee," is the word that is typically used to express nations other than the nation of Israel. [104] It is from the people of all nations that remain on the earth, after the rescue or rapture of the elect of God, and after the Battle of Armageddon that King Jesus will divide the "sheep" from the "goats." He will decide who will remain and inhabit the earth along with the "144,000" descendants of Israel that have been miraculously protected.

<u>**Matthew 25:34**</u>

Then shall the King say unto them on his right hand, Come, ye blessed of my Father, inherit the kingdom prepared for you from the foundation of the world: (KJV)

Then, the King will say to those on his right hand side, "come, you blessed of my Father. Inherit the kingdom prepared for you from the foundation of the world." (DHT)

Verse 33 tells us that the "sheep" are the ones that had been separated and placed on the right hand side of the King. In verse 34 we learn that even though this group had not been rescued by Jesus earlier with the elect, that they, like the Church that has previously been raptured, are also considered "blessed by God."

Those considered to be "sheep," will be rewarded by being invited to "inherit the kingdom prepared for" them. At this point in the future, "the kingdom," means a literal earthly kingdom. It is the Kingdom of Heaven; which Jesus has brought with Him to this world. This is the same "world," that is referred to in verse 34 ("foundation of the world"). This kingdom will bring about the world, that from the "foundation of the world" was designed and created by God to support.

Any survivors of God's judgment that had taken the mark of the Antichrist will be counted among the "goats" and will not inherit the new earthly kingdom. Next we learn of the criteria that Jesus uses for the selection of those who He placed on His right, who will inherit the kingdom.

Matthew 25:35-40

For I was an hungred, and ye gave me meat: I was thirsty, and ye gave me drink: I was a stranger, and ye took me in: Naked, and ye clothed me: I was sick, and ye visited me: I was in prison, and ye came unto me. Then shall the righteous answer him, saying, Lord, when saw we thee an hungred, and fed thee? or thirsty, and gave thee drink? When saw we thee a stranger, and took thee in? or naked, and clothed thee? Or when saw we thee sick, or in prison, and came unto thee? And the King shall answer and say unto them, Verily I say unto you, inasmuch as ye have done it unto one of the least of these my brethren, ye have done it unto me. Matt 25:35-40 (KJV)

For I was hungry, and you gave me something to eat. I was thirsty, and you gave me something to drink. I was a stranger, and you took me in. I was naked and you clothed me: sick, and you looked out for me: in prison, and you came to me.

Then the righteous will answer Him saying, "Lord, when did we see you were hungry and feed you or thirsty and give you drink? When did we see you as a stranger and take you in, or naked and cloth you? When did we see you sick or in prison and come visit you?

And the King will answer them saying, "believe me when I tell you that in as much as you did it for the least of one of these brothers of mine, you did it for me." (DHT)

So far within this parable, Jesus has referred to Himself as "the Son of Man," a "shepherd," and now "Lord" and "King." It is clear this parable is about Him, and an event that takes place at His return.

Jesus gives a list of physical acts of love; hospitality, providing food, drink, clothing, visiting the sick, visiting the incarcerated. Initially, Jesus makes it sound as though these things were done directly for Him. Eventually, Jesus clarifies in the parable that when these things were done for a group of people known as His "brethren," that it was the same as doing these things directly for Jesus.

Three of the needs that Jesus has enumerated are very basic, scoring in the top seven in Maslow's hierarchy of physiological needs; food, water, and clothing.[105] The other three needs have more to do with meeting emotional human needs; visiting someone in prison, taking in strangers, and visiting or caring for the sick.

I don't believe that this was intended to be a comprehensive list of everything that someone should feel obligated to do for others. I think Jesus was conveying the spirit of what he was talking about. He could have just as easily added, "when I was depressed, you cheered me up. When my car was broken down, you gave me a ride. When I couldn't buy or sell because I wouldn't take the mark of the beast, you traded with me. When I was fleeing the Antichrist, you hid me…"

After listening to all of the loving things that the King lists that they did, the "righteous" or the "sheep" who have been separated out to the right-hand side ask a question of the King. They did so as if His statements about what they had done for Him surprised them. "*When did we ever do any of these kind things for you that you are saying we did, your majesty? After all, we just met?*" The King answers that whenever the righteous did it for "one of the least of these, my brethren, you did it for me." Acts towards the "brothers" of Jesus equate with acts done towards Jesus Himself.

Who Are The "Brethren" Of Jesus

Who are the brethren of Jesus? All humankind? Is this parable simply about following the golden rule? Those whom treat others as they want to be treated will inherit the kingdom of God? Wouldn't that then mean that people could obtain salvation by merely treating others in this manner? Does this scripture support "salvation through works?" Can we "do" our way into heaven?

The "brothers of Christ" may be the 144,000 descendants of Israel who are "sealed" with God's protection and left on the earth during the outpouring of God's wrath. The group of "sheep" may be like those who lived in Nazi Germany and surrounding nations that were under Nazi control in World War II, who hid Jews in their attics, fed them, and helped them to escape. This is the view of Robert Van Kampen in his book *The Sign.*[106]

Certainly the "brothers of Christ" would include any descendant of Israel left on the earth after Jesus has returned, but in my opinion, that definition is a little too narrow. Anyone who is going to inherit eternal life and partake of Jesus' Kingdom, would likely be considered the "brothers of Christ." Anyone who is to be counted "righteous" in the end is part of that brotherhood. I would include all of the "sheep" in that group, along with the descendants of the tribes of Israel who are on the earth during the Day of the Lord.

Perhaps the most popular interpretation of this parable, is that it applies to the entire Church age we are currently living in, and not just the end of the age. The "brothers of Christ," according to this view, are any people who are in need. Howard Clark Kee, contributing author to *The Interpreter's One-Volume Commentary on the Bible*; says that some interpreters believe that this verse originally only applied to the disciples that were "received in Christ's name," but that now it applies to all mankind: "*anyone in need.*" [107]

Sheep

Surely those descendants of Israel, which are sealed by God and remain on the earth after the rapture, will be counted among the "sheep." But who else might be?

There is nothing in what Jesus is saying here that would hint at this group being judged having already been declared righteous due to being saved by grace. Clearly this group is being judged, in essence according to the "law," based on their works alone. In this judgment, not doing good works results in "eternal punishment." From what we know from the whole counsel of biblical scripture, the Sheep and Goats judgment criteria is not a part of the "good news" whereby one becomes "saved" in the age we live in, it is only by the grace of God.

The people symbolized by "sheep" that will be subjected to this judgment will have been alive during the time of the Antichrist and not taken his mark. They will have lived under fear of persecution since the penalty for not taking the mark will be death. This group will have survived the outpouring of God's wrath on the earth. Christians are not appointed to suffer God's wrath. In the middle of all of the tribulation at the hand of the Antichrist, and God's judgments being poured out on the earth, this group of "sheep" will manage to serve the needs of the "brothers of Christ." Jesus will reward their good behavior.

Despite some reason that this group is now worthy of "inheriting the kingdom" for, they were not worthy of eternal salvation when Jesus came to rescue His Church.

It seems reasonable, even necessary, that these people have had a change of heart after Jesus returned, and the Church was rescued. Scripture indicates that most will turn away from God with hardened hearts, and believe the lies of the Antichrist after God's wrath has begun to be poured out on the earth. Yet, the Sheep and Goats judgment story seems to indicate that there will be some who turn to God and live in fear of Him. Perhaps this group of righteous people are the ones who have responded to the proclaiming of the Eternal Gospel by the angel mentioned in Revelation 14:6-7.

It is through responding to the Eternal Gospel that this group of "sheep" manifests their belief in and respect for the Almighty through works consistent with the fear of God. First, they loved God with all of their heart, soul, and mind, and secondly, they loved their neighbors as themselves. This is precisely Jesus' summation of all of the Old Testament writings (See Matthew 22:36-40).

It is clear that anyone who followed after the Antichrist will be declared to be a "goat," and separated out to the "left" and be sentenced accordingly. It is also clear that the criteria for being a sheep is not that you are a "born again Christian" because any true followers of Christ have already been declared to be an elect child of God and raptured prior to this point.

The criteria for being separated out to the favored right hand side of the Shepherd at this judgment, beyond showing kindness to the "brothers" of Jesus, is finally recognizing that Jesus is in fact the Messiah and King of the world. Jesus will be recognized for being the one the New Testament of the Bible declares that He is: God, in human form.

Look unto me, and be ye saved, all the ends of the earth: for I am God, and there is none else. I have sworn by myself, the word is gone out of my mouth in righteousness, and shall not return, that unto me ***every knee shall bow, every tongue shall swear****. Surely, shall one say, in the Lord have I righteousness and strength: even to him shall men come; and all that are incensed against him shall be ashamed. Isa 45:22-24 (KJV)* (Emphasis added)

*But why dost thou judge thy brother? or why dost thou set at nought thy brother? for we shall all stand before the judgment seat of Christ. For it is written, As I live, saith the Lord****, every knee shall bow to me, and every tongue shall confess to God****. So then every one of us shall give account of himself to God. Rom 14:10-12 (KJV)* (Emphasis added)

Naturally, having feared God, seeing Jesus miraculously return in awesome splendor, they would recognize Him for who He is: God, and bend their knee and will to Him. This then will result in eternal salvation.

Goats

Just as those that do good things for the brethren of Christ, will do it vicariously for Jesus, those that will do wrong by doing nothing for the brethren of Christ, will be considered as having done nothing for Jesus.

Matthew 25:41-45

Then shall he say also unto them on the left hand, depart from me, ye cursed, into everlasting fire, prepared for the devil and his angels: For I was an hungred, and ye gave me no meat: I was thirsty, and ye gave me no drink: I was a stranger, and ye took me not in: naked, and ye clothed me not: sick, and in prison, and ye visited me not. Then shall they also answer him, saying, Lord, when saw we thee an hungred, or athirst, or a stranger, or naked, or sick, or in prison, and did not minister unto thee? Then shall he answer them, saying, Verily I say unto you, inasmuch as ye did it not to one of the least of these, ye did it not to me. Matt 25:41-45 (KJV)

Then He also said to those on His left, "depart from me, you who are cursed, into the eternal fire prepared for the devil and his angels. Because I was hungry, and you gave me no food. I was thirsty, and you didn't give me anything to drink. I was a stranger, and you didn't take me in. I was naked, and you didn't clothe me. I was sick and in prison, and you didn't come see me."

And then they will answer and say, "Lord, when did we see you hungry, or thirsty, or a stranger, or naked, or sick, or in prison, and did not take care of your needs? Then He will answer them saying, "believe me when I tell you, in so much as you did not do one of these things to the least of these, you did not do it for me." (DHT)

Lack of taking action can result in what we know as sin. Apathy or standing by and doing nothing while the brothers of Christ are in need will net the "goats" who are on the left of the King, "eternal punishment." As this scripture points out, this is true even if you call Jesus "Lord." A title such as "Lord" is just a word unless it has appropriate actions or righteous intention behind it.

"Eternity" or into "the Age to Come?"

According to this parable, if we are to believe there is "eternal" life, we also must believe that there is eternal punishment.

For those who say that eternal punishment will not last forever it is important to consider that the same word for "eternal" is used for both "eternal life" and "eternal punishment."[108] If it does not really mean eternal punishment, how can it really mean eternal life? (Please see the end notes for a discussion this)

Why this is important, is to point out that we are clearly talking about eternity future and more importantly, that however "long" eternity lasts, it applies to both "punishment," for the wicked, and "life" for the righteous. Some would like to believe that souls will not be eternally punished but instead be destroyed in the "lake of fire" (See Revelation chapters 19 & 20).

To think that God would show some mercy by destroying a soul rather than punish one forever makes Him "easier" for some to "sell" to unbelievers. How could a "good God" torment souls for eternity? Surely the merciful thing to do would be to put them out of their misery and simply destroy them? However, taking this route of interpretation regarding eternal punishment is taking scripture where our human minds want to go, rather than allowing scripture to take our human minds where the truth appears to lead.

Being creatures and not the Creator, we have a finite sense of justice and when showing mercy is appropriate. God is most merciful. However, I will choose to trust God's judgment and not my own or some other human's sense of what is "right," even if "eternal punishment" really means forever.

Matthew 25:46

And these shall go away into everlasting punishment: but the righteous into life eternal. (KJV)

And these will go away into eternal punishment, but the righteous into eternal life. (DHT)

Just as in the *Parable of the Talents*, where the lazy and wicked servant, who failed to show love to others, was assigned a place in hell, so also are those "goats" that fail to do the same.

What Does This Parable Mean for Christians?

Visiting the imprisoned, feeding the hungry, clothing the naked are all great ways to "spend our talents," or plainly speaking, show the love of Christ. These things would be great demonstrations that we understand the "Golden Rule," which is to love our neighbors as ourselves, or to do to others, as we would like to have done to us. As great as all of these activities are to communicate the love of Jesus, the eternal salvation of followers of Christ will not be determined by whether or not they do these things.

The elect of God: The Church, will not be judged according to the criteria of the Sheep and Goats judgment. There is no condemnation for those who are in Christ Jesus (Romans 8:1). Because the elect of God have been bought with a great price by Jesus, they will have been previously declared righteous and gathered to Him.

The Sheep and Goats judgment takes place after the rapture of the Church, at the very end of the tribulation period, after the wrath of God has been poured out on the earth. It will indeed be a judgment based on "works," or the actions that the involved people took in their lives.

Is The Church There?

Even though Christians will not be judged at the Sheep and Goats judgment, will they be present? I don't know. The Bible doesn't tell us. It is clearly the "King" who does the judging and separating of the "sheep" and "goats," but Revelation 20:4 indicates that there will be others present at this judgment who will be seated on "thrones," and have "the authority to judge." One of the future responsibilities of the *Elect* of God after the return of Jesus will be that of serving as a judge.

Do ye not know that the saints shall judge the world? and if the world shall be judged by you, are ye unworthy to judge the smallest matters? Know ye not that we shall judge angels? how much more things that pertain to this life? 1 Cor 6:2-3 (KJV)

Although it is clear that the "saints," or elect of God, will have the authority to judge, it is unclear whether this authority will be put to work at the Sheep and Goats judgment. The authority to judge may only come into play as "the Saints" serve King Jesus later during His millennial reign on earth.

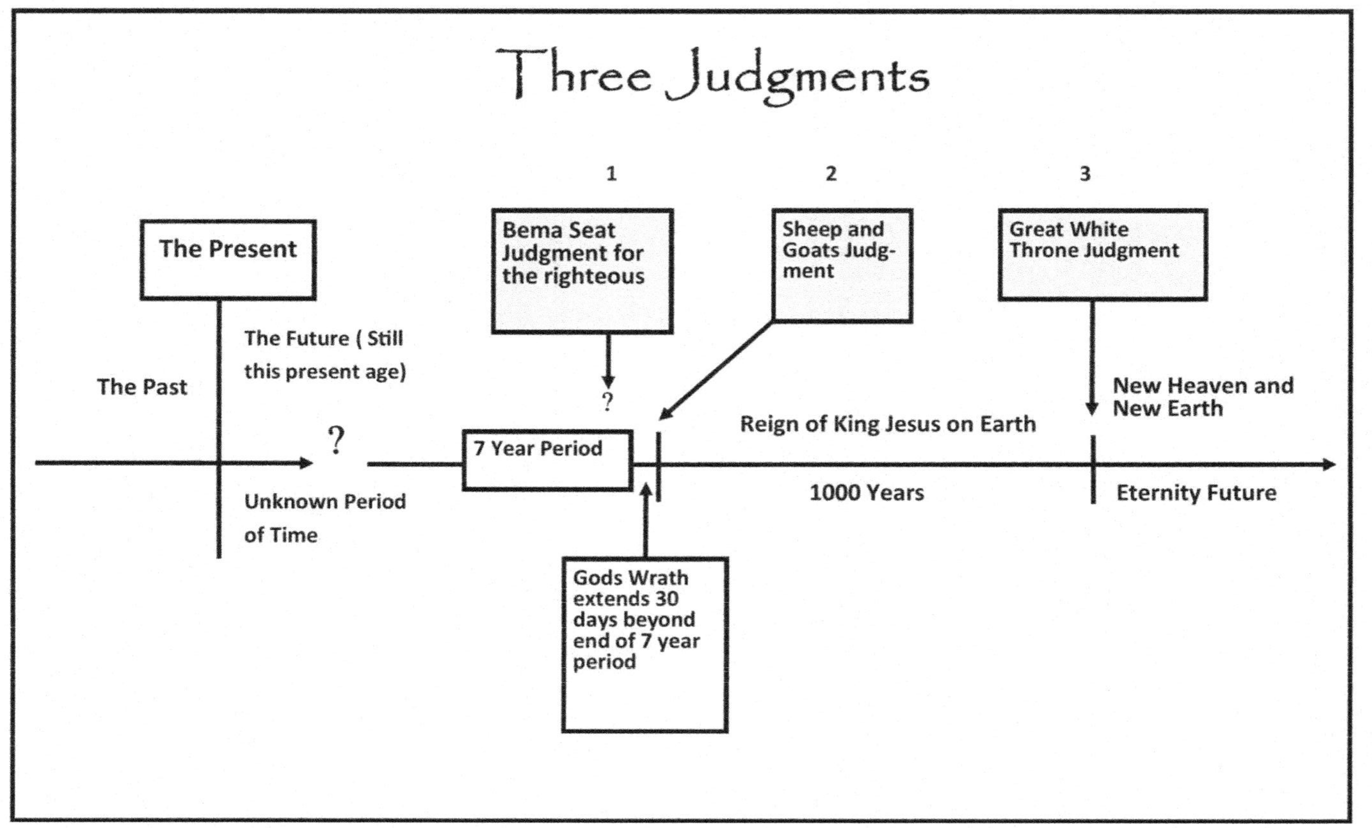
Three Judgments
1
2
3
The Present
Bema Seat Judgment for the righteous
Sheep and Goats Judg-ment
Great White Throne Judgment
The Future (Still this present age)
The Past
?
?
New Heaven and New Earth
Reign of King Jesus on Earth
7 Year Period
Unknown Period of Time
1000 Years
Eternity Future
Gods Wrath extends 30 days beyond end of 7 year period

Why Sheep and Goats Are Different Than "Talented" Servants

Some may notice similarities between the *Parable of the Talents* and the Sheep and Goats judgment. Jesus plays the part of the Master in the *Parable of the Talents*, and is the Judge presiding over the Sheep and Goats Judgment. In both stories, Jesus goes away for a long time. In both stories Jesus returns and makes judgments of people based on what they have done in His absence. In both stories, people are seemingly either rewarded or penalized based on their actions.

From these similarities, it would be very easy to lump the two stories together and assume they are basically saying the same thing. However, apart from the things above, I believe they are two separate stories for very good reasons.

First, please note the dissimilarities between the two stories. In the *Parable of the Talents*, the master places the servants in charge of his affairs. The servants know they are servants and what is expected of them. When Jesus left the earth, He left those that knew they were His followers, His disciples, behind to take care of His affairs in His absence. He gave them responsibilities to care for and be in charge of many things.

There is no indication that the people that are gathered from all over the world, who are compared to "sheep and goats," ever previously considered themselves to be under the authority of Jesus.

In the *Parable of the Talents*, the expectation for the servants is that they will act in a wise manner with what they have been given. There are no specific instructions or list of rules. In the end they are either declared to have been faithful servants, or they are considered to have been no servant at all.

Those who are servants of Jesus were chosen and purchased by Jesus. They act as faithful servants because they are called to be faithful. It is their new character and nature. False servants will be found out by the Master and he will deal with them.

The people that stand in front of Jesus in the Sheep and Goats judgment will be judged according to a list of behaviors as if they are being held accountable to some form of "law." It is as though the Sheep and Goats judgment is intended to determine who is a "good person" rather than someone who has relied on grace for salvation and then became a "good servant."

Good and faithful servants are placed in charge of many things and enter into the joy of their Master. This is consistent with being a "co-heir" with Jesus and ruling and reigning with Him.

"Sheep," are invited to "inherit the kingdom" prepared for them. That is, they are allowed to enter into the Kingdom of Jesus, which will have been brought to this earth. There is nothing indicating that they will be joint heirs with Jesus or ruling and reigning with Jesus in that future kingdom.

Something for Everyone

If not for including all of the stories and parables contained in the Olivet Discourse, one or more groups of people would have been left out of the epic end of the age story.

The Olivet Discourse, along with parallel passages of prophetic scripture, contains information for all of those living on the earth at the end of the age. This includes the descendants of Abraham, the Church, *and* the lost. It includes information for those who are removed from the earth before God's wrath, those who go through God's wrath, those who are found worthy to inhabit the earth at the beginning of the Millennial kingdom of Jesus, as well as those who will not be found worthy.

The Olivet Discourse tells us that just after the sign in the Sun, Moon and Stars, the elect of God ("faithful servants") will be raptured. The Parable of the Talents tells us that they will be put in charge of many things and enter into the "joy of the Lord."

In the Parable of the Talents, the Olivet Discourse tells us that people that were servants, or Christians in name only, will be found out and be treated like the rest of the unbelievers.

In the Parable of the Ten Virgins and related passages in the Book of Revelation, we see the faithful remnant of the tribes of Israel receive God's divine protection from the Antichrist and God's judgment as they are left on the earth.

The "Sheep and Goats" judgment gives us the judgment criteria for the non-elect of God, who were not raptured, but that are still alive at the end of the tribulation period, after God's wrath has been poured out. According to scripture in Revelation, those who have taken the mark of the beast will be thrown into the lake of fire. According to the Olivet Discourse, the rest will be judged based on their behavior. The "sheep," will inhabit the new Millennial Kingdom of Jesus, the "goats" will be cast into "everlasting fire."

The Olivet Discourse Comes to A Close

Jesus ended his discourse on His return and the end of the age by reminding His disciples that He, just like the master in His parables, was about ready to leave them.

Matthew 26:1-2

And it came to pass, when Jesus had finished all these sayings, he said unto his disciples, Ye know that after two days is the feast of the passover, and the Son of man is betrayed to be crucified. (KJV)

And it came about that when Jesus had finished saying all of this, He said to his disciples, "you know that after two days, the Passover will be here and the Son of Man will be delivered to be crucified." (DHT)

All of the parables about a master going away should have made sense to the disciples at this point as their Master reminds them that in only two days, He indeed is going away by means of crucifixion.

Summary

The parable of the Sheep and Goat Judgment builds on the Parable of the Talents. In both parables, those that chose to ignore the needs of others and show love were penalized with eternal torment.

The "Son of Man," in this parable is Jesus. The "sheep" in this parable are identified as those that have shown love towards the "brothers of Christ" through meeting at least some of their physical needs. For their actions, this group is promised to inherit the Kingdom of God. The Kingdom of God they will be inheriting starts with the 1000-year Kingdom of Jesus on earth. The "goats" in this parable stand for the unrighteous who stood by and took no action to help the "brothers" of Christ. The "goats" will also certainly include those who aligned themselves with the Antichrist and took his "mark" during the tribulation period.

The Sheep and Goats judgment takes place after Jesus returns, but before the new Millennial Kingdom begins. It is not to be confused with a second, "Great White Throne" judgment that will take place at the end of the Millennial Kingdom. The Sheep and Goats judgment is reserved for those who survive to the end of the Great Tribulation period. It is there that Jesus, as judge, will determine who will be the first inhabitants of the Millennial Kingdom, besides the 144,000 descendants of the tribes of Israel, who were already selected for that honor.

Although this parable may be a good lesson to all Christians throughout time concerning what Jesus considers to be "good" works, this specific "Sheep and Goats" judgment and the people involved does not appear to deal with the Church, which will have already been raptured. This is a judgment that is based on the things that people do on earth, rather than a judgment based on what Jesus did for those whom He called, bought, and purchased with His blood.

Jesus is coming back, just as He said He would. When He does, He will rescue His followers and then clean up the mess we have all made. This will involve judgment. The Judge will generously reward those whom He declares righteous. However, the penalties for not following Christ will be stiff: endless, relentless, punishment and torment.

24. Wrapping Up the Olivet Discourse to Go

It was Tuesday evening when Jesus spoke the words of the Olivet Discourse to His twelve disciples. By Friday night, He was dead. He overcame death and rose again to live forever on Sunday morning and He would only be in and out of the lives of His Disciples for the next forty days before He left the earth. The Olivet Discourse is one of the precious things that the Master, Jesus, entrusted to His servants to use and take care of while He is gone.

Having studied the Olivet Discourse, you have learned how to cut through end times deception. You can identify the signs which indicate that His return is near. You also have learned what things, as fantastic and disastrous as they are, do not necessarily mean the end of the age is close. You know how important it is for a good and faithful servant to await the return of Jesus with certainty and expectancy. It's going to happen! That means taking care of the Master's business until we see Him face to face.

The world apart from God is spiritually dark. It is currently being ruled by Satan. It is no wonder why people are so unsatisfied with the world the way it is. Everything appears to be falling apart around us. Pain, suffering, deterioration, the aging process, poverty, and evil surround us. Everyone experiences discomfort from time to time and hopes for something they don't have: better health, more wealth, more wisdom, more degrees, longer life, more time, a bigger house, more talent, a better job, better behaved children, better elected officials, less crime, a "greener" world, or better relationships. People long to live in a perfect world. It is as though everyone both sinner and saint, is always looking for or seeking something they don't have.

To paraphrase Reverend Timothy Keller, the founding pastor of Redeemer Presbyterian Church in Manhattan, human beings seem to have a memory of something or someplace that we have never personally experienced, and we are all trying to get back to it.

What we seem to be "remembering," as Reverend Keller put it, is the way the world was prior to the fall of Adam. It was the world in the state originally intended for humans, where total contentment and satisfaction were possible, and where humans could commune face to face with their creator. Although we were created to live there, none of us has ever lived in such a place. We want to live in the home where no one after Adam and Eve has ever lived. Being made to live in such a place appears to be a part of every human's DNA. We all long to go back to the garden.

The reborn follower of Jesus is twice vexed with the feeling of longing for another place and time. In our humanness, we not only want to return to the perfect world that we have never known, but those who have been saved by the blood of the Lamb and are spiritually reborn recognize that they are also citizens of the Kingdom of Heaven. Citizens of Heaven, while still in mortal bodies on this earth, have the immigration status of being "strangers in a foreign land."

Christians may feel "homesick." They don't completely fit in with the worldly culture that exists in this current age. Although Citizens of Heaven are immortal, the confines of the physical temporary body are cursed to ultimately break down and die. Being an immortal in a mortal body doesn't *feel* right. Citizens of Heaven yearn for the time when this will no longer be the case.

What Christians instinctively look forward to is the way the world will be again when Jesus returns and establishes His kingdom on this earth. What the lost inhabitants of the earth are looking for is a world that will never exist-a utopia where they call all the shots.

People Are Looking for Answers

Lack of contentment with this world drives people to look for answers. Ever since Jesus' feet left the Mount of Olives and He ascended into the clouds, people have been looking for answers regarding His return. Because most lack knowledge about what God's Word says on the subject, many have been deceived about the correct answers. This is not necessarily for lack of enthusiasm, passion, or yearning for His return.

In our role of "priest," we are to be "lights" to the world and ready with well-studied answers regarding God's plan when people have questions. As you have seen in our study of the Olivet Discourse, Jesus gave us the answers to the questions we ask about His return.

What Now?

Maybe you have previously studied the Olivet Discourse or perhaps you came to a deeper understanding of it through this book, but now it's time to ask the 'what now?' question. What should you do with the knowledge you have gained? The answer is go forth and be Biblically watchful! Continue to study the scriptures to gain **knowledge**. Use that knowledge in **wisdom** as you observe and experience the world around you, and wait for Jesus' return, like Noah waited for the flood- with certainty and **expectancy**.

Biblical Knowledge

I encourage you to continue your study of prophetic scripture utilizing a sound set of rules of interpretation (hermeneutics). The Olivet Discourse is *the* place to start when learning about the return of Jesus. It sets the foundational framework for the rest of prophetic scripture. Jesus ties the Olivet Discourse to the Old Testament when He directly mentions the prophet Daniel. He also references the Old Testament by quoting and paraphrasing passages. Be prepared to use what you have learned from the Olivet Discourse as a springboard to take you all over the Bible.

The Apostles Paul and Peter add additional details to what you have read in the Olivet Discourse. With careful study you can see the consistency of scripture and determine how their writings fit in perfectly with the information Jesus gave. The Apostle John's vision in Revelation, fills in many more details concerning Jesus' return, including the rapture of the Church and the end of the age.

Finally, studying the major and minor Old Testament prophets will complete and strengthen what you have learned about the end of the age. You will recognize a great deal of imagery used in the New Testament. These Old Testament prophetic books are especially important to completely understand the prophetic promises God made to Israel concerning the millennial kingdom and the Day of the Lord.

If you are interested in reading more books concerning the rapture of the Church and the end of the age, I recommend reading:

- *The Rapture Question Answered* and *The Sign*, by the late Robert Van Kampen.
- *The Pre-Wrath Rapture of the Church*, by Marvin Rosenthal.
- *Antichrist Before the Day of The Lord*, by Alan Kurschner.
- *God's Elect and The Great Tribulation*, by Charles Cooper.
- *The Sign of The End of the Age*, by Paul Kalbach

Wisely Applying Biblical Knowledge to the World Around Us

The Bible is the Story of King Jesus: why He created us, His family history, what is wrong in the world, why we need Him so badly, what He is like, what His expectations of us are, and what He intends for our future with Him.

There are many characters and groups of characters included in His story that require watchfulness. Although there are only a few "main characters," ultimately, the information contained in the Olivet Discourse, like the entire Bible, has meaning for, and will impact, the entire world.

One significant character group in the story of Jesus, is the Church. They will go through great persecution prior to being raptured. So, watch for the persecution of the Church at the hands of an Antichrist figure and a subsequent large falling away from the faith.

Another extremely important character group, will be a remnant of the descendants of the tribes of Israel that God chooses to seal and protect. They, like the raptured Christians, will be protected from God's wrath. However, they will remain on the earth. These people are Jews that will accept Jesus as their Messiah and follow Him wherever He asks them to go. Although "all of Israel will be saved," not everyone in Israel or every descendant of the tribes of Israel will be saved. God will decide who will make up "all of Israel."

Israel will enter into a seven-year "covenant of death," with the Antichrist. This seven-year covenant will be interrupted half way through by an act committed by the Antichrist, known as the Abomination of Desolation. This act will include the termination of the daily sacrifice in the Jewish temple, or holy place, and the Antichrist setting himself up to be worshipped as a god. The watchful will be looking for the covenant, and the Abomination of Desolation to occur exactly 1,260 days after the covenant is initiated.

The act of the Abomination of Desolation necessitates that a holy place, that does not exist now, will exist in the future. So, prior to Jesus' return, the "holy place," where a reinstituted Jewish daily sacrifice will be taking place, must be constructed. One can easily watch for such an event.

Jesus is going to return to this earth sometime within a 3 ½ year period after the Antichrist commits the act of the Abomination of Desolation. When Jesus does return, you won't be able to miss it.

As you are watching, along the way, events may come along that seem really bad, but "bad" relative to what? Nazi Germany? Stalin's U.S.S.R? Or how about Nebuchadnezzar's Babylon? Remember, followers of Jesus will watch for the "hard signs" and not be alarmed by the "soft signs" of the time.

Knowing that there are signs and a sequence of prophetic events lined out in the Bible prior to the return of Jesus, means that the return of Jesus *will not* overtake you like a "thief in the night." Tragically, that will not be the case for the unbeliever and for the elect that have been deceived and those Christians who are not watching.

Live with Certainty and Expectancy of Jesus' Return

Until Jesus comes back, His followers are to faithfully live with expectancy of His return. We know, without a doubt, He will return, and we know He will hold His servants accountable. The lesson of the Parable of the Talents tells us that the true servants of Jesus will receive eternal life and rewards commensurate with their achievements.

Millions of people are curious about how the "world will end." Christians are looking for answers regarding the return of Christ, and many pastors and teachers are answering "it really doesn't matter!" Yet, Jesus provided the real answers, and commanded His followers to put the information that He provided to use, by actively watching for His return. So, as we go forward and "make disciples," let us make complete disciples: one's who know the facts about the return of Jesus!

If you are a disciple of Jesus, it is not necessary for you to wait on anyone to tell you to teach what you know about Him to others. Jesus has already given you the go ahead. Once you have command of the things Jesus said in regards to His return, I encourage you to talk to others about it. However, please only do so utilizing love and the wisdom of Christ as your guide. Hopefully you have seen how important the topic is, and how much deception you may be up against when talking to others.

Don't ever be embarrassed for looking forward to the return of Jesus or talking about it. It is our great hope! I can't wait to see my Lord Jesus face to face and see what He wants me to do next!

The Big Payoff!

The return of Jesus will be no secret. The moon going dark or appearing "blood red" will accompany the return of Christ. The sun will also lose its light, and the stars will appear to fall from the sky. Then, the sky is going to "roll back like a scroll." If you miss all that, you won't miss the accompanying earthquake that will shake the entire planet, moving "every mountain and island" from its place. When these things occur, it is time to look up into the sky if you want to see Jesus coming on the clouds in great glory and splendor! Then…what a ride you will have!

Once Jesus returns, the first thing He will do is send out His angels through the entire earth to gather His elect. Those who are alive at the time will be changed in the blink of an eye into their immortal form. They will be gathered to Jesus together with those followers who have previously died.

Those who have previously died will be resurrected and in possession of their new, immortal body, a body like Jesus had upon His resurrection. A recognizable body you can touch. They will have bodies that still eat, but don't ever get sick, break or wear out. Bodies that can also pass through walls, travel great distances instantly, be invisible, and fly without the aid of machinery. Bodies that cannot be drowned or suffocated. We are going to meet many ancestors that loved Jesus before we were ever thought of or existed. What a sweet day that will be!

Once Jesus returns, for His followers, there will be no more sorrow. No tears, no pain, no being overweight, no alcoholism. There will be no need for "Obama-care." The blind and lame…won't be. Abortion clinics will be forgotten. Aging parents and grandparents will not need to worry about what home their children are going to move them into.

Mankind's "science" will be rendered obsolete by the creator of everything. What we know about now, we only know in part. Then, when we see Jesus, we will know everything in full.

Jesus' government will be perfect. There will be real peace. No need for treaties. No need for the United Nations. The economy will flourish. There will be no injustice and no need for welfare.

Our Master will do all of this upon His return. That is the day we are watching for!

I am so excited to get to meet all my brothers and sisters in Christ one day. Each one of you are a treasure chest full of the unique life experiences God has given you, and there is so much for us to talk about, if not sooner, then after our Lord returns. I hope to see you then! Until that time, if my Master allows it, I will be spending more of His "talents" He has entrusted to me on taking care of my family and writing my next book. How you spend yours is between you and our Master!

And what I say to you, I say to all; Watch! Mark 13:37

Support of Our Ministry

May my Lord Jesus use this book according to His purpose. May you use it according to His purpose as well! If someone you care about could benefit from reading *Watch!*, please consider loaning them this book, or sending him or her another copy. If you would like to order copies you can do so through the Doug Hooley Ministry website at: doughooley.com, or Amazon.com.

If you enjoyed or learned anything from *Watch!*, please consider supporting this ministry by writing a review on Amazon.com. As there are so many choices of books to read, reviews help others to know what is worth reading, and it will mean a great deal to me. Angela and I try to read and learn from every review.

If you would like to receive updates on our future projects, you can sign up for our email list at doughooley.com. You can view videos which compliment this book, or read my blog on the website. We are also on Facebook and Twitter @DougHMinistries and would love to have you "follow" us as we together follow Jesus and watch for His return!

Appendix

Doug Hooley's Translation of the Olivet Discourse as Found in the Gospels of Matthew, Mark and Luke.

I. Translation Methodology

My desire and goal is that both the first century reader of the original copies of the Greek texts containing the Olivet Discourse, and the 21st century reader of the English translation of those texts, would understand them in the same way. Transcending culture, idioms, continents and time means that in order to do so, sometimes literal word for word translation is not the way to accomplish that goal. There are often no single English word equivalents to the Greek words, and there are many times multiple meanings of a Greek word to choose from. Translators have been making those choices for years.

In translating the involved texts, I utilized the Biblesoft electronic version of the parsed version of the 27th Nestle-Aland (NA 27) edition of the *Novum Testamentum Graece* and the 1550 edition of the Stephens/Scrivener *Textus Receptus.* I secondarily consulted the electronic version of the *Wescott-Hort Greek New Testament.* Where there were meaningful differences in these texts I decided what to include by the context. Where there was more information in one text than another, I generally included that information.

For the parsing of Greek words, I relied on the Biblesoft version of the Interlinear (NA 27) and the principles set out in William Mounce's works.

I am not an expert on the Greek language. I heavily relied upon:

- The New Strong's Exhaustive Concordance; James Strong. Thomas Nelson Publishers © 1990 and the Biblesoft Electronic Version.
- Vines Complete Expository Dictionary; W.E. Vine. Thomas Nelson Publishers © 1996 and the Biblesoft Electronic Version.
- Thayer's Greek Lexicon (Biblesoft Abridged Version)
- Young's Analytical Concordance to the Bible 22nd edition; Robert Young. WM.B. EERDMANS PUBLISHING COMPANY.
- Basics of Biblical Greek, Third Edition: William D. Mounce. Zondervan © 2009

The Doug Hooley Translation of the Olivet Discourse scriptures is solely a work of Doug Hooley. However, since it is based on the same original works as most other translations of the Bible, it is to be expected that it will be similar to other English translations. In order to "consult" with others on the translation of scripture, I mainly relied on the King James Version of the Bible. I also regularly reviewed the New International Version, The English Standard Version, The New King James Version, and the American Standard Version of the Bible.

II. The three gospel compilation of concurrent scriptures

The Doug Hooley Translation (DHT) of the individual verses that make up the Olivet Discourse, taken from the books of Matthew, Mark, and Luke, are found throughout this book. The following DHT *compilation* is based on a combination of the three different gospel accounts. Each new "verse" that results are a combined summary of the corresponding related verses. The resulting new "verses" have been renumbered. The verses of each gospel that are used in the new combined "verse" are identified by either "M" (Matthew) "K" (Mark), and "L" (Luke), followed by their original verse number. Matthew chapter 25- 26:2 is not included in this compilation since it is entirely unique to the other two gospel accounts.

Jesus' Olivet Discourse (DHT Concurrent Gospel Compilation)

1 (M1, K1, L5) As Jesus was leaving the temple, some were speaking about how the temple was adorned with magnificent stones and offerings. One disciple said to Him, "look Teacher, what remarkable stones and buildings!"

2 (M2, K2, L6) Jesus replied to all of them, "do you see these buildings? There will come a day when not one of these stones that you are looking at will be left on another. Every one of them will be destroyed."

3 (M3, K3&4, L7) As Jesus sat on the Mount of Olives, directly opposite of the Temple, Peter, James, John, and Andrew came to question Him privately. "Tell us," they said, "when will these things occur, and what sign will there be when these things come to pass, and what will be the sign of your arrival and presence here, and of the completion of the age?"

4 (M4, K5, L8a) Jesus answered, saying, "watch out, that no one deceives you.

5 (M5, K6, L8b) For many will come in my name, saying, 'I am the Christ, and the time is close at hand' and will deceive many. Do not follow them.

6 (M6&7a, K7&8a, L9&10) But when you will hear of wars, rumors of wars, and disturbances, don't be terrified or troubled. These things must happen, but it is not the end." Then He said to them, "For nation will rise against nation, and kingdom against kingdom.

7 (M7b&8, K8b, L11) And there will be mighty earthquakes in places, and hunger, and pestilence and fearful sights and wonders in the sky. They will be exceedingly great, but only be the beginning of childbirth-like pain.

8 (M9, K9, L12) Now, before all of these things, watch out for yourselves, for they will lay their hands on you and persecute you, betraying you and delivering you to the councils and assemblies on my behalf to testify against them, and taken to prisons, and you will be brought before kings and rulers, and you will be hated by everyone, and beaten for my name's sake.

9 (K11, L13-15) So, when they take you, and deliver you over to the custody of others, it will come down to your testimony on my behalf. Don't take any thought beforehand about what to say, but speak whatever you are given at that time. For I will give you a mouth and wisdom that all of your adversaries won't be able to reply to or oppose, because it is not you that speaks, but the Holy Spirit.

10 (M10, K12&13a, L16&17) And at that time many will fall away, and shall betray one another, and hate one another. Brother will betray brother to death and the father his son. And children will rise up against their parents and shall cause them to be put to death. And you will be detested by everyone on account of my name.

11 (M11) And many false prophets shall rise up and shall deceive many.

12 (M12&13b, L18&19) And because lawlessness will abound, the love of many will be made cold. But, the one who patiently suffers to the end, that same person will be saved. Not a hair on their head will be lost.

13(M14, K10) And this gospel of the Kingdom must first be publicly proclaimed to all the world as a testimony to all peoples, and then the end will come.

14 (M15, K14a, L 20) Now when you see Jerusalem surrounded by armies, then know that it's desolation is near. Moreover, when you see the foul and detestable thing that causes desolation, set up in the holy place, spoken of by the Prophet Daniel, (let the one reviewing it understand).

15 (M16, K14b, L 21a) Then let those who are in Judea flee to the mountains.

16 (M17-20, K15-18, L21b-23a) And, let him who is on the housetop not come down to take anything out of his house. Neither let the one in the field return back to take his clothes. And let those who are in the middle of it, leave. And let the ones who are out in the country, not go in. And how awful for pregnant women and nursing mothers in those days! And pray that your flight not be in the winter or on the Sabbath. For these are the days of vengeance, that all that is written may be fulfilled.

17 (M21-22, K19-20, L23b-24) For then there will be such exceedingly great anguish, such has not been since the beginning of the world, or will ever be. For there shall be great distress in the land, and passionate violence on this people. And they shall fall by the edge of the sword, and will be led away captive into all the nations. And Jerusalem will be crushed under foot by the nations until the times of the Gentiles is fulfilled. And except that the Lord cuts short those days, no one will be saved. But for the elect's sake, who He has chosen, He has cut short those days.

18 (M23-28, K 21-23) At that time, if anyone says to you, look, here or there is the messiah, don't believe it. For there will arise false messiahs and false prophets and they will show great signs and wonders, so much so that they will deceive, if it's possible, even the elect. So you watch out and pay attention! Look, I have told you everything ahead of time. So, if anyone says to you, "look, he is in the desert," don't go out, or "see, he is in a secret room," don't believe it! For as lightning comes from the east and shines to the west, so shall also be the coming of the Son of Man. For where ever the corpse is, there the eagles will gather.

19 (M29, K24-25, L 25-26) Immediately after the persecution of those days there will be signs in the sun, and the moon, and the stars; the sun will be darkened and the moon will not yield its light, and the stars shall fall from heaven. Looking forward with expectation to what is coming on the earth, the powers of heaven shall be shaken and the waves of the sea will roar. The nations of the earth will be distressed and perplexed.

20 (M30-31, K26-27, L27-28) And then the sign of the Son of Man shall be seen in heaven; all of the tribes of the earth will mourn as they see the Son of Man coming on the clouds of heaven with power and great glory. And when these things begin to happen, lift your heads and look up, for your deliverance and redemption is drawing near. And He will send His angels with the sounding of a great trumpet, and they will gather together His elect from the four winds, from the uttermost part of the earth to the uttermost part of heaven.

21 (M32-33, K28-29, L29-31) Now learn a parable of the fig tree. When its branch is still tender and it puts forth leaves, you know that summer is near. So also you, when you see these things happen, you know that the Kingdom of God is close at hand; right at the doors.

22 (M34, K30, L32) I am telling you the truth; this same generation will not pass, until all of these things take place.

23 (M35, K31, L33) Heaven and earth shall pass away, but my words shall not pass away.

24 (M36, K32-33, L34-35) But no man knows the day and hour. Not the angels of heaven, nor the Son, but my Father only. Pay attention to yourselves, lest at any time your hearts be overcome by revelry, and drunkenness, and distractions of this life, so that day catches you off guard. Stay awake, and pray; for you don't know when the time is. For that day will come like a trap on everyone that dwells on the face of the entire earth.

25 (M37-39) But like the days of Noah, so will also be the coming of the Son of man. For like in the days before the flood, they were eating, and drinking, and marrying, and giving in marriage until the day Noah entered the ark. And they didn't know until the flood came and took everyone away. So shall also be the coming of the Son of Man.

26 (M40-42) At that time, two will be in the field; one will be taken and the other left. Two will be grinding at the mill; one will be taken, and the other left. Therefore, be vigilant, because you don't know what hour your Lord will come.

27 (M43-44) But understand this, that if the head of the household would have known at what time the thief would come, he would have watched and not had his house broken into. The same goes for you. Be ready, for at such a time when you don't think, the Son of Man will come.

28 (M45- 51, K34) It is like a man taking a far journey, who left his house and gave his servants authority and told every man what to do and told the gatekeeper to watch. Who then is a faithful and wise servant who the Lord has made ruler over his household, to give them food at the proper time? Fortunate is the servant who is found doing so when the lord comes. I am telling you the truth; he will give him authority over all of his possessions. But if the evil servant says in his heart that the master is delayed, and he begins to beat his fellow servants, and begins to eat and drink with the drunken, the lord of that servant will come in a day that he is not looking for him and at an hour that he is not aware of. There will be wailing and grating of teeth.

29 (K35-37, L36) So likewise you watch, because you don't know what time the master will come: in the evening, or at midnight, or when the rooster crows, or in the morning. God forbid he comes suddenly and finds you sleeping. Stay awake therefore, and always pray that you might prevail and escape all of these things that are going to happen, and to stand before the Son of man. And what I say to you, I say to everyone; watch!

Bibliography

Ankerberg, John and Weldon, John, *Cult Watch.* Harvest House Publishers. Eugene, OR © 1991

Aurelius, Marcus. *Meditations. Marcus Aurelius and His Times.* Walter J. Black, Inc. Roslyn, NY © 1945

Bercot, David W., ed. A *Dictionary of Early Christian Beliefs.* Hendrickson Publishers Peabody, MA © 1998.

Ellinger, Karl and Wilhelm, Rudolf eds. *Interlinear Translated Bible (NA27).* NESTLE-ALAND, NOVUM TESTAMENTUM GRAECE 27th Revised Edition. Biblesoft, © 1997-2011.

Ellinger, Karl and Wilhelm, Rudolf eds.. *Interlinear Translated Bible (TR).* TEXTUS RECEPTUS (STEPHANUS 1550): DISCOVERY BIBLE EDITION. PCStudy Bible formatted Electronic Database. Biblesoft. © 1997-2011.

Capps, Charles. *End Times Events.* Harrison House. Tulsa, OK ©1997

Cheetham, Nicolas. *Keepers of the Keys. A History of the Popes from St. Peter to John Paul II.* Charles Scribner's Sons. New York. © 1983.

Coogan, Michael D. *The Oxford History of the Biblical World.* Oxford University Press. New York © 1998

Cooper, Charles. *God's Elect and the Great Tribulation.* Strong Tower Publishing. Bellefonte, PA © 2008.

Dowley, Tim. *Introduction to the History of Christianity.* Fortress Press. Minneapolis, MN. © 1995

Foxe, John. *Foxe's Book of Martyrs.* Whitaker House. New Kensington, PA © 1981

Green, Jay P ed. *The Interlinear Greek-English New Testament, Third Edition.* Baker Books, Grand Rapids, Michigan ©1996

Gregg, Steve. *Revelation: Four Views, A Parallel Commentary.* Thomas Nelson Publishers. Nashville © 1997

Grun, Bernard. *The Time Tables of History.* Simon and Schuster. New York © 1975

Hagee, John, *Four Blood Moons*, Worthy Publishing. Franklin, TN © 2013

Halley, Henry H. *Halley's Bible Handbook 24th Edition.* Zondervan Publishing-House. Grand Rapids, Michigan. ©1965.

Hunt, Dave, *Global Peace and the Rise of the Antichrist.* Harvest House Publishers. Eugene, OR © 1990

Hunt, Dave. *How Close Are We?* Harvest House Publishers. Eugene, OR © 1993

International Standard Bible Encyclopedia, Electronic Database Copyright © 1996 by Biblesoft

Jeremiah, David. *Jesus' Final Warning; Hearing the Savior's Voice in The Midst of Chaos.* Word Publishing. Nashville, TN © 1999

Kalbach, Paul. *The Sign Of The End of the Age.* Crossbooks. Bloomington, IN. © 2013

Keller, Werner. *The Bible as History. Translated by William Neil.* William Morrow and Company Publishers. New York © 1956

Kurschner, Alan. *Antichrist Before the Day of the Lord.* Eschatos Publishing. City© 2013

Laymon, Charles M. The *Interpreter's One-Volume Commentary on the Bible.* Abingdon Press eds. Nashville. © 1971

Lindsey, Hal. *The Apocalypse Code.* Western Front Ltd. Palos Verdes, CA. © 1997

Lindsey, Hal. *The Late Great Planet Earth.* Zondervan Publishing House. Grand Rapids, Michigan. © 1970

The Lockman Foundation. *New American Standard Bible.* La Habra, CA. © 1995

Martin, Walter R. *Kingdom of the Cults.* Bethany House Publishers. Minneapolis. © 1977

McGee,J. Vernon. *Through the Bible with J. Vernon McGee.* Thru The Bible Radio. Pasadena, CA 91109 ©1983

Maier, Paul L. *Josephus, The Essential Writings. A New Translation.* Kregal Publications. Grand Rapids, MI. © 1988.

Mounce, William D. *Basics of Biblical Greek Third Edition.* Zondervan. Grand Rapids, MI. © 2009

New Unger's Bible Dictionary. Moody Press. Chicago, Illinois. © 1988

New Nelson's Bible Dictionary. Thomas Nelson Inc. Nashville, TN. © 2000.

Packer, J.I., Tenney, Merrill C., White, William. *Nelson's Illustrated Encyclopedia of the Bible.* Thomas Nelson Publishers. Nashville, TN. © 1980.

Platt, Rutherford H. ed. *The Forgotten Books of Eden.* Bell Publishing Company. New York. © 1980

Richardson, Joel. *The Islamic Antichrist.* WND Books. Washington D.C. © 2006

Richardson, Joel, *Mideast Beast.* WND Books. Washington D.C. © 2012

Ritmeyer, Leen and Kathleen, *Secrets of Jerusalem's Temple Mount.* Biblical Archeology Society. Washington D.C. © 1998

Rosenthal, Marvin. *The Pre-Wrath Rapture of the Church.* Thomas Nelson Publishers. Nashville. © 1990.

Ryrie, Charles Caldwell. *The Ryrie Study Bible New American Standard Translation.* Moody Press. Chicago ©1976.

Smith, Sam A. *The Olivet Discourse.* Biblical Reader Communications. Raleigh, N.C. © 2009

Shelton, Bob. *Prophecy in Context. A Look at the Olivet Discourse.* Journey Forth. Greenville, South Carolina © 2008

Steinsaltz, Adin. *The Essential Talmud.* Basic Books. New York © 1976.

Tragelles, Samual Prideaux. *The Hope of Christ's Second Coming: How Is It Taught in Scripture? And Why?* Whitstable Litho Ltd. Whitstable, Kent, Great Britain. Originally published in 1864

Van Kampen, Robert. *The Rapture Question Answered.* Fleming H. RevellBaker Book House Company. Grand Rapids, MI © 1997

Van Kampen, Robert, *The Sign.* Crossway Books. Wheaton, Illinois © 1992.

Ventors, Chad. *The Olivet Discourse in Mark's Gospel.* Self-Published, Amazon Books © 2011

Vine, W.E. *Vines Complete Expository Dictionary.* Thomas Nelson Publisher. Nashville, TN. © 1996.

Westcott-Hort, *Greek New Testament.* PC Study Bible formatted Electronic Database. © 2006, 2011 by Biblesoft.

The King James Version of the Holy Bible. World Publishing Company. New York

The New International Version of the Holy Bible. Zondervan Publishing House. Grand Rapids, Michigan © 1988

Endnotes

[1] Ryrie Study Bible. Pg. 1443

[2] Ryrie Study Bible. Pg. 1503

[3] Ryrie Study Bible. Pg. 1503

[4] Ryrie Study Bible. Pg. 1540

[5] Halley's Bible Handbook. Pg. 414

[6] Wikipedia. Jim Jones. http://en.wikipedia.org/wiki/Jim_Jones November 9, 2014

[7] Wikipedia. Waco Siege. http://en.wikipedia.org/wiki/Waco_siege#The_initial_assault November 9, 2014

[8] Wikipedia. Heaven's Gate. http://en.wikipedia.org/wiki/Heaven's_Gate_(religious_group) November 9, 2014

[9] Martin, Walter, M.A. Ph.D. The Kingdom of the Cults. Bethany House Publishers. Copyright 1977. Pg. 27

[10] Wikipedia: T .http://en.wikipedia.org/wiki/Demographics_of_Jehovah's_Witnesses. Taken January 24, 2014.

[11] Martin, Walter, M.A. Ph.D. The Kingdom of the Cults. Pg. 362

[12] http://en.wikipedia.org/wiki/Harold_Camping Accessed January 27, 2014.

[13] Jeremiah, David, Jesus' Final Warning; Pg.8 & 9

[14] Grace Faith, *Ask a Bible Teacher*, https://gracethrufaith.com/ask-a-bible-teacher/much-bible-prophecy/ Accessed 4/04/2016. This website was citing "*The Encyclopedia of Biblical Prophecy*" by J. Barton Payne: "there are 1,239 prophecies in the Old Testament and 578 prophecies in the New Testament for a total of 1,817. These prophecies are contained in 8,352 of the Bible's verses. Since there are 31,124 verses in the Bible, the 8,352 verses that contain prophecy constitute 26.8 percent of the Bible's volume."

[15] Grun, Bernard, The Timetables of History. Page 24. Grun places the death of Jesus in the year 30. Others including historian Paul Meier place it somewhere between 30 and 36 A.D.

[16] Keller, Werner, *The Bible as History. Pgs. 368-370*

[17] Matthew 21 says that Jesus sent the two disciples for both a colt and a donkey. It also makes it sound like he rode them both. Luke 19 and Mark 11 only mention a "colt."

[18] Nelson's Bible Dictionary

[19] Venters, Chad. *The Olivet Discourse in Mark's Gospel.* Self-Published Amazon Books. © 2011. Pg. 2

[20] Ritmeyer, Leen and Kathleen, *Secrets of Jerusalem's Temple Mount*, Biblical Archeology Society © 1998. Quoting Josephus Antiquities of the Jews 15.11.3

[21] Wikipedia. List of People who claimed to be Jesus. http://en.wikipedia.org/wiki/List_of_people_claimed_to_be_Jesus Accessed January 30, 2014

[22] Wikipedia. List of Messiah claimants. http://en.wikipedia.org/wiki/List_of_messiah_claimants Accessed January 30, 2014

[23] Dowley, Dr. Tim. Introduction to the History of Christianity. Fortress Press. Minneapolis, MN. Copyright 1995 Page 68.

[24] New Advent Organization. The Epistle from Ignatius to the Magnesians. http://www.newadvent.org/fathers/0105.htm Accessed January 30, 2014

---

[25] Cheetham, Nicolas. Keepers of the Keys. A History of the Popes from St. Peter to John Paul II. Charles Scribner's Sons. New York. Copyright 1983. Page 266.

[26] Wikipedia. List of Popes. https://en.wikipedia.org/wiki/List_of_popes August 19, 2015

[27] Richardson, Joel. *The Islamic Antichrist.* Pg. 20-71

[28] Wikipedia. List of wars by death toll. https://en.wikipedia.org/wiki/List_of_wars_by_death_toll January 5, 2016

[29] NT Strong's word:5604 "oodin." (from Thayer's Greek Lexicon, Electronic Database. Copyright © 2000, 2003, 2006 by Biblesoft, Inc. All rights reserved.)

[30] Lindsey Apocalypse Code. Pg. 107-108

[31] USGS: http://earthquake.usgs.gov/

[32] For example, the English Standard Version (ESV) has not chosen to include the word "pestilence" in their translation. This discrepancy is likely because the ESV is translated from a Greek Bible version known as the *Novum Testamentum Graece* (27th ed.). That version of the Greek New Testament does not include the Greek word for "pestilence."

There are several different versions of the Greek Bible that our English versions of the Bible use to translate. The *Novum Testamentum Graece* is one of them. The *Textus Receptus* is another widely used book. Translators are forced to make decisions. The first is which versions of the original language documents to use. The Greek word for "pestilence," or "disease," is "loimov." It is transliterated into English as "loimos." That word is included in the Textus Receptus. Loimos is also included in the Luke account of this passage in the Novum Testamentum Graece. That, to make a long story even more confusing, is why I chose to include "pestilence" in my translation of Matthew 24:7 and Mark 13:8.

[33] From Wikipedia, the community-written free encyclopedia. http://en.wikipedia.org/wiki/Pandemic#Pandemics_through_history

[34] It Is Well with My Soul, by Horatio Spafford 1828-1888 and Philip P Bliss 1838-1876

[35] *Foxes Book of Martyrs* Pg.10

[36] *Foxes Book of Martyrs*, Pg. 13

[37] National Geographic Channel website. How Did the Apostles Die? Article by Patrick J. Kiger, February 19, 2015. http://channel.nationalgeographic.com/killing-jesus/articles/how-did-the-apostles-die/ Accessed August 25, 2015

[38] Strong's word number 1161. From Teknia online Greek Dictionary found at https://www.teknia.com/greek-dictionary/de Accessed 8/25/2015

[39] McGee, J Vernon, Through the Bible with Dr. J Vernon McGee Volume 4. Through the Bible Radio, Pasadena California. Copyright 1983. Page 126.

[40] Strong's word 646. Meaning "defection from truth."

[41] Dowley, Tim, *The History of Christianity.* Fortress Press, Minneapolis, MN. Copyright 1995. Pgs. 82-83.

[42] Strong's word 166 aionios (ahee-o'-nee-os); from 165

[43] Strong's word 4352 proskuneo (pros-koo-neh'-o); from Strong's word 4314

[44] Marcus Aurelius. Meditations VII: 49

[45] Prouty, Guy. Eastern Oregon University Anth 410, *Sustainability and the Rise and Fall of Civilizations* Class Lectures. Fall 2004

[46] Don Coyhis (Mohican), the founder of White Bison organization: www.whitebison.org

[47] Cooper, Charles. *God's Elect and the Great Tribulation.* Pg. 328

[48] The Secrets of Enoch XXXIII:1. / Barnabas (c.70-130 AD) / Justin Martyr (c. 160 AD)

[49] Van Kampen, Robert. The Sign. Crossway Books.1992. Pg. 29

[50] Josephus, Jewish Antiquities X, *Josephus The Essential Writings. A New Translation* by Paul L. Maier. Kregal Publications, Grand Rapids, MI. © 1988.

[51] Nelson's Bible Dictionary and the International Study Bible Encyclopedia regarding the "abomination of desolation"

[52] From New Unger's Bible Dictionary:

[53] Strong's word number 314

[54] Vines Complete Expository Dictionary. Thomas Nelson Publisher. Nashville, TN. © 1996. Pg. 507

[55] Vines Complete Expository Dictionary. Thomas Nelson Publisher. Nashville, TN. © 1996.

[56] Josephus Book of Wars I and Jewish Antiquities XII. *Josephus The Essential Writings. A New Translation* by Paul L. Maier. Kregal Publications, Grand Rapids, MI. © 1988. Page 209.

[57] Cooper, Charles, *God's Elect and the Great Tribulation*, Strong Tower Publishing. © 2008. chapters 10-13.

[58] Ibid.

[59] Israel Ministry of Foreign Affairs website. http://www.mfa.gov.il/mfa/foreignpolicy/peace/guide/pages/israel-palestinian%20negotiations.aspx accessed August 30, 2015

[60] http://www.temple.org.il/

[61] http://www.templemountfaithful.org/

[62] http://templemountfaithful.org/index.php

[63] *A Dictionary of Early Christian Beliefs*. David W. Bercot, Editor. Hendrickson Publishers © 1998. Page 24

[64] INDIEGOGO web site. https://www.indiegogo.com/projects/build-the-third-temple--3#/story Accessed August 30, 2015.

[65] Parrett, Christopher M., *LDS Preparedness Manual* version 8.0 Handbook 2: Provident Living, June 2012, 15th Anniversary Edition.

[66] *New Unger's Bible Dictionary* (originally published by Moody Press of Chicago, Illinois. Copyright (C) 1988.) Regarding Judea.

[67] 780,517 as of 2010 according to google https://www.google.com/?gws_rd=ssl#q=jerusalem+population on September 25, 2014

[68] Ankerberg Pg. 81.

[69] Martin Pg. 86

[70] "Practicing members". This is taken from the official Jehovah's Witness website which says, "While *other religious groups count their membership by occasional or annual attendance, this figure reflects only those who are actively involved in the public Bible educational work.*" http://www.jw-media.org/people/statistics.htm accessed 1/2/06.

[71] Rosenthal, Marvin. *The Pre-Wrath Rapture of the Church*. 1990 Pg. 40-41

[72]. McGee, J. Vernon *Through the Bible with Dr. J. Vernon McGee*, Volume IV, Pg. 130

[73] Gregg, Steve *Revelation Four Views, A Parallel Commentary* Pg. 172

[74] Baird, William Edited by Laymon, Charles M. Abingdon. The Gospel of Luke contained *in The Interpreter's One-Volume Commentary on the Bible*, Pg. 696

[75] Matthew 24:28, MATTHEW HENRY'S COMMENTARY ON THE WHOLE BIBLE. PC Study Bible Formatted Electronic Database. Copyright © 2006 by Biblesoft, Inc. All rights reserved.

---

[76] Gregg, Steve. Revelation *Four Views, A Parallel Commentary* Page 103

[77] Gregg, Steve. *Revelation Four Views, A Parallel Commentary*. Page 103

[78] Blessed Assurance, Jesus is Mine: Words by Fanny J. Crosby, 1873, and music by Phoebe P. Knapp, 1873

[79] *Although Revelation 6 & 7 do not specifically refer to the revealing of the Antichrist, elsewhere in Revelation the Antichrist is mentioned and a solid case can be made that the timing of his activities at least in part precede the Second Coming of Jesus (See chapters 10& 11).

** Olivet Discourse does not say that the angels do not gather those who are dead. In fact, the language pertaining to "vultures" gathering "bodies" points in that direction.

*** Although it doesn't mention the gathering of the elect, it mentions those whom "the Lord calls."

[80] Thompson, Jeff, PhD. Psychology Today. Is Non-Verbal Communication a Numbers Game? https://www.psychologytoday.com/blog/beyond-words/201109/is-nonverbal-communication-numbers-game Accessed 10/10/2015

[81] Wikipedia http://en.wikipedia.org/wiki/Rayleigh_scattering 10/15/14

[82] Earth Sky website http://earthsky.org/space/what-is-a-blood-moon-lunar-eclipses-2014-2015#tetrad 10/15/14

[83] Earth Sky website http://earthsky.org/space/what-is-a-blood-moon-lunar-eclipses-2014-2015#tetrad 10/15/14

[84] Amazon.com http://www.amazon.com/Four-Blood-Moons-Something-Change/dp/1617952141/ref=sr_1_1?ie=UTF8&qid=1413402280&sr=8-1&keywords=blood+moon Accessed 10/15/14

[85] Laine, David C. Demand Media, Web-site: Synonym, *Examples of Volcanoes Blocking the Sun*. http://classroom.synonym.com/examples-dust-volcanic-eruptions-blocking-sun-14361.html Accessed January 20, 2016

[86] Vine's Complete Expository Dictionary. Page 144-145 Strong's word #4654

[87] Ask an Astronomer http://curious.astro.cornell.edu/eclipses.php#questions 10/15/14 broken link

[88] DateandTime.com http://www.timeanddate.com/eclipse/in/israel/jerusalem 10/15/14 broken link

[89] *The Bible Almanac* J.I. Packer, Merrill C. Tenney, and William White, Jr., Thomas Nelson Publishers. Copyright 1980. Page 254

[90] Coogan, Michael D., The Oxford History of the Biblical World. © 1998 Pg.564

[91] Kurschner, Alan, *Antichrist Before The Day Of The Lord*, Eschatos Publishing © 2013

[92] *Ryrie Study Bible*. Note on 2 Thess. 2:7, 1706

[93] "nor the son" is included (as it is in the English Standard Version) because the words are included in the Novum Testamentum Graece. The King James Version does not include the words because it is reliant on the Textus Receptus, which does not include the words.

[94] Among many others is: Henry, Matthew. *MATTHEW HENRY'S COMMENTARY ON THE WHOLE BIBLE*. PC Study Bible Formatted Electronic Database. Copyright © 2006 by Biblesoft, Inc. All rights reserved.

[95] See the following websites for proponents of this theory: http://www.gospelminutes.org/rapture.php Accessed 02/20/2016, http://biblelight.net/psttrib.htm Accessed 02/20/2016, http://www.amatteroftruth.com/the-rapture-one-taken-and-one-left Accessed 02/20/2016.

http://unknown shapedbythestory.blogspot.com/2014/06/the-righteous-are-left-behind.html All were accessed 02/20/2016

[96] From a blog: *How Big is the World's Black Market.* By Freakonomics. Based on the work of Economists Cayhun Elgin, and Oguz Oztunali. http://freakonomics.com/2012/06/25/how-big-is-the-world-black-market/ Accessed April 14, 2016.

[97] *Strong's* NT:59 from NT:58; properly, to go to market, i.e. (by implication) to purchase; specially, to redeem:

KJV - buy, redeem. (Biblesoft's New Exhaustive Strong's Numbers and Concordance with Expanded Greek-Hebrew Dictionary. Copyright © 1994, 2003, 2006 Biblesoft, Inc. and International Bible Translators, Inc.)

[98] *Vines.* Page 562

[99] Halley, Henry H, *HALLEY'S BIBLE HANDBOOK*, 24th edition 1965 (pg. 447)

[100] Broken linkhttp:/www.peshitta.org/ The Teaching of Matai: Chapter 25 verse 1. *then let be likened the Kingdom of Heaven to ten virgins now those five of them were wise and five foolish who took their lamps and went out for the meeting of the bridegroom and the bride*

[101] Capps, Charles, *END TIMES EVENTS*, 1997 (Pgs. 105-132)

[102] Steinsaltz, Adin *THE ESSENTIAL TALMUD*, 1976 (Pg. 130)

[103] On March 12, 2012, The United States Census Bureau estimated that the world population exceeded 7 billion people. According to Revelation 6:8, when the fourth seal of the scroll containing God's will be broken by Jesus, a rider named "Death" rides out on a pale horse with the authority to kill a quarter of the earth's population. If there are seven billion people on earth at that time, there would be 5.25 billion survivors after the rider of the pale horse completes his mission.

According to the Pew Research Center in 2010, there were an estimated 2.18 billion people in the world that call themselves "Christians." Assuming that a quarter of them die along with the rest of the world's population as a result of the fourth seal of the scroll being opened, that would leave about 1.6 billion people who claim to be Christians.

There is no way for us to judge the hearts of those who claim to be Christians to determine who is Christian in name only, and not a true follower of Jesus. Remember there will be a great "falling away" from the faith during this tribulation period (see chapter 8). However, I will make a large, baseless assumption that about half of those who claim to be Christian, are so in name only (God only really knows this number). That would mean that about 800 million true followers of Christ would be alive on the earth, at the time of His Second Coming. After this 800 million would be gathered to Jesus at the rapture of the Church, there would still be around 4.5 billion inhabitants left on the earth.

An unprecedented, science-defying earthquake that will move every mountain from its place on the planet will accompany the Second Coming of Jesus. This earthquake will trigger mass tidal waves. Cities will be leveled. According to the United States Geological Survey, 2,319,716 people have died in earthquakes between 1900 and 2014. This is only counting the number of people who have died in earthquakes that have killed over 1000 people. One earthquake in Haiti in 2010, killed over 316,000 people alone.[103] There is no way of telling how many people would die in such a quake. Limiting the death toll to 10% seems very conservative. 450 million earthquake related deaths would leave 4.05 billion survivors on the planet.

Once the rapture of the Church has taken place, as God's wrath is poured out, several enormously horrific events occur as the first five "trumpets" are blown by angels in Heaven (Rev. 8:6-9:12). These events will result in widespread death on the earth. However, there are no specific death toll numbers mentioned in the Bible related to most of these judgments. It would be impossible to accurately estimate the impact on human life, but it will be great.

As the sixth trumpet is blown, four angels are released to "kill a third of mankind" (Rev. 9:15-18). A third of 4.05 billion would leave approximately 2.67 billion people left living on the earth.

The amazing thing is that even after all of this, with about 62% of the world's population having perished, the 38% that remain will refuse to repent and turn to God. *(Rev 9:20-21)*

It is estimated that there are currently over 49.6 million people involved in active and reserve military duty in the world today. If they have been subject to the same levels of casualties as the rest of the world's population, that would leave about 25 million military personnel throughout the entire world (using today's numbers) that could end up making it through to the end of the tribulation period.

Serving as a great warning against only relying on what we know to be true today, Revelation 9:16, indicates that there will be significantly more people involved in the military at the end of the age.

An army of "200,000,000" to be exact. When that entire army alone perishes at the battle of Armageddon, under 2.5 billion inhabitants will possibly remain on the earth.

[104] Strong's word 1484 ethnos (eth'-nos); probably from 1486; a race (as of the same habit), i.e. a tribe; specially, a foreign (non-Jewish) one (usually by implication, pagan): KJV-- Gentile, heathen, nation, people.

[105] Wikipedia http://en.wikipedia.org/wiki/Maslow's_hierarchy_of_needs Accessed 03/13/06

[106] The Sign Pg. 388-389.

[107] The Interpreter's One-Volume Commentary on the Bible Pg. 640

[108] Strong's word # 166 aionios (ahee-o'-nee-os); from 165; perpetual (also used of past time, or past and future as well): KJV-- eternal, forever, everlasting, world (began). We have previously seen the word transliterated from the Greek as "aion" in the discussion of Matthew 24:3 (see chapter 6). I chose to interpret the word there as "age" as opposed to the King James translation which translated that word to mean "world." "World," has an implied meaning which brings to mind a place (Planet Earth) rather than a period of time.

Aion can mean several different things depending on the modifying words that surround it, as well as the context. It is sometimes translated as an "age." It can mean "eternity," "perpetual," "everlasting age," or "into the age." However, it is always used in reference to a period of time or a period of "unendingness" or "no beginning."

In the Bible aion is used to describe "eternity" prior to the beginning of time (1 Corinthians 2:7). It is used to denote past "ages" that have existed since creation up until Jesus' time (John 9:32, Ephesians 3:8-9). Aion is used to describe this present age we are living in (Matthew 13:22, 24:3, 28:20, Mark 4:19). When aion is in the plural form, "αἰώνων," transliterated as "aionon," it may refer to ages that have been from the time of creation up to the end of the current age (1 Corinthians 10:11, Hebrews 9:26). The use of aion can be for the purpose of denoting a combination of eternity past, all time since creation, all future time, and eternity future. This occurs in 1 Timothy 1:17, where "aionas ton aionon" is translated as "forever and ever." (New Testament Word Studies. http://www.ntwords.com/eternal.htm. Accessed 5/10/ 2016).

The word Aion is used twice in Matthew 25:46. Both times, the word is preceded by the Greek word "εἰς," transliterated as "eis," meaning "into." The combination of the words can mean "into the age," "into the next age," "into the eternal," or "into perpetuity," depending on the context. We know that the current age we live in will end. When it does, it will be replaced by the age in which Jesus will establish His kingdom and rule "forever and ever," (eternally). To go "into" that age, is the same as going into an "eternal" age. That is why the English Standard Version of the Bible and I, translate the meaning of aion to be "eternal," rather than translating it as "into the next age." The King James version translates aion once in this passage as "everlasting," and once as "eternal." To translate the combination of words as "into the next age," could imply to the reader that the next age is limited to a period of time that could have an ending like all preceding ages. My understanding of the age in which Jesus will rule is that it will be without end.

The two complete phrases in question here in verse 46 are transliterated as "eis kolasin aionion," which literally means "into punishment eternal," or "into punishment age," or "into punishment everlasting." The second phrase is translated "eis zoe aionion," or literally "into life eternal," or "into life age," or "into life everlasting." Given that the coming age is the everlasting, eternal, unending, perpetual reign of Jesus, a safe interpretation of both phrases is as stated in the King James translation and my translation of Matthew 25:46.

About the Author

Doug and his wife Angela, raised their three children (now all adults) on three beautiful acres in the foothills of the Oregon Cascades, where they still live today. Doug is a retired 25-year veteran of the Lane County Sheriff's Office. He received a B.A. in Liberal Studies with minors in Anthropology and Sociology from Eastern Oregon University. To find out more, please visit doughooley.com.

CPSIA information can be obtained
at www.ICGtesting.com
Printed in the USA
LVOW13s0708150617
538225LV00016B/482/P